Building Blocks of Modern Society

Building Blocks of Modern Society

History, Information Ecosystems, and Infrastructures

James W. Cortada

ROWMAN & LITTLEFIELD
Lanham • Boulder • New York • London

Published by Rowman & Littlefield
A wholly owned subsidiary of The Rowman & Littlefield Publishing Group, Inc.
4501 Forbes Boulevard, Suite 200, Lanham, Maryland 20706
www.rowman.com

Unit A, Whitacre Mews, 26-34 Stannary Street, London SE11 4AB

British Library Cataloguing in Publication Information Available

Library of Congress Cataloging-in-Publication Data

Names: Cortada, James W., author.
Title: Building blocks of modern society : history, information ecosystems, and infrastructures / James W. Cortada.
Description: Lanham : Rowman & Littlefield, [2020] | Includes index. | Summary: "This book proposes a way to look at the history of information and to history as a whole that is simultaneously relevant to observers in other disciplines and familiar to historians of business, economics, sociology and technology. The author presents that advocacy in two ways: with theoretical and historiographical discussions of what information ecosystems and infrastructures are and their value for this kind of research, second, through a range of case studies applying those concepts"— Provided by publisher.
Identifiers: LCCN 2020031067 (print) | LCCN 2020031068 (ebook) | ISBN 9781538148549 (cloth) | ISBN 9781538148556 (epub)
Subjects: LCSH: Information technology—History. | Information technology—Social aspects. | Information technology—Economic aspects.
Classification: LCC HC79.I55 C68 2020 (print) | LCC HC79.I55 (ebook) | DDC 303.48/33—dc23
LC record available at https://lccn.loc.gov/2020031067
LC ebook record available at https://lccn.loc.gov/2020031068

Contents

Preface

For over five decades observers have declared we live in the Information Age. Sociologists, media, and many in the public have signed on to that view of modern times, but not so many historians. They see many problems with that paradigm. They find evidence of extensive use of information in many periods of history, not just in modern times. Evidence is mounting that by criteria used by many observers and the public, humankind has lived in an Information Age for a long time, while scientists and biologists are finding that animals and plants did too. A second problem a historian encounters involves definitions. What would an Information Age look like if we were living in one? A great deal of debate has taken place since the 1990s over that issue. I engage in a bit of that in the first chapter and sporadically through others. Put those two problems together and one quickly gets to a third: How should historians go about the work of understanding the role of information in society?

This book is an early attempt to answer that question. It advocates for a very specific, tactical approach for dealing with definitions and research methods relevant at this time. I recognize that as the field of information history expands and evolves, what I advocate will need to change. Meanwhile, we have to move forward. That means proposing a way that can encourage a larger community of historians, scholars, and students in other disciplines to participate. To strengthen my argument, this book presents case studies as demonstrations of what results look like, what in the parlance of computing one would call the "output," what in business and management one thinks of as the "end results."

Briefly, I argue that an effective approach to the study of information's role in society can be facilitated by understanding the role of information ecosystems and information infrastructures, how these evolved over time, how people used them and became dependent on them. Information ecosystems are about what information is embedded and used by people doing other things, such as working, raising children, or participating in civic affairs. Information infrastructures are about how information is created and delivered, for example, such as by using roads, a postal system, or the Internet. Examining both in a simultaneous integrative manner leads to a more precise understanding of the role of information, and to the specifics of what one might mean when they sense we live in an information-rich era. To do this, we have to discuss historiographical issues—the questions one needs to investigate—then apply specific research efforts to demonstrate the approaches presented here. These are building blocks for constructing a new understanding of history.

The case studies are important not just because of the chosen topics; rather, they demonstrate the broad applicability of using notions of ecosystems and infrastructures with which to understand myriad aspects of human behavior. These cases are largely narrow in scope, some broader, much as one would find historians writing when exploring new topics in history. The first chapters set up the work accomplished in subsequent case studies. Since a new field, too, needs its own infrastructure, chapter 3 tells the story of how another recently created field developed its own to suggest what is possibly coming for historians of information. Subsequent chapters present case studies. Note that they come from different periods in time and can be thematically linked to administrative structures and social communities.

The chapters containing case studies (2 through 8) were selected to illustrate how the proposed research approach can be applied to several aspects of information ecosystems and infrastructures currently attracting the attention of historians practicing their craft in more traditional ways. Chapter 2 looks at the role of information in business enterprises and industries, which to date have recently been animated by discussions about the role of information technologies (computers and communications) as an adjunct to issues concerning strategy, organization, and product marketing, for example. Since the use of information technologies has so animated research about information, it would seem interesting to see how historians dealt with the issue of computers as they, too, form an information ecosystem. To that end, chapter 3 describes their emerging ecosystem and infrastructure, paralleling what was occurring across industries and firms. Since governments were always massive users of information, often also building infrastructures used by protagonists in all our case studies, following the lead of what happened with computer historians, we look at the behavior of a long-standing profession—diplomacy—over an extensive time to see how our approach plays out. For that purpose chapter 4 discusses one diplomatic corps; it could have been French or British, military or legislative, no matter, as they all behaved the same when it came to the use of information. We learn that the behaviors evident in late twentieth-century information-intensive work were evident even over two hundred years ago. Chapter 5 then goes to the other extreme—groups of people who do not have to interact with each other (as required of diplomats and employees in corporations) to illustrate how the research might go. In our example, we provide a far more detailed case study, this one involving farm wives and their children. All the issues identified in the first four chapters are in evidence in this fifth one. It is purposefully detailed and lengthy to demonstrate that even groups one might think would be difficult if not impossible to research about their use of information, turn up at least as much evidence and documentation as what one would expect from diplomats, companies, and academics. Chapters 6 and 7 explores what happens in communities of highly specialized experts, IBM sales staffs, and then computer scientists. Both had to learn and exchange information. The story told of them illustrates how they behaved like the ladies and children of chapter 5, but within the context of their own ecosystems. We see that Spanish diplomats, farm wives, salesmen, and computer scientists are so similar in their behavior that our approach to the study of their information ecosystems and infrastructures has merit across wide swaths of the human experience. With chapter 8, we explore what occurs at the tiny level of one or few people, asking how they deal with information. The answer reinforces the value of the approach, because their behavior and ecosystem parallels what is presented in earlier case studies. Each serves the dual purpose of demonstrating the use of our approach and supporting it. After preparing these case studies, I concluded that many other hundreds of cases could have been chosen for inclusion, but that these seven were sufficient to make my point. I hope the reader will conclude that information ecosystems and infrastructures apply at the individual, community, firm, industry, and national levels across many periods of time and geographies. The approach is not proposed as a replacement for other ways of studying human behavior and especially history of people and societies. It is merely another technique constructed out of the accepted methods of historical research and which builds on what historians have learned about the history of information since the late twentieth century.

I end the main body of the book with a chapter summarizing the evidence in favor of studying information history using the proposed approach and muse about the future of the subfield of information history. A short bibliographic essay offers a starter kit of sources for those beginning to look at the history of information. The approach offered in this book is not intended to be a catchall model that can be applied universally; rather, it represents one way of approaching what an anonymous reviewer of this book called "the undoubtedly tricky research subject of information." What makes the history of information "tricky" is its ambiguous, sprawling nature. This book offers a path toward more certainty and specificity in studying the subject, to make research manageable within the realities with which historians, sociologists, and humanists work.

Several experts on information and technology have been especially influential on my thinking and encouraged my work. William Aspray, Thomas Misa, and Toni Weller over the years have been most helpful. As these case studies were put together, protagonists eagerly contributed and nowhere was this more the case than the ladies of Madison County, whose story I tell in Chapter 5. I tapped into their information ecosystem, flowing through it almost as a particular floating on water, as they handed me from one to another to make sure I got the story "right." I want to acknowledge the help of Clare K. Lillard, the current Extension Agent for Family and Consumer Sciences, Virginia Cooperative Extension, assigned to Madison and Orange Counties for opening doors to individuals interviewed for this study and to the half-dozen Virginia 4-H All Stars that opened doors and old boxes of evidence to me. I also appreciate the help provided by the interviewees who had never been questioned by a historian about their food activities. The library staffs at Virginia Tech, at the University of Minnesota, University of Wisconsin, and at the IBM Corporate Archives were generous in providing materials, advice, and help.

A number of the chapters began life as articles in this emerging field as I worked out the ideas presented in this book. I want to thank journals I originally published earlier versions of some of the material presented in this book. I would like to thank the University of Texas Press and *Information & Culture* for allowing me to publish a portion of my articles: "Shaping Information History as an Intellectual Discipline," in Chapter 1, "A Framework for Understanding Information Ecosystems in Firms and Industries" in Chapter 2, and "The Information Ecosystems of National

Diplomacy" in Chapter 4. Thanks also goes to the IEEE and the *IEEE Annals of the History of Computing* for allowing me to repurpose my article, "Studying History As It unfolds, Part 2," in Chapter 3, and finally *Enterprise and Society* for allowing me to do the same with "When Knowledge Transfer Goes Global," as the basis for Chapter 7. All those essays, however, have been substantially revised to reflect my current thinking and to fit into this book.

I want to thank the publishing team, especially Brennan Knight, our production editor on this project and the editor who supported this project, Jon Sisk, Vice President and Senior Executive Editor at Rowman & Littlefield. Errors and poor judgments are of my own making, for which I apologize. The views expressed here are mine, not necessarily of the Rowman & Littlefield Press or the University of Minnesota. If the reader wishes further discussion with me, I can be contacted at jcortada@umn.edu. In the meantime, welcome to an exciting new way of viewing history.

James W. Cortada

Part One

APPROACH

Chapter One

Information History as a Research Topic

The greatest thing in this world is not so much where we are, but in what direction we are moving.

—Oliver Wendell Holmes, 1870s

The study of information as a subject in its own right is a broadening field of interest to citizens, public officials, and scholars in many industries and disciplines. Historians are just coming to the subject. This chapter acknowledges that they face problems in defining the subject of information history, but argues that the topic can be coherently addressed. Six questions are posed for historians to answer that can assist in their study of this new subfield of history. Three strategies suggest what they can do to make the topic a fresh field of inquiry, called "information history," by drawing on the historiographical experience of other areas of historical inquiry. Then chapter 2 extends the conversation further by introducing the concepts of information ecosystems and infrastructures, two essential features of information history, using a case study. These two features are core subjects of this book, because the notion of "ecosystems and infrastructures" as an integrated idea provides the essential conceptual scaffolding needed to describe how facts are circulated, used, and modified. The idea also provides a path to the linkages—consequences—of the use of information in how people and their organizations behave. The objective is to move from a fuzzy idea—information—toward a more concrete appreciation of the centrality of its use in human affairs. This approach builds nicely on what biologists, for example, have come to understand about the behavior of animals, plants and weather, how sociologists and anthropologists study social ecosystems, and how businesses understand their commercial opportunities and competitive threats. In short, what is proposed in this book will seem familiar to researchers working in other fields of scholarship and thanks to the last case study, presented in chapter 8, familiar to individual readers.

Information, like a beautiful painting or a simple meal well cooked, is difficult to define, but, you know it when you experience it. The subject does not have to be obscure or difficult to define. Facts, such as your birthdate, are information, so too that George Washington was the first president of the United States. Every profession, hobby, and subject of interest has collections of information, some published in articles or books, others spread by word-of-mouth, still others scribbled in notebooks or stored on a spreadsheet, available on film and video, or as voice recordings or pictures. The key insight, however, is that pieces of information—facts—tend to cluster together in ways that make sense to humans. Weather data is rarely stored with information about sports, but could be; statistics on election outcomes are not stored with instructions on how to assemble a toy. Information is clustered together because it then becomes relevant and useful. That practicality spills over into the physical tools one uses to get to information, such as articles or books on a topic, use of databases and PCs, smartphones, even old fashioned file cabinets and their paper folders. Studies of the history of information build on this fundamental feature—facts grouped together for practical reasons—allowing us to connect what people do with information they use. Historians can then track the evolution of the collection and use of information over time.[1]

Does a consensus exist on what to study, and how? Of course not, because the subject is diverse and covers all human activity. Information is a new subfield of history, so scholars are still sorting out what to study, what questions to explore, and how best to present the results of their research and teaching. Historians are asking questions about such matters, just as they have for all other subfields of history.

We should begin by understanding three basic problems historians work with before jumping to questions to answer or to the development of a research strategy. The first involves defining what we mean by "information." Every historian working on the problem attempts to resolve this difficulty, yet finds it challenging due, in the words of one, to the "width of the proposed field."[2] One must still come to the table with some definition, as that view tells the researcher what to look for, what to study. The second problem is to document information's role in society, how it has been used, and the consequences that result. That is the heart of what someone does who looks at the history of information and how it fits into the history of any field or what society does. The third is to conduct historical research to explain the context in which information flourished and existed. Focusing on these three problems represents a useful a start. How to take steps two and three is the subject of this book.

This chapter is designed to perform some essential housekeeping and to introduce a way to study the history of information. First, we establish a definition of information as it is used throughout this book in a collection of case studies. Second, six questions are described that can inform the research agenda of an historian. I do not claim that these are THE six, rather six useful ones for the study of information's history. These questions helped guide the work done to prepare all subsequent chapters. We then move beyond housekeeping discussions to introduce the ideas and definitions of frameworks, information ecosystems, information infrastructures, and information flows, arguing that exploring these topics carries a researcher a long way in reconstructing the history of information. Armed with the concepts and their definitions we can begin discussing a strategy for exploring them. A reasonable question to ask is: how is what we propose so different than what historians do as a normal course of action? It is a crucial question—not a criticism—of the research proposals. They are different, but similar as well, which makes the pursuit of the history of information less uncomfortable or alien to an historian, for example. With these conversations completed, we move through a series of chapters that present case studies applying the ideas discussed here.

While all of this may appear to be an introduction to a user manual, a historian's cookbook, it is not that precise, because every research project is unique. However, at the risk of repetition, it is not necessary to offer a singular definition of information, but rather, to offer a multi-purpose framework for working with differing definitions and circumstances. Each historian has to shape their own definitions of the issues involved, especially what is information for their purposes. Historians can apply their differing definitions upon this proposed framework. However, for every project, historians cannot avoid committing to a definition as their first step. I propose one to get things started; the reader will want to reshape it, and defend their definition, as appropriate to their work.

WHAT IS INFORMATION? WHAT IS A FACT?

First, it helps to settle on a working definition of information that can be applied in this book. There is no widely accepted definition among historians and other scholars; however, the differences among them are narrow.[3] For our purposes, a simple definition is applied: information consists of data, in another word, facts. Each is an independent entity, such as a number or name. Because historians also speak about knowledge, let us agree with the users of that term that this word is about the idea of integrating together numerous facts and their context, as occurs, for example, when we discuss how many copies of this book were purchased last year through Amazon .com, or what weather New Yorkers experienced last night, and possibly the implications of those data points. Wisdom is a third word often used in discussing information and normally refers to understanding context in considerable detail in which a piece of information perches, such as patterns of book purchases in the United States or the kinds of weather one can expect in New York at this time of the year. When we circle back to information—facts—they become practical, relevant, and informative when they describe a situation, individual, place, or event. This is how we come to the notion of "I know it when I see it," because facts can describe situations, offer instructions on how to do something, or describe an unfolding event. Note that useful information is by definition, therefore, practical. For the study of the history of information it is useful to look for its practical application for doing something or to understand a situation. A map with facts about how to get from point A to B, or a text on how to prepare a spaghetti dinner, are practical examples of facts in use. A lecture on the evolution of polling practices in America and how they affected a national election is an illustration of facts providing context. Context is needed to make useful decisions about what actions to take or to develop an understanding about a circumstance.

The nature of information evolves over time. In the seventeenth century one might have described the weather with no use of numbers, but by the early 1800s, one could use numbers to describe temperature ranges or when the sun rose and set. Facts almost take on the feature of being an object, such as one's name, or as a tool to be used when needed, such as cooking recipes. But facts are also malleable, as they change over time, such as how the British defined democracy in the early 1900s versus how they see it today. Facts can be fuzzy, such as the idea of what democracy is, or very precise, such as that a democracy exists when citizens can vote for their senior public officials in the United States or Canada. As the centuries unfolded the features attributable to facts evolved. In the Middle Ages, religious causes of events were considered facts, such as "God did this." In the 1800s, humans were more responsible for facts, such as "pioneers populated the Western United States." In the twentieth century, the adjective began a long retreat from the world of facts, replaced with numbers, such as "95 percent of Americans believe in the existence of God." A hard fact is today the most sought after: the temperature is 72 degrees. A soft fact is less desirable, although still useful: the weather is quite nice.

Information is also in the eye of the beholder. An impoverished African American living in the South in the 1920s might believe that only white citizens were well off economically, while white sharecroppers might state as a fact—and be right—that they were having a tough time, too. The fact of poverty might have felt acceptable to an African American farmer, since he probably believed there was nothing he could do about it. A white farmer voting for Franklin D. Roosevelt for president could feel otherwise, because in the 1930s his family needed/demanded government support. Gender, race, and ethnicity influenced what constituted facts. They were made malleable by the context in which they appeared and were used.

In human behavior, facts encourage action. The revelation that there is a new flavor of ice cream on a hot summer day posted on a window of an ice cream parlor will cause someone to take an action: to try the new flavor. The revelation through a notice from one's bank that their account is overdrawn would probably cause a person to stop spending until more money appeared in their account. A parent wishing to give their child a new toy will be motivated more to do so if the instructions for putting it together are practical, understandable, and do not require a great deal of time or effort. The notion of facts stimulating actions is crucial to understanding the history of information, because by looking for the relationship between facts and action, one can identify the techniques, tools, and sources for access and application of information. If studying the role of blacksmiths in eighteenth century England, we could assume members of that profession had access to information useful in plying their trade. That assumption would help a historian to understand what facts (skills) someone had to be effective in this trade, to identify how they learned (acquired) that information, and how they applied it. The reverse also occurs: the individual has a new situation that requires he or she acquire facts with which to deal with it. For example, the kitchen faucet starts to leak and, in fact, the individual cannot afford to hire a plumber to fix it. So, they go to Youtube and find a video that explains exactly how they can make the repair. In practice in any period of history there is a back-and-forth movement of facts that are called up to support an action or that when they appear cause people to do something they otherwise might not have.

To sum up how the word "information" is applied in this book we rely on three observations. First, people use the words information or facts more frequently than older terms, such as knowledge or skills. Information can be assets, possessions, think physical objects.[4] We have patents and trademarks to protect these. We buy e-books on history, while information about competitors provides advantages in selling one's products over those of another. Facts are treated as things, much like a hammer or a pencil sharpener. Second, the amount of data that has accumulated over the centuries is staggering and the quantity of money people have been willing to spend to obtain and use that growing collection of facts is also remarkably high.[5] The closer one gets to the present, the more facts people used to make decisions, to take actions, or to form opinions. Your great grandmother may have only known how to prepare two to three dozen dishes, today you can prepare many hundreds of meals, thanks to the convenient availability of recipes that both men and women can access and apply.

Third, there is a growing body of studies on how people have used information conducted in multiple disciplines that can be used, copied, or improved upon by those studying history. That capability to borrow from one another's studies of information is what this book is about. Computer scientists and biologists taught us the concept of feedback loops, which in turn facilitated development of computers, which in turn made the collection of data—numbers—in vast quantities convenient, timely, and affordable, thus increasing our reliance on greater bodies of facts than our ancestors. Students of media developed theories on the social uses of information, librarians and scientists on how to organize bodies of information, and software engineers on how to create databases in ways effective for use by scientists, business professionals, and medical doctors.[6]

QUESTIONS OF INTEREST TO HISTORIANS OF INFORMATION

What questions—research topics—can historians of information pursue? Answering this query is a useful first step in studying information as a topic all of its own, because information can be ambiguous, comes in many forms, and is constantly changing all before even coming to any discussion of how people have used it or responded to its presence. So, an early useful task has to be to put a stake in the ground about what we want to study. Good history offers clarity about a situation, argued with sound evidence, and increasingly invigorated by acceptable and believed theory, but at a minimum with well-thought out arguments buttressed with facts. Think in terms of a Christmas tree as a metaphor. It is not more than a green tree standing in someone's living room until adorned with electric lights and decorations. Then we have a Christmas tree. Until then we have boxes of lights and decorations, possibly a tree stand and a small green tree leaning against a wall. What lights should we put on it? Do the lights go on before or after the decorations? Should the decorations convey a message, a theme? Why? We face the same issues with the history of information.

In a paper I published in 2012,[7] I proposed several questions that fit directly into the discussion here about what information is and how it became part of ecosystems and infrastructures. They are not necessarily the most crucial or only questions one might ask, but they seem to be standing the test of time. I offer them as a starter set, recognizing that as the field of information history evolves, other questions will certainly need to be asked. Many future ones will probably emerge from our experience with the Internet, a technology that in less than one generation has influenced our thinking about the nature and role of information, including the half-dozen questions presented here.[8]

First, what vessels were used to collect and store information in many different societies and times? This question engages the very long history of the study of books and archives. In the twentieth century other "vessels" or mediums were used, such as disk drives and e-publications, and long before the book, tablets made of clay. Today, machines are creating and storing information faster and in greater quantity than humans, so the question is far more complicated than ever. It is also important because the physical ephemera of information, including digitally-based ones, affect the nature and use of information ecosystems and infrastructures. Vessels can also include schools, universities, libraries, industrial research centers, publishers, associations, and government agencies.[9] Think broadly about the diversity of vessels.

Second, by profession, job, or other human activity, what information was collected, used, and shared? There are several aspects to this question. Building on the progress made over the past half century concerning feedback loops, students of information are learning what happens when we receive and react to facts in an interactive way. This insight, and the notion of feedback loops, emerged from studies in biology, cybernetics, artificial intelligence (increasingly called cognitive computing), and computer science.[10]

While historians are engaged, too, they remain outnumbered by so many other disciplines, including the librarians and computer scientists. Yet the question is central to what historians do, because it is their job to fill in many of the details, notably the activities of individuals, groups, and whole communities and nations. In the process they are responsible for identifying patterns of use, behavior, and consequences over time. Complicating the issue is that scholars in many other fields also think the history of information is important and are looking at it through the lenses of their disciplines.[11] When viewed by historians through those of, say, their or some other community, each with its own identity and patterns of behavior, the possibilities for historians of information become nearly endless, but crucial. Obvious early candidate organizations to view through the lens of information's history include libraries, publishers, booksellers, and schools, and that is before we get to the professions, such as law, medicine, and business. Just answering this question could consume generations of historians. What they know, so far, is that the bulk of what professionals did over more than two centuries was to collect, store, analyze, and apply information.[12]

Third, what were the patterns of adoption and use of information over time? The answer to this question often lies in exploring how the institutions in the second question collected and used information. People relied upon information variously in different times and places. A seventeenth century avatar in the minds of a Pilgrim in North America would have resembled a figure out of the Bible; for a twenty-first century Korean, an image lodged in the Internet. Yet, both found value in using avatars and the information associated with these in their personal lives and in how they interacted with the world around them. The key notion is that there are three facets—think spaces—of one's life in which facts play a role: work, leisure, and identity. Overlaying these are other activities requiring use of information, such as hobbies, community involvement, religious practices, and vacationing. Information generally used in one facet of life often also spills over into another. The worker who uses spreadsheets to track budgets as part of her job may well do the same to manage personal finances, or those of a church or non-profit to which she belongs. Historical research can describe these activities, their flow from one to another, and their influence on each other over time.[13] Historians can identify patterns of information use.

Examples exist that can be ported over to the history of information. The oldest of these, of course, are the descriptions of the rise and fall of civilizations made so popular originally by Edward Gibbon in describing the decline of the Roman Empire (he famously attributed it to lead piping to some extent, yet one could just as easily have criticized the role of asymmetric flows of information) and Arnold Toynbee in the early twentieth century, who kicked off decades of discussions about patterns of rise and fall. But the discussions continue.[14] Timothy H. Parsons, in examining various empires, argued that these rose based on temporary advantages that one party had over another in military technologies, wealth, and political power, all of which required explicit bodies of information.[15] Another historian, Ian Morris, described longer patterns of why Western societies—namely, Europe and North America—dominated global events, identifying arrangements of effects, largely geographic, much as was argued by Jared Diamond in his examination of what caused societies to thrive and fail.[16] Recently, Carmen M. Reinhart and Kenneth S. Rogoff, two economists, discussed the role of information in combination with other patterns of behavior to explain major financial crises over the past eight hundred years, building, in the process, a typology of financial problems that one could use to explain repeated common behaviors over time.[17]

More specific to the history of information, we also have the example of Joel Mokyr, who has written on the "knowledge economy," using a label in wide use among economists.[18] In this latter instance, knowledge and information are partially interchangeable, and Mokyr covers many centuries. An earlier study of his on the role of technology, which he likened to a lever that facilitated the creation of wealth in the Western world, was also about information—in this instance, technological and economic themes.[19] In his most recent book, Mokyr connects the role of information, publishing the rise of a "market for ideas" and the "Republic of Letters" made possible by new technologies (printing press) and infrastructure (postal systems) resulting in the creation and use of far more information in the Western World.[20] With this study we have a broad-based connecting of the role of information across centuries of human history. Daniel Headrick has also discussed such themes in three books, all of which consciously dealt with information. The first, *The Tools of Empire* (1981), described how the acquisition of information about technology and its use facilitated the growth of European imperialism in the 1800s. In *The Invisible Weapon* (1991) he discussed the role of telecommunications in international affairs from 1851 to 1945, and, finally, he published an excellent example of a study on how Europeans organized information from 1700 to 1850 in *When Information Came of Age* (2000).[21]

Fourth, how did the use of information affect the work and lives of specific individuals and then of groups? There are well known examples of people answering this question: sociologist Harley Shaiken looking at the effects of automation on factory workers, historian Richard Gillespie with the Hawthorne experiments, and historian JoAnne Yates in looking at the role of communications in corporations as part of the information story of the late 1800s–early 1900s.[22] I too became sensitized to the issue of information flows when examining how computers were used in nearly two dozen American industries. While I thought largely in terms of processes, not information, the work was overwhelmingly about moving information about and reacting to it.[23] What we all had in common was an interest in how people went about their work in an information-rich environment, but without overtly thinking in terms of information to the extent described in this chapter. What this fourth question calls forth is to do just that, make information the central theme.

These various approaches to historical research suggest that information history may be as much a perspective as a topic. By taking a process-centric view of knowledge work in *The Digital Hand*, I was led to relegate information to a lesser role in favor of other questions, such as how information technologies affected the tasks and economic behavior of whole industries. That approach involved trade-offs. For example, it meant spending less time describing what information—data—was gathered and its intrinsic forms or the cognitive or intellectual effect it had on people's behavior, let alone effects in creating community within firms and industries. In exchange, I was able to highlight the importance of industries in the economy and demonstrate that it was possible to identify personalities of industries and patterns of their behavior as large ecosystems of social and economic communities. Mokyr did a similar thing but on a much broader basis, drawing in entire civilizations. In the case of *The Digital Hand*, the approach offered a prize worth pursuing from the perspective of either economic or business history, and to that end information history played an important, albeit supporting, role. Other historians have confronted trade-offs when situating the role of information in some larger story, an issue evident in many historical eras.[24] One other important finding, however, was the significance of focusing on the spread of information's use in society: what was deployed, how much of it, how fast, to whom, when, and why.

Linked to this fourth question is the idea of information diffusion, the notion that information moved about within a group, an office, an organization, across society and that knowing how that happened, how quickly, and to whom, for instance, becomes a crucial component of any history of information. Richard D. Brown provided an influential approach to the matter when he looked at how information flowed through North America from 1700 to 1865 by examining specific professions and how they acquired and used such material.[25] These are themes also addressed by a new generation of researchers who have looked at the role of institutions such as those of the post office, telephone companies, and other communications technologies and, more recently, how information technology spread around the world. In all these cases, information's artifacts were instruments for the diffusion of information.[26] Diffusion of information as a candidate for research, however, represents an emerging opportunity for students of information's history not yet fully explored, but essential nonetheless to the task at hand.

Fifth, what other historical discourses should be viewed as information history? Would we include histories of the clock or of maps? Both are vessels containing information, both play crucial roles in affecting the behavior of individuals, and each does it in its own way. Clocks were not as important as the information they gave out—time—because time—a form of information—put people on a schedule to work and play, the key point made by historian David Landes in *Revolution in Time: Clocks and the Making of the Modern World*.[27] Elizabeth Eisenstein argued that politics and the activities of early modern Europe changed because so much new information became available through the invention of book printing.[28]

Sixth, what are the intrinsic features of facts themselves and how did those affect the creation and use of other facts? How did descriptions of things and circumstances evolve over time? What happened when information began evolving from narrative descriptive forms to numerical and statistical discourse? Back to our example from before, how did we move from "the weather was nice" to the "temperature was 72 degrees?" What happened when we went from "everyone is out of work," to "25 percent of the American workforce was unemployed in 1932?" How did we evolve from using a few pieces of data to inform a decision to relying on massive databases, today called Big Data, to develop mathematical models of options, before one made a decision? Information also has its own issues, such as the role of privacy, data security, cost, availability, and access. The list is quite long and can range across philosophical and literary considerations to economic and statistical/mathematical perspectives, from humanistic and sociological approaches to scientific ones. Professions come into play too: is business a discipline, does it have empirically based theories of best practices, or does it remain a craft, an art? These issues all represent grist for historians of information.

DEFINITIONS CENTRAL TO THE STUDY OF INFORMATION IN BUSINESS HISTORY

Keys to a useful paradigm are the concepts of *frameworks*, *information ecosystems*, *information infrastructures*, and *information flows*. Because the definition of what constitutes an *industry* is also subject to imprecise definition, it too needs clarification. All are related, yet have distinct meanings and purposes. To make the discussion simple, I define the term *framework* as a loosely structured approach to the study of a subject, offering a path, possibly a map, for organizing the exploration of an idea or topic. The concept of a framework has built into it assumptions about what might be discovered and possibly hypotheses to be challenged or proved. Their purpose is transitory, a temporary intellectual scaffolding to assist in the identification of what to study in the way of information's history in business.

The dominant overarching concept is "information ecosystems." Elsewhere, I have defined an information ecosystem as

> a collection of knowledge, experts and users much as academics think of a discipline (i.e., economics, history, or physics), but with the important difference that this body of knowledge and associated communities were far broader (larger too) than an academic discipline, the latter which would be more populated with academics and R&D practitioners in government and corporations.[29]

Over time information ecosystems became denser and larger. Density in business means more information, current knowledge of relevant technologies, and activities of a greater variety of participants (industries, vendors, public agencies, schools, and universities).

As the Industrial Revolution and new industries emerged, the use of foreign and domestic published sources of information grew as did literacy and the quantity and variety of publications, along with expanded experience in international trade and local training.

Simultaneously, learning experiences integrated across borders, such as what occurred in IBM research and development laboratories populated by many nationals, literally under one roof in a growing number of company campuses around the world, beginning in the 1930s.[30] Just as books and other publications flowed across borders and industries, so too did people, especially in these kinds of industrial research centers across Europe and the United States.

Embedded within information ecosystems is another notion of "information infrastructures." Historians have often expressed more interest in defining infrastructures rather than ecosystems, because it is often the physical manifestation of the ecosystems, consisting of the "things" that make possible the movement and use of information. These components of an infrastructure can include information and communications technologies, including networks, such as telephone lines, and today, the Internet.

Not all infrastructures were electronic, as they took many forms. Part of the infrastructure in business included reports, books, magazines, internal newsletters, spreadsheets, and various paper documents from train tickets to thick reports prepared by a consulting company for a client. An information infrastructure could also include buildings, such as libraries, magazine editorial headquarters, printing plants, classrooms, the ubiquitous office, and organizational schemes. Whole institutions can also be part of an information infrastructure (also its ecosystem), such as a university, a school, training center, headquarters, library, or publisher. Information infrastructure is both a term and a concept.

One group of scholars defined an information infrastructure as "a broad category referring to pervasive enabling resources in the networked form."[31] Keying off that definition, Megan Finn thinks in terms of analyzing these "pervasive enabling resources" that "help" people to do their work, but also acknowledges the physical feature of infrastructures as "tubes and wires."[32] Others contributed to the definition of information infrastructure by arguing that it included non-physical elements, such as organizations, information standards, and practices. Examples include time keeping (standardization) that make possible coordination of work over time and distances; practices in the way information is collected and used (best practices or the way things are done in a profession); and the role of institutions in formatting and delivering information as practiced by an organization. Finn reminds us that another historian, Paul Edwards, wants scholars to look at what appears at the bottom of an organization, things and activities that have "become standard, routine, transparent, invisible."[33]

How should one think of the role of information within an organization's information infrastructure? Information circulates within an organization used by a defined set of individuals with which to do their work. Participants include employees, their customers, suppliers, and others with whom they interact in the course of their work. All these people communicate information back and forth with each other on a frequent basis and depend on this shared information to conduct their activities. Their business or work ecosystem includes documents formatted in familiar ways about shared interests, other publications, knowledge, even value systems and worldviews, all bonded together as common experiences laden with information and knowledge too.

One can begin research on the topic of the flow of information within an organization's information ecosystem by describing its components, leaving to others to opine later on consequences and about its intrinsic features and their implied contingencies. Karl E. Weick, a professor of organizational behavior and psychology, and a growing coterie of like-minded scholars, have demonstrated over the past forty years that organizations have cultures and practices that influence how they learn. Their thinking has much to lend to the study of information's role in firms. Central to Weick's thinking is that organizations make "sense" of their surroundings by understanding activities and circumstances, placing these in a relevant context. Historians could borrow his examples and approaches, because they are compatible with the discussion of information, although he uses phrasing from other academic disciplines often not familiar to the historian.[34]

Infrastructures have been likened to "information systems," the subject of useful examination, as they existed in business enterprises.[35] In these instances, historians focus on the use of knowledge, monitoring of operations (managing), and strategies (the work of senior management). For historians of information in business, it has largely been about the production and use of information to control operations of a firm.[36] Bud-Friedman has usefully thought about such infrastructures in two ways. "At the *micro*-level" it is about "the information structures of organizations and systems, primarily within firms," although other types of organizations can fit here too, such as a government agency. She also thinks in terms of the "*macro*-level," which is about "the underlying foundation of information in society or the fixed information capital within an economy."[37] The macro-element is useful for the study of information at an industry level.

Since companies operate within industries, and industries are largely defined by the firms with which they identify, both micro- and macro-approaches to the study of information's history are related, indeed co-dependent. But, let us be clear about what we mean by industries as the word is often used loosely. For our purposes we use Walter Kiechel's simple, yet practical, definition, drawn from an interview with an important American management consultant, Philip Evans:

> What's an industry? A small number of largely similar organizations, internally collaborative, externally competitive, that connect to each other through the mechanism of a competitive market, and connect upstream to suppliers, downstream to customers.[38]

Add in the various social and economic constructs of nations on top of industries, and the conversation about the use of information takes one directly to the globalization of the work of firms and industries. That combination constitutes the information ecosystem and its myriad information infrastructures that constitute modern global economies.[39]

Another important informational term crucial to our understanding of information in business and economic settings, used less by historians and more by economists and business managers, is the notion of *information flows*. If one thinks of information as if it were an object, a "thing," we can ask, what does it do? Where does it go? Who does things with it? Why do its handlers do what they do? Information flows are the movement of information from one spot to another for different purposes and consequences. For example, a salesman obtains an order for a computer (the order is a collection of facts, such as the size of the machine and when it is needed). It is then entered into the company's order system, and the facts of the order are sent to a factory as one grouping of information. At the factory that order and its information is used to create a production schedule, while the same data goes to headquarters where it is tracked as a forecast of future business. Once the computer is installed at the customer's facility, the data involved in the original order is converted into accounting and financial data accumulating with that of other sales that appear within quarterly and annual reports to stakeholders. Information flows are about the creation and movement of data (facts), with emphasis on action. They are about activity, not descriptions of the informational artifact itself.

These concepts about information can now be joined. Thinking about the order just presented, essential to our understanding of the role of information in businesses and industries is the notion of *co-location*. In our case, multiple locations were involved: customer's office, sales person's office, factory, and headquarters. Most corporations have multiple locations, indeed some have thousands. Since the creation of firms that had more than one location, a piece of information could be located (physically deposited) in multiple places. Second is the idea that different people could be using the same information concurrently or in different ways at the same time. For example, Ford Motor Company's automobile salesmen could rely on the same information about the features of a particular model of a car in 1948 in their simultaneous attempts to sell that specific model to customers in five cities. Yet another feature of co-location is the availability of the same information for use by different companies and people, such as information about the state of the economy, "best practices," and the history of rivals.

There is a substantial body of literature on the symmetry and asymmetry of information in business that has drawn much attention by economists, less so by historians.[40] Back to our example of a computer sale, a customer might buy that product without knowing that there was a better, or less expensive, alternative. That disconnect between critical pieces of informa-

Table 1.1. Definitions of Information History Concepts

Information Framework: An approach to the study of a subject, offering a path, possibly a map, for organizing the exploration of an idea or topic.
Information Ecosystems: A collection of knowledge, experts, and users much as academics think of a discipline, but with the important difference that this body of knowledge and associated communities are far broader than an academic discipline.
Information Infrastructures: Networks of physical items that make the movement and use of information possible, such as the Internet and laptop computers.
Information Flows: The movement of information from one spot to another for different purposes and consequences.

tion may even exist in the same firm when, for example, people in one office might be aware of alternative products to acquire while those doing the acquisition did not. Historians should acknowledge that access to the same information by contentious groups (e.g., one's competitors) and by those not in contending situations (e.g., the same information about a biological phenomenon used by the medical profession and pharmaceutical companies) also exist simultaneously. The histories of technology and the work of business management professors are rife with examples and solid historical research on this characteristic, but this has not yet been part of the study of information history.[41] To summarize, table 1.1 provides our key definitions of informational constructs for historians.

A STRATEGY FOR PURSUING INFORMATION HISTORY

These are six broad questions but they represent the start of a strategy for addressing the nebulous issue of what constitutes information history. Since "everyone" uses information and so much of it is on paper, verbalized, listened to, or seen on a screen, a researcher needs a plan that makes a project specific enough to make sense of it. That is why these questions can serve as a first step and why they are proposed as a lens through which to see the topic. These also move a research project into the format, call it structure, of how much historical research is done: by event, person, group, organization, and nation. In short, information history offers another facet, another dynamic to existing approaches to the study of history. The cases presented in this book illustrate a broad range of possibilities. It is a way a reader can identify connections to information by the fact that if already an expert on the subject of a case study, looking at it from the perspective of information, it seems familiar. A Spanish diplomatic historian or another of twentieth century business will find much that is already familiar, but now augmented by a discussion of the information plumbing that supports otherwise familiar events and activities.

A sufficient amount of work has already been done by historians of information to make it possible to define next steps, if you will, and that also draws from techniques applied successfully by historians of military, diplomatic, economic, business, and social themes. While historians favor choosing their own topic and the research strategy they wish to deploy, they share common methods and tell stories of prior events and circumstances. Those work well, too, in writing information history. Three actions, in particular, stand out: document processes, what people did; describe the context in which information was used; and conduct historical research and publish the results. Each step forward contributes to a growing set of practices, a community of like-interested individuals, and an expanding bibliography of examples and insights on the role of information. At the risk of being too prescriptive, each step merits further discussion.

On the recommendation that one should document processes, the key idea is that professions and organizations do work, normally in some common, relatively repetitive fashion. That work—called processes here—is often well documented and normally sustained by a large body of facts needed in order for a participant to perform their work. It can be as simple as the process for applying for a driver's license, which requires an applicant to provide the government with a certain collection of facts about themselves (e.g., name, address, birthdate) and for the state to do the same (e.g., conduct driver training, score a test to determine the extent of knowledge an applicant has of driving laws, document increased use of public roads) all the way to a complex international supply chain.

A supply chain can involve the participation of hundreds of companies providing parts, partial manufacturing, total fabrication of a product (such as a car), and its distribution to retail outlets around the world. Rarely is a car manufactured today of which more than 50 percent of all its thousands of parts originates from one country. To operate this supply chain requires coordination and collaboration and those two actions only occur if there is an understanding of roles and actions. That understanding only happens if information is shared and managed. So, viewing work as organized activities buttressed by the creation, use, analysis, movement, and storage of information is essential. Historians can document those elements, describe how they have evolved over time (such as how cars are made today versus in the 1920s) and the kind of information used, how events and information changed over time, and the decisions and effects of those actions.

This proposal to study processes builds nicely on a long-standing tradition of historians documenting the work of such literate professions as lawyers, teachers, public officials, priests, factory workers, business managers, fellow scholars, scientists, and engineers, as well as children and housewives. The starting-off point for modern studies of professions and, hence, the information that buttresses them, continues to be the work of Andrew Abbott, the sociologist who suggested that professions were composed of experts and that their expertise could be described and understood.[42] How people went about their work reveals a great deal about the information they needed and how they acquired it. Too many professions remain unstudied in their use of information (or knowledge), particularly those that were not considered literate, such as blacksmithing, farming, and soldiering, before World War II. Yet, in each case, one can probe and find a knowledge base, transmitted either orally, through written text, or through some combination of the two. There are many hundreds of professions to examine across several thousand years in some two hundred countries.

Even in modern times, not all information is acquired through the printed word. A survey done of senior executives by business school professors in the early 1990s documented, for example, how little information the executives gathered from printed sources; rather, they learned and gained information by talking with people whom they trusted.[43] Reijo Savolainen has done more than anyone in recent times to argue the case that non-institutional distribution of information, such as conversations with friends, neighbors, and colleagues, is much more important than institutional sources, suggesting even further the need to account for everyday information-sharing practices.[44]

The same exercise can be performed to document the activities of entire communities of practice, because they share common interests and play pivotal roles in promoting the use of specific types of information in equally specific ways (processes). All rely on large bodies of information shared by their members. In fact, the diffusion of specific types of information within an organization is often the primary function of such an association. Historians have the American Historical Association (AHA), doctors their two dozen "colleges" by specialty, labor unions their own nearly two hundred groups in the United States and others in Europe, and so it is with thousands of nonprofit associations, professional societies, and industry lobbying groups. They all essentially do the same thing: promote their members' interests and skills, and the only tool they have for that mission is the use of information. Historians know how to study these bundles of people. Walter Friedman has studied the development of salesmanship as a profession in the United States, Nathan Ensmenger early computer programmers, Olivier Zunz entire corporations, Lars Heide the activities of entire nations in their use of data processing.[45] Hundreds of such examples can be cited. So many exist that one journal has already started the practice to annually publish bibliographies of information history, *Library & Information History.*

Some groups have been more studied than others, such as librarians, doctors, lawyers, scientists, teachers, and their associations. But it is surprising how the role of information has appeared in the studies of other associations and professions: waitresses, automotive mechanics, salesmen, nurses, paper manufacturing workers, metal workers, Antebellum Southern U.S. plantation foremen, publishers, and soldiers, among others. But so many have not, representing opportunities for historians: booksellers, dry cleaning managers, butchers, farmers, and of course all new professions, such as management consulting, astronauts, and biotechnologists, for example. Normally, sociologists and business professors, and later historians, are the first to study the newer ones, following the paper trail to see how information is used. They normally focus on the work and circumstances of the individual or association, not on information. What is different now is that information or processes can be the lead protagonist with the individual or organization playing a supportive role.

This shift quickly gets us to the second task, that of understanding and describing the context in which information and its use took place in those professions, organizations, nations, and circumstances suggested above. Historical research has always been about enriching our understanding of events through a careful reconstruction of the context of events and the activities of people and organizations, the answering of the question, "why?" That is not news, but for the history of information it is all new news, because, often, context was about what someone knew or believed was happening, on the one hand, and what historians argue was occurring, on the other. We are learning that by studying the history of information, historians are being presented with a number of opportunities to expand their understanding of the role of context itself.

Several examples illustrate the opportunity at hand. Abstract types of knowledge work quickly come to mind, such as theoretical physics and economics, the work of mathematicians, or, on a more mundane level, that of mechanical and civil engineers, software programmers, and software engineers. We can trace what these practitioners knew before and during their work, especially on specific projects. For instance, many early developers of computers and software grew up as amateur radio operators or as mathematicians before turning their hands to the development of computers. Those prior disciplines, bodies of information, and practices influenced how they approached their work with computers.[46] Tracing this intellectual path dependency helps to understand how people applied information, even what types they collected and valued, and explain why. Every modern profession has an antecedent that can be studied. We already know that armed with information, its users learn to gather and use it differently over time. They leave behind a paper trail whose contents can be studied, as is demonstrated in every case study in this book. Biographers have long done this; historians can do the same about information.

One example of how this can matter came to light when historians began to study what military cadets, later officers, learned in the 1800s and early 1900s in military academies in Spain, France, and Germany. Thirty years later, when these individuals commanded armies and directed wars, historians observed that they did not have a widely shared worldview of their work and the politics of their time, going far to explain their highly divergent actions.[47] Yet in the second half of the twentieth century, they did, largely attributable to their personal participation in NATO and in the new practice of attending military training in other countries, such as French, Spanish, Dutch, and German cadets and officers at U.S. military academies and officer training facilities. The result of the shared context and bodies of belief and information resulted in behavior quite different than those of their pre-World War II predecessors.[48]

Historians also observed that simultaneous with the influence of events, training, and attitudes—context—people in many professions reflected on past events and their meaning, thereby affecting their future actions. The late science historian Michael Mahoney documented an example of this intellectual path dependency by exploring the role of software engineers. That exercise enabled him to demonstrate how clusters of information and beliefs affected behavior and use of data in a different profession, in this instance how these engineers misappropriated the notion of Henry Ford's mass production of cars to inform their own practices.[49] The most obvious example of this kind of retrospection relying on memory and information are personal memoirs, which document an individual's changing views, skills, and actions over a long period of time. Often they describe what facts they had at the time they made a decision, using the availability or lack of these in defense of their actions.

Longitudinal documentation of what people did as suggested by memoirs can be applied more formally by historians examining the values and experiences of generations of workers, or cohorts, and how those affected the scope of information. What does that mean? Essentially, this turns out to be a hunt for what information existed at a particular time to an individual or group and how they used it. The widely cited examples of this kind of research on information dominated the scores of studies conducted on what the American government knew before the Japanese attacked the U.S. Navy at Pearl Harbor on December 7, 1941, and again when the events of 9/11, 2001, unfolded in the United States. Winston Churchill's use of decoded German military messages during World War II has now emerged as one of a half dozen reasons why the Allies were able to defeat Hitler's armies. In each instance, behavior was influenced by both narrow contextual considerations, such as what information the American president had with respect to planned Japanese attacks on the United States. Similar responses can be documented of whole nations of citizens, such as the cautious fiscal behavior of Americans who lived through the Great Depression of the 1930s, and for the rest of their lives avoided debt and sought material security. In the process of implementing this behavior they acquired and used a great deal of information to inform their financial decisions and who to vote for. The point is, the study of contextual influences is largely an examination of what people knew—their facts—and therefore, what information they had to use.

The study of context presents a third opportunity that can be extracted from the behavior of economic and business historians. They are largely influenced by the concept that activities of human beings, and their use of information, can be explained as a world filled with supplies of things, experiences, or information balanced against the demand for these, such as for a product or some other asset. On the supply side, we want to know what information is being created and for what purpose. These are contextual agents. Then on the demand side of the equation, we want to understand how information is received and used, followed by resulting consequences. Business and economic historians have borrowed from the biologists and cybernetic experts the idea of feedback, which in our example informs those who are supplying new information and then measuring how the demand side (customers, users) responds. Because of the work already done by economic and business historians, we can begin to impose on the history of information formal models and theories, just as Abbott did to professions. In other words, these historians have provided methods that can be used to study the role of information in institutions such as industries, companies, military forces, government agencies, nonprofit organizations, and even informal groups such as neighborhood associations and farm wives' "demonstration clubs" for sharing information about food preparation and child rearing.

HOW DIFFERENT IS THIS APPROACH FROM NORMAL HISTORICAL PRACTICE?

Historians are loath to change their methods of work. There have been only several fundamental changes in their practices in the past 150 years: the introduction by German scholars of the primacy of archival research and use of citations and footnotes in the nineteenth century; application of statistics and numerical data in the mid-twentieth century; and just emerging now, use of the Internet and its capabilities to aggregate massive quantities of numbers, facts, and electronic impulses, while engaging in ever-larger networks of collaborative research and authorship.[50] In essence, historians describe what happened. That is their core deliverable. Barbara Tuchman may have provided the shortest description ever given of what historians do: they "tell stories." Another great historian, David McCullough, made a similar comment: "That's what history is: story."[51] But history is also about explaining why events happened, how they affected people and other activities. Like a well-written newspaper article, good history addresses the "who-what-when-where-why" dictum. A historian must, thus, tell a story, explain why it unfolded as she thought it did, and leave us with an understanding of its context.

Another feature of historical research is that answers are not definitive. This circumstance stands in contrast to the practice of scientists who seek explanations for some phenomena that are widely accepted by colleagues as absolute. In contrast with history, uncovering new information, or connecting together facts in new ways, provides opportunities to explain what happened differently. As events unfold, new insights become possible, accumulating over time, making it possible, for example, to write biographies of famous people different than earlier efforts. For example, hundreds of books have been written about why World War I occurred, each arguing that it was closer to the truth, and yet as more facts or points of view unfurl, new interpretations unfold. In their discipline, there is no absolute, ultimate truth about what caused World War I, only momentary consensus at best.[52] As a result, historians continuously find new typologies, tools, methods, perspectives, and primary source materials standard fare for them, continuously offering them new ways to look at events, their causes, and the consequences.

While stubborn about how they practice their trade and even slow to adopt new approaches (e.g., use of statistics in the 1930s–1950s, Big Data in the 2000s, computers in the 1980s–2000s), historians welcomed the Internet, which has made possible so many new practices for them, reinforcing their fundamental mission to tell a story and to make it understandable and relevant. By the time the Internet became a practical source of information for them after the turn of the century, they had learned to use personal computers, spreadsheets, and word processors, creating the necessary preconditions to take advantage of the Internet. Two students of how scholars use the Internet for research concluded that "humanities scholars have by and large responded enthusiastically to the availability of digital resources."[53] One byproduct of using the Internet has been to raise the consciousness of all disciplines about the importance of information ecosystems and networks. That insight, born out of the experience of using the Internet for over two decades by scholars in dozens of fields, boils down to several insights relevant to our argument.

The first involves a slowly discernable shift from the "lone wolf" model of the single researcher/author to a new style in which either multiple historians collaborate on the research and writing of a narrative, or that depend on a growing network of colleagues at different points in their work. For example, historians of computer science often reach out to virtual communities to obtain immediate insights from colleagues about an issue such as through the American Historical Association's "Members Forum" where scholars ask each other for help on a research or teaching issue and for sharing insights.[54] In other words, historians have become conscious of the existence of an ecosystem surrounding their work and rely on it more today than in earlier decades. It is a phenomenon that emerged in other disciplines and has acquired various names, such as "social informatics."[55] Historians and colleagues in the humanities and social sciences have also proven aggressive in shaping the behavior of such ecosystems and, in the process, the nature of information technologies—applications, data sets—and how they are used.[56] As they become self aware that they live and work in an intellectual ecosystem, they ask if such ecosystems existed before the arrival of the Internet. The cases of Spanish diplomats and IBM employees answer with a resounding "yes" to the question. Historians bring to light entire social and operational aspects to the work and play of earlier generations that they have not studied methodically. By applying insights from their personal involvement and that of colleagues in other disciplines they can look back to earlier times. A conclusion we can reach is that historians looking at information ecosystems are doing business as usual—telling a story—but also uncovering new ways to understand the past.

All of which leads us to a second question: Haven't historians always had information infrastructures, such as libraries, bookstores, postal services, publishers, and journals-of-record? Indeed, haven't they always used these in support of their work? At the operational level of historians collecting information, exchanging ideas, and publishing their writings, the answer is again, "yes." Yet, in the past they did not have the ability to optimize, to shape their information infrastructure. Today they do. They can control what data sets they look at within existing online files, what websites they rely upon, self-publish their own work, or create their own journals and blogs. It is all quite dynamic, quick, and ever changing. In the process, historians become aware of the characteristics of infrastructures, something they would hardly have paid attention to in the past. Examine any "how-to" historiography text of the pre-Internet era and you will not find discussions about information infrastructures. The mailbox was always out front, the *American Historical Review* has been published for over a hundred years, most key journals for at least a half century, and so forth. One adapted to them, not them to the historian. As that circumstance evolved, historians and scholars in other humanities and social science disciplines have become conscious observers of infrastructures.

The subject itself has been a topic of discussion in most disciplines for over two decades.[57] Scholars have come to realize that even physical infrastructures are socially constructed, involving objectives, issues to study, problems to solve, application of new methods (as we do in this book), acquiring appropriate technologies, defining new theories and hypotheses, and uncovering exemplary examples and artifacts.[58] That immediate personal experience presents today's historians with a body of insight and experiences they can use to revisit old stories of the past to see events in new ways.[59] The behavior of the ladies of Madison County, Virginia, described in chapter 5, reveals that they purposefully created and nurtured information infrastructures that were both physical (e.g., newsletters) and social (e.g., meetings) in ways reminiscent of what scientists do today long before the Internet became available.[60] So, we are again presented with the situation that historians are becoming aware of information-driven infrastructures by going about their daily lives and can use that experience to ask if such infrastructures existed in earlier times, what they looked like, how important they were, and how they used them, knowing what to look for and how to weave their findings into the stories they tell.

So, to the potential criticism that exploring information ecosystems and information infrastructures is not a new way of doing history; in fact, looking at such issues is both an extension of tried-and-true practices of the discipline but also the application of new ways of interacting with information and in the process making information the protagonist of a story. How is that done? Our six framing questions serve as ways of reaching answers to that question. As Wiebe Bijker argued so well, frames (in our case the six questions and the focus on information ecosystems and infrastructures) are similar to Thomas Kuhn's use of the idea of scientific paradigms.[61]

A WAY FORWARD

Ultimately, it comes down to practicing history, of doing the work. Carefully prepared case studies of how people created and used information are a tried and proven method for exploring all manner of history, including information. Historians have the ability to define ambiguous situations to make sense of events, their origins, and the consequences. All are required for the study of information. As awareness of information as central to the activities of any modern society increases, so too does demand for histories of information. Treating information as an object as real as a hammer or smartphone, then embedding these into the context of work done by people and organizations, is how the history of information is done. We no longer have to justify the need for such history, as just a few years ago.[62] We now have to move broadly into the implementation phase of doing historical research on the subject of information. The subject still needs shaping, possibly more precise definition, and certainly its role needs more understanding. These three tasks are complicated by the fact that so many disciplines are engaged in that effort, not just historians, each bringing to the task their own methodologies and perspectives. The questions and strategies presented in this chapter are intended to facilitate the move from ambiguity to specific actions, from historians working here and there in isolation from each other to a more purposeful collection of knowledge about the role of information in human history. Now that we have the broad questions before us, we turn to a methodological scaffolding to assist in the bread-and-butter actions of the historians. To that end, we move to the fundamental issue of how information ecosystems and infrastructures assist studying the history of information in detail and to our first example of how to use them in the next chapter.

NOTES

1. See, for example, the important work of Mary Poovey, *A History of the Modern Fact: Problems of Knowledge in the Sciences of Wealth and Society* (Chicago: University of Chicago Press, 1998), and its link to books in the equally impressive

scholarship of Adrian Johns, *The Nature of the Book: Print and Knowledge in the Making* (Chicago: University of Chicago Press, 1998).

2. Alistair Black, "Information History," *Annual Review of Information Science and Technology* 40 (2006): 445.

3. For a fuller discussion of definitions and issues related to it, James W. Cortada, *All the Facts: A History of Information in the United States Since 1870* (New York: Oxford University Press, 2016), 1–21.

4. M. K. Buckland, "Information as Thing," *Journal of the American Society for Information Science* 42 (1991): 351–360.

5. Explored in more detail in James W. Cortada, *Information and the Modern Corporation* (Cambridge, MA: MIT Press, 2011).

6. James Gleick, *The Information* (New York: Pantheon, 2011); Paul Ceruzzi, *A History of Modern Computing*, 2nd ed. (Cambridge, MA: MIT Press, 2003): 1–12; M. K. Buckland and Z. Liu, "History of Information Science," *Annual Review of Information Science and Technology* 30 (1995): 385–416; Frank Webster, *Theories of the Information Society*, 3rd ed. (London: Routledge, 2006); Brian Kahin and Dominique Foray, eds., *Advancing Knowledge and the Knowledge Economy* (Cambridge, MA: MIT Press, 2006); Cortada, *All the Facts*, 1–27.

7. James W. Cortada, "Shaping Information History as an Intellectual Discipline," *Information and Culture: A Journal of History* 47, no. 2 (2012): 119–144.

8. For an early rigorous study of the Internet's effects, see Eric T. Meyer and Ralph Schroeder, *Knowledge Machines: Digital Transformations of the Sciences and Humanities* (Cambridge, MA: MIT Press, 2015).

9. Communities of scholars can also be seen as repositories of information, Anthony Grafton, *Worlds Made by Words: Scholarship and Community in the Modern West* (Cambridge, MA: Harvard University Press, 2009): 1–8.

10. Gleick, *The Information,* 8–9, 238–39, 298–300, 205–6.

11. Meyer and Schroeder, *Knowledge Machines*, 125–174.

12. A key finding after looking at the specifics of individual professions in the trades, professions, and in the public sector, Cortada, *All the Facts.*

13. A major research priority in Cortada, *All the Facts.*

14. An accessible modern edition is Edward Gibbon, *The Decline and Fall of the Roman Empire* (New York: Penguin, 2001); see also Arnold Toynbee, *A Study of History*, 2 vols. (Oxford: Oxford University Press, 1987).

15. Timothy H. Parsons, *The Rule of Empires: Those Who Built Them, Those Who Endured Them, and Why They Always Fall* (New York: Oxford University Press, 2010).

16. Ian Morris, *Why the West Rules—for Now: The Patterns of History, and What They Reveal about the Future* (New York: Farrar, Straus and Giroux, 2010); Jared Diamond in two books: *Collapse: How Societies Choose to Fail or Succeed* (New York: Viking, 2011), and his earlier *Guns, Germs, and Steel: The Fates of Human Societies* (New York: W. W. Norton, 2005).

17. Carmen M. Reinhart and Kenneth S. Rogoff, *This Time Is Different: Eight Centuries of Financial Folly* (Princeton, NJ: Princeton University Press, 2009).

18. Joel Mokyr, *The Gifts of Athens: Historical Origins of the Knowledge Economy* (Princeton, NJ: Princeton University Press, 2002).

19. Joel Mokyr, *The Lever of Riches: Technological Creativity and Economic Progress* (New York: Oxford University Press, 1990).

20. Joel Mokyr, *Culture of Growth: The Origins of the Modern Economy* (Princeton, NJ: Princeton University Press, 2017).

21. Daniel R. Headrick, *The Tools of Empire: Technology and European Imperialism in the Nineteenth Century* (New York: Oxford University Press, 1981); Daniel R. Headrick, *The Invisible Weapon: Telecommunications and International Politics, 1851–1945* (New York: Oxford University Press, 1991); Daniel R. Headrick, *When Information Came of Age: Technologies of Knowledge in the Age of Reason and Revolution, 1700–1850* (New York: Oxford University Press, 2000).

22. Harley Shaiken, *Work Transformed: Automation and Labor in the Computer Age* (New York: Holt, Rinehart & Winston, 1985); Richard Gillespie, *Manufacturing Knowledge: A History of the Hawthorne Experiments* (Cambridge: Cambridge University Press, 1991); JoAnne Yates, *Control through Communication: The Rise of System in American Management* (Baltimore, MD: Johns Hopkins University Press, 1989).

23. James W. Cortada, *The Digital Hand*, 3 vols. (New York: Oxford University Press, 2004–2008).

24. See, for example, Toni Weller, *Information History in the Modern World: Histories of the Information Age* (New York: Palgrave, 2011), and her earlier study, *Information History—an Introduction: Exploring an Emerging Field* (New York: Neal-Schuman Publishers, 2008).

25. Richard D. Brown, *Knowledge Is Power: The Diffusion of Information in Early America, 1700–1865* (New York: Oxford University Press, 1989).

26. Richard R. John in two books, *Spreading the News: The American Postal System from Franklin to Morse* (Cambridge, MA: Harvard University Press, 1995) and *Network Nation: Inventing American Telecommunications* (Cambridge, MA: Harvard University Press, 2010); and in my own work on a global history of how information technology spread to many countries, James W. Cortada, *The Digital Flood: The Diffusion of Information Technology Across the U.S., Europe, And Asia* (New York: Oxford University Press, 2012). A group of scholars looked at the role of information in the United States from literacy and diffusion to the effects of information on work with an emphasis on the supply side and with a detailed bibliographic essay: Alfred D. Chandler Jr. and James W. Cortada, eds., *A Nation Transformed by Information: How Information Has Shaped the United States from Colonial Times to the Present* (New York: Oxford University Press, 2000).

27. David Landes, *Revolution in Time: Clocks and the Making of the Modern World* (Cambridge, MA: Harvard University Press, 1983).

28. Elizabeth Eisenstein, *The Printing Revolution in Early Modern Europe* (Cambridge: Cambridge University Press, 1983).

29. James W. Cortada, "When Knowledge Transfer Goes Global: How People Public and Organizations Learned About Information Technology, 1945–1970," *Enterprise and Society* 14, no. 1 (2014): 68–102.

30. Arthur L. Norbert and Jeffrey R. Yost, *IBM Rochester: A Half Century of Innovation* (Rochester, MN: IBM Corporation, 2006).

31. Geoffrey C. Bowker, Karen Baker, Florence Millerand, and David Ribes, "Toward Information Infrastructure Studies: Ways of Knowing in a Networked Environment," in *International Handbook of Internet Research*, ed. Jeremy Hunsinger, Lisbeth Klastrup, and Matthew Allen (Dordrecht: Springer Science+Business Media B.V., 2010): 98.

32. Quoted in Margot Finn, "Information Infrastructure and Description of the 1857 Fort Tejon Earthquake," *Information and Culture* 48, no. 2 (2013): 196–197," 196.

33. Paul N. Edwards, *A Vast Machine* (Cambridge, MA: MIT Press, 2010): 20; discussed by Finn, "Information Infrastructure and Description of the 1857 Fort Tejon Earthquake," 196–197.

34. His major works have been collected into two volumes, Karl E. Weick, *Making Sense of the Organization*, 2 vols. (Malden, MA: Blackwell Publishing, 2001 for volume one) (Hoboken, NJ: John Wiley & Sons, 2009). Volume two is the more useful one for historians of information; but see also Karl E. Weick, *Sensemaking in Organizations* (Thousand Oaks, CA: SAGE Publications, 1995): 63–82, 184–185, and the extensive bibliography in ibid., 198–217.

35. H. T. Johnson, "Managing by Remote Control: Recent Management Accounting Practices in Historical Perspective," in Peter Temin, ed., *Inside the Business Enterprise: Historical Perspectives on the Use of Information* (Chicago, IL: University of Chicago Press, 1991): 41–70; M. Levenstein, "The Use of Cost Measures: The Dow Chemical Company, 1890–1914," in Peter Temin, ed., *Inside the Business Enterprise: Historical Perspectives on the Use of Information* (Chicago, IL: University of Chicago Press, 1991): 71–116.

36. Alfred D. Chandler, Jr., *The Visible Hand: The Managerial Revolution in American Business* (Cambridge, MA: Harvard University Press, 1977); Yates, *Control through Communication*; James R. Beniger, *The Control Revolution: Technological and Economic Origins of the Information Society* (Cambridge, MA: Harvard University Press, 1986); Cortada, *The Digital Hand*, 3 vols. and *Information and the Modern Corporation*; Lisa Bud-Frierman, ed., *Information Acumen: The Understanding and Use of Knowledge in Modern Business* (London: Routledge, 1994), 7–25; Johnson, "Managing by Remote Control: Recent Management Accounting Practices in Historical Perspective."

37. Both quotes, Bud-Frierman, *Information Acumen*, 7–8.

38. Walter Kiechel III, *The Lords of Strategy: The Secret Intellectual History of the New Corporate World* (Boston, MA: Harvard Business Press, 2010): 293.

39. Emily S. Rosenberg, ed., *A World Connecting, 1870–1945* (Cambridge, MA: Harvard University Press, 2013); Alfred D. Chandler, Jr., *Scale and Scope: The Dynamics of Industrial Capitalism* (Cambridge, MA: Harvard University Press, 1990); John H. Dunning, "The Key Literature on IB [international busi-

ness, ed. Note] Activities: 1960–2006," in Alan M. Rugman, ed., *The Oxford Handbook of International Business, 2nd ed.* (New York: Oxford University Press, 2009): 39–71. Although not an historian, rather a business management professor, the work of Michael E. Porter is seminal to any understanding of late twentieth century business practices, and in particular for global issues see, *Competition in Global Industries* (Boston, MA: Harvard University Press, 1986), *The Competitive Advantage of Nations* (New York: The Free Press, 1990).

40. One of the first economists to examine the issue through many articles is Joseph E. Stiglitz, *Selected Works of Joseph E. Stiglitz*, vol. 1, *Information and Economic Analysis* (New York: Oxford University Press, 2009): 29–94, 481–648, and the large bibliography that follows in this volume. 649–688.

41. For an excellent collection of case studies, see Clayton Christensen, *The Innovator's Dilemma* (Cambridge, MA: Harvard Business School Press, 1997).

42. Andrew Abbott, *The System of Professions: An Essay on the Division of Expert Labor* (Chicago, IL: University of Chicago Press, 1988) In addition to his examples, his bibliography is a veritable starter kit for the subject of information-rich professions. See also, for another example by yet another person who was not an historian, Shoshana Zuboff, *In the Age of the Smart Machine: The Future of Work and Power* (New York: Basic Books, 1984). She interviewed "blue-collar" workers.

43. Sharon M. McKinnon and William J. Bruns, *The Information Mosaic: How Managers Get the Information They Really Need* (Boston, MA: Harvard Business School Press, 1992).

44. Reijo Savolainen, *Everyday Information Practices: A Social Phenomenological Perspective* (Metuchen, NJ: Scarecrow Press, 2008).

45. Nathan Ensmenger, *The Computer Boys Take Over: Computers, Programmers, and the Politics of Technical Expertise* (Cambridge, MA: MIT Press, 2010); Walter A. Friedman, *Birth of a Salesman: The Transformation of Selling in America* (Cambridge, MA: Harvard University Press, 2005); Olivier Zunz, *Making America Corporate, 1870–1920* (Chicago: University of Chicago Press, 1992); Lars Heide, *Punched-Card Systems and the Early Information Explosion, 1880–1945* (Baltimore, MD: Johns Hopkins University Press, 2009).

46. Memoirs are excellent sources; see, for example, one written by an early developer of computers, Maurice Wilkes, *Memoirs of a Computer Pioneer* (Cambridge, MA: MIT Press, 1985); for a more philosophical and intellectual example, a good model is Robert Wright, *Three Scientists and Their Gods: Looking for Meaning in an Age of Information* (New York: Times Books, 1988); by a historian of IT, Ensmenger, *The Computer Boys Take Over*; and for an anthology focused on one group, see Thomas J. Misa, ed., *Gender Codes: Why Women Are Leaving Computing* (New York: John Wiley & Sons—IEEE Computer Society Press, 2010).

47. Stanley G. Payne, *Politics and the Military in Modern Spain* (Stanford, CA: Stanford University Press, 1967).

48. This is a pattern of professional development not limited to the military. On Spanish diplomats, see Juan Carlos Pereira, ed., *La política exterior de España* (Barcelona: Ariel, 2010), 240–52.

49. His paper was recently reprinted in Michael Sean Mahoney and Thomas Haigh, *Histories of Computing* (Cambridge, MA: Harvard University Press, 2011): 90–105.

50. Matthew K. Gold and Lauren F. Klein, eds., *Debates in the Digital Humanities* (Minneapolis, Mn.: University of Minnesota Press, 2016); Eileen Gardiner and Ronald G. Musto, *The Digital Humanities: A Primer for Students and Scholars* (Cambridge: Cambridge University Press, 2015), and the earliest of such studies, Dennis A. Trinkle, *Writing, Teaching and Researching History in the Electronic Age: Historians and Computers* (London: Routledge, 1998).

51. David McCullough, *The American Spirit: Who We Are and What We Stand For* (New York: Simon & Schuster, 2017): 113.

52. A search on Amazon just on the phrase "Origins of World War I" shows up over 230 titles, while some of the most important books on the subject do not even use the word "origins" in their titles.

53. Meyer and Schroeder, *Knowledge Machines*, 147.

54. For example, https://communities.historians.org/home (Accessed October 20, 2020).

55. Rob Kling, "What Is Social Informatics and Why Does It Matter?" *D-Lib Magazine* 5, no. 1 (1999); Rob Kling, Geoffrey McKim, and Adam King, "A Bit More to IT: Scholarly Communication Forums as Socio-technical Interaction Networks," *Journal of the American Society for Information Science and Technology* 54, o. 1 (2003): 46–67; Wiebe E. Bijker, Thomas P. Hughes, and Trevor Pinch, *The Social Construction of Technological Systems: New Directions in the Sociology and History of Technology* (Cambridge, MA: MIT Press, 1987).

56. Geoff Cooper and John Bowers, "Representing the User: Notes on the Disciplinary Rhetoric of Human-Computer Interaction," in Peter J. Thomas, ed., *The Social and Interactional Dimensions of Human-Computer Interfaces* (Cambridge: Cambridge University Press, 1995); Nelly Oudshoorn and Trevor Pinch, eds., *How Users Matter: The Co-construction of Users and Technology* (Cambridge, MA: MIT Press, 2005).

57. For example, Wiebe E. Bijker, *Of Bicycles, Bakelites, and Bulbs: Toward a Theory of Sociotechnical Change* (Cambridge, MA: MIT Press, 1995).

58. Wiebe E. Bijker, "Social Construction of Technology," in Neil J. Smelser and Paul B. Baltes, eds.), *International Encyclopedia of Social & Behavioral Sciences* (Oxford: Elsevier Science, 2001): 15522–15527.

59. I went through the same experience of researching before the arrival of the Internet and afterwards, describing the differences between the two, James W. Cortada, *History Hunting: A Guide for Fellow Adventurers* (Armonk, NY: M. E. Sharpe, 2012): 30–32, 53–55, 64–70.

60. Meyer and Schroeder, *Knowledge Machines,* 39–40.

61. Thomas S. Kuhn, *The Structure of Scientific Revolutions* (Chicago, IL: University of Chicago Press, 1962); Bijker, "Social Construction of Technology," 15526.

62. As I felt compelled to do with "Shaping Information History as an Intellectual Discipline" in 2012 and earlier in *How Societies Embrace Information Technology* (New York: John Wiley & Sons, 2009).

Part Two

EXAMPLES

Chapter Two

How to Understand Information Ecosystems and Infrastructures in Firms and Industries*

There is a huge need and a huge opportunity to get everyone in the world connected, to give everyone a voice and to help transform society for the future.

—Mark Zuckerberg

Information is the glue that holds together organizations and their industries. Understanding their information ecosystems and their infrastructures is essential if we are to appreciate how companies, government agencies, and entire industries function. Yet the role of information in companies and industries remains understudied. This chapter defines concepts historians should understand, discusses challenges faced in the study of business information, and suggests approaches. In chapter 6 we pursue the topic further by examining what the ecosystem and infrastructure looks like in one large corporation, IBM. Historians studying firms or industries deal with complex and varied communities that operate within these two types of organizations: companies and their industries. These communities can consist of sales and production within a firm, or a collection of companies that collaborate and compete within an industry. Each plays a different role, some collaborative, others at cross-purposes. But all such communities operate in an environment in which information is collected, analyzed and used, influencing their interactions within a firm and across an industry. Information is the glue that binds organizations together.[1]

*Part of this chapter is a revised and updated version of an earlier paper published as "A Framework for Understanding Ecosystems in Firms and Industries," *Information and Culture* 51, no. 2 (2016).

Understanding the informational ecosystems of both firms and industries is essential. One cannot understand what went on in these organizations, what motivated people's intentions and behavior, how they were influenced by events, or what individuals did on a day-to-day basis, and why, without understanding information ecosystems.

But why approach the topic of information history through the lens of an industry or company? Why not through a religion, political movement, hobby, or other grouping of people? Examining those other collections of people and organizations can be done in the same way discussed here about companies and industries. But going through industries, in particular, is useful since all employers are part of some industry, including churches, non-profits, and governments. Much of their behavior transcends any one industry and is in evidence in others.[2] Second, using the United States as an example, nearly half the nation is employed full-time in the private and public sectors (127 million as of 2017) and another 27 million part time, so we are speaking about the lives and actions of over 150 million people in a nation of 326 million souls. Similar proportions of employees within an industry out of a nation's total population could be cited for any industrialized economy. Industries are not invisible constructs of economists or business professors. They are real, have their own identity and practices, and have been visible as industries for two centuries.[3] So, they constitute a social configuration attractive and important for historians to study.

Historians are increasingly studying the role of information in businesses and industries, leading to various approaches. Lisa Bud-Frierman emphasizes the importance of the "information infrastructure."[4] JoAnne Yates examined the role of information both in companies and in one industry. She is partial to the development of systematic managerial practices that promote efficiency of operations at the firm level, with a particular emphasis on the role of communications within an enterprise. She is also sympathetic to the use of theoretical constructs.[5] Others studying industries and international organizations emphasize information flows across spaces, economies, and firms.[6] So the rudimentary basis about how to look at companies within industries and industries in aggregate is beginning to be formed. How does one go about exploring the role of information in companies (governments and organized religions too for that matter) and industries this way? Answering that question is our central purpose in this chapter.

This chapter is also an extension of the first one, in which we discuss the case for studying information history and lay out basic steps and issues to explore. In this chapter, we dive deeper to see what is required when the research must be more specific, moving from generalized notions of looking at information through the lens of ecosystems and infrastructures—the key theme of this book—here through companies and industries. Subsequent chapters demonstrate the approach through specific case studies to demonstrate the universality of its applicability.

In this chapter we work through the approach by discussing four fundamental issues. We begin by piecing conceptually together what the study of information in firms and industries looks like. This is not invention—historian, and especially economists have already started down this path; we can learn from them. Then we describe the elements of a firm-level information ecosystem followed by a review of the elements of an information ecosystem at the industry level. Subsumed in those discussions are the roles of infrastructures. Armed with a perspective on those two topics we move to a broader discussion of similarities, differences, and co-dependencies between firm and industry ecosystems as none operate in isolation from each other. Because the emphasis on information in businesses and industries remains a relatively new field of history, despite early pioneers already at work on these topics, there is much to say about the implications for future work on the topic, so we conclude with such a discussion.

Beginning here we move away from historiographical and theoretical methodological discussions and start practicing what we have discussed earlier with a half dozen case studies. One might argue that two of these—chapter 5 about farm wives and chapter 8 about family historians—do not fit the model demonstrated in all the other chapters about firms and industries. But by the time one reads those chapters, it should be evident that farm wives and family genealogists behave much like historians of businesses and industries, information technology, salesmen, and scientists. It should also be evident that the methods deployed in this book would be applicable to, say, studies of the Catholic Church, a national army or navy, a university, or a community.[7] My essential point is to demonstrate how the historian's skills are directly applicable to the study of information, specifically using the case of business history in this chapter, while illustrating the relevance of the vast quantity of sources available to scholars in the field. Another concern is to demonstrate the process by eliminating the ambiguity that still envelopes the study of the history of information in the history of business.[8]

CHALLENGES AND ISSUES: PIECING IT ALL TOGETHER

The study of the use of information within organizations, firms, and industries, while relatively immature, now is acquiring a growing literature.[9] Yet, four circumstances make the subject immature. The first is a lack of definitions agreed to by the majority of students of information on the terms used: information ecosystems, information infrastructures, and information itself discussed in the previous chapter.[10] Second, how information is situated in people and organizations remains the domain of case studies of which there are too few to discern patterns. Third, the identification of how information (data, facts, numbers, text, and so forth) moves about and is used by individuals, institutions, industries, and societies remains in its infancy. Fourth, there are no unifying theories to inform research methodologies across multiple disciplines.[11] While historians are normally least interested in conforming to an overarching theory of how information operates, other disciplines welcome theories as a way to develop "best practices" and to identify behaviors that can be empirically validated, largely by statistical and mathematical means and through repeated observation of behavior.[12] Extant theories are largely discipline-specific. Yet, they can serve as an assist to historians, particularly those developed by economists and economic historians.[13]

Frameworks are required to help access widely believed paradigms and to help structure research agendas. Historians are attracted to frameworks because they fit neatly within extant methodologies and approaches in historiography, making it possible to raise open-ended questions scholars can attempt to answer. Research agendas and ways to go about conducting such investigations are normally prized more than some grand historiographical theory on the use of information.

There has been a growing appetite for such approaches to the study of information's historical role by historians, political scientists, and economists, cutting across many aspects of society's activities: warfare, diplomacy, library science, computing, and literature.[14] Historians, in particular, have demonstrated a growing interest in the role of information at the firm and institutional level (e.g., university or government agency), and across a few industries.[15] At firm and industry levels much discussion has centered on the role of accounting, financial, and inventory control data and about the use of data processing equipment to more efficiently and quickly collect and move information, using everything from the telegraph and post offices to computers and the Internet.[16] With focus dominantly centered on the role of computing in the past half century, insufficient attention has been paid to the whole purpose of using that technology, namely, to inform what Nobel Prize economist and early student of information Herbert Simon considered essential: "decision-making."[17] The act of decision-making involves using information to define a problem or opportunity, define options for a decision, discuss among various constituencies of such a decision,and then take, communicate, and implement the actual decision. Each step is laden with information. One needs to include a logical sequence to that focus: understanding results of actions taken.[18] In individual firms, as within their industries, both the making decisions and understanding the results of those decisions became increasingly formalized processes imposed by management on their enterprises, beginning in the nineteenth century. That process of formalizing decision-making became essential with the establishment of large organizations, with industries creating their own self-identities and supporting organizations for sharing of information, and with the emergence of customers as self-identified cohorts (i.e., consumers).[19]

Lest we forget, the central issue regarding our subject, in the words of economist/historian Bud-Frierman, is that "information is a resource that requires wise husbandry and an element of craft practice," because information is created by people and social groups, not just by massive uses of computing (although that may change with the introduction of "learning" computers).[20] The history of information is not dominated by the experience with computers; that technology is increasingly being situated into a broader texture of human activity, more as a handmaiden than as a leading actor, with growing emphasis on its use and effects on human behavior.[21] Business and economic historians borrow methods used by their subjects in the performance of their work, such as the growing use of charts and graphs, while economic historians are facile in their reliance on statistics and calculus, and in displaying information in logarithmic forms.[22]

How do all the pieces of a framework for the study of information in firms and industries conceptually fit together? There exists a well-defined ecosystem comprised of firms supplying goods and services to each other (often called the supply chain) introduced briefly in the previous chapter: enterprises that sell to other companies, institutions, and individual customers, and firms that collaborate in the sale of their products and services to people and organizations (often called business partners). Firms identify with each other as members of an industry if they sell the same goods and services, compete, and also occasionally partner together. Industries provide a larger sense of identity, such as providing training and information relevant to its members through conventions, associations, educational standards, and publications (usually industry magazines and newspapers). Other participants in this information ecosystem include departments within educational institutions (such as academic centers that specialize in the work of an industry) and local, state, and national government regulators responsible for the activities occurring in specific industries (as in banking and financial industries). Increasingly over time other participants have included industry associations and customers within other industries that interact with an industry (such as IT managers related to the computer industry). Figure 2.1 schematically illustrates these complex relationships.

None of the participants operate in isolation; each is affected by the activities of others. Customers inform companies about their needs, which affects new product developments. Sellers introduce customers to new products, trends, and ways of using goods and services. All stay in constant motion, sharing, collecting, and communicating information about all aspects of each other's activities. In Figure 2.1 the arrows between communities within the information ecosystem are suggestive of where information flows to and from on a more-or-less continuous basis. Seen this way, one can situate the work of individuals, departments, and whole en-

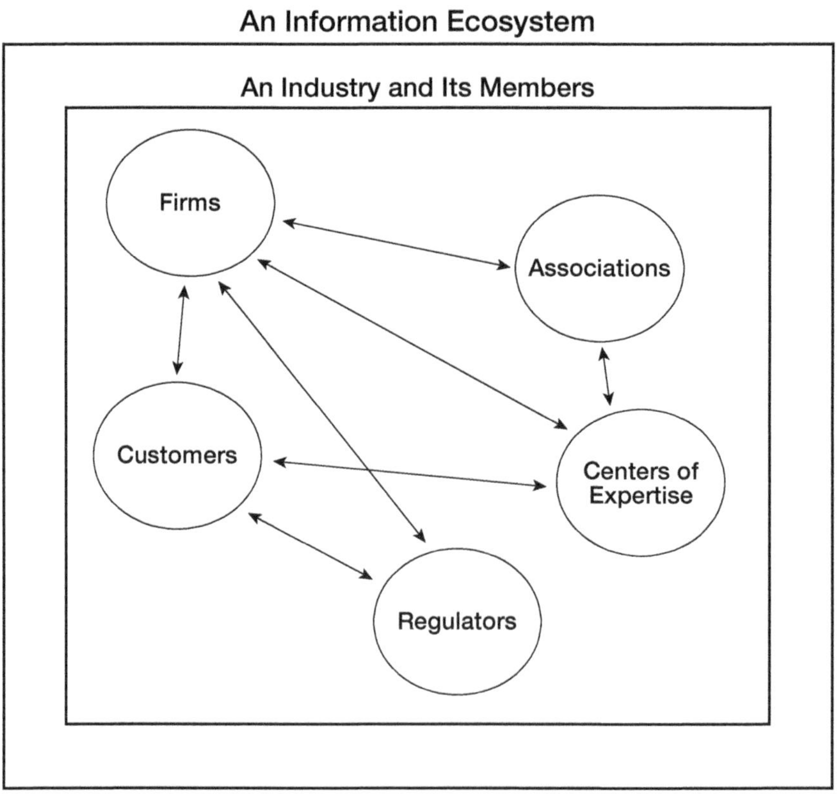

Figure 2.1. Information Ecosystem

terprises within a broader framework of an information ecosystem. Many questions can be asked about the collection, use, and flow of information, some of which we address later.

A second element of the framework is the recognition that underpinning this information ecosystem is an information infrastructure. Key elements can be categorized as a physical infrastructure filled with content. The physical infrastructure can include railroads and trucks (transportation of content), buildings in which it was kept (such as books, newsletters, sales literature), and supporting players, such as delivery services (e.g., UPS, Federal Express, postal systems). Another involves non-paper communications, such as telegraphy since the 1840s, telephony since the 1870s, PCs since the 1980s, the Internet since the 1990s, and, of course, such paper-based physical elements as newspapers, books, and other corporate ephemera.[23] One can easily see a great deal of physical information infrastructure at the personal, institutional, and industry level. The first two are obvious as the examples just cited illustrate. But even at an industry level they exist, such as the central banks that serve as conduits for the movement of information about funds from one bank to another (e.g., U.S. Federal Reserve, which has been in service since 1913). Military communications systems linked to their suppliers and R&D communities comprise another example (e.g., early Internet users).[24]

Figure 2.2 suggests the physical infrastructure that can exist within an information ecosystem. It also calls out that information flowing through this infrastructure parallels and is de facto part of that infrastructure, what media experts refer to as "content." Scholars have written extensively about content flowing through the Internet, but historians know that content has moved through information ecosystems in many forms for centuries.[25] Historian William Aspray referred to this content and to its outward manifestations as "the invisible infrastructures" of American life. His notion applies as well to any other nation's activities.[26] Both the physical infrastructure and content are needed to support one another. The physical is justified as the way to move information—content—from one point in the ecosystem to another with which to conduct business. The more physical infrastructure or content there is, the more dependent people and organizations are on information.[27] The diversity of both physical infrastructure and content suggests the variety, indeed complexity, and influence of the information ecosystem on human activities. Our framework makes it possible to begin identifying the role of information and information's effects on human activities, most notably the work of individuals and the shape and actions of organizations.

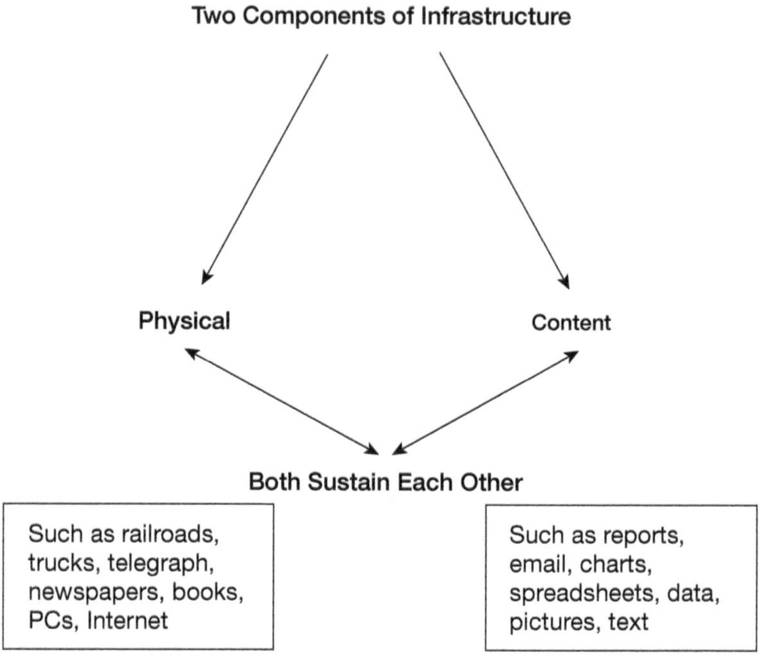

Figure 2.2. Information Infrastructure

To make the framework complete one must add the issue of professions, in other words, the role of individuals. While this chapter concentrates on the activities of firms and their industries, assuming interconnection—a basic assumption of the existence of information ecosystems—then the metaphorical atom, or basic unit of measure, is the individual. Much work has been done to describe the work of individuals, engaging in discussions about their reliance on information, development of skills, and application of knowledge to their work, play, and politics. The evidence is quite rich for the United States.[28] In fact, more research about the role of information has been done within professions than about information in organizations, let alone in industries. The remaining chapters of this book illustrate what that kind of research looks like. Additionally, of course, there is now a vast literature about modern nations forming into an "information society," operating in some "Information Age."[29]

Figure 2.3 conceptually places the individual within the framework so as not to lose them in our discussion. They personally create, use, and disseminate the vast majority of information. However, that is also not always the complete story. Sensors on an oil pipeline create and dis-

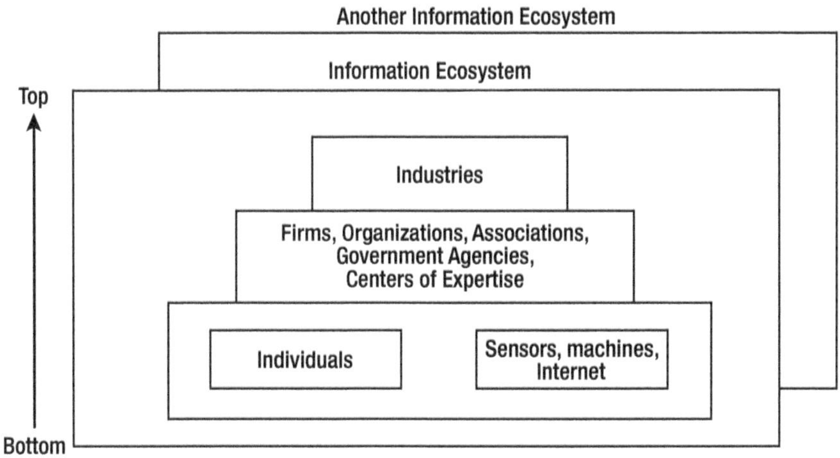

Figure 2.3. Hierarchy of Participants in an Information Ecosystem

seminate information about how much crude is flowing, its temperature, and its form, while video cameras in cities communicate traffic conditions over the Internet, further to officials and even to citizens on digital billboards and through telephone "apps." In fact, sensors and other computational devices generate more information (data) flowing through the Internet than humans.[30] While the history of the role of sensors has yet to unfold, its role as part of the information framework should, in time, become as important as that of people.

Figure 2.3 suggests a hierarchical nature to the relationships of people, organizations, and the flow of information. This representation of a hierarchy is intentional, since extant historical evidence suggests that it is the activities of people within organizations that drives the creation and use of information, while institutions larger than a company or university influence the work of people and organizations. One could just as easily conceptualize a framework that looks like concentric circles, but that would suggest that whatever is put in the middle of those circles is the dominant influence in the information ecosystem, while reality is different. In an information ecosystem multiple agents and circumstances are in constant motion, with some more influential at one moment than at another. So Figure 2.3, although a static graphic, should be seen as representative of communities whose influence (e.g., size in the graphic) expands and contracts, depending on events at any given moment. For the historian, the figure suggests that the study of the history of information must also be situated in a continuously dynamic set of circumstances, the latter comprising the information ecosystem. Failure to account for each of the components of that system either represents incomplete work or gaps yet to be filled as new evidence becomes available. Figure 2.3 also alerts historians to map flows of information from, to, and among individuals, within organizations, and through industries and economies.

We can begin to see that the movement of information through physical and process-based infrastructures (aka networks to some scholars) has implications that makes the subject a way of looking at the behavior of firms and industries. For example, large automotive manufacturers around the world have used such information infrastructures to make a large community of small parts suppliers dependent on them for their livelihood. Suppliers must connect to such infrastructures to provide information the large manufacturer wants, such as data on when tires will be shipped to a particular plant, production schedules for parts, or technical features and blueprints for other components.[31] The East India Company used that large enterprise's information infrastructure to gain control of downstream suppliers to them in earlier centuries.[32] The point is, there are many examples demonstrating the power of information infrastructures. So understanding their form and observing where the information travels and how can allow a scholar to uncover new connections, dependencies, and behaviors directly as a result of using such networks. To put a fine point on it, two historians argued that these infrastructures should be seen "as a thick soup of intentions, arrangements, and connections that facilitated business activity, a dish whose historical recipes and forgotten chefs are worth rediscovering."[33]

ELEMENTS OF A FIRM-LEVEL INFORMATION ECOSYSTEM

It is not enough to postulate that information is "everywhere" in an organization, even though this is undoubtedly true. The study of information and its role within an organization requires a structured approach. Traditionally, business historians, consultants, and managers examining activities of firms have found it useful to explore these within the confines of branch offices, regions, and divisions—in short, what was occurring within organizations, then possibly across organizations *within a company*.[34] An alternative way to probe the affairs of an enterprise is to examine the role of individuals and professions (roles) within it, such as that of the president, chief financial officer, shop floor worker, secretary, and so forth, although historians are predisposed to study these within the functions of an enterprise, privileging studies of actions not organizations.[35] Normally in the context of historical studies, one examines expectations of an individual worker (or profession), what they did, results, and consequences of their actions.[36] Since information was collected and used in support of work, it makes sense, when examining the role of information in various forms, to explore the use of data by employees within their job descriptions, performance plans, and operating work culture. This exercise complements the organizational/job-centric approach taken to study activities of enterprises. Management consultants, in particular, have learned that at a highly tactical level the merger of information, work, and organizational constructs are often best understood by examining workflows, specifically processes. They have developed extensive methods for doing this, which historians might benefit from appropriating for their studies of organizations, activities, and flows of information.[37]

Essentially, this activity calls for identifying and documenting all the steps in a process, describing roles and consequences of all participants (including variations), paper/data trails they create (electronic, oral, and paper), and actual information collected and used (i.e., numbers, descriptions, and facts). Often one extends the survey across the enterprise and even from one end of the "value chain" to the other. For our purposes, I define an enterprise as a company (or firm), such as IBM, General Motors, or Exxon. The term is often also used to include suppliers to a firm, such as for tires to General Motors, and business partners, those that sell a company's products but are separate firms themselves, such as an American automobile dealership owned by an individual selling GM products. The notion of a value chain can be described with an example. The sale or manufacture of an engagement ring can begin with miners digging a diamond and gold out of mountains. Next, other companies process these materials and deliver them to jewelers. These artisans, working in other enterprises, take these stones and construct rings. Their final act is to ship these to stores, where they are sold. The young man now has his role to play in the value chain: to acquire, present, and place the ring on his true love's finger. A number of options present themselves to historians for the study of value chains. One can study what happens only in mining companies, or in jewelry manufacturing environments, or in retail outlets. Regardless of the scope of the study, in each instance records are kept and insights acquired that lead to optimization of work, competitive pricing, and outcomes. Every form of work optimization involves collecting data. Understanding the entire value chain's activities became of particular interest to management since the 1870s, with the rise of complex organizations, multiple suppliers, and vendors. "Scientific management" methods began to surface to help impose order on these various activities, ultimately made famous as Taylorism. Named after Frederick Taylor, an American efficiency expert, he advocated understanding every task to be done and to define its activities and who was to do them. His ideas became the progenitor of mass production by the 1920s, statistical quality control, newer iterations of Taylorism (such as process engineering), and outsourcing.[38] Each of these evolutions gives historians of information much to research and to describe. It also calls for identifying tight links between work activities and roles of departments and other organizational entities that normally existed. Thus, one can imagine studies of the information infrastructure of supply chains within a particular firm, or comparative studies of the same process across an industry.[39]

Each major function of an organization is a potential subject. Candidates include accounting, finance, manufacturing, distribution, sales, product service, legal affairs, personnel management, training, public relations, advertising, and lobbying. These departments—candidates—house the information and work of an enterprise, linking together work and information needed for the enterprise as a whole to function. The activities of these major functional areas are where the bulk of what a firm does occurs. What of value they bring to an organization or market constitutes their "value proposition," which is to say their rationale for existing. Some of their activities have become increasingly standardized worldwide over the course of the twentieth century, such as how accounting is done. That standardization occurred across most functions of an organization, offering additional research opportunities for historians of information: how did this happen, why, what exactly occurred, and what were the standardization activities?[40] Historians are increasingly examining the role of standards and systems in processes, science, and technology. Historians of information should examine standards and systems, too.,[41]

A related approach to the study of information standards is to examine the work of individuals, or classes of workers. Exploring the role of people is the preferred approach taken by sociologists, and increasingly by historians of professions.[42] From the perspective of a framework, one documents the activities (including information spun off) from classes of workers of individual ones, examining the dynamics of work/information. These dynamics change over time as well. As products are changed, workers need to learn to work with new ones. For example, a Ford Motor Company shop floor employee in the 1920s would have learned to work with wood and metal in the highly repetitive Taylorist style in the 1950s with increasingly complex motors and electrical systems, and by the end of the 1980s, with the management of robotic devices and analysis of statistics for production results. Over time, the information they needed, how it was used, and the effects on their work, morale, income, and results evolved.[43]

Individuals in specific professions carried out all of these activities. Thus, one can envision studies of the role of salesmen, nurses, doctors, lawyers, papermaking shop floor employees, and home economists—indeed each has already been subjected to historical investigations.[44] However, a limitation of these kinds of studies is their insufficient or uneven discussion of four issues of interest to historians: what information these professions had, training needed to master this information along with skills to apply the data, facts acquired in the course of their work and how that changed over time, and the effects on the workers (physical, mental, income, career consequences).[45] To solve these limitations, models are emerging to suggest what issues to address, research to conduct, and how to present the results.[46]

A third approach, following explorations of processes and roles, is to study the role of information in how organizations are structured, because there has been little work done on this by historians.[47] Information affects how and what one organizes. In the 1960s and 1970s, historian Alfred D. Chandler, Jr. famously discussed the structure of railroads of the nineteenth century as a response to the need of these transportation firms to control the flow of information about train schedules (to meet customer needs and to avoid train crashes) and to monitor rolling stocks (i.e., where individual rail cars were and what they had in them).[48] His work stimulated many other studies of railroads that inherently were about information and management of that data, resulting in a wealth of business literature and debate about how an organization is structured, the notion of "form following function."[49]

A more recent trend concerns the effects of computers on both the nature of work and the information used to conduct any activity. As this technology evolved from large mainframes that could only be cost justified if situated in central locations to serve many users and departments to smaller units utilizing less expensive devices, such as personal computers and now tablets and cell phones, ultimately leading to the wide appropriation by individuals of personal computers by the early 1990s, work, delegation of authority, and physical dispersion of people evolved.[50] Large organizations located their major computer systems in few buildings with thousands of people or varied their approach to include a hybrid in which many employees still worked in large buildings, but also could now be geographically scattered.

These various evolving work environments call for historians to ask several questions:

- What data (facts) were needed to support the work of people, processes, and organizations?
- How was that information collected, analyzed, and stored?
- What information was tracked and how did that data affect subsequent actions, processes, and the work and nature of an organization?
- What information was physically diffused and used?

In each instance, the "paper trail" is often the first place to begin probing for answers. Historians ask, what data was recorded, who read it and was responsible for its accuracy, where did it go (information flows), and why was it saved? A second important tool is oral history techniques to fill in gaps between documents (including publications) to understand the use and consequences of having specific types of information. Oral histories enhance our understanding of the feedback loop so essential in appreciating the role of information in human and institutional activities.[51] We demonstrate the use of that tool in chapter 5 with an agricultural community.

Once we understand what was done and how information was saved, historians turn next to effects, to consequences, to results of such usage. The effects of where information could be accessed are more obvious, because one can track their ephemera and material manifestations, notably where computers functioned. Less obvious are the effects on work and individuals. Does remote access to information change the kind of data one needs and uses? What effects do access and that type of information have on work processes, work habits, attitudes of employees, security of corporate information, or the cost of collecting and diffusing it? These are central questions to ask.

In summary, any framework suggesting how to study information in a small or large enterprise should accommodate any of these three approaches: processes, roles, and organization. A sophisticated study of information history might include discussion of all three approaches to provide a more realistic holistic study of the role of information in a firm. We have yet to see such a publication, although a study of the U.S. National Science Foundation's massive research proposal system (FastLane) provides an pioneering model, albeit drawn from the public sector.[52] Table 2.1 summarizes the key firm research concepts to keep in mind.

Table 2.1. Elements of a Firm-Level Information Ecosystem

Jobs, professions	Each using/generating specialized information
Process/work flows	Documented activities/measures of performance and results
Functions/departments/organization	Specialized missions, information

Key Questions to Answer for Each Element

- What data (facts) were needed to support the work of people, processes, and organizations?
- How was that information collected, analyzed, and stored?
- What information was tracked and how did that data affect subsequent actions, processes, and the work and nature of an organization?

ELEMENTS OF AN INDUSTRY-LEVEL INFORMATION ECOSYSTEM

Industries are constructs of the mind. They are less evident physically than a firm, where at least one can point to buildings filled with workers, publications, products, and a big logo on the property announcing the name of the enterprise. Industries might have associations within them that have national headquarter buildings, industry-specific trade magazines and newsletters, and national conventions to which thousands of people may annually gather at some large hotel for a few days, then disperse back into their firms. Industries are social constructs too, in which people perceive that they share similar activities, compete against one another, or identify with each other. From a practical perspective, industries as communities help define the nature of work in a group of companies, identify and track their competitors and business partners, inform members about each other's activities and those occurring outside of the industry impinging on them, and train people in new technologies, managerial practices, and work processes.[53]

Two tangible manifestations of industries are information laden. The first consists of industry associations; most industries have one or several, much like clubs in which members are either individuals or companies from the industry. The American Banking Association (ABA) is one of hundreds of such examples; almost every bank in the United States is a member. It is a useful example because so many participants in the industry belonged to it and so used it as their voice to the outside world of regulators, media, and the public. It also became a model of how other industry associations should function. A variant can be a cross-industry, profession-centered association similar in mission, such as the Institute of

Electrical and Electronics Engineers (IEEE)'s Computer Society for IT workers, or the Society for Human Resource Management for personnel professionals. There is even an association of associations to help managers of these non-profit organizations.[54]

They provide another tangible manifestation of their existence: publications such as newspapers, trade magazines, white papers, proceedings, books, video tapes, podcasts, and websites dedicated to their association and industry filled with information and news, all grist for the historian. Associations hold annual conventions, where much networking (information exchanges) and training occurs. Conventions are extensions of the work of associations, as visible manifestations of their activities. Yet, historians have not studied extensively the collection and use of industry association information. A historian would be challenged to find historical analyses of training movies and videos, for example, yet tens of thousands of these were prepared by firms and industries.[55] Most industry trade magazines and newsletters have yet to be studied, or even collected by archives. Yet, many of these publications had large subscription rates, often running over two hundred thousand by the late 1900s, serving as rich sources of information.[56]

As with firms, processes, and individuals, industries have their members, ways of doing things across firms and with (and within) associations, and social and professional makeups of their members. In short, industries have their distinctive cultures. There are many historical information questions that can be asked of industries, quite similar to what one would explore when studying firms:

- What data (facts) were needed to support the work of people, processes, and organizations within an industry, including its associations?
- How was that information collected, analyzed, and stored?
- What information was tracked and how did that data affect subsequent actions, processes, and the work and nature of an industry association and the industry at large?
- How did use of information vary within an industry by firm, and what were the effects on enterprises and their industries?
- How did information flow among firms within an industry, and indeed also through their associations and important periodicals?
- What were the roles and effects of standards, pressures to conform to certain operational and managerial practices, in promotion of professionalization and credentialing of work?[57]

Table 2.2 summarizes key research issues for industries.

Table 2.2. Elements of an Industry-Level Information Ecosystem

Organizations, associations, members	Who they are, their demographics
Role of members and their associations	Process documentation, results
Communications practices	What they discuss, report
Industry-wide events	Conference information

Key Questions to Answer for Each Element

- What facts were needed to support the work of people, processes, and organizations within an industry, including its associations?
- How was that information collected, analyzed, and stored?
- What information was tracked and how did that data affect subsequent actions, processes, and the work and nature of an industry association and the industry at large?
- How did use of information vary within an industry by firm, and what were the effects on enterprises and their industries?
- How did information flow among firms within an industry, as well as through their associations and important periodicals?
- What role did standards play, and pressures to conform to certain operational and managerial practices, in promoting professionalism and credentialing of work?

SIMILARITIES, DIFFERENCES, AND CO-DEPENDENCIES BETWEEN FIRM AND INDUSTRY INFORMATION ECOSYSTEMS

Any attempt to define the total information ecosystem must consider the construct illustrated in Figure 2.1. However, an information ecosystem is bigger and more complex than a simple diagram can express. Summarizing similarities and differences can serve as a starting point for historians choose which information ecosystem to study, or at least to understand the contextual issues they face with either or both.

There are at least three obvious similarities between firms and industries. First, both companies and industries have firms, processes, and people that share practices, values, interests, and experiences within a company and across an industry. Historians can seek to identify what these are—they are glued together by information. Second, people organize their work, information, and interests into organizations, be it companies or associations. Third, their exchange of information is expanding to virtual associations, better known as chat rooms, websites, and social media communities. The concept is essentially the same: they are identifiable communities bound by shared information, interests, and activities.[58] They tend to use a shared specialized vocabulary. Phrases have meanings unique to them.

There also are differences. Firms are very precisely defined organizations with clear legal and operational boundaries within which specific pools of information flow, supported by infrastructures designed to function largely within those boundaries. Within strict operational boundaries, an Apple Computer employee uses information only available to them; the same happens within Zara, IBM, and millions of other enterprises. Boundaries are normally marked and reasonably obvious to an historian, providing a convenient control over the scope of their informational research.

However, it can also be the case that a firm may be a part of more than one industry, as is the case with a securities firm that sells stocks and also provides banking services, and thus is subject to two sets of regulators and participates in associations that focus on one or the other set of activities. Boundaries can be expanded to incorporate communities of suppliers, customers, competitors, and regulators, making the ecosystem's borders less precise, but their extensions controllable by the scope of an historian's research agenda. For example, one could study the information ecosystem and infrastructure of an IBM salesman (which we do in chapter six),[59] or the information the company takes and sends out to a set (or all) of its customers. The data that flows back and forth and how these are used changes in both content and volume depend on context. Information can be constrained by legal boundaries but, in practice, often bursts those bounds.[60]

Second, industries are fuzzy at best because there are potentially so many participants. Yet, government economists in industrialized nations have long tracked precisely what firms are in which industries.[61] A historian would find those lists limiting because they leave out customers who work in other industries.[62] There are informational exchanges within these loosely defined industries that historians will want to understand. Association economists and professors of economics and business management specialize in specific industries with this kind of data. They are allies for historians of a firm or industry's information ecosystem.

Compounding problems of definitions and scope is that industries are largely defined within the confines of a national or regional economy, such as the automotive industry in Japan or the automotive industry in the European Union. If an industry and its members operate in a globalized market, as does the automotive industry, one needs to consider participants from multiple countries that manufacture parts, assemble vehicles, and sell and support products around the world, all from a company that can be seen as originating in one country, but that operates everywhere. Is Ford Motors an American firm, even though parts come from dozens of countries and it sells its products in scores of nations? Yet another imposition is international associations, each with its own definition, such as the United Nations (UN), International Monetary Fund (IMF), European Union (EU), World Bank (WB), and the Organization for Economic Cooperation and Development (OECD).

Third, industries have missions different from those of firms, hence much of their activities vary too. Companies exist to make and sell goods and services to customers, generate profits, and offer returns to their investors. Industries are communities of practice in support of their members and, thus, are not in the business of making a profit. An industry's associations are not profit centers either, yet they play supportive roles to firms, and comment in a positive way about the attributes and activities of their memberships.

"Think tanks" are often adjuncts to specific industries, too.[63] So, their informational activities are different than those accumulating in an industry's ecosystem, or within a firm. They create aggregate profiles of all their members, summarize their issues, and increasingly lobby on their behalf with government officials, shaping information to meet their objectives. They often have enormous capabilities to generate and distribute information, such as global statistics. Historians need to be aware of the role of think tanks as they define their research agendas.

IMPLICATIONS FOR FUTURE HISTORIOGRAPHY OF INFORMATION IN FIRMS AND INDUSTRIES

What is unique about the study of information's history as compared to any other subfield of history? The answer is not that protagonists of the story are people, organizations, or information's ephemera (such as books or PCs). Rather, the center of our attention is the information that people and organizations used, and the objects that also contained messages, such as IBM coffee mugs. There is a fine line between information and the other elements, one that historians of information are going to have to define, then demonstrate they can understand. The trick is not to fall back on the safe histories of organizations and information technologies (both paper and electronic), or to traditional sociological histories. This problem exists, for example, in histories of education where, for instance, the political activities of school boards and national debates about the value and forms of education dominate the historiographical discussion, and rarely curricula, let alone what information is used in that industry and in the teaching profession.[64]

As suggested at the start of this book, information history can conveniently be seen as analogous to an object, with its own identity. Historians of software offer approaches for how to treat data as objects to be studied, handling them almost as physical things, like a book. They observe the research computer scientists do on software and, most specifically, databases.[65] The evolving role of computer science and study of information sciences by librarians and their scholars also suggests paths forward. In a recent issue of *Information and Culture* many of the ideas discussed in this chapter played out in articles. David B. Gracey described how cattle ranchers (corporate management), cowboys, and the cattle industry used information from the middle of the nineteenth century to World War I. Andrew Gross and Emeric Solymossy tracked the collection, organization, and dissemination of business information in the twentieth century, filling in details on how such an approach can be used in the study of any corporation. Alistair Black and Henry A. Gabb provided a case study of one type of information infrastructure by looking at the role of corporate libraries. Katie Pierce Meyer presented a case study of how a profession used information, in this case architects. Each author situated information technologies within the context of how information was used, from notebooks that trail bosses kept while herding cattle to architects using computer tools to design buildings. Collectively, they illustrate the rich possibilities of exploring roles of information in the private sector and within industries.[66]

The key point to keep in mind is that a convenient path into the history of information can be found through examining information organizations and their industries (ecosystems) used. They frequently left a paper trail familiar to historians that can be studied to see what happened to their content, how the ephemera circulated among people and organizations, and how they did that.

To start looking at the specific activities of information ecosystems, in the next chapter we look at how one group of historians created their own subfield, because as quickly as they turned to the history of information they wanted, indeed needed, some of the ecological and infrastructural support systems that made their work possible. How a most recently developed field—history of computing—did that shows us a useful path.

NOTES

1. I have described the role of information in firms in more detail in James W. Cortada, *Information and the Modern Corporation* (Cambridge, MA: MIT Press, 2011).

2. A fundamental finding of several previous studies I conducted, James W. Cortada, *The Digital Hand: How Computers Changed the Work of American Man-*

ufacturing, Transportation, and Retail Industries (New York: Oxford University Press, 2004), *The Digital Hand: How Computers Changed the Work of American Financial, Telecommunications, Media, and Entertainment Industries* (New York: Oxford University Press, 2006), *The Digital Hand: How Computers Changed the Work of American Public Sector Industries* (New York: Oxford University Press, 2008), and *The Essential Manager: How to Thrive in the Global Information Jungle* (Hoboken, NJ: John Wiley & Sons, 2015): 40–123.

3. W. Mark Fruin, "Business Groups and Interfirm Networks," in Geoffrey Jones and Jonathan Zeitlin, eds., *The Oxford Handbook of Business History* (New York: Oxford University Press, 2007): 244–267. For a more precise definition, see James W. Cortada, "How IT Makes Industries So Important," *Entreprises et Histoire* no. 60 (September 2010): 29–49.

4. Lisa Bud-Frierman (ed.), *Information Acumen: The Understanding and Use of Knowledge in Modern Business* (London: Routledge, 1994)

5. JoAnn Yates, *Control through Communication* and *Structuring the Information Age: Life Insurance and Technology in the Twentieth Century* (Baltimore, MD: Johns Hopkins University Press, 2005).

6. Geoffrey Bowker and Susan Leigh Star, "Knowledge and Infrastructure in International Information Management: Problems of Classification and Coding," in Bud-Frierman, *Information Acumen*, 187–213.

7. Your author is the president of the Arbor Hills Neighborhood Association in Madison, Wisconsin, USA, a community of just over 1,700 residents in houses, duplexes, and apartments surrounded by a school, businesses, and parks. When looked at through the lens of information ecosystems and infrastructures, it looks very similar in behavior to more formal organizations, such as a mid-sized corporation or small university. We are using the insights from this book to strengthen community bonds by building an information ecosystem evident to all its residents.

8. I began to demonstrate the applicability of our approach in business and industry in *All the Facts: A History of Information in the United States Since 1870* (New York: Oxford University Press, 2016) and continued in *IBM: How a Multinational Corporation Struggled for Success and Shaped the Modern World* (Cambridge, MA: MIT Press, forthcoming).

9. For examples, see Bengt Carlsson and Paul Davidsson, "Surplus Values in Information Ecosystems," *International Journal of Information Technology & Decision Making* 1, no. 3 (2002): 559–571; Shazia Rafiullah Miller and James E. Rosenbaum, "Hiring in a Hobbesian World: Social Infrastructure and Employers' Use of Information," *Work and Occupations* 24, no. 4 (November 1997): 498–523; Jacky A. Swan and Sue Newell, "The Role of Professional Associations in Technology Diffusion," *Organization Studies* 16, no. 5 (1995): 847–874; Paul Attewell, "What Is Skill?" *Work and Occupations* 17, no. 4 (November 1990): 422–448; James M. Bishop, "Institutional and Operational Knowledge in Work," *Sociology of Work and Occupations* 6, no. 3 (August 1979): 328–352; Matthew S. Weber and Peter Monge, "The Flow of Digital News in a Network of Sources,

Authorities, and Hubs," *Journal of Communication* 61 (2011): 1062–1081; Charles Williams and Will Mitchell, "Focusing Firm Evolution: The Impact of Information Infrastructure on Market Entry by U.S. Telecommunications Companies, 1984–1998," *Management Science* 50, no. 11 (November 2004): 1561–1575; James W. Cortada, *Information and the Modern Corporation* (Cambridge, MA: MIT Press, 2011); Ramesh Subramanian and Eddan Katz, eds., *The Global Flow of Information: Legal, Social, and Cultural Perspectives* (New York: New York University Press, 2011). For a bibliography of history studies published on a regular basis, see *Library and Information History*.

10. Every student of the subject feels compelled to still offer definitions as I have done in this article, for recent examples see: Marian Adolf and Nico Stehr, Knowledge (London: Routledge, 2014): 11–58; Cortada, *All the Facts*.

11. I discuss this issue more thoroughly in James W. Cortada, "Shaping Information History as an Intellectual Discipline," *Information and Culture* 47, no. 2 (2012): 119–144, which incudes extensive bibliographic sources.

12. For a useful, if slightly dated, introduction to some of the issues, see Frank Blackler, "Knowledge, Knowledge Work and Organizations: An Overview and Interpretation," *Organization Studies* 16, no. 6 (1995): 1021–1046; Toni Weller, *Information History—An Introduction: Exploring an Emergent Field* (Oxford: Chandos Publishing, 2008).

13. David Warsh, *Knowledge and the Wealth of Nations: A Story of Economic Discovery* (New York: W. W. Norton, 2006), but also by sociologists, most notably Niklas Luhmann, *Introduction to Systems Theory* (Cambridge: Polity Press, 2013).

14. The recent evolution of two library history journals to meet that need provides evidence of growing interest, and they serve as central hubs for historiographical discussions: *Information and Culture: A Journal of History* and *Library and Information History*.

15. For a collection of firm-level case studies, Lisa Bud-Frierman, ed. *Information Acumen: The Understanding and Use of Knowledge in Modern Business* (London: Routledge, 1994) with essays by her, JoAnne Yates, and Geoffrey Bowker defining the topic as well. For an early attempt to look at information and information technologies in several dozen American industries, James W. Cortada, *The Digital Hand*, 3 vols. (New York: Oxford University Press, 2004–2008).

16. In particular, about accounting and finance, Trevor Boyns, "Accounting, Information, and Communications Systems," in Geoffrey Jones and Jonathan Zeitlin, eds., *The Oxford Handbook of Business History* (New York: Oxford University Press, 2007): 447–469; K. W. Hoskin and R. H. Macve, "Knowing More as Knowing Less? Alternative Histories of Cost and Management Accounting in the U.S. and the U.K.," *Accounting Historians Journal* 27, no. 1 (2000): 91–149; M. Schweitzer, "The Significance of Production and Cost Theory for Costing Systems in the 19th and 20th Centuries," in *Accounting and History* (Madrid: AECA, 2000): 285–295; T. Tyson, "The Impact of Advancements in Manufacturing and

Information Technology on Management Accounting Systems," in T. A. Lee, A. Bishop, and R. H. Parker, eds., *Accounting History from the Renaissance to the Present* (London: Garland Publishing, 1996): 143–165; JoAnne Yates, *Control through Communication: The Rise of System in American Management* (Baltimore, MD: Johns Hopkins University Press, 1989).

17. Herbert A. Simon, *Models of Bounded Rationality*, vol. 1, *Economic Analysis and Public Policy* (Cambridge, MA: MIT Press, 1982): xvii.

18. A point of emphasis made by Peter F. Drucker, one of the twentieth century's most influential business management experts, particularly in *The Practice of Management* (New York: Harper & Row, 1954): 121–136 and in *Management: Tasks, Responsibilities, Practices* (New York: Harper & Row, 1974): 419–429.

19. Cortada, *The Digital Hand*; Yates, *Structuring the Information* Age, and the many essays in Jones and Zeitlin, *The Oxford Handbook of Business History.*

20. Bud-Frierman, *Information Acumen*, 23.

21. The discussion among historians is unfolding painfully slowly within the pages of two major journals, *Technology and Culture* and *IEEE Annals of the History of Computing*, over the past decade in over two dozen articles. In the spirit of candor, I have commented about this issue through four books, *Digital Hand* (3 vols), and *The Digital Flood: The Diffusion of Information Technology Across the U.S., Europe, and Asia* (New York: Oxford University Press, 2012). Sociologists have discussed this issue extensively, largely centered on whole theories of the evolution of the Information Society. For an introduction to this conversation, see Frank Webster, *Theories of the Information Society*, 3rd ed. (London: Routledge, 2006).

22. Economists and other disciplines are also beginning to create descriptions of information age economic activities that can be useful to historians, such as George Gilder, *Knowledge and Power: The Information Theory of Capitalism and How It Is Revolutionizing Our World* (New York: Regnery, 2013); Peter F. Cowhey and Jonathan D. Aronson, *Transforming Global Information and Communication Markets: The Political Economy of Innovation* (Cambridge, MA: MIT Press, 2009); Robert E. Litan and Alice M. Rivlan, eds., *The Economic Payoff from the Internet Revolution* (Washington, DC: Brookings Institution Press, 2001); Dominique Foray, *The Economics of Knowledge* (Cambridge, MA: MIT Press, 2000); Thomas H. Davenport, *Information Ecology: Mastering the Information and Knowledge Environment* (New York: Oxford University Press, 1997); and for collections of pioneering studies, see Dale Neef, ed. *The Knowledge Economy* (Boston, MA: Butterworth-Heinemann, 1998) and Dale Neef, G. Anthony Siesfeld, and Jacquelyn Cefola, eds., *The Economic Impact of Knowledge* (Boston, MA: Butterworth-Heinemann, 1998).

23. For an early attempt to integrate all of these into an historical context, see Alfred D. Chandler, Jr. and James W. Cortada, eds., *A Nation Transformed by Information: How Information Has Shaped the United States From Colonial Times to The Present* (New York: Oxford University Press, 2000).

24. Arthur L. Norberg and Judy E. O'Neill, *Transforming Computer Technology: Information Processing for the Pentagon, 1962–1986* (Baltimore, MD: Johns Hopkins University Press, 2000).

25. For a few examples, see David Hochfelder, *The Telegraph in America, 1832–1920* (Baltimore, MD: Johns Hopkins University Press, 2012); Walter G. Vincenti, *What Engineers Know and How They Know It: Analytical Studies from Aeronautical History* (Baltimore, MD: Johns Hopkins University Press, 1990); Edward W. Stevens, Jr., *The Grammar of the Machine: Technical Literacy and Early Industrial Expansion in the United States* (New Haven, CT: Yale University Press, 1995); Gary John Previts and Barbara Dubis Merino, *A History of Accountancy in the United States: The Cultural Significance of Accounting* (Columbus, OH: Ohio State University Press, 1998); Trish Loughran, *The Republic in Print: Print Culture in the Age of U.S. Nation Building, 1770–1870* (New York: Columbia University Press, 2007); Markus Krajewski, *Paper Machines: About Cards and Catalogs, 1548–1929* (Cambridge, MA: MIT Press, 2011).

26. William Aspray and Barbara M. Hayes, eds., *Everyday Information: The Evolution of Information Seeking in America* (Cambridge, MA: MIT Press, 2011).

27. A point made obvious in early studies of professions, most notably that of Andrew Abbott, *The System of Professions: An Essay on the Division of Expert Labor* (Chicago, IL: University of Chicago Press, 1988); Eliot Freidson, *Professionalism: The Third Logic* (Chicago, IL: University of Chicago Press, 2001); Luis Galambos, *The Creative Society and The Price Americans Paid For It* (Cambridge: Cambridge University Press, 2012); but there is an older study not to be overlooked, Oleson Voss, *The Organization of Knowledge in Modern America, 1860–1920* (Baltimore, MD: Johns Hopkins University Press, 1979).

28. Walter A, Friedman, *Birth of a Salesman: The Transformation of Selling in America* (Cambridge, MA: Harvard University Press, 2005); Kevin Borg, *Auto Mechanics: Technology and Expertise in Twentieth-Century America* (Baltimore, MD: Johns Hopkins University Press, 2007); Christopher D. McKenna, *The World's Newest Profession: Management Consulting in the Twentieth Century* (Cambridge: Cambridge University Press, 2006); Sharon Hartman Strom, *Beyond the Typewriter: Gender, Class, and the Origins of Modern American Office Work, 1900–1930* (Urbana, IL: University of Illinois Press, 1992); David M. Gordon, Richard Edwards, and Michael Reich, *Segmented Work, Divided Workers: The Historical Transformation of Labor in the United States* (Cambridge: Cambridge University Press, 1982); Mike Rose, *The Mind at Work: Valuing the Intelligence of the American Worker* (New York: Viking, 2004); Eliot Freidson, *Profession of Medicine: A Study of the Sociology of Applied Knowledge* (New York: Harper & Row, 1970); a set of two studies that broaden the scope of investigation beyond individual professions, Naomi R. Lamoreaux and Daniel M. G. Raff, eds., *Coordination and Information: Historical Perspectives on the Organization of Enterprise* (Chicago, IL: University of Chicago Press, 1995) and Lamoreaux, Raff, and Peter Temin, eds., *Learning By Doing in Markets, Firms, and Countries* (Chicago, IL:

University of Chicago Press, 1999); for an example of a contemporary discussion, Frank Levy and Richard J. Murnane, *The New Division of Labor: How Computers Are Creating the Next Job Market* (New York: Russell Sage Foundation and Princeton, NJ: Princeton University Press, 2004), and by an economist, Martin Carnoy, *Sustaining the New Economy: Work, Family, and Community in the Information Age* (New York: Russell Sage Foundation and Cambridge, MA: Harvard University Press, 2000).

29. For introductions to many of the arguments in favor, see Webster, *Theories of the Information Society*; Reijo Savolainen, *Everyday Information Practices: A Social Phenomenological Perspective* (Lanham, MD: Scarecrow Press, 2008), Manuel Castells, *Communication Power* (Oxford: Oxford University Press, 2011); and for a contrasting view, Christopher May, *The Information Society: A Sceptical View* (Cambridge: Polity Press, 2002).

30. Kevin Ashton, "That 'Internet of Things' Thing," *RFID Journal*, 22 July 2009 (last viewed 12/7/2016). For an early and innovative analysis of what content is in the Internet and a framework for assessing it, see Martin Dodge and Rob Kitchin, *Mapping Cyberspace* (London: Routledge, 2001).

31. Sally Clarke, *Trust and Power: Consumers, the Modern Corporation, and the Making of the United States Automobile Market* (Cambridge: Cambridge University Press, 2007): 238–274.

32. Philip Scranton and Patrick Fridenson, *Reimagining Business History* (Baltimore, MD: Johns Hopkins University Press, 2013): 181.

33. Ibid., 183.

34. As demonstrated by the contributors to Bud-Frierman, *Information Acumen*; and in Peter Temin, ed. *Inside the Business Enterprise: Historical Perspectives on the Use of Information* (Chicago, IL: University of Chicago Press, 1991), and by individual scholars, such as Yates, Structuring the Information Age; Margaret Levenstein, *Accounting for Growth: Information Systems and the Creation of the Large Corporation* (Stanford, CA: Stanford University Press, 1998).

35. There is an excellent collection of 7 essays on the current historiography of business functions, e.g., banking, technology, engineering, marketing, and so forth, replete with citations of the appropriate literature in Jones and Zeitlin, *The Oxford Handbook of Business History*, 319–497. Exceptions to this type of historiography are cited in various notes to this article.

36. Robert A. Rothman, "Deprofessionalization: The Case of Law in America," *Work and Occupations* 11, no. 2 (May 1984): 183–206; David H. Autor, Frank Levy, and Tichard J. Murnane, "The Skill Content of Recent Technological Change: An Empirical Exploration," *The Quarterly Journal of Economics* 118, no. 1 (November 2003): 1279–1333; Gary Alan Fine, *Authors of the Storm: Meteorologists and the Culture of Prediction* (Chicago, IL: University of Chicago Press, 2007); Elizabeth H. Gorman and Rebecca L. Sandefur, "'Golden Age,' Quiescence, and Revival: How the Sociology of Professions Became the Study of Knowledge-Based Work," *Work and Occupations* 38, no. 3 (2011): 275–302;

Bruce E. Kaufman, *Managing the Human Factor: The Early Years of Human Resource Management in American Industry* (Ithaca, NY: ILR Press, 2008) and his *Hired Hands or Human Resources?: Case Studies of HRM Programs and Practices in Early American Industry* (Ithaca, NY: ILR Press, 2009).

37. Histories of consultants focus on their enterprises, rather than upon their methodologies. One exception is Walter Kiechel III, *The Lords of Strategy: The Secret Intellectual History of the New Corporate World* (Boston, MA: Harvard Business Press, 2010), but even this author focuses only one way aspect of consulting—strategy work—while there are many other areas to explore, from early Taylorism to modern process reengineering. To get a sense of the work of process redesign, see Thomas H. Davenport, *Process Innovation: Reengineering Work Through Information Technology* (Boston, MA: Harvard Business Review Process, 1992). The literature on process redesign—a major activity of business consultants in the 1980s-early 2000s—is extensive. For useful examples, see Dorine C. Andrews and Susan K. Stalick, *Business Reengineering: The Survival Guide* (Englewood Cliffs, NJ: Yourdon Press, 1994); Raymond L. Manganelli and Mark M. Klein, *The Reegineering Handbook: A Step-By-Step Guide to Business Transformation* (New York: AMACOM, 1994); Robert F. Rhyder, *Manufacturing Process Design and Optimization* (New York: Marcel Dekker, 1997).

38. Kiechel, *The Lords of Strategy.*

39. The central task undertaken in Cortada, *The Digital Hand*, vol. 1, *How Computers Changed the Work of American Manufacturing, Transportation, and Retail Industries.*

40. Accountants seeing this phenomenon or globalization of standards and work practices, largely as a result of increased collaboration of banking and accounting regulators and industry associations since the 1980s. Already reflected in textbooks, which historically take a decade to codify and explain practices long underway, for example, see Donald E. Kieso, Jerry J. Weygandt, and Terry D. Warfield, *Intermediate Accounting*, vol. 1 (Hoboken, NJ: John Wiley & Sons, 2011): 7, 10–11; Thomas Johnson and Robert S. Kaplan, *Relevance Lost: The Rise and Fall of Management Accounting* (Boston, MA: Harvard Business Review Press, 1991); their sequel is worth examining too, *Relevance Regained: From Top-Down Control to Bottom-Up Empowerment* (New York: Free Press, 1992).

41. Examples include Tom McNichol, *AC/DC: The Savage Tale of the First Standards War* (San Francisco, CA: Jossey-Bass, 2006); Peter Gibbon, Stefano Ponte, and Jakob Vestergaard, *Governing through Standards: Origins, Drivers and Limitations* (New York: Palgrave Macmillan, 2011); Marc Levinson, *The Box: How the Shipping Container Made the World Smaller and the World Economy Bigger* (Princeton, NJ: Princeton University Press, 2006); George Barnett Johnson, *Drafting Culture: A Social History of Architectural Graphic Standards* (Cambridge, MA: MIT Press, 2008); Agatha C. Hughes and Thomas P. Hughes, eds., *Systems, Experts, and Computers: The Systems Approach in Management and Engineering, World War II and After* (Cambridge, MA: MIT Press, 2000); Wiebe E. Biker, Thomas P. Hughes, and Trevor Pinch, eds., *The Social Construc-*

tion of Technological Systems: New Directions in the Sociology and History of Technology (Cambridge, MA: MIT Press, 1987, reprinted 2012).

42. Many examples of this literature cited in earlier endnotes.

43. Much of the research has centered on job losses and obsolescence. Looked at another way, through the lens of information and skills history, one can find considerable documentation and discussion about the changing nature of information. See, for example, Amy Sue Bix, *Inventing Ourselves Out of Jobs?: America's Debate over Technological Unemployment, 1929–1981* (Baltimore, MD: Johns Hopkins University Press, 2001) and the growing literature on professions, such as Kenneth M. Ludmerer, *Time to Heal: American Medical Education from the Turn of the Century to the Era of Managed Care* (New York: Oxford University Press, 1999); Christopher D. McKenna, *The World's Newest Profession: Management Consulting in the Twentieth Century* (Cambridge: Cambridge University Press, 2006); Lawrence M. Friedman, *A History of American Law* (New York: Simon & Schuster, 2005); Kevn L. Borg, *Auto Mechanics: Technology and Expertise in Twentieth-Century America* (Baltimore, MD: Johns Hopkins University Press, 2007).

44. In addition to those already cited above, see for different approaches, Stephen R. Barley and Julian E. Orr, eds., *Between Craft and Science: Technical Work in U.S. Settings* (Ithaca, NY: ILR Press, 1997); Paul K. Conkin, *A Revolution Down on the Farm: The Transition of American Agriculture Since 1929* (Lexington, KY: University of Kentucky Press, 2008); Sarah Stage and Virginia B. Vincenti, eds., *Rethinking Home Economics: Women and the History of a Profession* (Ithaca, NY: Cornell University Press, 1997); Shoshana Zuboff, *In the Age of the Smart Machine: The Future of Work and Power* (New York: Basic Books, 1989).

45. A problem I have started to address, too, in discussing over a dozen professions in James W. Cortada, *All the Facts: A History of Information in the United States Since 1870* (New York: Oxford University Press, 2016).

46. These are beginning to appear on a regular basis, for example, in the pages of *Information and Culture: A Journal of History*; but see also, Weller, *Information History.*

47. Done more by business management experts, sociologists, consultants, and economists, but essentially none emphasizing information sharing. For a review of the state of historiographical research on big businesses, see Youssef Cassis, "Big Business," in Jones and Zeitlin, *The Oxford Handbook of Business History*, 171–193; also W. Mark Fruin, "Business Groups and Interfirm Networks," Ibid., 244–267, and Luca Lanzalaco, "Business Interest Associations," Ibid., 293–315.

48. Alfred D. Chandler, Jr., *The Visible Hand: The Managerial Revolution in American Business* (Cambridge, MA: Harvard University Press, 1977).

49. For example work by historians, John F. Stover, *American Railroads* (Chicago, IL: University of Chicago Press, 1997); H. Roger Grant, *Railroads and the American People* (Bloomington, IN: Indiana University Press, 2012); Steven W. Usselman, *Regulating Railroad Innovation: Business, Technology, and Politics in America, 1840–1920* (Cambridge: Cambridge University Press, 2002); Coleen

A. Dunlavy, *Politics and Early Industrialization: Early Railroads in the United States and Prussia* (Princeton, NJ: Princeton University Press, 1994).

50. Mainframes were large computers that included printers, various data storage devices, telecommunications controllers, and other peripheral equipment. These routinely cost millions of dollars, required many full-time employees to operate, and provided the bulk of computing for large organizations from the 1950s to the end of the century.

51. While there are many "how to" books on conducting oral histories, for a thoughtful discussion of its benefits, consequences, and methodological implications, see Per Lundin, *Computers in Swedish Society: Documenting Early Uses and Trends* (London: Springer-Verlag, 2012): 18–30.

52. Thomas J. Misa and Jeffrey R. Yost, *FastLane: Managing Science in the Internet World* (Baltimore, MD: Johns Hopkins University Press, 2015).

53. One of the first scholars (in this case, of business management) in modern times to raise the profile of industries as something to study is Michael E. Porter, most notably in *Competitive Strategy: Techniques for Analyzing Industries and Competitors* (New York: Free Press, 1980) and in a sequel, Porter, ed., *Competition in Global Industries* (Cambridge, MA: Harvard Graduate School of Business Administration, 1985). On the tension between professionalism vs. industry or firm perspectives, see Edward Layton, *Revolt of the Engineers: Social Responsibility and the American Engineering Profession* (Cleveland, OH: Case Western Reserve University Press, 1971).

54. http://www.shrm.org/Pages/default.aspx; American Society of Association Executives (ASAE), http://www.asaecenter.org/index.cfm (both last accessed 7/7/2013).

55. This community had a trade magazine for a while, *Business Screen* (1938–1972), containing statistics on the number of films made and shown, company case studies, discussions about how to make such films, suppliers of film equipment, and advertisements.

56. I used these as a core source material for my study of how three dozen industries used computers, 1950s–2000s, Cortada, *The Digital Hand*, 3 vols.

57. Abbott, *The System of Professions*; and for a history sponsored by a corporation that discussed standards and professionalization, see David Grayson Allen and Kathleen McDermott, *Accounting for Success: A History of Price Waterhouse in America, 1890–1990* (Boston, MA: Harvard Business School Press, 1993); Gary John Previts and Barbara Dubis Merino, *A History of Accountancy in the United States: The Cultural Significance of Accounting* (Columbus, OH: Ohio State University Press, 1998).

58. Eric T. Meyer and Ralph Schroeder, *Knowledge Machines: Digital Transformations of the Sciences and Humanities* (Cambridge, MA: MIT Press, 2015).

59. Partially accomplished by Cortada, "Carrying a Bag," forthcoming.

60. John Seely Brown and Paul Duguid, *The Social Life of Information* (Boston, MA: Harvard Business School Publishing, 2017).

61. In the United States, the U.S. Bureau of the Census and the U.S. Bureau of Labor Statistics are examples; OECD and central banks of all industrialized countries do the same. The *Monthly Labor Review*, a publication of the Bureau of Labor Statistics, has routinely discussed how to do this for decades, http://www.bls.gov/mlr/ (last accessed 12/7/2016).

62. Weaknesses in how economists track firms, industries, and economic activities in a time when information and its effects on society are of great interest were recently the subject of a useful study of the issue by George Gilder, *Knowledge and Power: The Information Theory of Capitalism and How It Is Revolutionizing Our World* (New York: Reagnery, 2013).

63. There is now a useful study of this type of information organization, Thomas Medvetz, *Think Tanks in America* (Chicago, IL: University of Chicago Press, 2012), especially on their role and structure, pp. 23–43.

64. Examples include Herbert M. Kliebard, *Schooled to Work: Vocationalism and the American Curriculum, 1876–1946* (New York: Teachers College, Columbia University, 1999); Joseph Watras, *A History of American Education* (Boston, MA: Pearson Education, 2008); Wayne J. Urban and Jennings L. Wagoner, Jr., *American Education: A History*, 4th ed. (New York: Routledge, 2009); Herbert M. Kliebard, *The Struggle for the American Curriculum, 1893–1958* (New York: Routledge, 1995); William J. Reese, *America's Public Schools: From the Common School to "No Child Left Behind"* (Baltimore, MD: Johns Hopkins University Press, 2005). Reese adds more about information content of curriculums than do the other authors, albeit quite little.

65. For a current set of examples of this kind of software history, see *IEEE Annals of the History of Computing*, 35, no. 2 (April–June 2013); the entire issue is devoted to publishing articles just on this topic, and earlier issues were devoted to the same topic, Ibid. 31, no. 4 (2009), Ibid., 34, no. 4 (2012).

66. All appeared in *Information and Culture: A Journal of History* 51, no. 2 (2016).

Chapter Three

Studying History As It Unfolds*

Computing's History, 1970–2017

Communities of practice are groups of people who share a concern, a set of problems, or a passion about a topic, and who deepen their knowledge and expertise in this area by interacting on an ongoing basis.

—Etienne Wenger

When a new field of study emerges, it comes with no supporting information ecosystem or infrastructure devoted to it. It must be created out of parts of preexisting resources. These parts include such components as libraries and funding from pre-existing foundations involved in supporting other fields of studies, meetings and organizations that facilitate communications among scholars, and journals where they can present their findings. Historians of computing needed tools and facilities just as scholars did in all fields. In the case of information technology's (IT) history, research had to be conducted in new ways as a new information ecosystem emerged, such as relying extensively on oral history and finding evidence from non-archival sources (e.g., using newsletters and industry trade magazines). It is a dynamic faced by those exploring new fields of study. An interesting, important feature of computing's history was a close and continuing collaboration among scholars, business executives, universities, and government agencies.

This case study focuses on the practical infrastructures needed to pursue the history of computing as an example of building an ecosystem and

*"Studying History As It Unfolds, Part 2: Tooling Up the Historian," (*IEEE Annals of the History of Computing* 38, no. 1 (January–March 2016): 48–59), published by the IEEE Computer Society. Used with permission of the copyright holder.

infrastructure.[1] I begin by looking at how research was done as the subject unfolded; then describe the evolving information ecosystem that emerged in response. I point out an academic-industrial-philanthropic nexus that emerged out of the process. This case study looks at a community as it became an information ecosystem, suggesting how that happened can become the basis of research on the history of information applicable to groups in a way similar to what is possible about firms and industries.

In this book we see several other related cases so, to put them into context relative to each other, it is helpful to return to our framing questions that asked what kind of information groups collected, what infrastructures they built to do that and to disseminate and use it, and what patterns and behaviors became evident by looking at their information, and begin to identify the intrinsic features of their information and ecosystem. These questions animate the discussion below, but as they do for all the case studies, can we also ask if these questions can be related? On purpose, our chapters appear integrated, yet each stands alone, demonstrating common practices and behaviors across various groups of people. This chapter concerns how historians created a new subfield of history to study the emergence of computing, its users, and vendors. Chapter 6 discusses the role of information at IBM, which did not have any significant interactions with historians of computing but was a subject of inquiry by them. Chapter 7 explores how computer scientists and their new scientific discipline came into existence, a subject that has drawn attention from the protagonists discussed in this current chapter. Each is a story, but also part of an even larger information ecosystem.

They are collectively an example of information ecosystems that can be clustered together. To encourage the reader to think of them independent of each other, so as to focus our attention on the specifics of how one can describe a particular information ecosystem and its infrastructure, several are separated by case studies that have nothing to do with computing to avoid running the risk of the three computing history case studies melding into one complex, confusing mass. Every group of protagonists in any grouping of people constitutes one or more members of an ecosystem; each system has to be identified and described, much as we do with the seven offered in this book. Then, they can be understood as collections of ecosystems. This approach is not so different than what historians do when building a larger history through inductive approaches. To write a military history of the American Civil War, for example, one would need to study each of the major battles in detail before conjoining them to write a credible history of a campaign that involved multiple battles, and then bring together a discussion of the major campaigns of that war into a comprehensive understanding of all the military events at a national level.

I assume readers of this book understand the concept of an academic discipline, such as physics versus library science, mathematics versus English literature, including subfields within each one (e.g., poetry versus novels). I present as the first of what might seem to be related chapters on computing a case of how this subfield of history emerged. It follows the same method used in the previous chapter, applying it to a circumstance that should be more familiar to the reader—an academic discipline—reinforcing the notion that the approach used for discussing firms and industries in Chapter 2 is universally applicable. So, when the rest of the case studies take off in various directions, the reader should be able to see through the narrative what approach I used. It will not require a leap of faith; merely an open mind and that you observe the signposts that guide us through the cases. It reinforces my contention that by looking at information ecosystems and their infrastructures we have an approach to the study of information's history and how it links intimately to other forms of historical discourse to such an extent that historical research should no longer ignore the centrality of the use of information and that it can be studied in a rationale manner.

HISTORICAL RESEARCH DURING THE "INFORMATION AGE"

The work of IT historians since the 1970s did not occur in isolation. We need to understand that context before delving into the heart of this chapter, as that helped shape their infrastructure. Beginning as early as the 1960s, economists and sociologists commented on the increasing importance of computing, knowledge, literacy, and office work, most intensely in the United States, but also in Europe.[2] A worldwide debate ensued on whether or not we lived in an "information age" conducted in universities, journals, and a string of widely read books, largely on both sides of the Atlantic Ocean, a process that continues in many parts of Asia, Latin America, parts of Africa, and the Middle East.[3]

Few historians of IT engaged in this debate, but they could not ignore it, especially after diffusion of the Internet began in earnest in the 1990s, which made the topic more evident to scholars across the humanities and social sciences. The Internet almost came to dominate research in media and communications by the early 2000s, with scores of books appearing for almost every one written by an IT historian. Historians of IT cautiously chose narrow topics to explore, but were increasingly confronted outside the printed word with impinging issues.[4]

Global history also became a widely explored topic. Discussions of Western colonialism had gone on since the early 1900s, but now global themes of other sorts gained attention: shared cultures, languages (e.g., expanded use of English, Spanish, Chinese, decline of French), the role of women, ethnicity, wars, diseases, technologies, political systems (e.g., expansion of democracy), migrations, integrated economies, and so forth, spawning fat books and a growing literature that increasingly looked at these themes as systems or ecosystems.[5] Electronic communications received early attention, beginning with accounts of telegraphy and telephony, then radio, paralleling a growing literature on expanded uses of various forms of transportation worldwide. Scholars reported that the costs of transporting information and goods declined sharply, while the speed of delivering messages and products increased.[6]

All disciplines had to consider the implications of these various activities. Historians not working in the history of computing thought in terms of diffusion of what historian Emily S. Rosenberg aptly called "circuits of expertise."[7] Implicit in such a framework was use of all manner of information tools by engineers, educators, doctors, and others available in their times, including computing and communications networks by the start of the last quarter of the twentieth century. The story was becoming complicated, diverse, and expensive to understand.

EVOLVING INFORMATION INFRASTRUCTURES FOR HISTORIANS

Historians need four types of information infrastructures to do their work properly, in addition to some organization paying their salaries. These are, first, libraries (museums too) stocked with publications (sometimes technological artifacts too) relevant to their research; second, archival collections that meet the same need; third, organizations and societies focused on their area of specialty; and fourth, a range of journals, book publishers, and research tools and guides. In short, historians need a broad range of support services from research to publication. Mature subject areas have had all of these in great abundance for a long time, such as in economic, diplomatic, and national histories. While historians of emerging fields have the same needs, they normally enjoy fewer of them. As a field emerges, so too do these infrastructural components; indeed, their creation is a part of that process of maturation. When historians have studied the process, they have done so by looking at pieces of the necessary informational ecosystem, such as the birth of a journal of record for a topic, development of a library, or establishment of a specialized society.[8]

Historians working in potentially new fields are, of course, not burdened with prior published accounts or influenced by existing archival records and sources of support that could influence their research agendas to such an extent as to compromise their ability to think freshly. However, as one of those historians who started without the four supporting infrastructures in any state of maturity, I am convinced that the counterargument about the benefits of not being burdened with a preexisting support structure—a suitable information ecosystem—is specious at best. While historians of new fields have to be creative in finding sources, even those in well-trodden fields have to do the same to push forward new thinking, research, and conclusions.[9] Ultimately, we are left with the lesson that historians need all four elements to do their work. As those emerged for IT, so did historians able to focus on the history of computing.

To better understand the historian's infrastructure, however, all four components of their intellectual and research environment should be considered as part of a larger process. Development of a subfield of the history of information technologies provides a real-time example of the four unfolding elements. Each is required, none is normally more important than another, and all emerge concurrently, although at various speeds and extent. They also interact and become codependent. For example, the Charles Babbage Institute (CBI) at the University of Minnesota is a library, an archive, a center with historians and students doing research and publishing, a host for conferences, and occasionally a publisher. It is a leading center for the study of IT history: a facility, a historian, a library of over ten thousand volumes, and some fifteen million pages of archival material, fellowships, and travel grants. A single CBI is not necessary, just very convenient. It is also not alone. There are other organizations that provide some or all four of the useful support structures. These include, for example, the Computer Museum in Mountain View, California, the Smithsonian Institution in Washington DC, and a variety of committees and other supporting organizations, such as ACM's History Committees, the IEEE Computer Society's history committee, and increasingly the Hagley Museum and Library, among others.

For most historians, the first infrastructures they think about are libraries stocked with books and journals in their field, followed immediately by archives. The first has secondary (published) materials while the second primary (manuscript) ephemera, although increasingly the lines are blurred because a library's magazines or collection of oral histories might be seen as primary materials for the history of computing too. When the field of IT history first emerged in the 1970s, there were no specialized collections of books and journals devoted to the subject. Libraries had large collections of technical proceedings and publications, and a few industry magazines and newspapers, such as *Datamation* and *Computerworld*. A handful of books on IBM were available, but the literature was sparse.[10] As a few history books appeared in the 1980s, formal collections on the subject still did not exist; the best were privately held by IT business professionals.[11] But, at least libraries were acquiring whatever became available as part of their broader collecting strategies, buying "everything" published by distinguished academic presses, such as MIT Press, Johns Hopkins University Press, Oxford University Press, and Harvard University Press, or by professional associations, for instance the ACM, Computer Society, and the IEEE.

In the 1990s, as the body of literature on computing continued to grow, library catalogs began to call out the topic as a new category of publications, such as WorldCat and the Library of Congress. Young historians reacted as many scholars do in such circumstances: they pressured university libraries to start acquiring on the topic. However, with severe budget cuts the reality of library administrations in both North America and in Western Europe over the past four decades, the process proved painfully slow.[12] Universities already active in the science and technologies of IT had growing collections, such as in the United States at MIT, others in the California system, Stanford, Harvard, Texas, Minnesota, and Wisconsin; in Great Britain at Warwick and Oxford; and at some Chinese technical and educational institutions. But these were small collections, because the literature remained limited. There was a chicken-and-the-egg issue involved with libraries and archives. Librarians and archivists could not collect what did not yet exist. Nor could one chastise them for not spending on these when budgets were being cut. It was also true that librarians and archivists, like historians, needed to learn what to collect, for example contemporary IT manuals and technical literature, and private papers.

A second group of libraries, about which almost nothing has been documented, are those in companies that created and sold computing and telecommunications products, such as IBM, Apple, Microsoft, AT&T, and a few European firms. As with academic libraries, their collections largely concerned the technology, while books and other ephemera on the history of IT were acquired as byproducts of those. Some of these collections were large, running into thousands of volumes. One normally only learned about them when they were discarded for being "out of date," such as occurred at AT&T and at IBM, where tens of thousands of volumes were acquired and disposed of in waves, beginning in the 1960s.[13] Another similar set of libraries was situated somewhere between the private and public sector, such as those operated by RAND, MITRE, and BBN. These often contained their own archives too, as did such professional societies as the ACM, Computer Society, and the IEEE. Historians rarely gained access to these, particularly to those of "think tanks" and corporations. Yet, they existed at almost every research and product development laboratory in the world, including over a dozen within IBM, many established as early as the 1930s.

Librarians and archivists at these institutions did not work in isolation. By necessity they created an *ad hoc* proto-information ecosystem of their own to advise each other on what they were collecting, what to collect, and even to advise donors of materials where to deposit them. Over time, this ecosystem incorporated more participants, initially librarians and archivists at academic institutions, later archivists and some librarians from the private sector. Historians and other interested parties participated, such as experts on media, telecommunications regulators, and journalists. Over time, instead of constituting a world of several dozen people, it had grown to several hundred, an ecosystem that continues to expand geographically and in the number of members.

A number of museums interested in the history of computing, too, began to collect ephemera on IT and about its history and in the process plugged into the emerging ecosystem. The Computer History Museum has been in operation since 1996 in Mountain View, California, earlier in Boston, Massachusetts. As part of its operations, it maintains a library largely comprised of user manuals for the machines they collect, other technical publications, histories, and a growing collection of archival materials.[14] The Smithsonian Institution in Washington DC started its collections of devices and ephemera in the 1950s (and a library on these, complete with rare, vital materials). The British Science Museum did too, beginning at approximately the same time as the Computer Museum.[15] The great German museum/library of technology, the Deutsches Museum in Munich, has both a collection of machines dating to the birth of the computer and a growing library of publications from around the world as part of its larger holdings of over seven hundred thousand titles on technology. Universities in Europe and North America have had either temporary or permanent exhibitions as well, such as at the University of Minnesota in the United States and Warwick in Great Britain.[16] By the end of the 1990s, there were an estimated dozen such collections available to historians in North America and Western Europe. Like libraries and archives, they often had primary and secondary materials, in addition to artifacts one most normally associates with them.

Archival collections normally build up slower than published materials, and so it has been with IT. Most are today housed in the United States, but to a growing extent in Europe too.[17] Western historians of IT know little of if there are collections in Asia, while for Latin America there are general corporate archives, which are only just now being consulted.[18] Initially, archivists focused less on the history of computing than on papers of local professors, as was (and is) the case at such universities as MIT, Harvard, and Stanford, or on the major activities of an institution, such as construction of computers at MIT in the early 1950s or U.S. Government projects, whose documentation resides in the U.S. National Archives and Records Administration (NARA), at the Smithsonian Institution, or in smaller agency archives (such as the U.S. Bureau of the Census). By the early 1980s, archival collections distinctly about IT and computing were being created, while existing ones grew in size.[19] Both were augmented with texts of oral history interviews conducted by the Smithsonian Institution and the Charles Babbage Institute (CBI), among others. These became available to historians, while others generally did not, such as those done at IBM. By the start of the new century, oral histories were surfacing online, such as those from CBI.[20] By the late 1990s many were online.[21]

Use of oral histories is a particularly new and important development that has needed support. Much modern history of IT relies extensively on interviews with the protagonists, as do other subfields of history that focus on the post-World War II period. They augment laboratory notes, slides, and scientific papers with background details, discussions of motivations, and ideas people had in mind when doing their work. It is an issue, think tool, or source, discussed by many historians.[22] Use of oral histories is a method of historical research that has matured since World War II with, for example, the establishment of the Oral History Association in 1966 and a stream of "how to" practitioner guides and seminars that historians of IT eagerly embraced as crucial to their work. The studies done by historians Janet Abbate, Arthur Norberg, and Leslie Berlin would have been impossible to complete without these.[23] Arthur Norberg launched an extensive program at CBI to create a collection of high-grade oral interviews. His work represents the Gold Standard for IT historians. Almost all book-length studies coming out of CBI are extensively based on interviews; their use is a hallmark of its work. In the post-2010 years CBI conducted a study of FastLane, the use of IT by the National Science Foundation for awarding funds for all manner of research. Researchers conducted some four hundred oral histories just for that one book![24] While this paragraph reads like an advertisement for CBI's oral histories, since many individuals were collecting oral histories, often not doing so many, early on Norberg at CBI campaigned for better quality work and made training of Ph.D. students using CBI's materials in the proper execution of oral histories an imperative. Corporations, the Computer Museum, even families of technologists created oral histories of uneven quality. To be sure, some were exemplary, such as those developed by the Smithsonian Institution that were comparable to CBI's. In the process, participants expanded the information ecosystem they needed.

Essential to the work of historians are organizations and societies devoted to preserving and supporting their subject areas that amass collections and publish journals and books. In the field of information technology a number of these appeared, almost all tiny and regional, with the oldest and most formally established in the United States and in Great Britain. The most important of these was the Charles Babbage Institute. Most historians of IT could not have done their work over the past two decades without its help. So, understanding its emergence is crucial in appreciating how IT historians came to have an effective research and publishing infrastructure. Close behind it in importance was literarily a communications infrastructure known as SIGCIS, discussed below.

In 1978, a group of industry executives, recognizing the need to preserve documentation on the history of IT and committed to supporting academic studies on its history, established the Charles Babbage Institute (better known as CBI, named after a British inventor of the nineteenth century) and a foundation to support it (the Charles Babbage Foundation). The foundation found a home for the institute at the University of Minnesota. It raised funds to endow a chair/directorship at CBI, then to support graduate students doing dissertation level research (Tomash Fellowships), while foundation members began to personally support efforts to stock CBI with books and archival materials.[25] CBI prospered and in time added a second historian and an archivist.

CBI houses over ten thousand volumes and fifteen million pages of archival materials dealing with the work of individuals, such as computer scientists; institutional records of companies, such as of Burroughs, CDC and some from IBM; of technical societies, such as of the American Association for Computing Machinery (ACM); trade associations, such as ADAPSO; and market research firms/market research reports produced by such firms as Auerbach and Gartner, among others. CBI's total collections consisted of over two hundred series and 150,000 photographs as of 2017.[26] Note that the types of records also reflect the ephemera spun off by other information ecosystems and infrastructures, such as those of the computer industry and trade associations.

CBF—its early fundraising arm—evolved into a membership society in the 2000s to include individuals working in the industry interested in the history of computing, and changed its name to the IT History Society (ITHS), broadening and changing its mission. Its members included historians, technologists, business managers, and other commentators on the history of IT. It launched projects to increase awareness and access to materials on the history of IT, building databases about hardware, software, and leading IT professionals. Most important for historians, it created a database pointing to archival collections around the world, acting as a macro finding aid to organizations having millions of pages of relevant materials.[27] It had several dozen institutional members too, such as corporations (e.g., IBM), non-profit members (e.g., Smithsonian Institution) and over seven hundred individuals by 2014, most drawn from the IT industry in North America and Western Europe. CBI also established an outreach program, Friends of CBI, of some one hundred individuals and organizations that contributed financially to CBI; many participants belonged to both organizations. The evolution of the community interested in IT history created and integrated a thickening information ecosystem and infrastructure. The availability of information encouraged people to participate, while the availability of an infrastructure gave them the wherewithal to do so. It is an important observation for anyone studying the emergence of an information ecosystem.

Information ecosystems are difficult to define in precise terms because new participants will join those that are successful. That happened with the history of information technology. One of the IT industry's largest technical societies, comprised of IT professionals and academics, the IEEE Computer Society, has a history committee, while the organization to which the Computer Society is a member—Institute of Electrical and Electronics Engineers (IEEE) with over four hundred thousand members in 160 countries—has an IEEE History Center. Both promote preservation of IT history and involve academic historians in that process.[28] The British Computer Society supports work on history, called the History of Computing Collection, focusing like CBI on acquisition of manuscripts useful to historians. The Science Museum in London also collects materials, and has partially constructed Charles Babbage's design for a computer he conceived in the nineteenth century.[29]

What ultimately may eventually be seen as one of the most important of the groups established to support historians of computing came into existence in 2005 with the foundation of an online community made up largely of historians, but also others in different disciplines and industries, called the Special Interest Group Computers, Information and Society (SIGCIS), hosted by the Society of the History of Technology (SHOT). The SIGCIS-SHOT linkage is important for it affords historians of IT visibility and indirectly approval from the leading organization of historians of technology, while giving access at conferences to those not familiar with IT to the work of this new group of scholars. It is a facilitative force for all. Historians have led SIGCIS. In recent years Thomas Haigh (University of Wisconsin—Milwaukee) energized the organization into a highly active one as the population of IT historians increased. It rapidly became where historians learned about the activities of colleagues, could find online resources for teaching and research, prizes, and travel grants. They could discuss issues relevant to its hundreds of members. SIGCIS also hosts day-long sessions at annual SHOT conventions to discuss issues and to coach doctoral students and young academics.[30]

Think of SIGCIS as an online history society for historians of computing. Its formation came approximately twenty years after initial recognition that the history of information technologies and computing was an emerging field of history, giving community and focus to the activities of what was now either the first or second generation of historians working in this subject. Had this subfield of history emerged fifty years earlier, historians would have probably formed an academic society devoted to IT history and most important to them, probably launched a journal devoted to the subject. Today a convenient alternative is an online group.

The fourth requirement for historians—reference tools—became an early priority for those organizations and some individuals working in the field. One of the most useful early in a research project is a good bibliography, followed by written descriptions of various archival collections, better known as finding aids. The process of developing both of these tools only began in the 1980s. A series of bibliographies relevant to the history of computing appeared.[31] Eventually some of these were made available online through CBI's website, and in particular, one on software.[32] Other tools appeared quickly. Biographical encyclopedias and other references tools began appearing during the second half of the 1980s.[33] Guides to archival materials were published as articles and books, an activity that continues in such traditional formats as articles and books, but increasingly in ones which are online, such as those of CBI, ITHS, and SIGCIS. As in other fields, initial availability of these kinds of materials came in the form of books and articles, but quickly historians embraced the digital tools they studied. While much work remains to be done to document online bibliographies and archival and oral history finding aids, much is already available online.

One development that facilitated academic disciplines was the availability online of academic journals (such as the *IEEE Annals of the History of Computing*). Another involved online posts by historians of their resumes, which often included links to their publications, making their writings available online. It is now universal practice for historians to post their vita and list of publications (when possible with links to these) at their departmental websites in universities.[34]

THE ACADEMIC-INDUSTRIAL-PHILANTHROPIC NEXUS

The information infrastructure described above suggests that just as in all manner of historical work, the larger issues swirling in their profession's intellectual firmament influenced historians of IT. We can also discern an evolving engagement between those academics engaged in the history of computing with those organizations that supported their work. The "academy," as universities in the West frequently called themselves, had increasingly become dependent on national governments for research and other project funding, beginning during World War II, massively so during the Cold War, and most spectacularly in the United States where, by the end of the 1950s, nearly 85 percent of all academic R&D was funded by federal agencies.[35] A similar story could be told for other countries.[36] In the 1980s—when professional historians began earnestly looking at the history of computing—their employers (higher education) reoriented themselves to draw closer to the private sector for support, a process familiar to contemporary scholars in many disciplines.[37] Part of that process involved focusing on specific projects and, to use widely used business phrases popularized by business gurus such as Peter Drucker, on measureable "results" that were "outcome based" or "results oriented."[38] Philanthropists tied contributions to activities they could shape and that would generate results relevant to them. They were looking for facts normally not produced by historians and academics in other fields, but that were routine types of information emanating from their information ecosystems. This process began decades earlier, and historians of computing were not immune to it.

The story told about the creation of CBF and CBI is an example of this process at work. Industrialists set out to create both a new field of history and to ensure that it had sufficient resources to flower. Historians did not come to Irwin Tomash and his colleagues; the latter came to them. This scenario stands in contrast to the image of university fundraisers constantly extending their palms for funding, a model more closely aligned with earlier government funding practices. CBI's case illustrated other features of this style of philanthropy and industrial connections. CBF placed conditions on its largesse, such as the funding of research grants for doctoral students, republication of minor classics in the field of computing's technology, and in the early 2000s, requested (not ordered) that historians start examining the history of software.[39] Historians would tell the story differently, of course, that they drove these initiatives, but only after industrial leaders proposed them.[40] Yet, all shared values too. Industrialists wanted to preserve their history, hence their interest in building archival collections, funding research, and supporting computer museums. They also wanted to promote historical research of the type conducted by professional historians, hence endowment of a professorship at CBI. Most of these industrialists had advanced STEM or business management degrees and experience developing science- and engineering-based products, so they understood the nature of academic research.

In the case of CBI, business executives sought out examples of how to approach structuring of the new field of history (e.g., from the Chemical Heritage Foundation), discussing what requirements were needed with university officials in over a dozen institutions, and with academics the scope of activities that should take place. In establishing CBF, they recruited academics onto its board, including a historian of science, a Nobel Prize scientist, and engineers. Representatives from IT firms familiar with industrial research participated, such as from IBM, the industry's largest company at the time. In classic business style, once these individuals had a mental model of what they wanted to create, they welcomed universities too, in effect, to bid on the work of establishing and hosting a research institute, inviting over a dozen institutions. They visited them to explain the value of their initiative. Their process, which mimicked how business executives worked with potential commercial partners and customers, serves as a model of how industrialists could do this for other subjects.[41] It is all about building an infrastructure that will facilitate a community to go about its work.

Defined projects were specific in requirements. For instance, IBM hired historians Arthur Norberg and Jeffery Yost of the University of Minnesota to write a monograph-length history of its laboratory and manufacturing facility in Rochester, Minnesota, published on the occasion of that site's fiftieth anniversary. IBM required that it be a research-based scholarly study (not a celebratory piece, although positive comments were welcomed), and that it be completed by a prescribed date within budget. In exchange, IBM donated cash and laptops to CBI. IBM made available to these historians personnel in Rochester for oral histories, gave them access to local and national corporate archival materials, and later, use of the company's connections with Minnesota's public officials and IBM's marketing and public relations organizations to distribute over ten thousand copies of the publication worldwide.[42]

The model for support was never purely for the sake of supporting knowledge for knowledge's sake; it shifted to some extent from a civic model to an economic one. For those interested in developing support for a new subfield, the implications are relatively clear. Traditional infrastructures needed by historians can be funded by industry, often in sufficient volume to accomplish a great deal over a sustained period of time, encompassing decades through a string of grants for projects, but also via endowments that are more general as long as they focus on the specific subfield, in this case the history of computing. Scholars and their institutions needed to reach out to industrialists and their foundations rather than directly to companies, but had to find sympathetic listeners capable of taking action. Academics needed to speak about projects and specific outcomes, and to be willing to be inspected to make sure they were performing as promised. The focus of funders is athe inspection of project progress, not inspection of points-of-view or even the quality of the scholarship and writing, which they acknowledge they are not qualified to judge, and which is normally inappropriate for them to do. Industrialists, however, are perfectly capable of shutting off funding rapidly if an academic does not perform as committed. The computer case illustrates that a positive nexus can exist among scholars, their institutions, and the business community.

PATTERNS, LESSONS, AND IMPLICATIONS

The emergence of IT history followed an identifiable course. Initially, protagonists of our story reflected on their roles and history, such as engineers building computers and industry executives forming IT companies.

When historians began commenting on IT, they focused largely on devices and technologies, followed by exploring the history of relevant institutions (such as IT vendors), the thorny issue of how to write the history of software, then studies about national institutions, communities of practice (such as programmers, women in computing), and national and global IT histories. Each thread of research continues, accounting for the increasing volume of publications and research materials on the subject.

Over the past three decades institutional infrastructures were created in support of the subject, from associations to journals, as well as the appointment of professors in the subject in North America and Western Europe. In an interesting turn of events, in the United States a number of historians were hired into what used to be Library Schools at universities. As these schools evolved into Information Schools, they needed staff with Ph.D. degrees in IT sciences, humanities, and history, and fewer librarians with MLS degrees. It was an important transformation affecting the history of IT. Into that new part of the academic organization came historians, such as William Aspray, Thomas Haigh, and Nathan Ensmenger, among others. The lesson one can draw from this is if a discipline is changing from a highly vocational orientation of an old order (in this case, librarians and books) to some new structure and focus (here to information management and use of IT tools such as databases and query tools), they may need more historians of IT. As a harbinger of things to come, CBI's historians work in the College of Science and Engineering at the University of Minnesota. It is a structure inconceivable to deans of a technical college forty years ago.

Likewise, new sources of funding for research emerged, from the Tomash Fellowship at CBI to others in support of specific projects coming from such diverse sources as the National Science Foundation, the Sloan Foundation, and the European Union. As historians began to think about the scope of their subject, they also developed—and shared—syllabi and other course outlines with each other, largely through SIGCIS. The subject has yet to reach the critical mass necessary to define the scope and issues IT historians can rally around to the degree reached in such other fields as diplomatic or economic history. Like historians of technology in general, they engage in exploring a continuously expanding set of issues, hence information.

Simultaneously, there continues to appear a massive worldwide wave of articles, books, courses, and television programs from many other academic disciplines commenting on the history of IT. One could argue that this circumstance is unique to historians of IT, but probably more convincingly so after many disciplines began examining the nature and effects of the Internet in their areas of concern. Journalists, in particular, wrote extensively on the history of IT companies and biographies, media experts on the role of communications and information in society, and economists and sociologists about implications of it all. The lesson that can be drawn from this activity is that popular history is popular, has a role to play, and can be useful to historians and to those other individuals interested in the history of computing.

Existence of this large milieu of people writing about computing's history suggests public and academic interest in the subject is finally taking off. Historians will need to account for it and respond, or be influenced by it in their future work. While we wait, for example, for a scholarly history of Google, nearly a dozen books have already been published on the firm; the same is true of such other major players as eBay, Twitter, and Facebook. Quality issues complicated this phenomenon, some involving historians. For example, Kevin Maney, a journalist, wrote an outstanding biography of IBM's nearly half-century leader, Thomas J. Watson Sr., based on archival research. It was a thorough well written biography anyone would have been proud to author. In the same year in which his book appeared, an academic historian published a thin biography based only on secondary research.[43] In short, competition for quality scholarship exists in this subfield, coming from many corners. That is a healthy development for the history of IT. In the process, IT history's information ecosystem and infrastructure thickens.

A limiting problem from the beginning is the lack of as much financial support from the IT industry as proponents in its ranks of such assistance have advocated. They were willing to fund establishment of museums, less so academic research, although some did as the CBI case demonstrated. This pecuniary stinginess could possibly be attributed to two factors. First, the industry feels and acts young and its leaders do too, so they have not had the time or the interest to deal with historical perspective with the exception of museums.[44] Second, the Computer Museum and the Charles Babbage Foundation (later ITHS) kept running into recessions in the industry during the late 1990s, early 2000s, Great Recession of 2008–2011, and the fallout of the pandemic in 2020, all of which made it difficult for companies or individuals to support activities as generously as in the 1980s and early 1990s.

New subfields in the history of technology and science are appearing, while preexisting ones inject information on the history of IT into their spheres of work. One is left with the interesting question: Is there a natural evolution in how historians study a subject area, or even just a new technology? As the story told here suggests, it might be difficult to fully answer this question without comparing experiences of other modern topics, such as nuclear energy, automotive, and air travel technologies. The AIP Center for the History of Physics, itself an information infrastructure hub, was a useful model for CBI, one of many explored. The question is further complicated by the fact that use of IT is continuing to spread rapidly, with no slowdown in its evolution, diffusion, uses, and consequences fully in evidence. Historians are caught up in that tsunami of technologies and consequences as much as billions of other people, and the volume of information they are producing and using. As a community, they have not acknowledged that they were as much a group of IT pioneers as the software and hardware veterans we applaud in books and articles.

Their story suggests either a logical construction of a narrative or that there was a process of emergence underway in this field with its own internal logic. It consisted of identification and definition of the topic and its issues within the context of how historians worked and what questions their generation focused upon. It was, and is, a stream of activities in developing research tools, publications, archival collections, oral histories, institutions and jobs in teaching and archiving, and financial support. All the while, the historiography evolved, played out in conference presentations, organization and content of courses taught, and by the topics and issues discussed in journal articles and books.

The IT case study for historians and industry is instructive in several ways. First, it proved to be a successful startup for a new subfield, although not necessarily unique but rather a recent one, demonstrating collaboration among industry, academic institutions, and scholars, all recognizing the need to establish an information ecosystem buttressed with an infrastructure of sufficient size and capability to sustain the community. These features of our case may be the most valuable to those interested in what best to glean from this story. But second, it concerned an extraordinarily important modern technology massively deployed around the world, hence, a potentially big area of academic interest now and deep into the future that will attract academic and business attention in scores of countries. Third, it is an ongoing experiment in which contemporary events still unfold, dealt with by historians as they occur in their intellectual pursuits, work, and personal activities. Fourth, its story is increasingly being documented, while many of the protagonists are still alive with many willing to share their experiences with scholars in other branches of the history of technology.[45]

GETTING TACTICAL IN CREATING A NEW FIELD OF STUDY

Historians about to face new potential subfields can learn from what historians of IT experienced, possibly now historians of information. To be sure, lessons could also be drawn from looking at other historical fields and technologies. But for our purposes, the lessons are drawn intentionally from one area—IT history—because it seems so particularly analogous to such fields as bioengineering, pharmacology, nanotechnology, space travel, and environmental history, among others. My point also applies to historians of IT that may emerge in countries that do not yet extensively study the topic, notably India and China, and in Latin America; these three regions combined account for over a third of the world's population. Scholars in these areas will have to replicate many of the experiences of North American and West European historians in creating information ecosystem components such as institutions, libraries, archives, and publishing outlets for their studies of computing, because they will want to have their own intellectual infrastructures, rather than rely just on those of the pan-Atlantic community.

They will do what historians always do: inject into the process unique features of their cultures and economies. How IT is diffused in a country varies, driven by the nature of the technology, wealth of the local economy, levels of education, and what industries and size firms, government agencies, and academic institutions exist.[46] Historians will study those realities. They have all of Asia, swaths of Europe, all of Latin America, and the massive continent of Africa with its fifty-some nations to study. In each, computing and modern IT-based telecommunications have a significant presence, providing endogenous influences on the history of computing.

Finally, what are the lessons for historians of information ecosystems and infrastructures? Going back to our six strategic questions from the first chapter offers insights. With respect to what media and mediums were used, historians used all the normal ones—books, articles, videos, lectures—also two others not to be overlooked: oral histories and Internet-based communications. The first is well understood; the second is unique but part of current historical practice.[47] An example illustrates the point. Periodically a historian will raise a question seeking engagement or information, such as when a term was first used, what sources one would recommend for students, or about the truth of assertions of a "first." For several years a debate has been underway on when e-mail first began to be used, who invented it, and so forth, resulting in much presentation of evidence and claims followed by a lawsuit settlement on who was THE inventor of e-mail, to the consternation yet great interest of historians. Much new data came out of hiding during the discussion. In the first ten years of SIGCIS, its most enduring feature may have been these kinds of discussions. Often someone would tee up an issue, say early on a Friday, and by Monday morning dozens of comments would have poured in from all over the world from knowledgeable experts, generating in a matter of hours the equivalent of a book chapter's worth of new information.[48] So the vessels and how they are used can change. We encounter that with the ladies of Madison County in Chapter 5.

The second question was about who collected information and what kind. IT historians were traditional: biographical, information about events and business issues of companies; industry and economic data; facts about programmers and other IT professionals; some on the nature of software, operating systems, and programming; considerable amounts about the physics, engineering, and construction of specific computers and their peripheral equipment; how people used computers at work, in their private lives, and in public spaces, with the amount of data regarding the Internet dominating the new information. Also quite traditional was how they collected information. Funded by grants, they visited archives and libraries, interviewed protagonists, published in conventional academic outlets, and came to know each other as friends, colleagues, and reviewers of each other's works. They paid attention to the intellectual and informational tools and issues protagonists in IT's history dealt with in the course of developing and diffusing the new technology. Much of it, so far, involved physics, electrical engineering, mathematics, biological feedback, studies of the brain's activities, economics of digitally-based businesses, work flows and accounting/manufacturing data enabled by computing, and a vast amount of discussion and study of information systems, such as the construct of databases, files, and their transmission over communications systems.

Our fourth question focuses on the effect of information on the work and lives of individuals and groups. Historians of IT have begun to address those, but less so than "technologists," media experts, business management professors, CEOs of IT companies, public officials, and economists. Historians would argue either that it was too soon to have the perspective wrought by the passage of time, or that they have not yet been able to begin assessing effects of IT information on people and groups. That is probably a fair claim, but not if examining how information affected people in earlier times. In the next chapter we do that by exploring how Spanish diplomats used information between 1815 and 1936.

Our fifth question, which called on identifying other historical discourses, has started. Instead of maps and clocks, blueprints of machines, wire diagrams of electrical circuits, source code for software, and programming languages are new, massive, rich in every conceivable way, and essential to a proper understanding of the emergence and evolution of computers and software. Indeed, software, like maps or clocks, represents a new subject area yet to be taken on by historians to an appreciable extent. The ephemera left behind to be studied is also vast: thousands of "how to" and user guide books, tens of thousands of articles, thousands of programming guides, and, increasingly becoming available, old printouts of programs and their reports. From a historical perspective, it represents virgin territory barely examined by historians as technical history, largely only as business history so far.

Finally, the issue of intrinsic features of facts and their effects on the creation and use of other information is an unfolding area of discussion centered on the development of databases with its growing body of literature. This is largely in the form of articles published in the *IEEE Annals of the History of Computing* over the years, massively so in the technical/scientific literature and Big Data, the latest iteration of massive databases, which is a subject almost too new for today's historians to take on. But the central effect so far was the creation of many professions historians would need to study. These include computer salesmen, managers of IT companies, Chief Information Officers (CIO), data processing managers, systems analysts, programmers, tape librarians, systems operators, teleprocessing managers, field engineers, and IT auditors, not to mention more traditional roles but played in an IT setting, such as lawyers, accountants, public relations experts, communications and media specialists, advertising specialists, and even truck drivers delivering large mainframe computers.

This case study of how a new subfield of history developed its own information ecosystem and supporting infrastructure reminds us that new subjects require these too in order to function. Once established they affect the conversation, the subject of study, the language used, and the information that is generated as a result of their work. Think of this chapter's subject as about the observers of a community at work, in this instance, historians of IT.

There remains the lingering question of whether the emergence of new ways of studying the history of information is analogous to the experience of the IT historians. It is an interesting issue to ponder. It is both simple to consider yet complex. If a sub-specialty develops, say, call it Information History, as distinct as IT or diplomatic history, then yes, it seems quite clear that its practitioners will need the four components to be able to go about their work. These elements of their ecosystem are universal in all academic disciplines and are not limited to history, humanities, or social sciences.

Then there is the larger issue raised by this entire book—that the study of information's history is new, representing a fundamental addition (or change) in the agendas and methods of historical research—what do the ecosystem and infrastructures look like? Two possibilities exist. The first is that large portions of the history community turn their attention to the study of information in their existing subfields, such as the role of information in Italian political history, in military activities during World War II, in how Philip II ruled Spain in the 1500s, and so forth. In each instance, techniques and agendas described in this book would probably be imposed on existing ecosystems and infrastructures, as happened in economics every generation or so as new ways of thinking and researching the subject emerged.[49] History journals would then start publishing on the history of information that rarely, if ever, did before. In fact, that has started.[50] The second possibility, and I believe the less likely one, is that old subfields would whither in the face of the New History. This problem occurs all the time and so cannot be fully dismissed. For example, there is less interest today among historians of technology in examining engineering in the Roman Empire or the Middle Ages than two decades ago. Most technology historians would rather deal with the Second Industrial Revolution and all manner of Twentieth Century technologies. But, old topics never disappear fully, which is why we could see new studies about information infrastructures of pre-agricultural times in early human history, or discussions about how Roman engineers shared information from one end of the Empire to another. In archeology, its practitioners aggressively embraced all manner of science and engineering methods, increasing their knowledge at a breathtaking pace, resulting in a massive growth in their understanding of early human societies.[51] Any of those specialties would reflect much of the behavior described in this chapter and book.

We turn, now, to the first of five chapters that delve into the activities of communities bound to each other by their shared use of information, beginning with Spanish diplomats. These chapters are intended to reinforce the observations explored in the first three chapters of this book. Their tone begins to shift from advocacy to more formal demonstration of the proposed approach to the study of the history of information. There is no better way to do that than to back out of the present into what must seem a distant past, to a time when Napoleon Bonaparte still lived, although no longer a threat to the peace of Europe—1815.

NOTES

1. For an analysis of the intellectual side of the development of the new subfield with much on its information content, see James W. Cortada, "Studying History As It Unfolds, Part 1: Creating the History of Information Technologies," *IEEE Annals of the History of Computing* 37, no. 3 (July–September 2015): 20–31.

2. For an extensive review of the literature, James W. Cortada, *The Digital Flood: The Diffusion of Information Technology Across the U.S., Europe, and Asia* (New York: Oxford University Press, 2012): 733–768.

3. Marc Uri Porat, *The Information Economy: Definition and Measurement* (Washington, DC: U.S. Department of Commerce, May 1977); William J. Baumol, Sue Anne Batey Blackman, and Edward N. Wolff, *Productivity and American Leadership: The Long View* (Cambridge, MA: MIT Press, 1989); Shoshana Zuboff, *In the Age of the Smart Machine: The Future of Work and Power* (New York: Basic Books, 1988) are a few examples out of hundreds.

4. Geoffrey Nunberg and Umberto Eco, *The Future of the Book* (Berkeley, CA: University of California Press, 1996); on archives see Bruce I. Ambacher, *Thirty Years of Electronic Records* (Lanham, MD: Scarecrow Press, 2003); and Lawrence J. McCrank, "History, Archives, and Information Science" *Annual Review of Information Science and Technology* 30 (1995): 281–382. Even the American Historical Association began to host sessions about the "death of books" at annual conventions. See, for example, http://www.hnn.us/articles/121910.html#Day1 (Accessed 10/10/2019).

5. For a massive summary of the literature and issues, Emily S. Rosenberg, ed., *A World Connecting, 1870–1945* (Cambridge, MA: Harvard University Press, 2012).

6. Ibid., various essays.

7. Rosenberg, *A World Connecting*, 919. Her book devotes over a thousand pages to these historiographical discussions.

8. Described by Ludimilla Jordanova, *History in Practice* (London: Arnold, 2000); see also, Robert H. Townsend, *History's Babel: Scholarship, Professionalization, and the Historical Enterprise in the United States, 1880–1940* (Chicago, IL: University of Chicago Press, 2013): 37–54.

9. The point made recently by two highly experienced historians, Philip Scranton and Patrick Fridenson, *Reimagining Business History* (Baltimore, MD: Johns Hopkins University Press, 2013).

10. James W. Cortada, *History Hunting: A Guide for Fellow Adventurers* (Armonk, NY: M. E. Sharpe, 2012): 60–70.

11. In addition to mine, Erwin Tomash had an important collection, now housed at the Charles Babbage Institute; neither of us was a professor, both worked in business.

12. A severe problem at the moment is the practice of libraries discarding old IT books as "out of date," which historians will need in future decades. These are

turning up at online second hand bookstores; about 25 percent of your author's library of old IT literature are discards of American and West European libraries.

13. I rescued several thousand volumes from IBM over the years, and acquired discarded volumes from AT&T's Bell Labs.

14. http://www.computerhistory.org/about/ (Accessed 10/10/2019). In an earlier incarnation from the 1970s it had operated on a smaller scale in Boston, Massachusetts.

15. On its activities with computing, http://www.sciencemuseum.org.uk/Search.aspx?keywords=computers&results=10 (Accessed 10/10/2019).

16. Historians of computing have relied on the *IEEE Annals of the History of Computing* for reports on such exhibits published in each issue of the journal for over three decades. There are routinely at least a half dozen such exhibits around the world each year.

17. IT History Society, "IT Historical Resources Sites," http://www.ithistory.org/resource_sites/resource-sites.php (Accessed 10/10/2019).

18. For a useful example of these materials, in this instance relating to Mexican banks and their use of IT, see Gustavo A. Del Angel Mobarak, "Computerization of Commercial Banks and the Building of an Automated Payments System in Mexico, 1965–1990," in Bernardo Bátiz-Lazo, J. Carles Maixé-Altés and Paul Thomas, eds., *Technological Innovation in Retail Finance: International Historical Perspectives* (New York: Routledge, 2011): 92–115.

19. These collections have grown so rapidly that all published surveys of archival collections are badly out of date. The only major inventories of these collections that seem to stay current are those listed by the IT History Society, per Bátiz-Lazo, Maixé-Altés, and Thomas (eds.), *Technological Innovation in Retail Finance*. However, once at an archive, finding aids are widely available for local collection, many online and most quite current.

20. In 2013, the IT History Society made the decision to add yet another database to its collection of online references devoted to cataloging all oral histories available worldwide over the next several years.

21. CBI has over three hundred oral histories, the largest collection in the world, http://www.cbi.umn.edu/oh/index.html (Accessed 10/10/2019), while other large collections now exist across North America and in Western Europe, Per Lundin, *Computers in Swedish Society: Documenting Early Use and Trends* (London: Springer Verlag, 2012): 25–29.

22. Lillian Hoddeson and Vicki Daitch, *True Genius: The Life and Science of John Bardeen* (Atlanta, GA: National Academies Press, 2002).

23. Janet Abbate, *Inventing the Internet* (Cambridge, MA: MIT Press, 1999); Arthur L. Norberg, Judy E. O'Neill, with Kerry J. Freedman, *Transforming Computing: The Pentagon's Role, 1962–1987* (Baltimore, MD: Johns Hopkins University Press, 2000); Leslie Berlin, *The Man Behind the Microchip: Robert Noyce and the Invention of Silicon Valley* (New York: Oxford University Press, 2006).

24. For a current list of their nearly 20 projects using oral history methods see http://www.cbi.umn.edu/research/index.html (Accessed 10/10/2019). On NSF FastLane see Thomas J. Misa and Jeffrey R. Yost, *FastLane: Managing Science in the Internet World* (Baltimore, MD: Johns Hopkins University Press, 2015); it is one of two current projects, the other is about computer security's history. These four hundred oral interviews are in addition to over three hundred done earlier by the staff at CBI.

25. For details on its history, mission, and collections, see http://www.cbi.umn.edu/about/index.html (Accessed 10/10/2019).

26. http://www.cbi.umn.edu/collections/archmss.html (Accessed 10/10/2019); Thomas J. Misa, "Charles Babbage Institute: Glimpses of the Founding," *CBI Newsletter* 34, no. 2 (Fall 2012): 4–8.

27. http://www.ithistory.org/resource_sites/resource-sites.php (Accessed 10/10/2019).

28. http://www.ieeeghn.org; http://www.computer.org/portal/web/cshc (both accessed 10/10/2019).

29. Doron D. Swade, "The Construction of Charles Babbage's Difference Engine No. 2," *IEEE Annals of the History of Computing* 27, no. 3 (July–September 2005): 70–88.

30. On membership, see http://www.sigcis.org/?q=user/register (Accessed 10/10/2019).

31. James W. Cortada, *An Annotated Bibliography on the History of Data Processing* (Westport, CT: Greenwood Press, 1983), *A Bibliographic Guide to the History of Computing, Computers, and the Information Processing Industry* (Westport, CT: Greenwood Press, 1990), *Second Bibliographic Guide to the History of Computing, Computers, and the Information Processing Industry* (Westport, CT: Greenwood Press, 1996), and *A Bibliographic Guide to the History of Computer Applications, 1950–1990* (Westport, CT: Greenwood Press, 1996); Jeffrey R. Yost, *Bibliographic Guide to Resources in the History of Scientific Computing, 1945–1975* (Westport, CT: Greenwood Press, 2002).

32. Charles Babbage Institute, "Software History Bibliography," http://www.cbi.umn.edu/research/shbib.pdf (Accessed 10/10/2019).

33. For examples, James W. Cortada, *Historical Dictionary of Data Processing* in 3 vols. (Westport, CT: Greenwood Press, 1987); John A. N. Lee, *International Biographical Dictionary of Computer Pioneers* (New York: Routledge, 1995).

34. See, for example, those of the staff at CBI, http://www.cbi.umn.edu/about/index.html (Accessed 10/10/2019).

35. Kenneth Flamm, *Targeting the Computer: Government Support and International Competition* (Washington, DC: Brookings Institution, 1987): 42–92.

36. Overviewed for many countries in Peter Hall and Paschal Preston, *Carrier Wave: New Information Technology and the Geography of Innovation, 1846–2003* (London: Unwin Hyman, 2004); Richard Coopey, ed., *Information Technology Policy: An International History* (Oxford: Oxford University Press, 2004).

37. Gaye Tuchman, *Wannabe U: Inside the Corporate University* (Chicago, IL: University of Chicago Press, 2009).

38. Peter Drucker published over a dozen books and some 35 articles in the *Harvard Business Review*, all of which influenced substantially the thinking of two generations of business executives. Jack Beatty, *The World According to Peter Drucker* (New York: Free Press, 1998).

39. I commissioned the task force while chairman of CBF, comprised of industry executives and historians of IT, to define the role of software history in 2000. That led to a series of software projects by CBI, documented on its website, http://www.cbi.umn.edu. For a list of the MIT reprints, http://www.cbi.umn.edu/research/reprints.html (both accessed 10/10/2019). Documentation on the task force is located at CBI, but in a closed file.

40. Jeff Opt, "An Introduction to the NCR Archives at the Montgomery County Historical Society Dayton, Ohio," *Charles Babbage Institute Newsletter* 25, no. 1 (Fall 2002): 12–14; Doron D. Swade, "Collecting Software": Preserving Information in an Object-Centered Culture," in *Electronic Information Resources and Historians European Perspectives* (St. Katharinen: Scripta Mercuturae, 1993): 93–103; Charles Babbage Institute, *Charles Babbage Institute Archival Collections* (Minneapolis, MN: CBI, 2001); Misa, "Charles Babbage Institute," 4–8.

41. I chaired CBF for a decade (1997-07) and fielded a number of telephone calls from industrialists and a slew of deans and vice chancellors in the United States and in Western Europe in other fields inquiring about how CBF created CBI, and continued to have such conversations as recently as 2012. I spent 38 years as an employee of IBM in sales and consulting, in addition to having been trained as a historian.

42. Author L. Norberg and Jeffrey R. Yost, *IBM Rochester: A Half Century of Innovation* (Rochester, MN: IBM Corporation, 2006).

43. Kevin Maney, *The Maverick and His Machine: Thomas Watson Sr. and the Making of IBM* (Hoboken, NJ: John Wiley & Sons, 2003); Richard S. Tedlow, *The Watson Dynasty: The Fiery Reign and Troubled Legacy of IBM's Founding Father and Son* (New York: HarperBusiness, 2003).

44. Many senior executives are under the age of forty, such as the CEOs at Yahoo! and Facebook, for example. Your author has called on dozens of such individuals over the past two decades to raise funds for IT history and draws his conclusion from this experience.

45. Sharing lessons learned was a formal goal of CBF, and is today at CBI and the ITHS.

46. Key findings of the global study of IT diffusion in Cortada, *The Digital Flood.*

47. Following the practice of scholars in scores of academic disciplines. For that practice, see Eric T. Meyer and Ralph Schroeder, *Knowledge Machines: Digital Transformations of the Sciences and Humanities* (Cambridge, MA: MIT Press, 2015).

48. Per a series of emails to the author. Similar discussions had been underway over the prior three years.

49. About which is a brilliant history by David Warsh, *Knowledge and the Wealth of Nations: A Story of Economic Discovery* (New York: W. W. Norton, 2006).

50. *Library and Information History*, a key journal in the field of information history, publishes a bibliography on the subject each year. See for example, Katherine Birkwood and Eric Howard, "Bibliographies," *Library and Information History,* 34, no. 1 (2018): 85–86.

51. For an overview of examples, see T. Brughmans and M. Peeples, "Trends in Archaeological Network Research: A Bibliomeatric Analysis," *Journal of Historical Network Research* 1, no. 1 (2017): 1–24; Mara T. Horowitz, "Recent Trends in the Study of Late Bronze-Age Ceramics in Syro-Mesopotamia and Neighboring Regions," *Journal of the Council for British Research in the Levant* 49, no. 2 (2017): 226–229.

Chapter Four

The Information Ecosystems of National Diplomacy*

Spain, 1815–1936

To be absolutely certain about something, one must know everything or nothing about it.

—Henry A. Kissinger

Workers in information intensive professions live in an information ecosystem in which they create, analyze, store, control, and communicate information as their core activities. This chapter illustrates how to write a history of a group that is cohesive, working in one highly regimented organization. Their information ecosystem was extensive, encompassing institutions, tacit and explicit knowledge, and routine and ad hoc collections of information. Looking at the work of individuals is the centerpiece of the study.[1] In the two centuries following the end of the Napoleonic Wars in 1815, the number of information-based professions increased sharply, constituting one of the most obvious evolutions in the nature of work to occur during these years, often simply called office workers.[2] Historians are pushing back in time their hunt for examples of work and professionalization of labor, with many examining that of public officials who, among others, are the quintessential knowledge workers in almost any century.[3] That is why linking the work of individuals to the history of information ecosystems and infrastructures is a useful strategy for historians to pursue.

The case of diplomats offers an excellent vehicle with which to study the role of information, professionalization, and the dependence of the key

*A longer, earlier version originally published as "Information Ecosystems of National Diplomacy: The Case of Spain, 1815–1936," *Information and Culture: A Journal of History* 48, no. 2 (2013): 222–259.

agents on data, information, and insights. It allows us to explore their use of information in both written and verbal communications and how facts were organized, maintained, and accessed. Diplomatic activity has left one of the richest, most detailed paper trails of any profession, reaching back to the earliest written records. The profession long required its members to read and write well, analyze situations, and articulate points of view, much as was required of high Catholic Church officials, lawyers, and academics. Spain was no exception to that pattern. Diplomacy was a profession that required documentation of its activities in considerable detail,[4] because that documentation, in turn, was used to do further work by others located in other countries, even in future years. While much of the work of a diplomat could be likened to that of a salesman or politician in that they had to tell a story and persuade people to do things, it was also analogous to the legal profession, in that they worked with documents, kept meticulous records with which to formulate future views and actions based on precedent and history, and had a profoundly legalistic culture, bound by governmental regulations, national laws, and, of course, the most obvious of diplomatic documentation, treaties.[5]

The Spanish case is informative for several reasons. Like other diplomatic corps, it left behind a very detailed paper trail dating back to the Middle Ages. The Spanish diplomatic profession and how it worked paralleled other European and American diplomatic corps. That similarity itself is part of the information ecosystem, because for centuries nation states worked to standardize diplomatic practices. Their success depended on their ability to exchange information and conduct conversations that made possible political and economic collaborations, the conclusion of wars, payment of reparations, and servicing of the needs of their citizens in foreign lands. All diplomats shared common identity from one country or another. It was formally enshrined through treaties articulating aspects of their jobs (such as who could be called a Minister or an Ambassador), all through the nineteenth and early twentieth centuries. It was reinforced through the process of credentialing and training diplomats, practices that became increasingly formal and structured in the two centuries following the Congress of Vienna (1815). While this case study on Spain ends with the start of its seminal civil war of 1936–1939, the process of harmonizing practices and shared values continued, for example, with the establishment of a formal training school for diplomats, paralleling that of other nations in the post-civil war years, and publication of training materials and other ephemera essential to the work of today's diplomats, much of it similar to archetypical information domains of prior centuries.[6]

While informationalizing work was well underway before the start of the French Revolution in 1789 along French lines in Spain, one can conveniently identify the growing thicket of Spanish information activities by looking at the post-1815 period. This is possible in spite of the fact that this is a long period filled with national wars, civil wars, economic crises and transformations, and other forms of political and social churn. That churn did not disrupt the movement and use of information. One data point on the matter: Between 1800 and 2010, the Spanish foreign ministry (variously known, but largely as the *Ministerio de Asuntos Exteriores*) had 265 cabinet level ministers, or roughly 1.26 ministers per year, in some years up to seven in one year (1822, 1840, and 1847), and nine in 1823. This churn in leadership was a direct result of the political instability of public administration that, while reducing the effectiveness of Spain's ability to implement foreign policies, did not stop the daily work of its diplomats.[7] That fact suggests an observation about the profession: it continued to professionalize and use more information over time despite events. Their information ecosystem displayed a remarkable resilience and ability to thrive. The information infrastructure upon which these workers relied never collapsed. The Ministry kept working, its records increased, and its embassies and consulates did their assigned missions. That was even the case during the highly disruptive occupations of the nation's capital during the Napoleonic invasion of Iberia (1808–1814) and during the Spanish Civil War (1936–1939).

These ideas are explored by examining several interrelated topics. First, we identify participants and the information ecosystem in which they worked. This process involves describing institutional supporting elements, such as the library and archival features of the Spanish foreign ministry. Second, because I argue that professionalization of work leads to codification of a necessary information infrastructure, we next describe how that came to be for Spanish diplomats. Third, the early role and activities of Spanish diplomatic historians is introduced, because their work was a byproduct of the diplomatic information ecosystem and part of it, as history helped reinforce professional expertise and insight, making it far more important than one normally would acknowledge is the case for historical writings.

Diplomatic information ecosystems consist of documents and publications which circulate within a community, but also shared knowledge, worldviews, and values its members have accumulated through experience and education, all of which comprise an ecosystem. Derived from that notion, then, conversations about what occurs in that intellectual, idea-driven, information environment, which is how often one then spills over into discussions about knowledge management (KM).[8] For our purposes, we avoid the term knowledge management and stick, instead, with a more elementary description of the environment. As Alistair Black observed when examining the work of British diplomats over the course of several centuries, a member of that profession was less of a negotiator than "knowledge manager," and more "a collector and conduit of information designed to enhance the knowledge of policy-makers," just as is found in the work of Spanish diplomats.[9] Finally, the concept and term, ecosystem, makes the connection between how and what information flows in a community. The effects of that process on individual players are important. It is that link which makes the study of information so important.

THE PARTICIPANTS AND THEIR INFORMATION ECOSYSTEM

There are several communities comprising the Spanish diplomatic world. They interacted closely with each other, often daily even in the days before the telegraph, telephone, and e-mail. None could perform their duties without interacting with each other. Those interactions were collaborative for the most part, but political vicissitudes prevailed too—the subject of so much diplomatic and political history—all of which contributed to their invisible information ecosystem whose traces remain in the form of the ephemera that has so dominated diplomatic history for centuries. Figure 4.1 introduces the majority of the participants in this ecosystem. Their informational roles and dependencies are next described.

The first and *primis* organization is the nation's foreign ministry, a cabinet level department located in the capital. Following the French model, the *Primera Secretaría de Estado* was established in 1714 as part of a major reorganization of the national government. The constitution of 1837 introduced the nomenclature of ministers as heads of departments, in this instance the *Ministerio de Estado*, which remained in force until 1938. During the Civil War of 1936–1939, General Francisco Franco's Nationalist government created the *Ministerio de Asuntos Exteriores*, while the Republic still had its *Ministerio de Estado*. After Franco won the war, the two were folded into his organization. In 2004 the department had its mission expanded, as was customary in these years at many other national foreign offices, and was renamed the *Ministerio de Asuntos Exteriores y de Cooperación* (MAEC).[10]

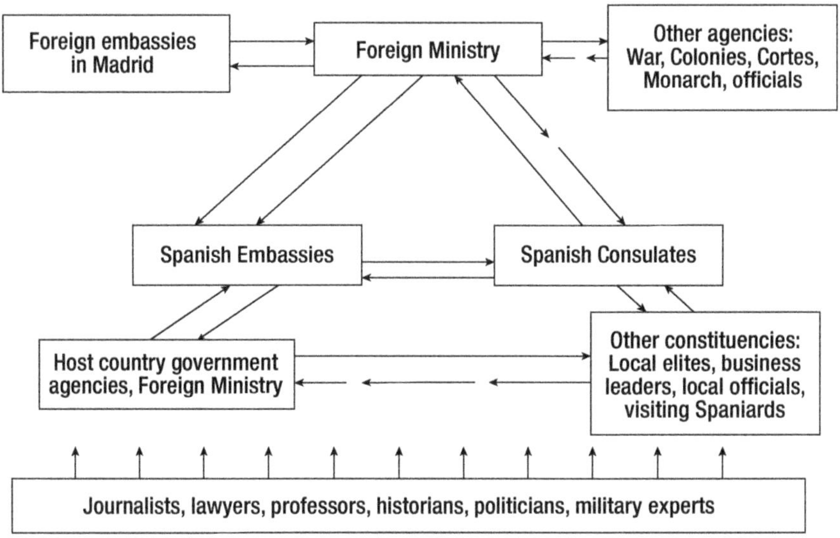

Figure 4.1. Spanish Diplomatic Information Ecosystem, 1815–1936

The "home office" in Madrid was responsible for helping the monarch and more frequently the prime minister and the minister of state to recruit diplomatic staff, fund embassies and consulates, train their staffs, collect information presented to kings, queens, cabinets, and the parliament (*Cortes*) to inform them about the nation's diplomatic and foreign trade situations, and to recommend policies and take actions.[11] Records of diplomatic activities were kept throughout the period. A local library was established to serve as a source of additional information, and specialists on various regions of the world were located in Madrid, interacting with all diplomatic posts around the world.[12] Two other cabinet level departments participated in this ecosystem from time to time as well: the *Ministerio de la Guerra* (War), later called the *Ministerio de Defensa Nacional* and *Ministerio de Defensa*, and the *Ministerio del Ultramar* (established in 1863), which managed the nation's colonies.[13] The Cortes injected itself into this world in much the same manner as legislatures in other European and North and South American countries, also leaving a paper trail that reflected who used diplomatic information.[14]

A second cluster of participants in this ecosystem consisted of diplomats assigned to embassies. Prior to the 1600s, embassies were groups of people who visited another kingdom to negotiate on some issue, then returned home. Afterwards, a full time presence was increasingly needed in major countries, because the volume of communications, business, and knowledge required to conduct diplomatic work had grown. As that activity increased so did the number of embassies and the size of their staffs. In the early decades embassy staffs were small, several clerks and an assistant to an ambassador or minister, in addition to servants. In 1830, Spain had two major embassies, one in Paris and the other in Naples, each headed by an ambassador. In 15 other nations it had embassies (legations) headed by a minister (slightly lower in rank than an ambassador but the same role), scattered across Europe and in the United States. By 1876 there were 38 embassies around the world, with most of the additional ones in Latin America. By 1931 Spain had embassies in 49 countries, and 85 by the end of the Franco regime in 1975. Today it has 123 embassies.[15]

The role of diplomats was to observe local political and international conditions and to report regularly on them with analyses about their implications for Spain's national interests and foreign policy. Unless there was a war going on in a minister's country, which meant possibly multiple daily communications, this often meant writing a weekly report. They were to communicate messages prepared by the home office to be delivered either to an official in the local foreign ministry or to a higher level dignitary (such as a king or prime minister), using such occasions to drive home points using whatever persuasive communications skills they had. Messages were precise and required that, following immediately such meetings, the Spaniard reported the details of what transpired to Madrid. A third role was to network socially with local elites who could influence the outcomes of events and relations, such as economic cabinet officials, members of the legislature, leading commentators in the press, and leaders in business. This type of activity occurred normally every day.[16]

Beginning in the eighteenth century and certainly by the early 1800s, these various tasks were being codified in Spain and other European foreign ministries.[17] Following another round of institutional transformations in foreign ministries during the 1840s and 1850s that essentially remained intact until after World War II, diplomats gained access to increasingly detailed information on how they should do their jobs, reflecting the kinds of advice one now often hears referred to as "best practices."[18] These codifications of information proved important because too few Spanish diplomats were careerists who became experienced in the day-to-day work of a diplomat until the second half of the nineteenth century. Many were political appointees, or people that some cabinet level minister wanted to get out of the country so as to block a political rival. Some were members of the literati as well. For example, the minister assigned to the United States during the American Civil War, Gabriel García Tassara, was a poet;

he also turned out to be an astute observer of the American scene and a prolific commentator on events in the country.[19]

Over the course of the nineteenth and twentieth centuries embassies assumed additional responsibilities, such as the task of issuing visas to foreigners who wanted to visit Spain or its colonies. They assumed a growing role in influencing their local country's economic policies in support of Spanish commerce, affecting the release of or arranged for legal representation of Spanish nationals accused of violating local laws, and promoting cultural exchange programs and tourism, the latter initially in the 1870s and 1880s, and most notably between the 1920s and the start of the Spanish Civil War.[20] This pattern of expanded facilities, more diplomats, and greater reporting was as a result of more nations coming into existence, expansion of colonies, and further globalization of trade.

Consulates comprised a third cluster of agents in this diplomatic information ecosystem. These were tiny organizations, often staffed with a part time consul who was a local businessman always located in large urban centers, normally ports, which had economic ties to Spain. Their primary role was to facilitate trade between their local port (and country) and Spain. They reported on economic matters and the number of ships coming in and out of ports, collected fees and duties, facilitated trade deals, extricated arrested Spanish sailors from jail, and entertained wealthy Spanish visitors and local elites.[21]

There were more consulates than embassies and their number varied over time. In the United States, for example, a major trading partner in both centuries, consulates were established soon after the Revolutionary War in such obvious trading centers as New York, Boston, Philadelphia, Charleston, and New Orleans.[22] The United States did the same in Spain in Cadiz, Malaga, and Barcelona.[23]

Consuls served at different ranks, from vice-consul to Consul General and, as with ambassadors and ministers, had their social pecking order too. They networked tightly into the elite power structure of their city and region. As with staffs in embassies, they too became more professionalized with their own unique set of information requirements. These included knowledge about how to perform their tasks, conduct economic analysis, analyze and report on local non-diplomatic events, and about Spain's local foreign policy initiatives. As in other countries they had career paths up the consular ranks, although increasingly by the late nineteenth century it was not uncommon for consular diplomats to serve in embassies, and also in jobs located in the Ministry of State in Madrid. For most of the two centuries, the role and needs of consuls were separated from those of embassies.

Not until the twentieth century did these two variants of the foreign service integrate, merging into one fundamental profession with shared values, knowledge, and information needs.[24]

Figure 4.1 reminds us of the institutional participants in the diplomatic information ecosystem. The core members were the foreign ministry, embassies, and consulates. Other participants were also active and, depending on events, could be viewed as core as well. Solid arrows indicate an intense, essential, ongoing, and voluminous exchange of information, while dashed arrows suggest a less voluminous, often occasional participation in the Spanish diplomatic information ecosystem. The model is Spain centric; that is to say it implies that the foreign ministry in Madrid was the gearbox, the engine that kept the ecosystem functioning. The ministry initiated or managed diplomatic activities either out of a royal court or secretary to a monarch until the seventeenth century, afterwards through the specialized cabinet department devoted to foreign affairs. It also controlled staffing, budgets to pay the costs of diplomacy, and the way in which information was collected and diplomatic work done, just as was done by other national governments. That these looked similar reinforces the argument that interdependence of national diplomatic communities was an essential feature of their work that required compatibility in they way they functioned and in what information they collected, used, and even shared with ministries of other nations.

THE DIPLOMATIC INFORMATION ECOSYSTEM

The structure of diplomatic archives and the comments made by diplomats in their memoirs represent rich veins that can be mined for evidence to understand the role of the information ecosystem at very precise times in history, by location and by individual. Spain's diplomatic archives have been described, and finding aids to these various collections have been appearing for a century, and are now moving to the Internet.[25] Scores of memoirs by Spanish diplomats cover the entire period, although as in other nations, more than half cover the period since the 1940s. Some are memorable for their tactical descriptions of the daily work of a Spanish diplomat. Fewer exist describing work done back in the home office in Madrid.[26]

At Spain's embassies, ambassadors and ministers and usually a couple of staff, possibly only scribes, informed Madrid about domestic political issues, and wrote other reports on the economic status of the country, including data about volumes of trade. A second class of correspondence involved activities of diplomatic personnel, describing meetings held by them with local government officials and the results and consequences of those, their assessments of people's thinking about issues relevant to Spain, and any intelligence gathered about what other diplomats were doing or learning.[27] Their reports often included extensive collections of newspaper clippings, broadsides, political tracts, maps, and, more rarely, books, deemed of interest to the home office. Periodically, an official in Madrid would request information about a specific activity or topic, as occurred frequently in the 1850s as various governments in Europe compared notes on how their diplomatic services were evolving, salary levels, and other operational matters. Transmittal of information by the government to which a diplomat was assigned was routinely sent on to Madrid in its original form or as a copy or summary of the message. Often such correspondence would lead to a dialogue back and forth on some matter of policy or practice, usually with the ambassador attempting to influence the position of his government about an important issue, such as whether to recognize the legal and practical legitimacy of a new local regime.

In Madrid, information from the embassies came in every day and was distributed to appropriate staff for analysis. These individuals engaged in extensive correspondence back with the embassies, normally to instruct them about actions to take and information to collect, sharing less new facts than did the embassies with their home office. The volume of information coming in varied, but in aggregate grew between 1815 and 1936. For example, in the case of the United States, several thousand pages were written during the American Civil War, but only about one tenth as much in the 1870s and 1880s, only to pick up in volume as the two nations addressed the intensifying Cuban crisis in the 1890s that resulted in the Spanish-American War of 1898. We know about the volume because the archival record of that correspondence is complete, and the bundles of records (called *legajos*) can be counted.[28]

As the nineteenth century progressed and the information coming into Madrid increased, officials began to think of their data, hence their files, by topic, not just by country of origins. Political correspondence, discussions about slavery and economics, and military affairs were examples of topics discussed. Budgetary and personnel information were collected and preserved for the same reasons as a large organization would today.[29]

An extensive correspondence also took place with consulates, although more narrowly focused on local economic issues, business problems and opportunities, and other topics related to individuals. Consuls engaged in conversations with local business and political leaders, reporting those to both Madrid and their embassy, the latter institution the one to which consuls "officially" reported to for budgets and instructions. Because most consuls served part-time, usually non-career diplomatic representatives, they varied in the degree of commitment to their diplomatic duties.[30] When a consulate closed, some records were not returned to Spain. Sometimes they were preserved, however, as occurred with the Spanish consular records from the office in Charleston, South Carolina, and another set from Savannah, Georgia, for the entire nineteenth century, now at Duke University. They constitute two of the most complete long runs of records of any Spanish consulate.[31]

In the particular case of Charleston, we have consular staff witnessing the first eruption of warfare at the start of the American Civil War, providing a highly detailed description of the event and analysis of the consequences. Given that it took two to three weeks for mail to move across the Atlantic, officials in Madrid became some of the first in Europe to understand exactly what had happened from a reliable eyewitness. This reporting arrived in Madrid a few days sooner than the second hand reports of the same event from its embassy in Washington, DC that relied on press reports, and additional communications from the consulate in Charleston. But combined, the information from Washington and Charleston gave officials in Madrid a good account of events and confirmed their growing realization that the United States was in a serious crisis.[32]

Since the role of consulates was to stimulate business, provide passports, permits, and letters of introduction, collect taxes, verify inventories, and ensure conformance to local and Spanish laws, there was much to do. On occasion, Madrid would launch a global campaign to have their consulates collect information relevant to business establishments both in the Iberian Peninsula and in the colonies. For example, by the end of the nineteenth century the Ministry had an office devoted to collecting information useful to Spanish business firms, the *Centro de Información Comercial*. During World War I, this office requested and received economic information, which made it possible to publish scores of pamphlets on trade relations between Spain and these countries based on consular and embassy data. These often ran 20–50 pages in length, some to over one hundred pages, all with statistical data on different types of goods, imports, and exports, and practical information about local laws and general economic conditions and practices. Combined, they represented a large amount of specific current details about the global economy in the period between 1910–1916, all presented in a consistent format suitable for use by both the government and businesses.[33] During the twentieth century, this practice of globally collecting information about a topic, usually economic, became a routine practice of both embassy and consular communities and later of departments or ministries of commerce and trade.

Because reports from consulates, embassies, and others from Madrid included references to news reports or actual news clippings on political and military affairs, we know that those forms of non-manuscript sources of information entered into this Spanish information ecosystem. No student of Spanish diplomacy of the nineteenth and twentieth century can avoid that reality, even though extant administrative and budgetary records did not document the cost of subscriptions to local newspapers. However, the existence of so much ephemera makes it clear that these sources were important inputs into the reports written by local diplomats that affected their views of events. On this last point, almost all diplomatic memoirs refer to this source of information.[34]

It was no different for diplomats of other nations that, like the Spaniards, read the same newspapers, political tracks, and broadsides, and formed in their cities tight communities that talked constantly to each other about their profession and shared interests. These "communities of practice" were so intimate that by the late nineteenth century one's social ranking within that community, even where one sat at a dinner party, was based on their seniority of appointment to a particular city. That community even had a spokesman that would represent all of them to the local foreign ministry, called the Dean of the Diplomatic Corps, who was always the longest serving ambassador in that country. They discussed local issues ranging from housing and traffic conditions to passports, permissions to travel within a country, and even schooling for their children.[35] Spanish diplomats routinely reported activities and conversations of this virtual community to Madrid. Diplomats from other countries did the same, so a historian can compare reports from two or three different diplomats from two or three different countries about the same event and thereby trace the evolution of an idea. Today, this is called "group think."[36]

The *Ministerio de Estado*, like any corporate headquarters or ministerial office, constituted an ecosystem of its own, aligned to, but somewhat distinct from, the larger one that included embassies, consulates, and other constituencies. Figure 4.2 reflects some of the major informational features of this institution. It is tentative, because only portions of the administrative history of the ministry have been studied, so we do not yet have a longitudinal institutional history that describes its informational ecosystem.[37] The figure reflects collections of activities that took place within the Ministry for most of the period under study, however. The

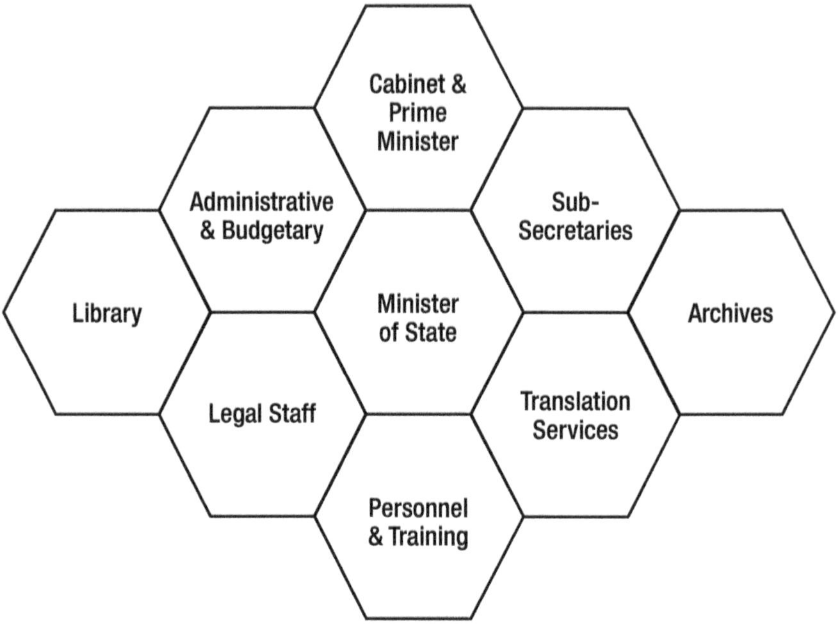

Figure 4.2. Information Ecosystem within the *Ministerio de Estado*

names of various agencies and functions changed over time, but essentially remained constant. Each generated large bodies of information preserved in the national archives of Spain, largely as categories of records, not necessarily as institutional records of a particular office or agency. That is why the figure is more valuable as a representation of the work, and hence information ecosystem, than as an administrative organization chart.

Officials in Madrid engaged in extensive sharing of information, following practices evident in diplomatic circles in other countries. Perusal of any of the various guides to the Ministry's internal records makes that patently clear; they communicated in writing as well as verbally in this large three-story building. Like other governments, this ministry established three sets of internal sources of information that it could rely upon. First, it stocked a library. Second, it maintained an archive that felt very much like a corporate archive, designed more for use by diplomats and lawyers than by historians. It was not until long after the end of the Spanish Civil War that scholars were able to access these records on a regular basis. The third was office files kept all over the building and only periodically surrendered either to the library or to the archive. Regulations regarding the deposition of files were published from time to time, a *de facto* recognition that these massive paper databases were essential to the work of this ministry.[38]

Employees at the Ministry relied as well on other sources and types of information for as long as this organization had existed in support of their work. Like military ministries, for example, they needed maps of countries, colonies, and cities and so, for several hundred years, acquired these, often requesting such materials from consulates, embassies, and colonial officials around the world. The requirement for new maps, in particular, remained constant and over time old ones became the property of archival organizations inside and outside this ministry. These also improved in accuracy and detail across the century.[39] Related and popular forms of cartographic information were globes of the earth. As these were updated with new information, old ones were retired, replaced with new ones. Europe's activities in Africa in the nineteenth century involved development of colonies and included Spain, although the latter was only in North Africa, requiring current maps and globes as sources of information on the region. Finally, a vast amount of information was needed on such issues as the history of a nation, accounts of a country's diplomacy, diplomatic histories of "everyone," including Spain, geographic and economic atlases of as many countries as possible, and other economic and demographic data.[40]

Requirements for such information increased during the course of the nineteenth century as a result of two circumstances. First, the number of embassies and consulates around the world grew, requiring local staff in Madrid to keep up with events and conditions in an ever-increasing number of places. Second was the evolution of the diplomatic corps from a relatively untrained crew into a more formal profession, requiring training of its diplomatic corps. Part of that training involved lectures on regions and issues that had to be empirically based, and that required a library.

ROLE OF THE MINISTRY'S LIBRARY AND ARCHIVE

This ministry made its first attempt to create a library as early as 1801, along with other administrative reforms that three decades later had evolved into a more organized archive. We know little about how much information was collected in the nineteenth and early twentieth centuries by the ministry for its own use. However, catalogs published in the 1940s for use by ministry employees makes clear that by the start of the Civil War there were at least 11,000 volumes in its collection. One could assume other books and ephemera were located in various offices in this large building.[41] Bibliographic citations in these catalogs make evident that the ministry was acquiring new materials on a regular basis, including, by the end of the nineteenth century, magazines and journals, reflecting an emerging genre of publications in such fields as international affairs, law, economics, and history. During the civil war, many of the materials at the ministry were moved to Barcelona and Valencia. Most of it was returned to Madrid after the war, and later some of it went to other libraries or became property of the ministry's archive.[42]

Of whether this library grew in importance during the nineteenth century there can be no question. So too the role of an archive, discussed further below, to such a point that by the end of the century it was decided to bring the two collections under one administrative head in 1901, directed by Manuel Flores Calderón, who managed this information ecology for the ministry for eight years. Subsequent directors had formal experience as librarians and archivists and often served for similar periods of time, with the exception of Federido Ruiz Morcuende (1932–1948), who served a long tenure and had the unenviable task of preserving both the printed and manuscript records of the Ministry during the civil war and the early years of the Franco Regime, while meeting simultaneously the informational requirements of local diplomats and other staff.[43]

A major part of the home office information infrastructure, however, was its archive, operating much like those of government ministries and corporations today all over the world. In the years from 1800 to at least the 1960s, these materials were intended to be used only by employees of the ministry, not historians; that second group would receive significant support in the subsequent half century. Thus, this function should not be seen as just a center for the preservation of the historical record, playing merely some passive role in contemporary events. Rather, it served as a central repository of information that could be shared by all in the building. From about 1807 to 1852, the archives and library were managed as one administrative unit, suggesting it did not matter to employees in the Ministry whether a piece of information was in the form of a letter from an embassy, a book, a map, or some other ephemera. While many diplomatic records dated before 1833 were located in other libraries and archives, the Ministry proved more interested in the most contemporary records, as those were the ones in greatest demand by active (meaning not retired) diplomatic employees. One can conclude that a combination of old and newer files was often required in order to inform cabinet and sub-cabinet officials and members of the Cortes about a circumstance unfamiliar to most of them, as well as officials in other interested ministries.

That such a circumstance could exist in which important information was not well known by groups of public officials is evidenced by the example of the peace treaty that brought to a close the Spanish-American War of 1898. During the negotiations, the question came up of what territories in the Pacific should be turned over to the Americans, and in the process of making that determination, it was initially unclear what islands Spain had in the region, which provided a bit of a surprise for both sides once the necessary research was completed. As a result of this work, the United States ended up with more property in the Pacific than it first thought it would get.[44] The Philippines, a massive collection of poorly mapped islands, is one example of that process. The occupying Americans spent years understanding the region as it established its administrative and military control over the ex-Spanish colony between 1898 and the start of World War II. In this instance, and with respect to Cuba and Puerto Rico, both sides relied extensively on the records in Madrid and others located in the colonies, of the Ministry of the Colonies, which, like the diplomatic ministry, also maintained records and collections of relevant information such as maps and publications.

One of the informational roles employees concerned themselves with involved the highly legalistic staff work of negotiating and writing treaties. Simply put, treaties are contracts among nations, and like a commercial contract, are considered binding in that their terms and conditions are carefully negotiated, meticulous in the precision of their language, and invariably involve the participation of multiple cabinet officials, heads of state, diplomats, and other agents of a government. Most need the informed services of both legal staff—hence development of international law since the sixteenth century as a field of knowledge and academic discipline—and of others familiar with a region. The Spanish-American War's information trail represented one of the most public in Spanish diplomatic history. The public and many officials in numerous countries wanted to understand the terms of the settlement, since it affected the Caribbean, the United States, Spain, Germany's interests in the Pacific, the Philippines, and other regions and nations. Both the U.S. Congress and the Spanish Cortes engaged in conversations about all facets of these events, and left a paper trail in the wake of their interest.[45]

The Treaty of Westphalia of 1648 was one of the largest, most complex of these kinds of documents ever prepared by European nations. It remains one of the most important in European history because, as an unintended result, many of the borders most nations maintained for centuries afterwards were originally defined in this treaty. Part of the exercise of drawing up this set of agreements required detailed drawings of maps articulating exactly where borders were to be, what towns were on this side or that side of a border, the role of rivers and roads as boundaries, and so forth. Many negotiators of this treaty came armed with maps from their respective nations, or commissioned new maps to be drawn as part of their work.[46] It was a very data intensive exercise that did not always lead to exactness. For example, along the Franco-Spanish border, the town of Llivia was, from a practical point of view, in France as a result of the treaty, but because it was not specifically listed in the detailed legal documents that emerged out of that treaty, it remained part of Spain. To this day, there is a road from Spain that goes to the town. The road and town are Spanish; the fields on either side are French. It is still referred to as the Spanish "enclave" of Llivia.[47]

During the nineteenth century, the archive/library organized its materials in ways that proved useful to the other secretariats in the building, such as correspondence organized by country and within country, and by type of information and agency providing it, such as consular or embassy. This arrangement was standard practice among other diplomatic archives in Europe, and was modeled in both the nineteenth and early twentieth centuries largely on the practices of the French Government, of the *Ministère des Affaires Etrangères*, and its *Archives*.[48]

Linked to the pooling of information into this combined library/archival structure were, from time to time, translation services all foreign ministries maintained. In Madrid's case, enough translating was going on that it required the consolidation of that function into its own office then connected to that of the archive and library in 1888.[49] Translation staffs had operated in the ministry since before its establishment as a formal organization in 1994.[50] Various reorganizations in the subsequent forty years after 1888 reaffirmed the role of these various functions as core constructs of the administrative support services of the Ministry.[51]

Evidence of how the library and archive organized its materials suggested further how diplomatic officials thought operationally about their information. Workers in all fields organize information in ways relevant to their work. That was recently affirmed in a stunning manner in a study of how computer scientists still relied on paper and organized it to fit their needs in what otherwise should have been a paperless office environment.[52] Historians examining the role of lawyers in seventeenth century Spain noticed the same, as well as in eighteenth and early nineteenth century North America.[53] The lack of significant reorganizations of information in the Spanish case also suggests that this typology, or data map, of

Table 4.1. Categories of Records in the Ministry of State, 1713–1970s

Ministry of State	
Subsecretary (1721–1930)	Correspondence (1821–1931)
Commerce (1713–1931)	Cultural relations (1881–1931)
Accounting (1816–1930)	Telegrams (1914–1932)
Passports (1824–1919)	Registers of correspondence
Court cases (1762–1932)	
Ministry of State/Ministry of Foreign Affairs Archives	
Interpretation of Languages (1875–1970)	
Accounting (1895–1964)	
Cultural (1922–1936)	
Institute for Hispanic Culture (1941–1960)	
Commission for Cultural Exchanges between Spain and the United States (1959–1962)	
Diplomatic Post Records	
Embassies, legations, consulates (records by city from founding of local Spanish presence)	

Source: Elisa Carolina de Santos Canalejo, *Guía del Archivo General del Ministerio de Asuntos Exteriores* (Madrid: Ministerio de Asuntos Exteriores, Secretaría General Ténica, 1997): 215–218.

how to organize information was not subject to much restructuring, despite that the operations of these functions reorganized from time to time.

Table 4.1 catalogs an extensive list of records with the dates for how long these records were augmented. Staffs organized information by institution (such as an embassy or sub-secretariat), function (e.g., translations), or topic (e.g., treaties). Very rarely was the material form in which information was collected and organized an influence on how data was managed and accessed. In Table 4.1 there is the category of telegrams, a form of communication that continued to come into the Ministry well into the last quarter of the twentieth century. But essentially, the organization of information was by topic (for instance, commerce), by agency generating or needing it (most commonly, administration and accounting), or by geography (an embassy or consulate), not by format.

As bibliographies of the library suggested, the subjects of diplomacy, international law, and history also became more structured and codified as the nineteenth century unfolded, occurring at the same time as the profession of diplomacy acquired its own codified set of practices and protocols about what one needed to know concerning the role and information essential to the work of these officials.

Table 4.2 offers a short list of the most frequently used information artifacts relied upon by Spanish and, by direct inference, all diplomats

Table 4.2. Types of Diplomatic Information Artifacts

Types	*Examples*
Dispatches	Reports to Madrid about meetings with local foreign ministry officials; instructions from Madrid to embassies and consulates
Correspondence	Letters by diplomats, local officials, citizens
Reports	Routine, periodic, such as economic statistics, ship registers, passports issued
Ministry publications	Collections of treaties, administrative guidelines, forms
Administrative records	Budgets, personnel dossiers
Local publications	Local foreign ministry publications, newspapers, magazines, local books on diplomatic themes
Telegrams	Regarding local political, military, and diplomatic events
Memoirs and diplomatic histories	Published by ambassadors, foreign ministry officials, historians, and experts in international law

between the end of the Napoleonic Wars and the early years of World War II. Telegrams came into use late in the nineteenth century, of course; telephones were increasingly used by the 1920s. Extant physical records make clear that the volume of such artifacts proved extensive, while this table reminds us of their variety. All were used concurrently as diplomats processed various types of information as a routine part of their work.

PROFESSIONALIZATION OF THE DIPLOMATIC CORPS AND CODIFICATION OF THEIR INFORMATION INFRASTRUCTURE

Over two centuries, the Spanish diplomatic corps slowly evolved into a professional organization, much as occurred with those of other European and North and South American nations, and in parts of Asia.[54] Diplomats increasingly trained in their profession and spent their careers in their nation's foreign service. The second evolution was the formal documentation of regulations and laws governing their work, most evidently observed in the activities of consuls. A third development involved their reliance on a growing collection of information relevant to their work, most notably treaties. In most decades all three activities were underway simultaneously, either as coordinated activities aimed at modernizing workflows or as a circumstance requiring a response to the evolving exigencies of their actions. Either way, the information environment proved dynamic and essential.

As the various ranks of diplomats were agreed to by European nations following the Napoleonic Wars, the Spanish defined the roles of each, with the most detailed articulation of the profession's status and duties introduced in a royal decree of March 4, 1844, which also laid out for the first time the career path of a diplomat, ranks, and so forth. This was supplemented with additional details in another royal decree on February 27, 1851, which further aligned the Spanish diplomatic service to the French style. By this time entrance into the diplomatic corps required a university education and, soon after, passing an entrance examination that tested, among other things, communication and knowledge of history. Merit became increasingly a critical basis for entry and success within the professional ranks, even though in both centuries it was not uncommon for ambassadors and ministers to be appointed who were not career foreign service officers, as we saw with Spain's emissary to the United States in the 1860s. Additional reforms that included training were initiated in 1883, with an entrance process and exams along the lines of the French *grand concours*. The organization of the profession varied over the years, of course, but an important transformation occurred in 1928 with the merger of the diplomatic and consular career paths, essentially making it possible for a consular officer to work in or run an embassy. That meant two sets of knowledge and experiences would be increasingly blended together. In 1932, the government began to require its diplomats be able to converse in French and English, following an increasingly European practice.[55]

In addition to mentoring diplomats at various stages of their careers, they could increasingly rely on information provided by the ministry or generated by academics and the legal community, often in collaboration with the ministry in Madrid or which it distributed. "User" manuals that taught diplomats how to do their work appeared all through these years, often written in French, which an educated Spaniard would have been expected to be able to read. Many citations of such materials appeared in the library catalog published in the 1940s.[56] Some were in such demand that they were translated into Spanish. One of the standard texts of the mid-nineteenth century was written by a Russian professor, but published in French—the universal diplomatic language until after World War II. In the 1880s a Spanish professor of law translated all three thick volumes.[57] As normal in the period, the text largely focused on international law of all kinds, not just war and peace, but rather the entire spectrum of diplomatic activities. It included insights on the art of negotiations.[58]

Because of the importance of international trade, making sure consulates were well informed on consular law proved crucial. The process of informing consulates about new practices and regulations was essentially communicating this information in the form of hand written correspondence scribed in Madrid until late in the nineteenth century. Consular records of the period are full of such instructions. By the last quarter of the century it had become too inefficient to hand scribe rules and insights needed because there were too many offices and so, like other governments, the Spanish began to publish anthologies of rules to guide consular work and to make available academic treatises on consular law.[59] In time, even consular personnel were commenting on their profession. For example, in 1889 Eduardo Toda y Güel, both a lawyer and consul, published an extensive monograph on Spanish consular law under the authority of the Minister of State, Antonio de Aguilar y Correa, with the seal of the Ministry on the title page, indicating that it was an official government document.[60] It discussed the consular profession, work of these employees, attributes of the work (legal, political, commercial, judicial, and record keeping), how to deal with the Ministry of State (what kind of information to send to Madrid and in what form, correspondence, telegrams, forms), how to work with other agencies and ministries, and what kind of information they exchanged, such as with the ministries of war and the navy. It included discussion about Spanish consular law.

Another source of information distributed to this community in the late 1800s–early 1900s was the widely used treatise on Spanish consular law written by Miguel Maluquer y Salvador, both a lawyer and a consular official, also published by the Minister of State in 1899.[61] It became the "official" user manual for Spanish consular officials. This nine hundred page encyclopedic work included a much larger array of information on specific Spanish regulations, currency exchange rates, how best to do one's work, personnel guidelines, samples of standard forms and letters to be used for specific situations such as the issuance of permits and passports, and reporting practices. Spanish publications of the period were singular in their insufficient use of indices, but not this one. Rather than a formal table of contents as the main entry into the material, one used a highly detailed index, suggesting that to do their work they would need to rely on continuous consultation of the volume about very precise pieces of information, rather than just on one's own personal experience or memory.

One major source of internal information circulating in both embassies and consulates was royal orders, such as those already cited dealing with the organization and structure of the diplomatic profession. But all manner of administrative information moved through the diplomatic information ecosystem by way of royal orders. These were not occasional reports. Between 1730 and 1834, the Spanish government published 11 volumes of such instructions, also covering non-diplomatic issues, that the diplomatic community needed to be aware of.[62] These discussed many topics and provided formal legal documents. Examples include Spain's new constitution promulgated in Cadiz in 1812, reorganization of the Ministry of State (1814), another soliciting information about the activities of other countries (1821), hundreds dealing with administration and reorganizations, and others that delineated what the Ministry was responsible for versus the Ministry of the Colonies (*Ministerio de Ultramar*), established in 1863.

In 1899 a royal decree provided a list of the functions within the Ministry's headquarters, shedding light on how it was an information gearbox for the diplomatic service. It had what amounted to a record keeping function, another devoted to analyzing political activities, yet others for juridical matters, commerce, translations, the library and archive, and personnel. It also had the Center for Commercial Information, previously discussed, which communicated with both embassies and consulates.[63] Others launched studies about the events of World War I and their implications for Spain and implementation of foreign policy.[64] Spain remained neutral in this war and enjoyed enormous increases in trade from both sides, with a stream of guidance and information circulating within diplomatic circles on what to do and how these actions related to trade. Embassies (often also referred to in these decades as legations) received and used all these various types of information prepared within the Ministry and by consulates.

TREATIES AND ROLE OF DIPLOMATS

Embassy staffs had another role apart from the other two entities: to negotiate and implement treaty terms, which, much like contracts between businesses and their customers or landlords and tenants, defined the nature of their relations and activities. For this reason it was essential that copies of relevant texts be made available to diplomats in embassies and, one can reasonable assume, at consulates. It was customary in Spain, as in the rest of Europe, to publish rapidly the texts of a treaty once consummated in the form of a pamphlet that one could carry and consult conveniently. This practice had gone on since the early 1600s.[65] It was not uncommon for an embassy or consulate to have scores of these in their libraries. Starting in the 1700s and extending to the present, European governments began to publish anthologies of these treaties in book form, and Spain followed this practice. Over time, this activity resulted in a substantial, but conveniently organized, body of information of two types: first, the treaties; second, studies of international laws governing treaties.[66] Diplomats were expected to know the terms and conditions of relevant treaties much the way a lawyer is expected to understand the specifics of a domestic law. The topic of treaties and their implementation was largely a legal conversation. Indeed, lawyers who, by the late nineteenth century, could also specialize in international law prepared all treatises and reference materials used by diplomats. The legalistic mindset of the topic made sense, of course, and continues to this day.[67]

These were routinely issued by the Ministry every decade or so as the accumulation of changes in existing treaties or new ones came into force. While of use to diplomatic historians, they were not published for them but for the diplomatic corps. These populated their office and personal libraries, and were available only on a limited basis to the general public for purchase. Non-diplomatic communities that also relied on these were largely professors and lawyers concerned with international law. But across both centuries, these other participants in the diplomatic information ecosystem also published commentaries on treaties, discussed above. For very important treaties, such as that which ended the Spanish-American War, both governments published proceedings and treaties resulting from the event and these were routinely exchanged to ensure accuracy and to avoid incidental misunderstandings that might have occurred in the negotiations and subsequent communication of results. In the case of a major treaty, such as that ending this war, it was customary to make such publications widely available to other ministries, the Cortes (or U.S. Congress in this case), and to the press and other interested parties.

OTHER ROUTINIZED BODIES OF INFORMATION

Two additional sources of information about which we have only anecdotal evidence that related to treaties, war, and diplomacy and economic issues among nations are substantial bodies of polemical literature—usually pamphlets—and small anthologies of documents relating to an issue put together and presented to the Cortes or some other legislative body, such as to the U.S. Congress or to the British Parliament, by their respective governments. Spanish diplomats routinely read these and often included copies, with commentary about them, in their dispatches to Madrid. Without methodically going through all the country archives in Madrid, it would be difficult to proffer a reasonable guess as to the extent of this material; however, since I have personally looked at those covering U.S.-Spanish relations from the 1700s to the 1940s, I surmise that a number of these were published nearly every several years in each country.

In the case of the United States, following a period of intense relations concerning Cuba in the mid-1830s, President Andrew Jackson sent to Congress a lengthy collection of correspondence between the two nations and, importantly for the Spanish, copies of instructions to the American legation in Madrid, all of which were published and dutifully sent to Spain.[68] The same kind of information became available to Spanish diplomats in 1854, following another increased period of tense relations after the seizure of the American ship, *Black Warrior* by Spanish officials.[69] The Spanish embassy in London informed Madrid about Great Britain's declaration of neutrality in the Spanish-American War (1898) as promulgated throughout the British Empire.[70]

In addition, polemical pieces, normally pamphlets, sometimes books, on critical issues of interest were published that added to the information pool of Spanish diplomats. One important topic concerned the American position prohibiting colonial activities in the New World, first enunciated in 1823, best known as the Monroe Doctrine. For over 150 years the issue stimulated much debate in Latin America and occasionally in Spain. For example, Fernando Jardón y Perissé published in 1903 a lecture he gave in Madrid on the Monroe Doctrine, which was acquired by the Ministry of State.[71] Such presentations continued. Another example: to the *Sociedad de Menéndez y Pelayo*, an academic organization, Rodolfo Schevill made a presentation in 1919 entitled "Menéndez y Pelayo y el estudio de la cultura Española en los Estados Unidos," published in Santander, but made with the king of Spain present, ensuring copies would make it into the Ministry of State and be duly examined.[72] As international issues caught the attention of the Spanish public and the extended circle of public officials, including the legal community, diplomats were increasingly exposed to additional discussions and information. For example, Spain played an active role in the League of Nations during the 1920s and early 1930s; just as it did decades later in the European Union. There was an extensive discussion about what that role should be for Spain in the League, and indeed, even what the League was.[73] In short, the information ecosystem expanded, initially with the crisis of the War of 1898, then subsequently with Spain's growing involvement in North African warfare, neutrality in World War I, role in the League, and ultimately, its civil war.

Following World War II the Ministry used these kinds of presentations in its training academy for diplomats, which it published, distributed to the diplomatic community, and made available for purchase by the general public, continuing a growing pattern of keeping somewhat open a few boundaries of the Spanish diplomatic information ecosystem.[74]

SPECIAL ROLE OF DIPLOMATIC HISTORIOGRAPHY

Much emphasis has been placed in this chapter on the administrative and juridical nature of the information governing the work of Spanish diplomats, and on the kinds of information they gathered and reported on with colleagues and Madrid. By the last quarter of the nineteenth century yet another form of information sharing emerged: historical perspectives on Spanish events. In the nineteenth century all over Europe it was quite common for erudite public officials to write history, and the Spanish were no exception, even though illiteracy in the nation remained high until after the civil war of 1936–1939. Spain's equivalent to Otto von Bismarck, Antonio Cánovas del Castillo, the prime minister for much of the last quarter of the nineteenth century, was also a historian, author of many histories, and owner of a private library on the subject.[75] Spanish diplomats began writing histories, sometimes memoirs, in this period, continuing this activity to the present.[76] Most were published in Madrid. Copies entered the Ministry's library, and others were acquired by diplomats. By the end of World War I, the volume of these kinds of introspective and historical narratives can be assumed to have contributed to the sense of identity and "lessons learned" from history informing the world-views of Spanish diplomats.

One writer in the years prior to the Spanish Civil War so stood out as an example of this kind of information moving through the diplomatic information ecosystem that his contributions need to be recognized: Jerónimo Bécker (1857–1925). Educated with a degree in philosophy and letters, he spent the bulk of his working career at the Ministry's archive, managing this facility from 1900 to 1924. In those years he also became a well-recognized celebrity in historical and other academic circles in Madrid. But most important about his role is that he wrote over a half dozen seminal works about Spanish foreign policy and diplomacy of the nineteenth century, and others to diffuse the "black legend" about Spanish colonial policies that had been propagated largely by English writers over the prior two centuries. His massive three-volume history of Spanish foreign relations of the nineteenth century, published between 1924 and 1926, was based entirely on the Spanish archives located in his building.[77] It was then and remains now a seminal work on Spanish diplomatic history. At the time of publication it served more as a recent accounting of events suitable as a work of reference for diplomats working in the 1920s, as it was a scholarly piece of historical writing. Given the practice of the day, this, as well as his other studies on diplomatic relations with the Holy See, North Africa, and the New World, among others, would have been distributed to various embassies and some consulates.

The timing of his observations, as reflected in the subjects of his books, makes clear that while using the tools of the historian, he was informing diplomats about the context of current events. His publications on relations with France, the United States, and Morocco all appeared during periods of intense national involvement in colonial wars and other international events with these areas.[78] Given the historical orientation of Spanish diplomats, these would have been read, influencing their view of prior events as context for current activities, following a long standing tradition in this profession of informing oneself about the historical context of contemporary events.

The Ministry's practice of publishing diplomatic history was interrupted by the civil war of the 1930s, but soon after began again through publication of journals, monographs, and later whole series of histories.[79] This pattern of publication has continued to such an extent that it accounts for nearly a third of all diplomatic histories published in Spain during the second half of the twentieth century, in addition to such working tools as anthologies of treaties and discourses on consular law and procedures. The Ministry now publishes other works related to Spain's role in the world sponsored by other ministries and agencies. That tradition has led to services intended to help historians beginning in the early 1970s.[80]

ARE THERE EXOGENOUS SHOCKS TO THE DIPLOMATIC INFORMATION ECOSYSTEM?

So far in this essay the diplomatic information ecosystem and the work of its participants has been defined very much like a smooth operating model of predictable, measurable activities that evolved slowly over time in response as much to external circumstances as to its own internal dynamics. Such an inward view of affairs seems obvious after the fact, because diplomats would argue that in their time events and circumstances were anything but endogenous, as evidenced by the scores of memoirs they published over the centuries. So, are there exogenous forces at work affecting the information ecosystem so cleanly described in this essay? The answer is not obvious. While formal definitions of exogamy in studying information in its political, social, and diplomatic contexts have yet to be solidified as descriptors of systems of exogenous information, the essential notion of forces or events occurring outside routine activities is useful to consider as part of the informational activities of these diplomats and their institutions.

The evidence presented here suggests that the diplomatic informational ecosystem and practices evolved over many centuries precisely to absorb quickly what might otherwise be considered exogenous events and circumstances, such as wars and sudden changes in government. These otherwise exogenous forces, one could argue, are part and parcel of the daily work of diplomats, and thus could be considered endogenous to the model presented in this chapter. Rapid changes in senior leadership at the Spanish foreign ministry and civil wars of the Napoleonic era, that of the early 1820s, Carlist civil wars of the 1840s and 1870s, and total civil war of 1936–1939, attest to the volatility of the diplomatic world. Add in Europe's own revolutions of 1848, that of the United States in 1861–1865, and myriad colonial contests in North Africa (1860s), Cuba (1868–1878, 1895–1898), and Morocco again between 1900 and the end of the 1920s, and we have more churn. Yet, through all these events—many of which were unpredictable or erupted quickly—the ecosystem held, the work of diplomats went on, and the foreign affairs of nations proved central to the actions of senior public officials.

Table 4.3 catalogs some of the most obvious potential exogenous forces at work in the diplomatic community. The list could be expanded. They all share several characteristics. They represent something new occurring to be accommodated either intentionally (such as use of a new communications technology) or unintentionally (a new government friendly or hostile to one's own nation). They led to unintended consequences for all concerned, results that became fodder for memoirs and diplomatic histories describing events unique to a time and place. Yet the underlying model of how information facilitated the activities of both endogenous and exogenous forces remained essentially the same, a point reinforced more thoroughly. They affected activities of all people and institutions that interacted with the diplomatic community or that provided it with information, from the points of view of individuals writing dispatches and letters, to what was published in local newspapers, to what terms and conditions were incorporated in treaties. Tied to the flexibility of the informational

Table 4.3. Exogenous Forces and Their Impact on Diplomatic Information Ecosystems

Forces at Work	*Effects on Diplomatic Information Ecosystems*
Changes in governments, such as elections, coups, civil wars, revolutions	Disrupts personal information networks, causes rapid shifts in diplomatic relations, temporarily blocks flow of information
Wars, such as between Spain and France, world wars	Severed diplomatic relations, severed flow of information, destruction of records, closing of embassies and consulates
Technologies, such as steam ships, telegraph, telephone, radio	Speeds up the flow of information through the ecosystem, often also the volume of accessible data, speeding up diplomatic activities
Shifts in international balances-of-power	Often not obvious as they emerge leading to analysis and actions based on earlier political paradigms, often both subtle or rapid (e.g., election of Hitler as Chancellor at same time as Roosevelt as US president)

ecosystem, due to its ability to take in and process information, was the reality that such activities never ended; there was always something new happening, much of which would have been unanticipated by diplomats, such as the appearance of steam ships that carried their mail faster or the telegraph which also sped up the flow of information. On the other hand, some were known about and so gradually embraced that they can hardly be called exogenous forces in the information ecosystem. Rather they proved endogenous, because they were embraced slowly. Individuals could anticipate eventually having to deal with these, such as the slow diffusion of the typewriter to diplomatic services all over the world, a tool that took nearly a half-century to become standard equipment. We are left with the puzzling question: how exogenous are exogenous forces in the diplomatic ecosystem? The evidence suggests that while it would seem obviously so, it also offers less than one might think, because of its robustness and elastic versatility.

TECHNOLOGICAL INNOVATIONS AS DISRUPTIVE FORCES IN THE WORK OF DIPLOMATS

By the end of the 1830s steam ships began to appear that, by the end of the 1850s, had made movement of mail worldwide faster than in earlier times. We saw an example of the consequences of that development with respect to Spanish reporting during the American civil war of the 1860s.

Not to be forgotten is that railroads had the same effect of speeding movement of mail, except over land, in the same half century. Then came the telegraph, both in its overland versions at mid-century and, nearly simultaneously, the underwater cable, with the result that by the 1880s, there was substantial access to fast electronic communications from all the major capitals and commercial cities in the world.[81] While telegraphy proved far more expensive than mail services, diplomats increasingly used it by the end of the nineteenth century, more so in the first two decades of the next one. They used this latest technology as a supplement to the others because telegraphic messages were short (due to cost), while dispatches and other forms of paper communications were more detailed. Historians studying the effects of telegraphy on diplomatic activities conclude that it led to more "micromanaging" of diplomatic personnel from the national headquarters and the speeding up of the transmission of news concerning diplomatic events as they unfolded. British diplomats pointed out that telegrams were not effective for communicating complex ideas and could lead to errors of facts and judgments being communicated.[82]

The role of changed transportation and of telecommunications on Spanish diplomatic communities awaits its historians. But several patterns were observable. As postal systems worldwide began using trains and steam ships, so too did Spanish diplomatic information travel. Use of diplomatic messengers, a long standing practice dating back hundreds of years to the establishment of diplomatic missions that continued to be used right through the twentieth century, declined in importance among all European diplomatic services during the second half of the nineteenth century. The speed of private transport systems improved and proved reliable. Their cost declined when compared to having dedicated employees for the task. Second, because of the slow global diffusion of telegraphy when compared to the rapid diffusion of railroads and steam ships, reliance on telegraphy took longer. Spanish diplomats were not using this technology to any great extent until the end of the 1870s, although it was common by the end of the Spanish-American War. However, as archival evidence makes clear, telegraphy, later the telephone, did not replace the written or published document.

To what extent did the availability of these various innovations in communications alter the balance of power between diplomats in the field and their home offices? The Spanish case makes it difficult to generalize. While the speed of moving mail and the cost of doing so declined across the nineteenth century, the volume of correspondence back and forth was dictated less by the technology than by the diplomatic and economic circumstances of the day. Thus, war and political crises resulted in more information and quieter times less so, regardless of the technologies. Instructions from Madrid via telegraph and later telephone seemed to increase after the Spanish-American War, but this generalization needs further validation. That the foreign ministry began to notice the effects of telegraphy on its work there is no question, as we saw in the evidence presented in Table 4.1. The historical evidence so far is of British diplomats complaining of London managing them more, but then Great Britain was both an early adopter of the technology in government and as a nation dominated the telegraph networks available around the world.[83] My tentative conclusion is that Spanish diplomats only began to see modern uses of all manner of information technologies significantly affect their work during World War I and most notably in the 1920s, several decades later than the British, Germans, and the French.

AN ENDURING INFORMATION ECOSYSTEM

This chapter demonstrates that one can examine the role of information within a profession by the method of constructing a description of the information ecosystem in which it worked. It is a method used in other disciplines, most notably in understanding the role of information in large enterprises, knowledge management, and process control.[84] The advantage of looking at information as part of an invisible ecosystem is that one can identify what data is coming in and moving about within a circle of users, the effects on their work and behavior, and the role they have within work processes. Ephemera left behind in the form of documents, books, and other media can then be viewed less as a topic in materiality and more as part of the dynamic of informational activity underway, in effect, as a form of informational archeology. The paper trail tells us more than what is written (published) within its pages, while dates on documents, postal stampings on envelopes, and time stamps in offices where they were received suggest when information became available and, thus, holds up the possibility of offering insights into the velocity with which information, decisions, and actions occurred. Studying ephemera this way should also set off alarm bells for those who worry about how to preserve or examine electronic files, notably e-mails, as their role in an information ecosystem is quite different than in the days of just pure paper.[85]

Examining work through the lens of a profession remains a useful method for understanding the role of information within an organization or society. Because the work of diplomats is ambiguous and dynamic, yet so thoroughly documented for reasons already discussed, we can learn about this research approach by looking at diplomatic history for almost any century. There are models of studies done on other professions to learn from, ranging from such examples as the study of typewriter clerks to telegraph operators, and more traditionally of lawyers, merchants, and ministers.[86]

Specific to the matter of Spanish diplomats, one should distinguish publications and issues discussed above from the history of diplomacy itself. The volume of material published on diplomatic history is extensive and most of it today is aimed at the general public (which can include diplomats, of course) and the scholarly community. These kinds of materials resided on the outskirts of the information ecosystem described in this chapter. Experienced diplomats routinely read diplomatic history of both their nation and of those to which they were assigned. They were not required to do so, nor was it necessary for their routine work. The extent to which diplomatic history *per se* was part of their information ecosystem depended on the idiosyncratic behavior of individual diplomats.[87]

Finally, I demonstrated in this chapter that the ecosystem of a diplomatic corps based on European and American traditions is comprised of some common elements in evidence around the world, and essentially that it became similar because of the interdependence of multiple diplomatic communities in nearly two hundred nations. These elements included a micro-information ecosystem within the headquarter ministry, what I called here the "home office," another within each embassy and consulate, and yet another with information coming and going into other ministries (Spanish or otherwise), as suggested in Figure 4.1. There was additionally that generated by the extensive social and political networking done with local elites around the world, and finally the influx of published opinions and data from books, magazines, pamphlets, legislative discourses, and publications, during the twentieth century various electronic media, from radio and telephone to television, and most recently e-mail and blogs. For if one material fact is certain, diplomats everywhere in every age used whatever information handling devices and media existed, often sooner than the private sector.

The model presented here was not fully described. Much remains to be explored, such as how to link more directly actions of an individual to a specific piece of received information or to a result of a growing and complex context built up over many years of richly informed experiences and circumstances, elegantly parsed into explicit and tacit knowledge as both types existed and evolved. Much more could be learned, however, by mining memoirs of diplomats who routinely discussed the coming and going of information and what they did with it. With so many diplomatic memoirs available, often written by individuals trained in the social sciences and humanities and able to write tightly argued points of view, the opportunity to learn how a profession works with information is substantial.

This tidy story is all well and good when everyone is forced to adhere to a set of conventions mandated by their employer and globally homogeneous profession. But what happens with a community of like-minded people who do not work for the same organization, who are not required to conform by law or to stay employed? Do they behave the same way as our diplomats or do they take a different path? Can we describe their activities using the same approaches as with the diplomats? We take up that question in Chapter 5. It is an important discussion because not all people exchange information within the context of a job. Often they do so in much broader, looser social circumstances, such as in voluntary organizations, interactions among friends and neighbors, and even family.[88]

NOTES

1. Alistair Black, Dave Muddiman and Helen Plant, *The Early Information Society: Information Management in Britain Before the Computer* (Hampshire, England: Ashgate, 2007); Mary Poovey, *A History of the Modern Fact: Problems of Knowledge in the Sciences of Wealth and Society* (Chicago, IL: University of Chicago Press, 1998); James W. Cortada, *Making the Information Society: Experience, Consequences, and Possibilities* (Upper Saddle River, NJ: Financial Times/Prentice-Hall, 2002); Andrew Abbott, *The System of Professions: An Essay on the Division of Expert Labor* (Chicago, IL: University of Chicago Press, 1988); Sharon M. McKinnon and William J. Bruns, *The Information Mosaic: How Managers Get the Information They Really Need* (Boston, MA: Harvard Business School Press, 1992). How the mind deals with information in its work is now moving from scientific discussions to the public, and to management and economists. See Nobel Economist Daniel Kahneman, *Thinking Fast and Slow* (New York: Farrar, Straus and Giroux, 2011).

2. Jorge Reina Schement and Terry Curtis, *Tendencies and Tensions of the Information Age: The Production and Distribution of Information in the United States* (New Brunswick, NJ: Transaction Publishers, 1995); James W. Cortada, ed., *Rise of the Knowledge Worker* (Boston, MA: Butterworth-Heinemanm, 1998).

3. Daniel R. Headrick, *When Information Came of Age: Technologies of Knowledge in the Age of Reason and Revolution, 1700–1850* (New York: Oxford University Press, 2000); Richard D. Brown, *Knowledge Is Power: The Diffusion of Information in Early America, 1700–1865* (New York: Oxford University Press, 1989).

4. Essentially the same task that in today's digital language we might say is "to capture the data" and put it into accessible databases, which is what the Spanish diplomatic establishment does.

5. The topic has a vast literature on the profession. On Spain, see Donald E. Quiller, *The Office of Ambassador In the Middle Ages* (Princeton, NJ: Princeton University Press, 1967); Luis García Guijarro, *Bases Para Una Reforma del Cuerpo Consular* (Madrid: Clásica Española, 1918); José Manuel Paz Agüeras, *La Adopción Consular* (Madrid: Ministerio de Asuntos Exteriores, 1990). Most of the research done on the Spanish diplomatic profession has focused on the modern period, Juan L. Pérez Ruiz, *Las depuraciones de la carrera diplomática española, 1931–1980* (Burgos: Dossoles, 1980); R. Valdivielso del Real, *La carrera diplomática en España (1939–1990)* (Madrid: Biblioteca Diplomática Española-Ministerio de Asuntos Exteriores, 1996); Angel Viñas, ed., *Al servicio de la República. Diplomáticos y Guerra Civil* (Madrid: Marcial Pons, 2010); Jeremy Black, *A History of Diplomacy* (London: Reaktion Books, 2010).

6. Luis Eugenio Togores and José Luis Neila, *La escuela diplomática: cincienta años de sericio al estado (1942–1992)* (Madrid: Escuela Diplomática, 1993); for listings of publications, see the annual catalog of the Ministry, *Publicaciones: Catálogo general* (Madrid: Ministerios de Asuntos Exteriores y de Cooperación, annual). See also, the Ministry's website, http://www.maec.es (Accessed 2/5/2019).

7. Carlos Sanz Diaz, "La Adminisración Exterior del Estado," in Juan Carlos Pereira, ed., *La Politíca Exterior de España de 1800 Hasta Hoy* (Madrid: Ariel, 2010): 187–188.

8. The literature about KM ecosystems is now vast. However, two anthologies edited by leading experts in the field provide useful introductions to the issues, Laurence Prusak, ed., *Knowledge in Organizations* (Boston, MA: Butterworth-Heinemann, 1997) and Eric L. Lesser, Michael A. Fontaine and Jason A Slusher, eds., *Knowledge and Communities* (Boston, MA: Butterworth-Heinemann, 2000).

9. All his comments and studies of diplomats are based on the experience of the British, Alistar Black, "Knowledge Management and Diplomacy: Reflections on the Demise of the Valedictory Despatch in the Context of an Informational History of the British Diplomatic Service," *First Monday* 16, no. 1–3 (January 2011), http://www.uic.edu/htbin/cgiwrap/bin/ojs/index.php/fm/article/vewArticles/3339/2757 (Accessed July 2, 2019).

10. Ibid., 186; I. Molina Alvarez de Cienfuegos and Fernando Rodrigo Rodriguez, "Las transformaciones organizativas de la política exterior española," *Revista de Estudios Políticos* (New Era) 17 (July–September 2002): 173–202; Presidencia del Gobierno, *Libro Blanco sobre la Administración Exterior del Estado* (Madrid: Presidencia del Gobrierno, 1986).

11. On support of requests from the Cortes, A. Remiro Brotons, *Las Cortes y la Política exterior española (1942–1976), con especial referencia a su participación en la conclusión de los tratados internacionales* (Valladolid: Universidad

de Valladolid, 1977); Carlos Secos Serrano, "Alfonso XIII y la diplomacia española des u tiempo," in *Corona y Diplomacia: La monarquia española en la historia de las relaciones internacionales* (Madrid: Escuela Diplomática, 1988): 183–211; and for a sense of the rythym of business and information exchanged in the Ministry, there is the diary of a minister, Francisco Gómez-Jordana Souza, *Milicia y diplomacia: Los Diarios del Conde de Jordana, 1936–1944* (Burgos: Editorial Dossoles, 2002).

12. Elisa Carolina de Santos Canalejo, *Guia del Archivo General del Ministerio de Asuntos Exteriores* (Madrid: Ministerio de Asuntos Exterores, 1997): 13–22, but see also José Lozano Rincon and Enrique Romera Iruela, *Guia del Archivo del Ministerio de Asuntos Exteriores* (Madrid: Ministerio de Asuntos Exteriores, 1981): 15–41.

13. In particular the Ministerio de Ultramar worked closely with consular officials and therefore can reasonably be included in the information ecosystem of the diplomatic community, A. Sánchez Andrés, *El Ministerio de Ultramar. Una institución liberal para el gobierno de las colonias, 1863–1899* (Morelia/La Laguna: Universidad Michoacana de San Nicolás de Hidalgo/Centro de la Cultura Popular Canaria, 2007); F. Tomás y Valente, *Inventorio de los Fondos de Ultramar (1835–1903) y estudio histórico* (Madrid: Boletín oficial del Estado, 1994).

14. For an example of the interaction of the Cortes and the Ministero de Estado from the 1860s, see James W. Cortada, "The New York Times, Spain and Cuba, 1851–1869," *Revista de Historia de America*, nos. 77–78 (January–December 1974): 61–75. See also the continuous presentation of reports to the Cortes by the Ministero de Estado, *Documentos presentados a las Cortes en la legislature . . . por el Ministerio de Estado* (Madrid: Ministero de Estado, 1876–1931), and for a recent example, *The Spanish Red Book on Gibraltar* (Madrid: Ministerio de Asuntos Exteriores, 1965).

15. Donato Fernández Navarrete, "El Papel del Sector Exterior en la Economía Española," in Pereira, *La política exterior de España*, 193–196.

16. While Spanish diplomats commented on their roles in their memoirs, other publications documented their activities, Alexandro Castro y Casaleiz, *Guía práctica del Diplomática español*, vo. 1 (Madrid: no publisher, 1886); Angel Martínez de Velasco, "La reforma del cuerpo diplómatico por Primo de Rivera," *Revista Internacional de Sociologia* 35 (1980): 409–44; Maria Casanova Gómez, "El ingreso en la carrera diplómatica durante la II República," *Cuadernos de la Escuela Diplomática* 1 (June 1988): 129–138. For a list of memoirs, see Pereira, *La política exterior de España*, 745–749.

17. Raymond A. Jones, *The British Diplomatic Service, 1815–1914* (Waterloo, Canada: Wilfrid Laurier University Press, 1983): 116–126; Magnus Mösslang and Torsten Riotte, *The Diplomats' World: A Cultural History of Diplomacy, 1815–1914* (Oxford: Oxford University Press, 2008).

18. Memoirs were of particular value to other diplomats, such as that of Augusto Conte, *Recuerdos de un diplomático* 3 vols. (Madrid: Imprenta de J. Gongora y

Alvarez, 1901) as were more prescriptive publications, such as Agustín de Letamendi, *Atribuciones consulares, ó manuel para los consules de España en paises estrangeros* (Madrid: no publisher, 1835); Antonio de Castro y Casaleiz, *Guía práctica del diplomático español* 2 vols (Madrid: no publisher, 1886); Eduardo Toda y Gúell, *Derecho consular de España* (Madrid: no publisher, 1889); Miguel Maluquer y Salvador, *Derecho consular español* (Paris: A. Roger & F. Chernoviz, 1899) for the Ministerio de Estado. The communication of changes in Consular law and treaties continued, for example, Ministerio de Asuntos Exteriores, *Tratados consulares de España* (Madrid: Ministerio de Asuntos Exteriores, 1958).

19. Mario Menendez Bejarano, *Tassara: nueva biografia critica* (Madrid: J. Pérez, 1928); for a detailed view of his work as diplomat, James W. Cortada, *Spain and the American Civil War: Relations at Mid-Century, 1855–1868* (Philadelphia, PA: American Philosophical Society, 1980); and for his poems, Gabriel García Tassara, *Poesias de Tassara* (Madrid: Rivadeneyra, 1872).

20. For a bibliography that touches on these issues, James W. Cortada, *A Bibliographic Guide to Spanish Diplomatic History, 1460–1977* (Westport, CT: Greenwood Press, 1977): 291–315.

21. Fernandez Navarrete, "El papel del sector exterior en la economía española," 194–196.

22. Sean T. Perrone, "The Role of Spanish Consuls in the United States, 1795–1898," in Brian D. Bunk, Sasha D. Pack, Carl-Gustaf Scott, eds., *Nation and Conflict in Modern Spain: Essays in Honor of Stanley G. Payne* (Madison: Parallel Press, 2008): 81–102.

23. Eula McDonald, "Highlights in the History of the United States Post at Barcelona, Spain, 1797–1959," *Cuadernos de Historia Económica de Cataluña* (Primer trimester 1969–1970): 21–63.

24. Togores and Neila, *La escuela diplomática*, 78–110.

25. Santos Canalejos, *Guía del archive general del Ministerio de Asuntos Exteriores*; http//www.maec.es (Accessed 2/5/2019).

26. Pereira, *Politica exterior de España*, 745–749; but see also for additional citations Cortada, *A Bibliographic Guide to Spanish Diplomatic History*, passim. Approximately a half dozen are published annually in Spain.

27. There are many examples of these reports which comprise the bulk of both what diplomatic archives preserve, and what historians rely on to produce their studies. However, the Spanish, as with so many Europeans, often published extensive collections of such correspondence, normally long after the events had been contemporary ones. However, some were almost contemporaneous. See, for example, the papers published by a diplomat, José Maria Campoamor, *La actitud de España ante la cuestión de marruecos (1900–1904)* (Madrid: Instituto de Estudios Africanos, 1951). The Ministry continues to publish such collections; see, for example, Nuño Aguirre de Cárcer, ed., *La neutralidad de España durante la primera Guerra mundial (1914–1918)* (Madrid: Ministerio de Asuntos Exteriores, 1995); Ana Mur Raurell, *Diplomacia secreta y paz: La cor-*

respondencia de los embajadores españoles en Viena. Juan Guillermo Ripperda y Luis Ripperda (1724–1727) 2 vols (Madrid: Ministerio de Asuntos Exteriores y De Cooperación, 2011).

28. Cortada, *Spain and the American Civil War*, 112; Santos Canalejo, *Guia del Archivo General del Miniterio de Asuntos Exteriores*, 82, 93, 96.

29. Made evident by how guides to the archive are organized and their lists of record types, for example, Santos Canalejo, *Guia del Archivo General del Miniterio de Asuntos Exteriores.*

30. Perrone, "The Role of Spanish Consuls in the United States, 1795–1898," 81–102.

31. Charleston Consular Papers, Duke University, http://library.duke.edu/rubenstein/research/guides (Accessed 2/5/2019). These consular papers were from 1794 to 1898 and consisted of over 4,600 items. The library also has a collection of Spanish consular papers from the consulate at Savannah, Georgia, covering 1835 to 1935.

32. Cortada, *Spain and the American Civil War*, 52.

33. A typical publication was entitled *Memorias diplomaticas y consulares: Suiza memoria commercial correspondiente al año de 1914*, número 550 (Madrid: Imprenta del Ministerio de España, 1916). Examples of countries reviewed include Canada, Venezuela, Peru, Italy, Tunisia, Portugal, Norway, Persia, Mexico, Guatemala, United States, and Great Britain.

34. A similar observation can be made about their value to foreign diplomats working in Spain. My research on nineteenth- and twentieth-century relations between Spain and the United States led me to examine scores of local newspapers cited by American, British, and French diplomats in their reports to their foreign ministries.

35. This practice was formalized in the treaty coming out of the Congress of Vienna in 1815 and reinforced over the next 150 years. The most recent formalization of this role and the collective responsibilities of a diplomatic corps are articulated in United Nations, "Vienna Convention on Diplomatic Relations 1961," *United Nations, Treaty Series*, vol. 500 (New York: United Nations, 2005): 95.

36. I constructed all of the major analysis conducted about U.S.-Spanish relations of the 1850s and 1860s in this manner, *Spain and the American Civil War*. A recent example of the practice is Joan Maria Thomàs, *Roosevelt, Franco, and the End of the Second World War* (New York: Palgrave, 2011). The same applied to the activities of foreign military attaches that were part of the diplomatic information ecosystem. For a recent example of their reliance on each other's information and insight, see James W. Cortada, ed., *Modern Warfare in Spain: American Military Observations on the Spanish Civil War, 1936–1939* (Washington, DC: Potomac Books, 2012).

37. While the nineteenth and twentieth century institutional histories of Spanish diplomacy await their great historians, the era before that reported on in this article has been studied, yet even this magnificent history has left room for future scholars

to explore the ministry's information ecosystem, Beatriz Badorrey Martín, *Los origenes del Ministerio de Asuntos Exteriores (1714–1808)* (Madrid: Ministerio de Asuntos Exteriores, 1999).

38. Discussed outside the Ministry on rare occasions through its archival guides which describe collections of prior and current retention regulations, *Disposiciones organicas 1705–1936;* Pereira, *Política exterior de España*, and in its annual publications catalog, *Cátalogo general.*

39. Headrick, *When Information Came of Age*, 99.

40. Ministerio de Asuntos Exteriores, *Cátalogo de la biblioteca del Ministerio de Asuntos Exteriors*, 9 vols (Madrid: Ministerio de Asuntos Exteriores, 1942–1948).

41. Ibid. Another bibliographic listing was of treaties and other international documents, and the sources for their actual text, J. López Oliván, *Repertorio diplomática española: indice de los tratados ajustados por España (1125–1935) y de otros documentos internacionales* (Madrid: Diana Artes Graficas, 1944).

42. Gustavo Castañar Marquardt, "Fuentes y centros de investigación," in Pereira, *Política exterior de España*, 93–113; M. L. Conde Villaverde, ed., *Archivo General de la Administración, 1969–1994* (Madrid: Ministerio de Cultura, 1995); C. Crespo Nogueira, ed., *Archivo Histórico Nacional. Guía* (Madrid: Ministerio de Cultura, 1989); A. De la Plaza Bores, *Archivo General de Simancas: guía de investigador* (Ministero de Cultura, 1992); and for related military records, *Guía de Archivos Militares Españoles* (Madrid: Ministerio de Defensa, 1999).

43. Santos Canalejo, *Guía del Archivo General del Ministerio de Asuntos Exteriores*, 16.

44. John L. Offner, *An Unwanted War: The Diplomacy of the United States and Spain Over Cuba, 1895–1898* (Chapel Hill, NC: University of North Carolina Press, 1992): 209–224.

45. Two key documents in addition to the normal publication of U.S. Congressional proceedings are essential to this story, 55th Congress, 3ed Session, Senate, *Message from the President of the United States Transmitting A Treaty of Peace Between the United States and Spain, Signed At the City of Paris, On December 10, 1898* (Washington, DC: Government Printing Office, 1899), which is nearly seven hundred pages in length, and an anthology of various declarations and notes from many countries relevant to the war, *Proclamations and Decrees During the War With Spain* (Washington, DC: Government Printing Office, 1899) probably put together by the U.S. Department of State. In Madrid, there was Ministerio de Estado, *Documentos presentados á Las Cortes en la legislatura de 1900 por el Ministerio de Estado* (Madrid: Ministerio de Estado, 1900), with a map. A large collection of documents were sent to the Cortes during the war and afterwards as the nation examined the causes for its disaster; some were reprinted recently in facsimile, Ministerio de Estado, *Libro Rojo Tratado de Paris: Documentos presentados a las Cortes en la legislature de 1898 por el Ministro de Estado* (Madrid: Ministerio de Estado, 1898, reprinted San Juan, P.R.: Editorial de la Universidad de Puerto Rico, 1988).

46. Peter H. Wilson, *The Thirty Years War: Europe's Tragedy* (Cambridge, MA: Harvard University Press, 2009): 671–747.

47. http://www.maplandia.com/spain/cataluna/gerona/llivia/ (last accessed 2/5/2012).

48. Vincent Confer, "France," in Daniel H. Thomas and Lynn M. Case, eds., *The New Guide to the Diplomatic Archives of Western Europe* (Philadelphia: University of Pennsylvania Press, 1975): 69–91, which includes a useful bibliography of finding aids and histories of the French ministry's archive.

49. Santos Canalejo, *Guía del Archivo General del Ministerio de Asuntos Exteriores*, 14.

50. Ibid., 112; but see also Miguel Santiago Rodríguez, *Los manuscritos del Archivo General y Biblioteca del Ministerio de Asuntos Exteriores (catálogo sistemático)* (Madrid: Ministerio de Asuntos Exteriores, 1974): 200, 234.

51. Santos Canalejo, *Guía del Archivo General del Ministerio de Asuntos Exteriores*, 14–19.

52. Abigail J. Sellen and Richard H. R. Harper, *The Myth of the Paperless Office* (Cambridge, MA: MIT Press, 2003).

53. Kagan, *Laws and Litigants in Castille*; Brown, *Knowledge Is Power*; Thomas C. Jepsen, *My Sisters Telegraphic: Women in the Telegraph Office, 1846–1950* (Athens, OH: Ohio University Press, 2000); Sharon Hartman Strom, *Beyond the Typewriter: Gender, Class, and the Origins of Modern American Office Work, 1900–1930* (Urbana, IL: University of Illinois Press, 1992).

54. On European patterns, Mösslang and Riotte, *The Diplomats' World*; and on public officials across many departments, Richard J. Evans, *The Pursuit of Power: Europe 1815–1914* (New York: Viking, 2016): 320–326.

55. Rocio Valdivielso del Real, "Orígenes evolución y organicación de la carrera diplomática española," in Pereira, *Politica exterior de España*, 237–238; C. Barrios, *El diplomático de carrera en España: Algunos consideraciones sociológicas*, Memoria (Madrid: Escuela Diplomática, 1978); additionally discussed from time to time over the past half century in the annual presentations published by the ministry, *Memorias de la Escuela Diplomática* (Madrid: Ministero de asuntos Exteriores y de Cooperación, annual).

56. Such as those collected by the ministry's library, *Catálogo de la biblioteca del Ministerio de Asuntos Exteriores*, 9 vols.

57. F. De Martens, translated with introduction by Joaqín Fernández Prida, *Tratado de derecho internacional* 3 vols (Madrid: La España Moderna, undated, circa 1880s).

58. Ibid., vol. 3.

59. Toda y Gúell, *Derecho consular de España*; Maluquer y Salvador, *Derecho consular español*; Ministerio de Asuntos Exteriores, *Tratados consulares de España.*

60. Toda y Gúell, *Derecho consular de España.*

61. Maluquer y Salvador, *Derecho consular español.*

62. Ministerio de Estado, *Colección de Reales Cédulas*, 11 vols (Madrid: Ministero de Estado, 1730–1834).

63. Valdivielso del Real, "Orígenes, evolución y organización de la carrera diplomática española," 239–248.

64. Ibid., 350–355, and for examples, 376–378.

65. For example, Consejo de Estado, *Tratado para continuación y renovacion de paz, y amistad entre las Corona de España y la Gran Bretaña* (Madrid, 1667); *Tratado de paz ajustado entre esta corona, El Emperador de Romanos, y el Sacro Romano Imperio* (Madrid, 1725); while other signators did the same, for example, *The Treaty of Peace, Union, Friendship, and Mutual Defence, Between the Crowns of Great-Britain, France, and Spain, Concluded at Seville on the 9th of November, N.S. 1729* (Dublin, 1729), all from the author's collection.

66. Alejandro del Cantillo, *Tratados, convenios y declaraciones de paz y de comercio . . . desde el año de 1700 hasta el dia* (Madrid: Alegria y Charlain, 1843); Florencio Janer, *Tratados de España. Documentos internaciones del reinado de Doña Isabel II desde 1842 á 1868* (Madrid: Imprenta de Miguel Ginesta, 1869); José Joaquín Ribó, *La Diplomacia española: colección de tratados celebrados entre España y las demás naciones desde 1801 hasta el advenimiento al trono de Amadeo I*, 2 vols (Madrid: Elizalde y Llano Editores, 1871–1872); Alejo García Moreno, *Leyes y tratados internacionales ó sea reseña histórico-crítica y texto de las leyes y tratados vigentes entre España y las demás naciones* (Madrid: n.p., 1885); Jerónimo Becker, *Collección de tratados, convenios y demás documentos de carácter internacional firmados por España (1868–1874)* (Madrid: Ministerio de Estado, 1907); Marqués de Olivart, *Tratados y documentos internacionales de España firmados por nuestros Gobiernos con los Estados extranjeros desde el reinado de Doña Isabel II hasta nuestros días*, 14 vols (Madrid: El Progreso Editorial, 1890–1911); Ramon Olivart, *Tratados, 1908–1910* (Madrid: Ministero de Estado, 1911); *Colección oficial de los tratados, convenios y demás documentos de caracter internacional firmados por España desde el año 1900 al 1905* (Madrid: Imprenta de la C.G.D. Artes Graficas, 1929). There were also monographs about these documents, such as the widely used one by Spanish diplomat P. Soler y Guardiolo, *Apuntes de Historica Política y de los Tratados (1490 á 1815)* (Madrid: Libreria de Victorioano Suarez, 1895), precursors to the many volumes published by Becker in the subsequent two decades.

67. Jesús Núñez Hernández and Xavier Martí Martí, *La Función Consular en el Derecho Español*, 3rd ed. (Madrid: Ministero de Asuntos Exteriores y de Cooperación, 2009).

68. "Message From the President of the United States," December 10, 1835, published in the *Congressional Record, 24th Congress, 1st Session* (Washington, DC, 1835). Also issued as an offprint.

69. "Seizure of the Black Warrior. Message From the President of the United States," March 15, 1854, *Congressional Record, 33rd Congress, 1st Session.* Also issued as an offprint.

70. "British Proclamation for the Observance of Neutrality in the War between Spain and the United States, April 23, 1898," *London Gazette*, April 26, 1898, 826–846. Also issued as an offprint.

71. Fernando Jardón y Perissé, *La Doctrina Monroe* (Madrid: Imprenta de los Hijos de M.G. Hernández, 1905).

72. Rodolfo Schevill, *Menéndez y Pelayo y el studio de la cultura Española en los Estados Unidos* (Santander: Sociedad de Menéndez y Pelayo, 1919).

73. Rafael Altamira, *El Congreso de la Sociedad de las Naciones* (Madrid: Editorial Reus, 1920); Francisco José Urrutia, *La evolución de principio de arbitraje en América. La sociedad de Naciones* (Madrid: Editorial-America, 1920); José Ramon de Orúe, *La Sociedad de Naciones* (Madrid: Góngora, 1925, 1932 expanded edition); Leopoldo Palacios, *Los mandatos internacionales de la Sociedad de Naciones* (Madrid: Librearia General de Victoriano Suárez, 1928); Luis Izaga, *El desarme y la Sociedad de Naciones* (Madrid: Razon y Fé, 1932).

74. These are listed in each annual edition of its *Catalogo general.*

75. Carolyn P. Boyd, *Historia Patria: Politics, History, and National Identity in Spain, 1875–1975* (Princeton, NJ: Princeton University Press, 1997): 66–69; a modern biography of this politician/historian does not exist, but see José Luis Comellas, *Cánovas del Castillo* (Barcelona: Editorial Ariel, 1965; reprinted, 1997).

76. For an incomplete, but nonetheless useful list, see Preira, *Política exterior de España*, 745–751.

77. Jerónimo Bécker, *Relaciones exteriors de España durante el Siglo XIX*, 3 vols (Madrid: Establecimiento Tipográfico de Jaime Ratés, 1924–1926).

78. His list of publications is extensive; however, some of his key works include: Jerónimo Bécker, *Historia política y diplomática desde la independencia de los Estados Unidos hasta nuestros dias, 1776–1895* (Madrid: n.p., 1897); *España y Marruecos. Sus relaciones diplomática durante el siglo XIX* (Madrid: n.p., 1903); *Relaciones diplómaticas entre España y la Santa Sede durante el siglo xix* (Madrid: Imprenta de Jaime Ratés, 1908); *Relaciones comerciales entre España y Francia durante el siglo XIX* (Madrid: n.p., 1910); *La política espaóla en Las Indias (rectificaciones históricos)* (Madrid: Imprenta de Jaime Ratés, 1920); *Acción de la diplomacia española durante la Guerra de la Independia* (Zaragoza: n.p., 1909); *España y Inglaterra. Sus relaciones desde los paces de Utrecht* (Madrid: n.p., 1906); *La independencia de América: su reconocimiento por España* (Madrid: n.p., 1922).

79. In its annual catalog of publications, *Catalogo general*, published every fall on its website, the Ministry lists publications that appeared decades earlier in addition to new titles, thus serving as a continuously updated bibliography of its publications and those of other agencies that are concerned with Spanish culture and international affairs.

80. *Publicaciones: Catálogo general* (Madrid: Ministerios de Asuntos Exteriores y de Cooperación, annual)

81. Daniel R. Headrick, *Invisible Weapon: Telecommunications and International Politics, 1851–1945* (New York: Oxford University Press, 1991): 29, 94.

82. David Nickles, *Under the Wire: How the Telegraph Changed Diplomacy* (Cambridge, MA: Harvard University Press, 2003); Jones, *The British Diplomatic Service*; Black, "Knowledge Management and Diplomacy."

83. Headrick, *Invisible Weapon.*

84. Sharon M. McKinnon and William J. Bruns, Jr., *The Information Mosaic: How Managers Get the Information They Really Need* (Boston, MA: Harvard Business School Press, 1992); Thomas H. Davenport and Laurence Prusak, *Working Knowledge: How Organizations Manage What They Know* (Boston, MA: Harvard Business School Press, 1998); Don Cohen and Laurence Prusak, *In Good Company: How Social Capital Makes Organizations Work* (Boston, MA: Harvard Business School Press, 2001); Richard E Neustadt and Ernest R. May, *Thinking in Time: The Uses of History for Decision Makers* (New York: Free Press, 1986).

85. Prior to the arrival of e-mail, diplomats communicated with their home ministries first by mail, then telegraphs, and later by telephone, in addition to reports and memorandum. As communications became faster and cheaper, their instructions from their home office became more frequent and prescriptive, reducing their individual latitude to determine what to do. The situation was exacerbated by the 1990s with the wide use of e-mail by most countries. Your author's father was an American diplomat who commented about this phenomenon during the transition from telegraphic communications to the frequent use of the telephone multiple times a day in the American foreign service underway by the early 1960s. For insights on the role of communications and its effects on activities and a diplomat's information ecosystem, see George L. Argyros, Marc Grossman, and Felix G. Rohatyn, *The Embassy of the Future* (Washington, DC: CSIS Press, 2007); Jozef Bátora, *Foreign Ministries and the Information Revolution* (The Hague: Martinus Nijhoff, 2008).

86. Brown, *Knowledge Is Power*; Walter A. Friedman, *Birth of a Salesman: The Transformation of Selling in America* (Cambridge, MA: Harvard University Press, 2005). For a collection of wide-ranging case studies, see Aad Blok and Greg Downey, eds., *Uncovering Labour in Information Revolutions, 1750–2000* (Cambridge, MA: International Review of Social History Supplements, 2003).

87. Based on anecdotal evidence as I have talked to hundreds of diplomats over the past forty years and found no exceptions; they all were interested in diplomatic, political, and economic history, and to a large extent, also in cultural anthropology.

88. These were also communities whose information ecosystems and infrastructures were the subject of a large investigation of American patterns of behavior, James W. Cortada, *All the Facts: A History of Information in the United States Since 1870* (New York: Oxford University Press, 2016).

Chapter Five

Information Ecosystems of American Homemakers in Madison County, Virginia, 1950–1995

Home demonstration has brought to thousands of rural women a belief in themselves, in their families, and in their communities.

—Home Economist, 1957

Central Virginia in the mid-twentieth century was largely rural, dotted with small farms of often less than three hundred acres in size, towns with less than three thousand inhabitants spread across a handful of counties (Orange, Madison, Louisa, Culpepper, and Green). It is sandwiched between Fredericksburg some 30 miles to the east (home town of George Washington), and a similar distance west to Charlottesville (home town of Thomas Jefferson and location of the University of Virginia). A mere 80 miles to the north and culturally and politically millions of miles away is Washington, DC. Nestled in the rural landscape at the foothills of the Blue Ridge Mountains was a vibrant society populated with between six thousand and fifteen thousand residents in most counties, the majority living on farms, others in small towns and unincorporated villages.[1] People knew almost "everyone" in their county and "drove into town" to do their shopping, except for special occasions when they went to Charlottesville.[2]

Membership in a church constituted a vital part of their social and informational ecosystem, with congregations scattered over every county. To understand one's social position, people would politely ask, "and what church do you belong to?" Episcopalians were the upper classes in towns (largely in Orange), Presbyterians slightly less so, Methodists squarely middle class with some farmers, Lutherans, Baptists, Christian church, and other splinter Protestant denominations middle class, mostly farming families, and working class congregations. The higher the social order of a denomination the more formal education one could find. Episcopal, Presbyterian and Methodist churches had the largest number of high school and college graduates. Madison County gravitated toward Baptist, Lutheran, and other smaller Protestant denominations, most organized into small congregations of 100 to 150 members, attending white clapboard wooden churches. These generalizations applied to both White and African American populations with church congregations the most segregated in the entire period, schools less so by the end of the 1960s.[3]

This case study focuses on the activities of girls and women in Madison County, but draws on activities in other parts of Virginia, too, to demonstrate that a vibrant information ecosystem and accompanying infrastructure existed that made it possible to share practical information and to provide people with a sense of local identity and purpose. Social and information boundaries among the counties were porous, characterized by inter-county marriages and sports rivalries among the high schools. Workers crossed boundaries between Madison and Orange counties, less so into other neighboring areas, with the exception of Charlottesville, which grew in population and footprint all through the period, and largely in the direction of Green and Madison Counties. Each of these circumstances affected the use of information by these two groups.

I describe largely the role of house and farm wives, most of whom lived on farms and in rural communities, many of which had less than two dozen homes each, concerning their activities involving the collection and use of information about food and cooking. But why look at these women, and why for the second half of the twentieth century? Does the reality that there are essentially two social styles of grouping people in the world facilitate understanding their role: those who live and work in highly defined communities under the authority of, say, a manager within a company or by accepted practices, such as within a nation's culture; and those who live in far looser constructs, such as in a community or "out in the country," where interactions are voluntary and behaviors emerge in a less structured way than mandated by a manger or a military officer, for example?

Studies exist about information used by professions and well-defined institutions, such as about diplomats or academics, the nineteenth century cattle industry, architects, companies, and the military.[4] Far less research has been conducted to understand the informational practices of less structured groups, such as homemakers, although that circumstance, too, is changing.[5] In theory, such groups did not have to interact with each other, nor share information of interest to them. But they did, so we need to ask:

Why? Equally interesting, what did they share and how much? Did they become dependent on each other for organized bodies of information? To address such questions, this chapter demonstrates that using the lens of information ecosystems and infrastructures provide a useful approach to get to answers. It provides a *contra pose* to those studies of more defined organizations and professions. By adapting the economic historian's shorthand rule of "follow the money" with a "follow the information" strategy, we can gain insight about the role of information in the lives of what appear to be loosely connected groups of people and, most usefully, about women and girls, two cohorts Donald O. Case rightly called out as understudied by those interested in information behavior.[6]

With those concerns in mind the women who lived in these rural communities made for an interesting case study. They lived close to Washington, DC, a one hour drive up Route 29; but that city might as well have been in California, as there was almost no interaction between them, despite proximity. The second half of the century was chosen because in those years the rural features of Madison County that had remained essentially unchanged since the second half of the nineteenth century began to experience the effects of new information technologies entering the lives of its citizens. These included, most notably, expanded use of the telephone from "party lines" to dedicated lines, almost universal adoption of television, more frequent travel to other communities, and college education for the first time for many in a generation of children born in the post World War II period.[7] In short, the community was sufficiently self-encased to document activities largely influenced by what went on within this and surrounding counties.

Our objective is to describe the information ecosystem and infrastructure of one community to add to our understanding of the role of information flows at a local level, applying the approach taken in the previous chapter about the role of information within a highly structured, disciplined, and defined community—Spanish diplomats—as another example of the research methods used in that previous exercise.[8] The surprise finding, here, is that regardless of whether one dealt with a loose confederation of participants in an information ecosystem or a highly defined one, as long as there existed mutual interests and perceived value in information exchanges, informational behaviors proved similar. I chose to use information about food as the lens through which to observe the behavior of girls and women, because of their extensive involvement in such subjects as nutrition, food preservation, and cooking, and learning about these subjects in both formal and informal social settings. Other informational topics that could have been studied, such as sewing, child rearing, or housekeeping, were subsumed in the broader interest in food displayed by these residents of Madison County. The post World War II period was a time when increased interest in the science of food and nutrition coupled to expanded initiatives by the State of Virginia to educate citizens about these topics. While behaviors described below existed prior to World War II, they intensified and became more inclusive after 1945. Additionally, but secondarily, the documentary evidence in support of such a study proved far richer, further evidence of the community's growing interest in such matters, applying information handling methods common to the period.[9]

Their local information ecosystem included conversations at regularly scheduled meetings, such as classes and home demonstration club meetings; publications, such as local newspapers, newsletters, community cookbooks, and government publications; and activities, such as food preservation, cooking demonstrations, and food projects. To demonstrate how information ecosystems and infrastructure concepts played out, I explore the participants and their food, describing their cooking information ecosystem (the heart of the study), the information itself, its codification over time, and the role of other routinized information that affected the central interest in nutrition, cooking, and recipes.

But why not use an existing framework? Many information behavior paradigms and models tend to frame research around information seeking activities, cost-benefit analysis, gratification and expectancies, and closest to our approach, discourse analysis. The vast majority of such studies were not conducted using the historian's perspective.[10] This one relied extensively on the historian's toolbox familiar to information scholars. All are useful, of course, but did not appear to square sufficiently with the need to understand the interaction between an ecosystem and its infrastructure when measured against the behavior of what appeared to be socially highly defined voluntary uses of information. Yet another set of lenses focuses on network analysis, the closest to our approach, as these tend to concentrate on behaviors of professions and other highly defined groups. Much that appears below will seem similar to those approaches except that I link my research to information ecosystems in broader terms with their information infrastructures. Having a group of women, and to a slightly lesser extent children through club memberships, who were not required to interact with each other and who did not have to embrace new bodies of information, makes the study of networks and social systems all the more interesting. Their behavior validates that these two features of information existed, indeed had to exist for them to go about their lives in ways relevant and enjoyable to them.[11]

We have much to do here. Our framing questions ask who participated in an ecosystem, and here we begin by answering that question. We want to know what media, mediums, and patterns of their adoption existed and to address those issues we discuss their sources of information, local information handling practices, and take an extensive look at cookbooks as they were specific and important sources of information, along with other forms of content. We asked an open ended question about what other historical discourses should be considered as part of information history and here demonstrate one not discussed in the other case studies: the physical location of information exchanges and how that subject can be discussed with respect to information ecosystems and their infrastructures. We also need to explore why a group of people not forced to interact with each other did. What were their motives for sharing and using each other's information? Did they form information ecosystems that had any durability comparable, say, to those of the Spanish foreign ministry, IBM, or academic departments?

This case is presented in more detail than all the others to demonstrate the level of probing one can engage in, even in subjects that initially might seem impenetrable. It should be clear by the end that it was almost irrelevant that we focused on women and children, that the important finding is less that gender was a crucial element affecting our way of looking at information ecosystems and infrastructures and more that relevant information is the shaping force at work. This is not to say that gender did not matter, because it did, just that it did not matter as much as the central focus of our attention: information ecosystems and their infrastructures. Both genders and individuals from childhood to old age participated in these.

A diverse number of people participated in information exchanges in this county, sharing facts about agricultural and other work related activities, and opinions and advice regarding illnesses, politics, and child rearing. The same held regarding homemaking activities, including storage and preparation of food, with the earliest publications in Virginia circulating at the dawn of the eighteenth century.[12]

PARTICIPANTS AND THEIR INFORMATION ECOSYSTEMS

In 1950, Madison County had a population of 8,273, essentially the same as the previous half-century. By 1980, the population had expanded to

10,232, a nearly 20 percent increase. Two decades later it reached 13,000.[13] Population growth mirrored the entire state's expansion, stimulated largely by economic prosperity following World War II. But the social construct of the county remained the same. Over the half century, 80 percent of the population was white, while African Americans made up between 10 and 12 percent.[14] Following World War II the county remained rural and agricultural, comprised largely of yeoman stock of Scottish, Irish, and German descendants of the original settlers, unlike next door, in Orange County, that had been populated by English stock. In the 1930s, with the creation of the Shenandoah National Park, hundreds of residents in what was now the park were moved by authorities to Madison County where they resettled, bringing with them their cultural heritage. Their practices included shared food preparation practices that endured to the end of the century. Cornbread, eating almost all parts of a hog, and consumption of fruit pies had a long history dating to the eighteenth century, as did eating corn that would have been familiar to residents of the late twentieth century.[15]

By the mid-twentieth century Madison County had over six hundred farms, the majority of which were small (less than two hundred acres each), concentrated overwhelmingly in raising cattle and other livestock, corn, and soy.[16] Across the half-century farms increased in size, as economies of scale needed to support family farming required more land or part time jobs elsewhere to bring in cash. Most farmers continued to provide much of the vegetables, dairy products, fowl, and meats required to feed their families. Arrival of supermarkets in nearby Orange and in other communities made available a wider assortment of foods by the 1950s, including A&P and Safeway, not to mention smaller groceries, such as Sparks' in Orange and Pratt's in Madison County. To put a fine point on farming, by 1975, when the majority of local Baby Boomers were reaching adulthood and sought employment outside the county; 17.1 percent of the adult residents worked on farms, down from 26.3 percent in 1970. Even sharply higher percentages prevailed a generation earlier, so economic changes were underway.[17]

The county had only one incorporated town: Madison, the county seat. It included the courthouse, a few stores, the county's public library, a fire department, and a number of community organizations (some discussed later). The Town of Orange served as the *de facto* economic center for the area, with its population of over three thousand in the 1950s–1980s, nearly six thousand by the end of the century; the town of Madison's hovered at less than 350 as late as 1990 and shrank nearly 25 percent by the dawn of the new century. There were 43 unincorporated communities in Madison County, most of which had less than one hundred residents each, many at one time anchored by a combination post office/country store.[18] Some of these country stores still function; however, most have closed. Over a dozen operated between 1950 and 1980.[19]

Farmers, farm laborers, and others in agriculture constituted one large cohort that shared information about their profession. A second group consisted of their wives and other women in their families, from roughly high school age on up. The vast majority of these women were interested in and concerned about agricultural themes, including cooking, food preservation, sewing, raising small farm animals, and child rearing. The female constituency equaled in size the adult male population throughout the period. Boys and girls made up a third cohort, from fourth grade (10–11 years old) on up exhibiting broader interests beyond those of their parents, but often encouraged by them. These interests included topics promoted by schools, scouting, patriotic organizations, and, increasingly, by what they saw on television. The latter began largely during the second half of the 1950s, with the major takeoff in television viewing by all groups occurring in the 1960s.[20] So, a modern urban population, consisting of what today is frequently referred to as "knowledge workers," did not exist in substantial numbers in the county during 1950–1995.

The county's agricultural population lived comfortably, but was not prosperous. They were cash poor, but endowed with fixed assets, notably land and cattle. Improvements to their quality of life came quickly, however, in this period. We do not know how many farms lacked indoor plumbing, but when compared to national standards, probably a quarter of all farmhouses went without these amenities at the end of World War II. Electricity did not come to many farms until 1943. By the mid-1950s it was difficult to find a farmhouse without indoor bathrooms and running water; the majority acquired electricity by the late 1940s, thanks to Federal and state rural electrification programs.[21] It seemed every farm family bought a radio or a refrigerator soon after acquiring electricity. WJMA Radio in Orange, Virginia, went on the air in the late 1940s, and people listened to it in Madison County, along with other stations that began broadcasting out of Charlottesville, some twenty miles down the newly built four-lane Route 29. Television became ubiquitous in the 1960s.[22]

Figure 5.1 summarizes who participated in the food information ecosystem. Arrows point to who directly interacted with each other and the general direction in which information moved. For example, newspaper-based information flowed to farm wives while among women it was back

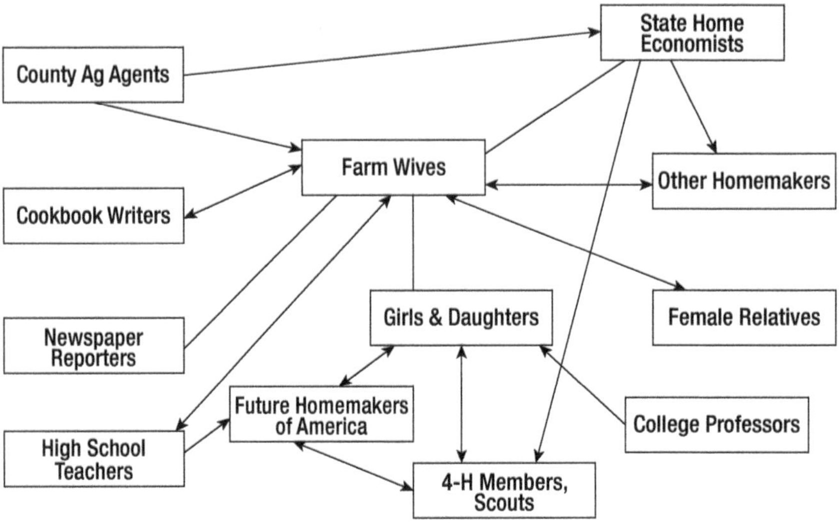

Figure 5.1. Participants in Madison County's Food Information Ecosystem, 1950–1995

and forth. The figure suggests there were many participants and their interactions remained complex and frequent. The figure demonstrates that the central coordinating person in disseminating information about food matters was the female homemaker who was a consumer of facts, played a vital role in educating future generations on the topic, influenced friends and neighbors, and contributed information to many through her civic, familial, and publishing activities. Their information ecosystem remained intact throughout the half-century; indeed, it had solidified by the 1920s and that describes the ecosystem as it exists today. Use of information became the glue that connected together many of the participants, particularly those outside the farm.

Close behind farm wives in diffusing information about food was a string of home economics extension agents responsible for teaching women safe food preparation methods, nutrition, and child rearing and health, among other topics. They ran 4-H programs for children where they, too, learned about similar topics and additionally about sewing and raising farm animals. These home economists were revered members of the community, often long resident in the county, even marrying into local families.[23] Upon their retirement those who stayed in the county volunteered as members of civic clubs, churches, beautification programs, and the in study of local history. We will have much to say about this group.[24]

PHYSICAL LOCATIONS OF INFORMATION EXCHANGES

Residents favored specific places for the exchange of information. Politics, economics, agricultural problem solving, and even discussions about health and social issues were the purview of country stores and civic organizations, such as at chapters of the Lions Club, Grange Halls, and churches. One of the largest spaces in the county, the War Memorial Building, located on Main Street in the town of Madison, housed the office of the home economics extension agents on the second floor for most of the period; it had a large meeting room and a kitchen. This facility was also a popular site for 4-H meetings and some demonstration club events that required more space than was available in someone's home.[25]

As in most American rural communities, country stores served as centers for the exchange of information of all kinds and Madison's experience proved no different. In 1972, when storeowner Harry Gibbs closed his establishment in Shelby, an unincorporated town, which had made his store the community center there, he described what used to go on at his shop beyond the buying and selling of goods:

> More importantly, the store kept a finger on the pulse of the community. Coming to the store for mail and few groceries was the customer's excuse to dawdle and listen to the elderly discuss many things. A young fellow could glean an education . . . if he listened carefully. He would hear politics discussed and studied, decisions made, business conducted and problems solved as neighbor helped neighbor. There would be practical remedies and advice on all medical problems, plans made for getting provisions to a homebound friend, and mercy trips to the ill. The church may have been the heart of the community, but the country store was the rest of the vitals. . . .[26]

He could have been describing any of several dozen country stores in the county.

Churches did more than serve the needs of the soul: they provided schooling and sites for meetings for community groups sharing information. Here women gathered to exchange information on rearing children, medical issues, raising food and animals, and cooking, and to organize community civic affairs. It was their space, although their husbands would chat with friends after Sunday services in the parking lot. Children's events were held there, too. In any given year there existed between 34 and 36 churches, almost all populated with congregations of one hundred or less, all quite small. The Baptists had the largest collection of churches with just over a dozen, Methodists ten congregations, Lutherans two, Episcopalians and Presbyterians one each.[27] All the others were various independent Protestant denominations, such as the Christian Church, Mennonites, and Pentecostals. All served the same information role. They got along with each other. Women in the community had established the Council of Church Women of Madison to facilitate coordination of programs and information exchange across the county. Because of the small size of these churches, everyone knew all the members in their own congregations.[28]

Another popular spot for gathering to exchange information were schools, which had auditoriums, libraries, and classrooms.[29] Much of the children's information ecosystems were situated in schools. The county had established its one high school just before World War I and had four elementary schools in the second half of the century. In those years the high school had over three hundred students and went from the eighth through the twelfth grades. Every child was required to attend school, and the majority graduated from high school. The community took seriously education of its children and invested in their schools through taxes and volunteer work in clubs for the young, such as in sports, scouting, and 4-H. Lunch menus for each school were published weekly in the *Madison Eagle* throughout the half-century. These menus were occasionally the subjects of community debate about their quality. School cooks were famous for their rolls. Homemakers were proud of theirs, too. Cookbooks from that period always carried these all-important kinds of recipes, but were consulted only for their slightly nuanced variations off a common way of baking them.[30]

The information ecosystem included other institutions that periodically engaged in exchange of information regarding food and cooking. These included the local newspaper, *The Madison Eagle* (established in 1924 and still publishing) and the *Orange Review* (established a few years earlier). Residents routinely read both. By the end of the 1970s, the Charlottesville newspaper, *The Daily Progress*, was also widely read in the county. Figure 5.2 catalogs many of the civic and other functioning organizations in the county; many had existed for decades, most were still active in the twenty-first century. Figure 5.2 also demonstrates the variety of organizations and physical places where information exchanges occurred. These were both public and private spaces, big and small, and physically dispersed throughout the county. It reminds us that an information infrastructure includes both content (facts) and physical components. Some were both providers and physical locations for the exchange of information, notably churches. Missing from the figure is another obvious physical component: transportation of information, such as automobiles, delivery trucks, and

Providers of Information	Physical Locations for Exchanging Information
Demonstration Clubs	Homes
Newspapers, Radio, TV	Churches
Scouts	Fire Department
4-H	Schools (K-12 & High School)
Future Homemakers of America	Country Stores & Post Offices
Future Farmers of America	Grange Halls
Church Clubs	Government Buildings
Women's Rescue & Fire Departments Auxiliary	Public Library

Figure 5.2. Organizations and Physical Locations in Madison County's Information Infrastructure, 1950–1995

telephones. The infrastructure represented in Figure 5.2, while including transportation, also mirrored the broader information infrastructure used by residents for all manner of collection, use, and exchange of information, such as that required for work and business.

Later we discuss those components of the information infrastructure that were part of the food information ecosystem. But notice how these organizations reflected local interests: the agricultural economy, women's concerns, and educating children. Some were formed after World War II, but many others flourished out of the surge of interest in community affairs that had swept the nation before and after World War I. Several groups in particular participated in sharing information about food. Farm wives dominated the food preparation ecosystem. They collected information about cooking, largely recipes, which they kept for personal use, but shared with their daughters and other relatives by copying them, sending these to them in letters, and by demonstrating to them how to prepare a dish or item. These women shared their recipes and insights in their spiral-bound recipe books published through their churches and local civic organizations, better known as community cookbooks. They gathered as groups, meeting monthly at each other's homes or in other public spaces in what were known as Demonstration Clubs, often following an agenda set by the local home economics extension agent. Local home economists in collaboration with club members published a two to four page mimeographed newsletter, *Extension Homemakers News,* on a monthly basis in the 1960s and 1970s to communicate meeting times and places, and to share information about the subjects discussed at these events.[31]

SOURCES OF INFORMATION

Farm wives gathered routinely at a neighbor's home in small groups to discuss food and other topics with county extension agents, overwhelmingly with home economists. So, it is important to understand these events. Home economists conveyed information about food preparation safety and tips, nutrition, clothing, child rearing, children's education, home safety, and health practices, among other topics. They were employees of the Virginia Polytechnic Institution (VPI), a land grant state university whose outreach programs were funded largely by the U.S. Department of Agriculture. These "home demonstrators" (better known locally as Home Extension Agents) held small meetings all over the county, and had done so since 1925 under the structure of Home Demonstration Clubs, which operated numerous chapters in almost every rural county in the United States.[32] They formed rapidly, spreading throughout Central Virginia in the 1920s and 1930s. By mid-century over 1.5 million women in over sixty thousand clubs dotted America's rural landscape.[33] By the early 1990s, Madison had approximately a dozen clubs, each with between 10 and 15 members. Home economists attached to these clubs were highly regarded and well known.[34] All were women. These gatherings were as much social events as learning opportunities. One resident of the time recalled that they were "a major social activity" where the hostess would "get out her best dishes."[35] Half met in the morning, the others in the early evening. One home economist reported that attendance at these events was "excellent."[36]

The Town of Madison's Home Demonstration Club spearheaded establishment of the local public library in 1937 and the initial accumulation of books for it. Virginia Rucker Crigler (1908–1990) served as the county's home economist from 1939 to 1968, and also ran the three 4-H clubs, which focused on farming practices and women's domestic activities.[37] In 1968, after her retirement, a new demonstration agent was appointed, Judy C. Fray, who served until 1973.[38] During the rest of the decade turnover increased as two young ladies subsequently served in the position.[39] The first, Laura Roach, served from 1973 through 1974, and her replacement, Helen Williams, worked in both Madison and Orange counties for several years. Those who served after Crigler had, too, been college trained as home economists.[40] Each became a trusted advisor called upon to answer questions about all manner of household, farm, and food issues at times beyond the demonstration meetings. They represented the most important source of new information about food entering the county during the entire half-century.

"Miss. or Mrs. Crigler," as she was known to many hundreds of children, was a highly regarded member of the community. Nearly a half-century after her retirement, members of her 4-H clubs, now in their '50s, '60s, and '70s spoke reverently of her influence on them: "Most patient woman I ever met," "gentle," "a fantastic woman." Members interviewed for this study spoke about the high standards she expected of everyone. Margaret Dawson's comments were typical. Crigler insisted on an "extremely professional level" of performance but in exchange was "totally interested" in helping children with competitions and demonstrations to make sure everything "was up to snuff" so that they put "their best foot forward" in representing their county and in building their personal confidence and knowledge. All the while, she was "so nice and gentle."[41] Another said she "knew everyone in the county and everyone knew her."[42] In 2018, late on a Saturday night in October, a flurry of Facebook postings about 4-H in Madison popped up—a first for that county's program on Facebook—celebrating what girls had learned. One of those girls, now a grandmother, posted: "The two main 4h ladies that inspired me were Mrs. V. Crigler who along with teaching sewing skills, taught us manners, grace and poise . . . your mother was the second [Dot Tappy]. I remember her telling and advising us about life itself while instructing us."[43] Another 4-Her from Fairfax County who went on to become a home economist reported in 2002 that Crigler "was probably one of the top agents in Virginia . . . highly respected by all the other Agents and the State Administration."[44] Today the Madison High School awards a $500 scholarship in her name to a senior active in 4-H. Her successor, Judy Ann Fray, was also highly regarded for her professionalism and patience with children, and, like Crigler, who she mentored under before taking over her responsibilities, maintained excellent relations with the women across the county. One 4-H member wrote in her "Member's Record" book in 1971 that Fray exhibited "patience" and offered "guidance" as the 4-Her matured during high school.[45]

In 1959 all four of Madison County's Extension Staff were recognized for their work with a Superior Service Award from the U.S. Department of Agriculture Cooperative Extension Service in Virginia. The recipients were Crigler (Home Demonstration Agent), Mrs. Sarah U. Gibbs (Extension Secretary),[46] G. Allan McLearen (County Agent),[47] and W. Rapley ("Rap") Owings (Assistant County Agent)[48] for their combined service to both the county and to the state. In the case of Virginia Crigler, the award recognized her for her accomplishments in promoting healthy practices through demonstration clubs, which organized clinics for children and education programs for adults. Her 4-H programs were "recognized State-wide as progressive and outstanding." During the 1950s, "Madison County 4-H members have been selected frequently to represent the State at National 4-H Conference, National 4-H Congress and to participate in the International Farm Youth Exchange Program." 4-H members of the 1960s interviewed for this chapter continued that pattern of representation and participation in national events. The same citation noted that home economists in many counties replicated Crigler's local programs during the 1940s and 1950s.[49]

Madison's home economists collaborated closely with the local newspaper, *Madison Eagle,* to ensure several types of information appeared regularly. Agents in most of these years published a weekly column discussing issues with which they were currently involved. Many dealt with food topics. The newspaper carried articles announcing the activities of the agent, 4-H club members, and anything that the children did that distinguished them at county fairs and at regional, state, and national 4-H conventions and camps. The newspaper routinely carried such articles about the children so that a member keeping a record book of activities normally had dozens of clippings mentioning them and their cohorts. The newspaper published the weekly school menus and announcements of culinary events in the area, such as demonstration club meetings held, or to be held, at the War Memorial Building. When radio programming became available in the late 1940s, they used this medium as well to communicate similar information in weekly broadcasts.

In addition to using media to communicate information, there were in every issue of the newspaper advertisements paid for by regional supermarkets, food banks, and stockyards. Publication of a community cookbook invariably led to an article about it to help promote its sales. County home economists knew how to work effectively with local media to communicate their messages. The vast majority of households subscribed to the *Madison Eagle* all through the half-century, ensuring that their messages would reach into most homes.

A third important source of new information that diffused throughout the county was the home economics teacher at the Madison County High School. The school offered a course in home economics throughout the half-century.[50] In the eighth grade students were exposed to all manner of topics in six-week modules, so they could later determine which elective classes they might want to take. These included exposure to food and nutrition, and to clothing and sewing. From the ninth through the twelfth grades, the school offered one semester on clothing (usually in the fall) and one semester on food (usually in the spring). Each year, course content became more sophisticated, but all classes involved food preparation, nutrition, cooking dishes basic to the region, and food preservation. In advanced classes one learned how to plan nutritious meals, budgeting, and household management.

One information theme that ran through classes, 4-H programs, Girl Scouts, and for grownups, the demonstration clubs, was an emphasis on being precise in measurements. Rather than a pinch of salt, it would be a teaspoon of salt. The rationale reflected the nation's overall embracing of greater precision in much of what it did in the twentieth century, in this case to ensure quality and consistency superior to what one's mother or grandmother practiced. This move to greater precision in food information was driven by changing technologies, not the least of which was the conversion from wood stove cooking to electric and gas stoves, a transition still underway in Madison County in the 1950s and 1960s. One could not control the temperature of a wood stove, but could with a gas or electric one. Those newer technologies encouraged a precision not possible before. As women moved increasingly into the nonfarm workforce, beginning in the 1960s, their need to prepare food right the first time and as efficiently as possible further encouraged this shift in the nature of the information disseminated to girls and women. This dissemination included farmwives who were constantly exposed to nutritional information by home economists which they otherwise might not have obtained through normal social interactions with neighbors. So students and grownups were being exposed to a similar new body of information from trusted sources.

Their instructors were college graduates trained as home economists and teachers. At Radford College, the women's version of VPI in Virginia, hundreds of home economists trained in these new bodies of information. Students majoring in home economics received instruction on safe food preservation and preparation involving fruits, vegetables, poultry, fish, and meats. They learned how to make precise measurements and to use new kitchen instruments. Their professors gave them a basic knowledge about nutrition. Particular emphasis was placed on application of information through projects, much as done in demonstration clubs and in 4-H.[51] Students received training in measurements, food buying practices, preparation, use of timetables, and physical properties of different types of ingredients bordering on chemistry. Such training for Madison County's home economists began after World War II.[52] College students received instruction on sewing and making clothes, too. They learned about the use of all manner of household appliances, management of a home, child rearing, and the socially appropriate ways to set a dining room table. Such information was designed for home economists to transfer to students in schools, additionally through 4-H programs, and to their mothers and grandmothers in Demonstration Club meetings.[53] The high school's total faculty in the 1950s through the 1990s ranged in size of between 18 and 23 teachers, and while a small number, there always was room for one of them to be a home economics teacher and another to be an instructor of agriculture. The former was always a woman, the latter a man.

While girls learned about home life, boys received instruction in agriculture and farming, an example of the collaboration among county agricultural agents and home economists. Each teacher—with the agricultural agent's assistance—advised high school clubs devoted to these two gender-defined subjects. Home economists managed the Future Homemakers of America (FHA) Club, which routinely had some 50 members in the 1950s and 1960s, fewer in the 1970s and 1980s. To put those numbers in perspective, the entire school's student population ranged from 290 students in the 1950s and 1960s to approximately fifty percent more by the mid-1970s.[54] The FHA explored food matters and hosted an annual tea for the faculty and a supper (evening meal) for the seniors. Often the teacher would collaborate with the county home economist, so "Mrs. Crigler," was a familiar figure at the school. She taught girls about food and about such things as how to create Christmas decorations for the home, set a table "properly," make up beds with precision, and, through modeling by her personal behavior, even how to write a thank you note. In 2018, the school still had a female home economics teacher, although now referred to as a Family Consumer Science teacher.[55] Boys could still take a course in agriculture, still taught by a man trained in agriculture that grew up on a farm.[56]

How many girls took home economics courses? Hard data on class sizes remain illusive; however, some calculations suggest an answer, especially when combined by looking at the number of people in high school yearbook pictures. Across these decades there were four classes about food, one for each grade. These had to be small, because students needed space for a kitchen in which they could experience preparing meals. That meant many of these classes only had 20 to 25 students. So approximately one hundred students per year could take such courses, or anywhere from 25 percent to over 30 percent of the female students. Since it was clear from yearbook photographs that student bodies were generally evenly split in number between boys and girls, roughly half the girls attended these classes. Many students who did not take classes, however, participated in 4-H programs that covered similar material, particularly subjects introduced in entry-level classes. 4-H required them to engage in projects involving preservation, preparing, measuring, and planning meals, supervised by the county home economist. Those girls were allowed to bypass the freshman class and go directly to the next higher elective, because they were considered to have already mastered the same material.[57]

Boys also learned about food, largely at home from their parents, but to a small extent too, through their high school Future Farmers of America (FFA) club. FFA focused on the production of food crops and raising farm animals, not on food preparation. FFA was always the largest organization at school. It was not uncommon for it to have 70 or more members. They represented a parallel universe to that of the girls, with the agricultural teacher, their advisor, and the local county agricultural extension agent involved closely in their activities. The agricultural teacher, a college graduate who majored in agriculture, grew up on a farm in Virginia. In the 1960s, for example, Joel B. Yowell served in that capacity. He was also an agricultural extension agent from a family that had long farmed in the county.[58]

There existed one more participant in the food information ecosystem: girls and boys who participated in 4-H. It would be difficult to overstate the importance of these clubs. They formed in elementary school and continued through high school. For the first half of the century members had to live on a farm to qualify for membership, and much of their training paralleled what Boy Scouts and Girl Scouts obtained: values, attitudes, work habits, and development of leadership skills and confidence, as well as experience working with agricultural projects. Some 70 million American children went through 4-H in the twentieth century, focusing on agriculture and home economics.[59] One of the most important of their projects involved raising an animal, such as a calf, pig, or lamb, which a child entered into a contest at the annual county fair. Judges awarded the top animal or crop in a class a blue ribbon for first place, other colored ribbons for second and third places. Prizewinners usually sold their winning animal to a local supermarket to be converted into meat products. The *Madison Eagle* would carry a story about what the children accomplished. Another project was raising a small crop, such as corn. These made up the normal cycle of events. Girls learned about food preservation and preparation and competed for prizes and recognition in these too.[60] They received public recognition for their projects by exhibiting at county fairs and at regional, state, and national events. Their exhibits ran the full gamut of projects, from pies, breads, and other dishes, to canning fruits, to more science-based research projects and care of animals. Many girls specialized in sewing, but even they also had to learn about food.

There were three design points crucial to the makeup of the 4-H movement. First, the children had to document their activities, keeping meticulous records of progress, say, in raising an animal or recipes used. There were national practices for recordkeeping implemented early in the century that remain in force to the present.[61]

Second, children competed for prizes as a way of encouraging their improved performance. To win a blue ribbon or some other prize in cooking, members prepared dishes in front of judges who were local ladies, showing how to prepare them, emphasizing the nutritional value of the ingredients as they were added. Children prepared for these demonstrations by writing out their verbal comments beforehand, rehearsing their presentations at home or in front of Mrs. Crigler to get it "just right." Facts they put on posters and in handouts had to be correct (verified). County, district, and state level competitions awarded scholarships to the winners. Girls in Madison County were active, and many were recognized at the highest level, as All Stars. Home economists interviewed for this study were All Stars. Local All Stars were given the opportunity to travel within the state and to other parts of the country, travel that otherwise would not have been open to them. These events broadened their horizons and improved their confidence in public speaking and working with others. For many, these would be their first trip outside of their county or state.[62] Cooking contests made it possible for girls to learn about other food preparation practices.

Third, 4-H, like Scouting, followed the practice of boys and girls "learning by doing," placing a premium on demonstrating how to do something, such as preparing a dish, a strategy also deployed by home economists and county agents in training these children's parents. It was the core pedagogical method used from the beginning of 4-H. 4-H, the U.S. Department of Agriculture, and state land grant universities, such as VPI, published extensively materials familiar to children and their parents, ancillary to the core method of learning.

4-H began in Madison in 1913, when Albion Waverly Yowell (1882–1974) established the first chapter in the county. At the time he was the principal at the Etlan High School (no longer in existence by the 1950s), running his "corn club" for boys; it was the first professional agricultural organization in the county. Thousands of American counties sponsored such clubs to teach boys and girls how to raise corn, later other crops and animals, and what to do with them.[63] By the time farmwives and their husbands were running their own households and raising children, largely in the 1940s and 1950s, many had already been trained through the 4-H process, and thus were comfortable in introducing their daughters and sons to the same system for acquiring information.

INFORMATION HANDLING PRACTICES

Life-long sharing of information occurred by acquiring much of their core knowledge at home from other female family members, most importantly their mothers, as women simultaneously learned about food through the practice of cooking in their own kitchens. Women verbally handed down their practices and insights. Many left a paper trail, too, of use to historians, if one could gain access to them, because these documents were so treasured as family heirlooms and sources of information for future generations' own cooking that they were not likely to make it to university archives. One small example that could have been pulled from many illustrates the exchange of information facilitated by these scrapbooks. Dorothy (known as "Dot") Tappy (1903–1982) lived on a 235-acre farm in Uno, a tiny unincorporated community consisting of a country store (where she daily worked as post-mistress for several hours), less than a dozen homes, one African American church, and another dozen farms. She had two daughters who grew up in 4-H and trained in college in home economics. In the 1970s many changes came to cooking practices: new ingredients, another generation of prepackaged food products and cooking instruments, and continued expanding emphasis on precision in measurements and cooking procedures, all of which generated much dialogue as everyone learned how to work with these.

Often, it was also a daughter who introduced the older woman to innovations. Tappy's reaction to a new cooking device in 1972 is an example of learning. Her daughter, Dora Jane, had recommended using a broiler oven, which Dot did:

> I tried our Broiler-Oven and it works fine and the little dishes you gave me are just right. I put my celery in the celery crisper you gave me and it really keeps it nice. The first time I go to C'-ville [Charlottesville, ed. note] I will take the red salt and pepper shakers back. I'm sure I can find something in a pretty red for the kitchen.[64]

Her daughter occasionally gave her measuring cups for both dry and wet ingredients and at family events they discussed cooking methods.

The familial cooking paper trail left out many details, such as how to prepare a meal for 10 or more people that involved making sure everything landed on the dining room table hot if it was supposed to be and cold if appropriate, and make it all look effortless.[65] Another undocumented nearly anonymous effort involved what had to have been many hours of safely canning fruits, vegetables, and meats. While techniques were continuously improved with new methods and technologies over the course of the twentieth century that were documented, missing from the historical record was the magic of how these cooks found the time to can hundreds of jars each year to sustain their families during winter. It raises the question of how much tacit knowledge is lost to the historian; but not lost is the fact that much of that knowledge was transmitted to daughters through observation, demonstration, practice, and oral transmission.

4-H record books, however, required girls to document some of that activity in the home. Mary Linda Lamb, a high school student, recorded that she baked bread 12 times in 1966, 14 times in 1967, and 15 times in 1968. In 1966, she recorded that she had "blanched and packed vegetables and fruit" and "used a pressure canner," canning six jars and helped her mother to "can 10 cans." She continued to log similar activities for the rest of the decade.[66] She acknowledged the role of her mother: "my mother spent many of her own hours, encouraging me and taking me to 4-H meetings and activities."[67] That kind of shared information was too precious to let time take away. The same held true for two culinary tasks required only of men: preparation of alcoholic beverages and teaching sons how to shuck oysters from the Chesapeake Bay, which were popular all over the state and an important component of any Thanksgiving meal and on Christmas morning in Madison County.[68]

INFORMATION AND COMMUNITY COOKBOOKS

To a large extent, facts (knowledge) circulating through the information ecosystem comprised of recipes, including this one:

PRESERVED CHILDREN

Take 1 large field, ½ doz. children, 3 small dogs, a pinch of brook and some pebbles.

Mix the children and dogs well together; put them in the field, stirring constantly. Pour the brook over the pebbles; sprinkle the field with flowers; spread over all a deep blue sky. Bake in sun until hot; set away to cool in the bathtub.[69]

It was further suggested that "a bit of something sweet is always handy, for instances: kisses, smiles and homemade candy."[70]

The recipe reflected the standard format for recipes that passed through the hands of Madison's women, with one exception. Overwhelmingly, recipes were signed by who contributed them to the community, usually in the form of an entry to a locally produced cookbook. While the preserved children's recipe is anonymous, the significance of attribution cannot be overstated, for no woman would offer a recipe with her name associated with it to her friends and peers without it being the very best she could do. It had to be truly very good, because her readers were experts in the foods they routinely prepared. In 1950 the variety of foods consumed in the county had not differed much since the 1930s, when frozen foods came into some use, and World War II when a few new canned goods, such as corned beef hash, became common fare. But essentially everyone ate the same dishes so they knew what a good pie recipe was or how best to prepare a cured ham.

By the early 1960s that circumstance began to change as people experimented with adding Italian food to their diet, such as spaghetti and meatballs, as well as Chinese food and new condiments in the 1970s. By the end of the 1980s, the variety of recipes had expanded to include these kinds of culinary changes, other new ingredients, and uses of condiments as they became available in local supermarkets.

For core foods enjoyed by generations of Madisonians, to offer up a recipe on one of those with one's name attached to it called for confidence and high professionalism. To be known for "your great pies" or your "rolls" was a status symbol among one's peers not to be dismissed as trivial. While this may sound superficial, we know from studies of professions that peer acknowledgment proved important to cohorts, earned through mastering the technical skills of one's work.[71] For a housewife who could cook well to be so recognized for that skill mirrored what occurred among lawyers, doctors, and professors through their specialized skills and knowledge. Like an academic needs to appear in the "journals of record" of her profession, so too, homemakers had to appear in the "right" cookbooks produced by their church or community organizations; failure to do so might raise eyebrows. They had to demonstrate their skills in important local events, too, such as in preparing dishes and entire meals for church and civic occasions.[72]

That demonstration went beyond preparing food to presentation, a point Mrs. Crigler hammered into the heads of her little charges for decades. Barbara Reddish, an All Star from the 1960s, recalled that her mother emphasized cooking well and "the presentation of the food." Reddish reported that, "in 4-H, we not only learned about how to prepare food, but how to present it in a pleasing and proper design. In those days [1960s], the grouping of foods at events, the container used for the food, the centerpiece, and the use of white pressed cloth tablecloths all contributed to one's status symbol." She taught her daughter how to display Queen Ann's Lace wild flowers, even how to have such flowers absorb a new color, such as pink from red dye added to the plant's water, so as to have pink flowers "to color coordinate the food table at an event." Her behavior was drawn from her own experience but that also of her mother's (and Crigler's) in Aroda and Radiant, where "my mom was the food presentation guru and everyone came to her asking her how to arrange this and that."[73]

Generations of women followed in each other's footsteps. Using the example of the cookbook from which the humorous children's recipe was quoted, the majority of farming households were represented in the volume, with mothers and daughters contributing content, such as the Clore and the Berry families. Dot Tappy persuaded her two daughters, Betty and Dora, to do so, too.[74] Similar patterns were evident in the two dozen local cookbooks examined for this study.

In addition to recipes, often community-created cookbooks offered other information convenient to a homemaker. These included oven temperature charts, guiding one on the heat and amount of time needed to cook certain classes of food, such as breads, pies, cakes, meats, and poultry. Sometimes a cook would find that she was out of an ingredient and thus needed a substitute. Often collections of this kind of information were located in the rear of a local publication, such as the substitute for 1 cup of sugar, "⅔ cups honey equals 1 cup sugar plus ⅓ cup of water."[75] Information about cooking for large numbers of people often led to useful lists. Such a listing might discuss how many pounds of baked beans were needed to feed one hundred people, hash for a supper (term for the evening meal) for one hundred, cabbage salad for 175, ham supper for 225, and turkey dinner (mid-day meal) for 250. This kind of information proved useful to someone responsible for arranging a community event in which people had to be fed, a normal expectation.[76]

For most women in the 1950s and 1960s, these kinds of information were often introduced into their homes by way of community cookbooks. By the 1980s, a homemaker would have had several of these volumes, now with extensive amounts of numeric information, such as measures of ingredients and appropriate cooking temperatures. Internet access remained rare in many parts of the county even as late as 2018, as the lack of telecommunications infrastructure held back access, much as the lack of electrical infrastructure had as late as the 1930s and early 1940s in this rural and mountainous part of Central Virginia. Therefore, beyond verbal communications and handouts obtained at demonstration meetings, even early in the twenty-first century much information still arrived packaged in community cookbooks.

What did the women of Madison County cook? What information did they share? As a baseline for answering these questions, Table 5.1 lists the general categories of food with examples of each from the late 1940s. The categories of foods remained essentially unchanged for the rest of the century, although ingredients and names of dishes evolved. Contributors came from Orange and Madison counties, all acknowledged with their names printed beneath their recipes, all wishing to support the fundraising involved with such books. Already interest in dieting existed. In the cookbook used to create Table 5.1, an entire section included recipes and advice on diets, an eighteen day menu encompassing breakfast, lunch, and dinner, another for those who had to eat out at a "soda fountain or restaurant," instructions on how to gain weight and build up muscles, high calorie diets, ideal weight charts for men and women, and caloric charts for various types of food and drink.[77]

Table 5.1. Categories of local recipes, with examples, circa late 1940s

Appetizers, Relishes, Garnishes
Slaw dressing, salad dressing, cherry pickle, cucumber pickle, pickled peaches
Soups, Salads, Vegetables
1-2-3 salad, vegetable casseroles, noodles and mushroom, asparagus with mushroom sauce, corn pudding, coleslaw, scalloped potatoes, potato salad
Meat, Fish, Poultry
Meat balls, salmon cakes, meat loaf, chili con carne, baked rice and meat, baked fish
Bread, Rolls, Pastry
Rolls, corn meal muffins, coconut pie, pecan pie, old fashioned custard pie, lemon chess pie, pineapple pie, spoon bread, potato pancakes, chocolate brownie pie, turn-over rolls, coffee cake, refrigerator rolls, ice box rolls
Cookies, Cakes
Dark chocolate cake, blackberry cake, fruitcake, fruit cookies, pound cake, spice cake, chocolate crispies, coconut layer cake, Jell-O dessert, lemon sherbet, fudge, banana walnut fudge
Beverages
Fruit punch, cranberry punch, cheese egg float

Source: W.S.C.S. of the Methodist Church, *Barboursville Treasure of Personal Recipes* (Barboursville, VA: Barboursville Methodist Church, undated, circa late 1940s).

A quarter century later such cookbooks had doubled in size, with recipes presented in the same format and length, just with more variety. More residents in the county contributed recipes. Table 5.2 does the same for the mid-1970s as Table 5.1 for the late 1940s. The variety of dishes had expanded, more than doubled, since the 1940s, to over four hundred. Old traditional recipes and dishes did not fade away, but women added to their core body of foods Italian, Mexican, and Chinese dishes. Casseroles came into their own, while appetizers increased in variety and became more elegant. As the influence of national media increased travel, and

Table 5.2. Categories of Madison County Recipes, with examples, circa 1975

Appetizers, Beverages, Soups	
	Developed ham puffs, cheese puffs, spinach dip, shrimp dip, cheese-sausage balls, crab tarts, cocktail sauce, summer daiquiri, punch, fruit punch, vegetable soup, celery soup, New England clam chowder, dried bean soup
Breads and Cereals	
	Corn light bread, English muffin, one-hour buttermilk rolls, sourdough rye bread, crescent rolls, sweet rolls, cinnamon twist coffeecake, oatmeal muffins, blueberry pancakes, spoon bread, corn bread, banana nut bread
Meats, Eggs, and Cheese	
	Steak, beef in cabbage rolls, lasagna, spaghetti, pizza, macaroni casserole, beef and noodle casserole, meat loaf, chop suey, barbecue, Mexican chicken, chicken salad, tuna casserole, deviled eggs, hard cooked eggs
Vegetables	
	Asparagus bake, green bean casserole, baked beans, broccoli and ham casserole, squash casserole, corn pudding, stuffed onions, potato and chicken soup, brown rice, baked tomato halves
Salads and Salad Dressings	
	Chicken mold, shrimp salad, tuna salad, four bean salad, beet salad, cabbage salad, slaw, sauerkraut relish, vegetable salad, fruit salad, orange jello salad, tossed salad dressing, mayonnaise dressing, French dressing
Desserts	
	Apple cake, banana cake, carrot cake, cherry cheese cake, chocolate cake, fruit cake, Italian cream cake, pound cake, rum cake, lemon pie, coconut raisin pie, apple pie, chess pie, moonshine pie, strawberry pie, stuffed baked apples, cheese cake, fruit cobbler, coconut bars, fudge
Pickles and Preserves	
	Orange marmalade, sweet cauliflower pickle, pickled peaches, okra pickle

Source: The Madison Cookbook (Madison, VA: Ladies Auxiliary, Madison Volunteer Fire Department, 1975).

arrival of new residents with different culinary experiences had their effects on the county's homesteaders, one could witness the transformation. The source for Table 5.2 listed over four hundred recipes, well over twice the number reflected in Table 5.1. A third table could have been constructed based on the categories of recipes found in community cookbooks published in the 1990s and early 2000s to demonstrate that the corpus of recipes were now settling down into a familiar compendium, much as had happened in the 1940s and 1950s after all the changes in foods and their preparation of the 1920s and 1930s had been integrated into Madison's cooking information ecosystem.[78]

Curiously, Jell-O survived the transition into the 1990s, despite growing interest in eating less sugar.[79] Why do we care about Jell-O? In American discussions about "good" and "bad" foods over the past half-century, Jell-O was routinely served up as an example of unhealthy food. Jell-O was the brand of packaged ingredients used to make this dish, and was probably embraced by the vast majority of women across the entire second half of the century.[80] However, the word had evolved into the generic phrase *jello*, much like *Xeroxing* to mean photocopying, although the term was part of a brand: Xerox. Finally, in these cookbooks we see the migration toward healthier alternatives in ingredients and substitutes for sugar evident in society at large.

Before continuing, it is useful to examine the grammar of the written recipe, even at the risk that every reader is already familiar with it—itself an observation about the extent of standardization in how such information was presented for nearly a hundred years—and that it diverts attention from the thrust of this chapter. What happened to recipes in Madison demonstrates that events there did not unfold outside of national trends. Two simple examples from 1957 show "old" and "new" content, but presented in similar format, with the old assuming a preexisting body of knowledge of the reader, the new one a more scientific, precisely measured format.

CHEESE TOAST

Put through grinder 1 small peeled white onion, 3 strips of bacon, raw, and ½ lb. American cheese.

Mix with a form and spread on bread strips which have been toasted on one side. This is enough spread for one loaf of bread. Place on a cooky sheet under broiler until the spread is bubbly and brown.

—Mrs. Edward M. Allen

CHEESE DROPS

8 oz. Cheese Whiz
½ stick butter
1 cup flours

Mix well. Make small balls. Chill. Pre-heat oven to 450°. Bake until brown and crisp.

—Mrs. James K. Barr[81]

Misspelling of the word *cookie* is intentional. In both, assumptions are obvious. Readers would have been expected to know what "bread strips" were, how to toast them (e.g., popup toaster or in an oven), type of bread to use, what a "cooky sheet" (type of pan) was, and how to preheat an oven (electrical or gas assumed, no longer wood stoves). While for twenty years the format remained similar, the content became more precise with respect to ingredients.

Women finally acquired their own identity, rather than remaining masked behind the name of their husband. An example from 1978 illustrates the evolution.

HOT CRAB DIP

6 oz. canned crab meat	8 oz. cream cheese
1 Tbsp. milk	1/1 tsp. horseradish
2 Tbsp. finely chopped onion	⅛ tsp. Worcestershire sauce
¼ t. salt	¼ tsp. pepper
toasted almonds	

Mix all ingredients together in small casserole or ramekin. Bake at 350° for 15 minutes. Top with almonds. Serve with crackers.

—Ann Plannenstiel[82]

Now readers were expected to know the language of measurement tools, such as that "Tbsp" meant tablespoon. The contributor assumed people had Worcestershire sauce or horseradish. Both were not always staples in Madison homes twenty or thirty years earlier. The cook was assumed to now own casserole containers, an addition to kitchens of the 1960s and 1970s, much like recipes in the 1980s and 1990s assumed kitchens had microwave ovens.

A third example of a recipe, this one from 1997, while lengthy, came from a cookbook with many recipes, and while in the same format as those of forty years earlier, contained more instructions and reflected the broadening variety of foods consumed in Central Virginia. The book was still published in spiral binding, printed by a press specializing in community cookbooks. The one from 1957 was manufactured by a local print shop, probably by the staff at the *Orange Review*, which published almost all other local pamphlets and booklets at the time.

NACHOS SUPREME

1 lb. hamburger	1 T. flour
1 pkg. taco seasoning mix	1 c. shredded lettuce
1 can pinto beans	1 c. diced tomatoes
1 sm. Onion	Sliced jalapeno peppers
12 oz. shredded cheese	Sour cream
1 T. bacon grease	

In a medium size skillet fry hamburger with chopped onions. Cook until meat is done. Drain grease, then add taco seasoning mix (use directions on package), then set pan aside. In another medium-size pan, put 1 tablespoon bacon grease in and let it get hot over medium heat. Once it starts to sizzle, add or sprinkle flour across to brown. When flour starts to brown, add the entire can of pinto beans and immediately start to mash them with a potato masher. Do this for approximately 5 minutes or until beans are mostly mashed. [Instructions continue for an equal number of words, ed. note].

—Dana Amos[83]

OTHER SOURCES AND TYPES OF INFORMATION

Community cookbooks did not reflect the full repertoire of available recipes. Missing from this paper trail were instructions on how to make coffee, prepare a cured country ham, or fry eggs and bacon. All three were staples of a Madison county diet for two centuries. Homemakers today would tell us that preparing these foods was so commonly known that there was no need to document them, unless someone came up with a novel way of preparing them.[84]

Other classes of absent items included alcoholic beverages. In rural Virginia prior to the mid-twentieth century it was customary for farm families to make their own hard liquor, various invigorated fruit drinks (including apple cider), and some even beer, but not wine.[85] Wineries came to Madison County in the 1960s and 1970s, but did not emerge as significant producers of quality wines until the 1990s, and even then, most of their output was sold into regional and national markets.[86] Madison County did not have a wine drinking tradition. Even after Prohibition lifted in the 1930s, making it possible to buy commercially manufactured hard liquor at state controlled A.B.C. stores, the tradition continued of making beverages out of corn and wheat, done almost entirely by men. Given the Southern and specifically Baptist and Methodist admonitions against alcoholic beverages, consumption was partially hidden, although with a wink and smile as most men in the county enjoyed their bourbon and their wives affected a look of disapproval, as expected of them. So, it is no surprise that "booze" never made it into the food ephemera as it did, however, in such rural communities as New England and the upper Midwest.

Other sources of information about food and cooking were widely available to women in Madison County beyond their locally published cookbooks. As early as 1915, for example, the Virginia State Horticultural Society disseminated information about how to cook apples. That information made it into Madison County for two reasons. First, like other Virginians, Madisonians and those in surrounding counties prepared apples for human consumption in many ways, only feeding leftover apples to their pigs. Second, Madison County grew apples for sale across the region. Most farms had a few apple trees to provide for a family's needs. In the case of the 1915 publication, we see the two reasons conjoined in the text accompanying information about apples: "for the purpose of increasing the consumption of apples and for exploiting in particular the superior quality of Virginia apples in flavor, appearance and square packing."[87] Orchards and packing plants existed throughout the twentieth century; that business still continues.

The Virginia Federation of Home Demonstration Clubs, too, produced information about cooking distributed through local clubs. Information gained in all parts of the state was shared in most of the state's 95 counties, including in parts of over three dozen cities. Members of these Virginia clubs, with over thirty thousand members by the early post-World War II period, continued functioning into the next century, although under a new name: Extension Homemakers Clubs. The county normally had a baker's dozen of these. As with local cookbooks, below each recipe published by the statewide organization appeared the name of the woman who submitted it and the identity of her home county. Five of the women who tested the submitted recipes in the 1940s came from Madison County, three others from nearby Louisa County; no other county in Central Virginia had even one judge. Over one thousand women contributed recipes from across the state; many had been handed down mother to daughter over several generations.[88] Table 5.3 catalogs the variety of recipes collected by the Federation. Nearly twenty years later, in 1964, the "Women's Club

Table 5.3. Categories of Recipes collected by the Virginia Federation of Home Demonstration Clubs, circa 1946

Beverages and Canapés	Salad Dressings
Fruits	Dessert Sauces
Breads	Pies and Pastries
Meats	Cake
Poultry	Frostings
Sea food	Cookies
Cheese and Eggs	Candy
Vegetables	Preserves, Relishes, and Pickles
Salads	Puddings and other Desserts

Source: The Virginia Federation of Home Demonstration Clubs, *Recipes from Old Virginia* (Richmond, VA: Dietz Press, 1946).

Leaders in the Virginias" circulated nine hundred recipes submitted by women from across the state. Mary Anne Rogers, a state home economist, commenting on Virginia recipes, observed that many "have been family favorites for many generations," and "have been handed down from mother to daughter over the years," while "others are adaptations of old recipes made by modern Virginia and West Virginia homemakers to fit their busy schedules."[89]

Yet another horde of information about food and cooking are the private files of rural cooks. These are collections of recipes, newspaper articles, and handwritten notes from friends or the owner of the files, altering someone else's recipes and comments. It seemed every woman had these, kept somewhere in their kitchen. They varied from a drawer full of papers to a file drawer somewhere else, but most had some sort of small "kitchen scrapbook" in which they wrote their notes and stored little pieces of paper. It was not uncommon for a woman to use these for thirty, forty, or more years before passing hers down to a female relative in the next generation. Dishes cooked frequently never made it into these little ephemeral collections, because their preparation was burned into the cook's minds, such as how to prepare a country ham, corn bread, French toast, or a popular recipe for hot rolls. Few of these scrapbooks from Virginia women make it into libraries, and to the best of our knowledge, none from Madison County.

The one owned by Dot Tappy now belongs to one of her daughters and dates its beginning to 1938, the year she married, and was used by her until her death in 1982. Her daughter, Dora, now consults it from time to time. The elder Tappy's filing system was a book entitled, *Kitchen Scrap Book: Designed to give the housewife a practical place in which to keep not only her own favorite recipes but those collected from her friends.*[90]

Her book has a few basic printed recipes, such as for biscuits (not to be confused with *rolls*), but then has empty pages where, in this instance, there is a recipe in her own hand for "rolls." The color of the ink in which it is written suggests she must have added it in the 1930s.[91] The next section was for Breads and there, too, she had her own recipes, including a very Southern dish, spoon bread, and among the others for breads, one for buttermilk rolls. Glued on other blank pages are printed recipes snipped from local newspapers. Tappy dated some recipes, such as the one from 1969 for Eggnog Pound Cake that her note said she obtained from Clara Leigh, a friend. It appears that she added recipes in two waves, a group in the 1930s through the 1940s, another batch in the 1960s, which would make sense. In the 1930s she was a bride and farm wife building her database and then later updating these when new ingredients and dishes began arriving in Madison County. In the 1970s she experimented far less than before, relying on her now tried-and-proven repertoire of dishes for which she had a positive reputation among her peers and relatives.[92]

Like her cohorts with their community cookbook recipes, she had mastered a body of cooking knowledge. Her written notes for preparing food were brief, concentrating instead on ingredients, cooking temperatures, and on subtle features of the process. For example, her hand written recipe for sugar cookies, dated 1963, came from a friend simply listed as "Helen;" she obviously knew which Helen. She listed the ingredients, such as two eggs, one cup of sugar, and so forth, then wrote, "mix the ingredients as listed. Makes a stiff dough. Chill 1 hr. or more. Roll on a mixture of half powdered sugar and flour. As you roll the dough out this mixture will stick to it [rolling pin?, ed. note] and this makes a nice crisp cookie when baked." She had no instructions on the baking process, because she knew how to bake cookies. Or, take as another example her recipe for damson preserves: "¾ to 1 lb. sugar (I use ¾ lb.), 1 qt. seeded damsons, 1 cup water. Mix the above. Cook until desired thickness." She noted that this recipe came from Ruth Roberts in 1967.[93]

Similar shorthand could be found in all Madison community cookbooks. Contributors knew the skill levels of their readers; that they too shared a common body of knowledge about ingredients and cooking, a collection of tacit knowledge both learned and discussed in similar ways. There seemed to be no controversy over the matter as they all shared a common set of values and similar knowledge and skills. Their mutual understanding began to fracture in the 1970s, however, as new residents brought different bodies of information into the county's information ecosystems and began integrating these into its collective databases, a process that could be seen in the evolving recipes published in local community cookbooks. Between that experience and a further codification of how to present recipes that professional cookbook publishers initiated in the 1920s (detailed list of ingredients and amounts first, followed by explicit instructions on what to do with them), cooks provided increased amounts of detail. For example, by the 1990s, one local cookbook was explaining that the oven had to preheat to 325 degrees, that wine had to be poured into a frying pan, and so forth.[94] But too much should not be read into that observation, because cookbooks kept appearing in the new century with shortened instructions too.[95]

Earlier I mentioned that other cookbooks and sources of information made their way into Madison, especially from nearby counties, mostly from Orange and Culpepper. They paralleled in form, organization, and content the Madison ones. Table 5.4 lists some of the more widely available ones in Madison County. Almost all were acquired in that county through clubs and churches or for sale in various shops. By the end of World War II, as a national format for presenting such information about food had spread to all four corners of the nation and to the local and in self-publishing operations of thousands of community organizations, these materials were presented in an almost universally familiar manner. They were bound as spiral publications in roughly 6 × 8 inch trim sizes, printed by local newspapers and small regional publishers, all of whom relied on presses often more frequently used for printing similar-sized weekly church bulletins, civic club newsletters, and pamphlets prepared by historical societies, churches, and civic clubs. Their distinctions often could only be found in their brief introductions that discussed motives for publication.[96]

Table 5.4. Cookbooks from Counties Neighboring Madison County, 1970s–1990s

Sponsors	*Title*	*Year*
Grace Episcopal Church	*Favorite Recipes of Jefferson's Country*	1971
Jr. Women's Club, Orange	*What's Cooking?*	1973
Walkers Methodist Church	*Favorite Recipes*	1974
Hinton Ave Methodists	*Recipes from Shadows of Monticello*	1976
Sycamore Park PTO, Culpeper	*Favorite Recipes from Sycamore Park*	1978
Extension Homemakers Clubs, Orange County	*A Taste of Orange County*	1979
Lake of the Woods Fire & Rescue Company	*Book of Favorite Recipes*	1981
Jr. Women's Club, Manassas	*The Virginia Hostess*	1991
Jr. Women's Club of Orange	*A Taste of Tradition*	1997
Orange Co. Nursing Home	*Sharing Our Best*	2004

MOTIVES FOR SHARING AND USING INFORMATION

Motives for using information have rich literature, as they have been the subject of considerable interest to students of information uses, and so need not detain us here. My findings align only somewhat with those of others, because mine suggest that social bonding was an extremely important motive, along with the practical need to learn in order to carry on one's daily activities, such as safe preparation of meals.[97] The experience in Madison County suggests that motives involved reinforcing one's social position within a community, too, in this case with other women, and in cementing their status within their families.

Simultaneous to social roles, county home economists working with the county agents coordinated prioritization of the kind of information they and the citizens of the county wanted. An internal report prepared by the Virginia Extension Service at the end of the 1950s described Madison's process:

> In recent years program planning in Madison County has been a cooperative venture on the part of the Extension workers and lay leaders. The needs and interests are expressed by the county people, following a close study of trends, outlook information, and general data, which are available about the county. The agents call in a group of county leaders who are representative of the agricultural interests, the different socio-economic levels, the various home economic interests, and other citizens who have a general knowledge of all areas of the county.[98]

This pattern of behavior remained intact for the rest of the century. It represented a departure from the earlier pattern of the 1920s–early 1950s of presidents of home demonstration clubs and a few local leaders setting priorities that were "loosely planned on the basis of spotty information."[99] Not to be overlooked were the intensity of the activities. One local home economist recollected a half century later that there were meetings with women almost every night somewhere in the county: "a 4-H function, a Home Demonstration Club function, a church function where we were representing Extension, a school function, a Lions Club function, or something," adding, "every night!" These events were widely attended by citizens.[100] In short, women and farmers owned the priorities and had "skin in the game." That commitment provides context for understanding the role of local publications.

The issue of motives raises interesting questions about the use of information in these publications and events. There are two sides to the issue:

why people bothered to submit recipes or participate in the production of such volumes and, second, why acquire these? Additionally, one might ask, were they used? Anne Bower, the historian most associated with the study of American community cookbooks, argued that these publications helped to establish a woman's authority as an *expert* within her home, much like publishing in another profession did in someone's line of work. She contended that publication of a recipe or cookbook enhanced her social *status* within her family.[101] One might add that publishing in such an anthology represented a form of self expression; yet conformed to a standard format for presenting ingredients with precise amounts (e.g., ¼ tsp. rather than "a pinch of salt"), followed by instructions for preparing a dish. Her argument held for younger women contributing to these publications, some recruited to do so by their mothers involved in a church or civic organization's publishing project. Her argument perhaps weakens, however, when applied to older women who already had established whatever reputations they were going to achieve in the sphere of cooking both within their families and wider community. These women were more likely to be motivated by a desire to help their church raise funds or for some other project in which publishing a community cookbook was a proven way to do that.

There is a more interesting question: Did people buy and use this class of information? After examining over two dozen community cookbooks from Madison and surrounding counties, the ephemera suggests a mixed answer. On the one hand, well over half were in excellent condition, as if never consulted. The others showed signs of use, but none were annotated with handwritten notes of the user. It has long been known that if someone used a cookbook of any kind, it was done in a kitchen while cooking, the evidence being grease spots on the pages from splattered butter or cooking oil, flower, or milk and water damage. Some exhibited these forms of evidence; others did not. The *Barboursville's Treasure of Personal Recipes* (published late 1940s), produced by the women of the local Methodist Church, is an example of a highly used one, with tape holding it together, the title page torn, and stains on many pages.[102] So, we can be certain some were consulted, probably on a regular basis. Since most were shelved in a kitchen cabinet, we can imagine that many were briefly consulted, at least for the data on measures and weights, since so many of them included such information in appendices.

A class of information barely touched upon, but for which a substantial body of literature exists, is the publications distributed by home economics agents, such as the pamphlet discussed earlier about Virginia apples.[103] Home economists distributed these at demonstration club meetings, especially if the Cooperative Extension Service at the Virginia Polytechnic Institute had published them. Their contents were discussed, often demonstrated too. A cook would not simply have acquired a publication to add to her collection. Rather, she had her interest in the subject piqued and her confidence reinforced in using that new information.

One example suffices to illustrate these collections of information. In May 1966, the Extension Service in collaboration with the U.S. Department of Agriculture published Bulletin number 271 of a series on food, *Curing Ham Virginia Style: With Recipes for Preparing.*[104] One would think all rural Virginia housewives who had been born since the 1600s knew how to cure, cook, and serve a ham; even their husbands knew how to do that. But such publications did more than provide recipes; in this one, only 3.5 pages out of 19 provided recipes. Rather, it described how to butcher a pig, normally done by the farmer and his wife in the fall once it became cooler outside, and discussed what ingredients were needed to cure it, followed by the latest thinking regarding curing techniques. This publication discussed how to bone and carve a ham. It contained over 20 photographs to demonstrate each step. Madison's home economics extension agent, Judy C. Fray, distributed copies, largely through her demonstration club meetings. Other publications discussed chicken, lamb, beef, and every conceivable type of vegetable grown in Virginia, as well as bees and fruits.

It is only a question of time before historians of information will want to discuss gender-related issues. Anne Bower, reflecting the burgeoning interest in women's history of the 1990s, waded in regarding community cookbooks. While it is not clear how fully information—facts—fit into the discussion as opposed to messages those communicated, Bower argued they were linked tightly together, because these publications were the provinces of women. In cookbooks produced in Central Virginia, the recipes were developed by women. Some attributions were by given names of individuals (e.g., "Shirley Hopkins") across the entire period, while most were cited by married name and frequently with their first given name (e.g., "Mrs. M. W. Weaver [Mary])," even in those published late in the century. On occasion, both full names were used, for example for a grits spoon bread recipe from "Mrs. Montie Rea Carpenter (Nancy Clore)."[105] Historian Jessamyn Nuehaus argued that even the table of contents demonstrated gender segregation of recipes, with sweets and desserts often appearing early in these books with numerous recipes as examples of women's culinary interests, while those of greater concern to men, largely meat recipes, received less coverage, usually later in cookbooks.[106] Virginia cookbooks did not reflect that pattern, however. Some started with ostensibly women's foods, such as salads and vegetables, others with supposedly men's foods, such as meats.[107] Still others were partially in the order in which foods were served, beginning with appetizers, followed by breads.[108]

Closer to women's roles were brief statements of intent for why they were published. For it was a fact that they did not produce many other types of books, with the exception of gardening guides, and even then on a far more limited basis. The vast majority of local community publications authored by women were contributed cookbooks. Church cookbooks usually provided a short history of the congregation, some of which dated to the eighteenth century, such as Walker's Methodist parish in nearby Albemarle County.[109] The ladies of the Madison County Rescue Squad inscribed their publication in the 1970s with as full an expression of the book's purpose and value as one can find in any of the regional publications and so is worth quoting in full:

> This book is dedicated to the modern home. In our home today, as always, life is centered around our kitchens. It is with this thought in mind that we, the sponsors, have compiled these recipes. Some of them are treasured old family recipes. Some are brand new, but every single one reflects the love of good cooking that is so very strong in this country of ours.[110]

A subtext inserted afterwards adds to the humor and fun associated with such a project: "The recipes in this book may not have been laboratory tested, but their merit has been established by civic and women's groups everywhere and the most critical group of all—husbands!"[111] Note, too, the reference to "laboratory tested," evidence of a changed view of how the validity of information was increasingly judged. Crigler's fingerprints were in evidence in such thinking.

Another publication from the same period spoke about how enthusiastically women all over the county contributed so many hundreds of recipes and that some of the nearly five hundred published had multiple attributions. The editors, all local women and the community's home economic extension agent, made it clear why they published the book: "Your purchase of this book will help to restore an historical site in Madison County and will benefit the Madison Fire Auxiliary."[112] This book also listed the names of 66 ladies, almost all "Mrs." who tested the recipes. The list reads like a *Who's Who* of the county, with families participating that had lived in the area for over a century and who were leading social, economic, and political lights in the community: Berry, Blankenbaker, Carpenter, Clore, Estes, Fray, Graves, Tappy, Weaver, and the Yowell clan, among others.[113] It seemed that not participating in this project would have been seen as a circumstance to be avoided. The spirit of community involvement and contribution to the pool of local information about cooking was not confined to the sentiments of one decade. A church publication from the 1990s introducing the volume commented that "the entries in this cookbook were submitted by members and friends of Pleasant Grove Baptist Church. Although they are not all original, they are dishes which have been used and enjoyed by the contributors."[114]

Many of these books were prolifically embellished with advertisements, paid for by local businesses in Madison and surrounding counties. While many included advertisements from businesses involved with food, such as the Piedmont Frozen Food Company, The Bavarian Chef (restaurant), and the Madison IGA Foodliner (small supermarket), the creators of these cookbooks were not necessarily endorsing one commercial enterprise over another. They gladly accepted advertising from gas stations, real estate firms, hardware stores, banks, automobile dealers, and even from a funeral home (Clore Funeral Home, Inc. of Culpeper County). One suspects that the wives of many local business owners imposed on the generosity of their spouses to fund publication.

The prior quote suggests that publication of a recipe did not mean it had to be original, as many were variations of widely used ones. Rather, a recipe—a piece of information—carried with it a social significance, because it came from someone the reader knew, probably respected for her cooking acumen, and that tied the purchaser to the wider community. Unlike scholarly writing, which strives for originality to justify publication, these could appear just fine if they were not novel, so long as they were personal and tied to the sentiment of community and clan. The women at another church may have caught that essence when describing how their collection was put together: "The publication of the cook book originated at our monthly fellowship suppers. Recipes for the dishes that had been brought were exchanged with the idea that good recipes are like kind thoughts, to be shared and remembered."[115] The women of Madison County used cooking information to build and sustain community.

Because we are discussing a Southern county during the period when the Civil Rights Movement was in full force and its consequences unfolding over the rest of the century, we should ask: What was the role of cooking information in the African American communities in Madison? These women lived in a parallel, if more impoverished, universe for the bulk of this period. Across the state their information ecosystem included their own county agents, home economists in some counties, churches, civic organizations, and segregated schools until the 1960s. Not until the 1980s did the two races mix in civic organizations. The Agricultural Extension Service at VPI ordered all its employees to stop offering segregated programs across the state in the mid-1980s, an edict that did not sit well in many communities.[116]

African American women learned to cook from their grandmothers, mothers, and aunts, shared recipes that were hand-written or verbally communicated, and less frequently than white women acquired new information from extension agents. Edna Lewis (1916–2006), an African American woman raised in Orange County, who went on to author several cookbooks in the 1970s that relied extensively on the culinary and food handling practices of Virginia, became a major source of information about how both White and Black farmers learned about food and how they handled and cooked it. The experiences were similar across the two races. For example, she wrote, "I learned about cooking and flavor as a child, watching my mother prepare food in our kitchen in Virginia. She took great care with the food she fed her large family and our assorted guests and I suppose I just naturally followed her example."[117] She reminded her readers that men played an important role, such as in the butchering of hogs and their preparation of hams and bacon, while women processed other parts of the pig in November or December in the same week that butchering took place.[118]

Publishing recipes as books was often beyond their financial means, although extant church bulletins from African American churches carried some recipes. Even these publications were rarely produced. Recall that the African American population in Madison County was quite small and their congregations tiny, frequently with less than a hundred members. But they received the same publications produced by VPI as well as instructions that came from its Black counterpart, Hampton Institute, which had trained African American county agents for decades. Ladies of both races also taught each other. An African American maid/cook for a white middle class farm wife was expected to be an outstanding cook, and also known for her specialties, such as preparation of fried chicken, in addition to specialties consumed less frequently by whites, such as pig intestines, known as *chitlins*.[119]

By the early 1970s, a few Black children began participating in 4-H programs and received instruction from their teachers about nutrition and food, particularly in the elementary grades. Home economist Judy Ann Fray recalled a particular interest in the Black community in learning how to sew, with homemakers participating in sewing demonstrations held at the War Memorial Building in the same decade.[120]

AN ENDURING INFORMATION ECOSYSTEM

Historians of information are apt to think of information as social glue bonding together professions, groups, communities, and nations. How women gathered, organized, stored, and used information in Madison County reinforces that thesis. Their history of information about food demonstrates that women more than men led the charge in using food facts to sustain community, reinforce one's own gender-specific role, and establish their competence. The closer their use of information applied to home life, the more women managed the movement of information to children, their peers, and the men in their lives. In the process, these women created a thick information ecosystem that relied on an extensive infrastructure of publishers and publications, organizations, and meeting places.

Their information ecosystem was not static. In the early 1990s, Demonstration Club attendance dropped sharply when the Extension Service made the decision to use those events to foster development of leadership skills among women, even renaming the clubs "Community Leadership." However, these women overwhelmingly rejected that change, most of whom were above the age of 50. They viewed the monthly meetings as occasions to get together with friends, and insisted on meeting at times convenient to them, such as in late mornings. Contributing to the decline in attendance was the fact that beginning in the 1980s, younger women could not participate during the day as they were working or had children to care for. By the end of the century, they also had many alternative sources of information; the Internet would soon be one of them. Declines in membership in 4-H clubs were discernable in the 1990s, too, but not to the same degree as in Home Demonstration Clubs. Class attendance in food preparation courses, always an elective, began to decline slowly in the 1990s as other interests competed for the attention of female students. None of these trends, however, indicated a diminution in the consumption of information regarding food, but rather a shift to other ways of obtaining and using it.

The information itself was quite comprehensive in that it covered all aspects of food management and consumption. It evolved in response to numerous exogenous forces, such as the arrival of electric and gas stoves, television, new ingredients, scientific information (particularly about safer canning methods, nutrition, and measurements), and recipes novel to the area.

Rising economic prosperity across Central Virginia in the second half of the twentieth century made it possible to expand school programs, to supply the wherewithal to publish cookbooks, and to acquire automobiles with which to attend increasing numbers of demonstrations and other civic events scattered around the county. A rising tide of formal education at both the high school and college levels made it possible to disseminate more information about homemaking in general, and specifically about nutrition, health, and safe food preparation. As Madison native and home economist Betty Barger emphasized, knowledge acquired by children and women over time became more scientific and precise, extending people's knowledge beyond what they had acquired from their mothers and grandmothers.[121]

A crucial facilitative force at work in the background was Virginia's land grant schools, VPI and Hampton Institute, which for nearly a century trained and deployed home economists all over the state, particularly VPI. As home economist Judy Ann Fray pointed out, VPI "pushed" new information and training out to the counties, using female home economists to teach women and girls, male county agents to work with men and boys. Both genders optimized their time by creating networks of clubs and organizations to disseminate information and teaching skills through demonstration clubs, 4-H, and class curriculums. By having much of the content for all groups and clubs essentially coming from one source—VPI—facts could be coordinated, timing their introduction, and contradictory data avoided. The end product for VPI and local political leadership was community and local economic development and the ability to improve lives. Areas of emphasis did not change for a century: plants, textiles, food, and farm animals. The strategy worked hardly unchanged until the late 1980s–early 1990s when new technologies, increased number of working mothers and women outside the home or farm, changing priorities of VPI, and more diverse sources of information led to changes.

Reflecting on the changes that began in the 1980s and intensified in the 1990s, Fray observed that the club system worked effectively in Madison County for its intended groups. The system worked for "accepting" information from VPI. But later there was a price to pay: loss of emphasis on the "proper way to do things" and the loss of "personal interactions," as people increasingly turned to the Internet or television, for example. Mrs. Crigler would have seen this as a "deterioration of standards."[122] The historian has to ponder: Was that a consequence or was it a new way of creating social structures in Madison less dependent on the exchange and use of information about food? Time will tell.

The ability of rural housewives to remain current in their consumption of new information was not slowed by any obvious circumstances, except perhaps declining health. At the other end of life, schools taught children, and 4-H did the same, along with the Future Homemakers of America chapters. Besides enjoying the benefits of delicious satisfying meals, men were included through their advertising support, adoption of modern farming practices, and participation in civic and religious affairs. People lived within the local food information ecosystem.

So, we come back to where we started, asking if a group of people could work together and become dependent on each other if they were not required to be part of an organization that could order them to behave in certain ways, like a company or a diplomatic service. What behavior voluntarily was in evidence in the women and children of Madison County? It turns out much of it was similar to what one could observe, for example, in the case of the Spanish diplomatic service, where there, too, existed information ecosystems, infrastructures, and regular flows of information.[123] People in Madison also shared information, respected each other, and willingly found value in the communal use of facts. Food was of interest to everyone, but also the social milieu it generated. Attendance at 4-H meetings and home demonstration clubs remained high for decades, suggesting there was value and enjoyment in the effort. The mechanisms for the exchange of information—VPI's publications, cookbooks, newsletters, and presentations—paralleled those found in corporations and governments. The changes that came in the 1990s paralleled what occurred in the wider American society in work lives and in private affairs.[124] Information ecosystems flourished, as did information infrastructures, and information flowed about the county at an observable rate, as documented by the frequency and regularity of publication of newsletters, newspapers, and cookbooks. The conclusion we can reach is that it is quite possible that many people in numerous circumstances relied on information as their tool and way of creating social structures, a point widely confirmed by students of information use.[125] The ladies of Madison County did not know about information ecosystems or infrastructures, let alone about information flows and constructs, but they certainly demonstrated their ability to create and use information within the context of their lives.[126]

Not discussed in this chapter, but repeatedly called out by veterans of the Extension Service or 4-H, were the life skills acquired in the process of participating in this information ecosystem. Let one 4-Her of the 1960s explain: "I can speak in front of groups without a care. That's a direct result from doing demonstrations each and every year since I was 8 years old. Competitive attitude. Yes, I am trained to compete, but also to recognize and applaud achievement in others. Self-confidence. I know I can do anything I set my mind to. I did it as a child in 4-H."[127]

We next turn to a far larger community, also held together by a homogenous culture and widely practiced norms, but situated within a corporation to see what its behavior was like with respect to information ecosystems and infrastructures. We will see that the ladies of Madison County had much in common with the salesmen at IBM.

NOTES

1. Except next door in Orange County, the most urban county among the rural communities, and the largest in population. Albemarle County was also rural except for the city of Charlottesville and surrounding neighborhoods. That county has been transforming into an urban one since the 1990s.
2. In the spirit of full disclosure, your author was from Orange County, located next to Madison County, and thus brings decades of tacit knowledge of the region to this chapter.
3. Overview of social structure based on observations by the author living on and off in the region since 1962. In the 1960s and early 1970s, author also worked for the *Orange Review*, which also owned and operated the *Madison Eagle*—the newspaper of record for Madison County.
4. For recent examples, see David B. Gracy, "Cowman's-Eye View of the Information Ecology of the Texas Cattle Industry from the Civil War to World War I," *Information and Culture* 51, no. 2 (May–June 2016): 164–191; Katie Pierce Meyer, "Technology in Architectural Practice: Transforming Work with Information, 1960s–1990s," *Information and Culture* 51, no. 2 (May–June 2016): 249–266.
5. I paid attention to this community in James W. Cortada, *All the Facts: A History of Information in the United States since 1870* (New York: Oxford University Press, 2016).
6. Donald O. Case, *Looking for Information: A Survey of Research on Information Seeking, Needs, and Behavior,* 3rd ed. (Bingley, UK: Emerald, 2012): 357.
7. Prior to 1950, more children went to college who lived in towns, because so many of their parents were knowledge workers, such as teachers, lawyers, bankers, ministers, and owners of local newspapers and radio stations. They valued college education but, just as important, could afford to send their children to a state college or university more easily than the more cash-strapped farm families of Central Virginia.
8. James W. Cortada, "The Information Ecosystems of National Diplomacy: The Case of Spain, 1815–1936," *Information & Culture* 48, no. 2 (2013): 222–259.
9. Described in considerable detail in Cortada, *All the Facts.*
10. For examples, see Solvveig Wikstrom et al., *Knowledge and Value: A New Perspective on Corporate Transformation* (London: Routledge, 1994); Kjell S. Johannessen, "Rule Following, Intransitive Understanding and Tacit Knowl-

edge: An Investigation of the Wittgensteinian Concept of Practice as Regards Tacit Knowledge," in Bo Göranzon, Maria Hammarén, and Richard Ennals, eds., *Dialogue, Skill and Tacit Knowledge* (West Sussex: John Wiley & Sons, 2006): 269–294; Marian Adolf and Nico Stehr, *Knowledge* (London: Routledge, 2014); Barry Barnes, *Elements of Social Theory* (Princeton, NJ: Princeton University Press, 1995); Daniel Bell, "The Social Framework of the Information Society," in Michael L. Dertouzos and Joel Moses, eds. *The Computer Age: A Twenty-Year View* (Cambridge, MA: MIT Press, 1979): 163–211; Harry M. Collins and Robert Evans, "The Third Wave of Science Studies: Studies of Expertise and Experience," *Social Studies of Science* 32 (2002): 235–296.

11. Information had to be practical, as called out earlier by F. Dretske, "Putting Information to Work," in P. Hanson, ed., *Information, Language, and Cognition* (Vancouver: University of British Columbia Press, 1990): 112–124 and which I make a central point in Cortada, *All the Facts;* on the limits of using an information needs approach, see N. J. Belkin and A. Vickery, *Interaction in Information Systems: A Review of Research from Document Retrieval to Knowledge-based Systems* (Boston, UK: British Library, 1985): 6. Yet that approach reminds us to pay close attention to the context of information use. Our study is most closely situated in methods used in network analysis, in particular used frequently by R. Marcella and G. Baxter, for example, in their "Information Interchanges," in K. E. Fisher, S. Erdelz and E. F. McKenchnie, eds., *Theories of Information Behavior* (Medford, NJ: Information Today, 2005): 204–209, supplemented with content analysis, such as suggested by K. Krippendorff, *Content Analysis: An Introduction to its Methodology* (Beverly Hills, CA: Sage Publication, 1980).

12. Linda L. Sturz, *Within Her Power: Propertied Women in Colonial Virginia* (New York: Routledge, 2002).

13. U.S. Bureau of the Census.

14. Ibid.

15. For an introduction to this history, see Elmer L. Smith, *Shenandoah Valley Cooking: Recipes and Kitchen Lore* (Middletown, VA: Shenandoah Valley Folklore Society, 1970).

16. U.S. Department of Commerce, U.S. Bureau of the Census surveys.

17. Margaret G. Davis, *Madison County, Virginia: A Revised History* (Madison, VA: Board of Supervisors of Madison County, 1977): 247–249.

18. U.S. Department of Commerce, U.S. Bureau of the Census surveys.

19. Author's personal knowledge based on living at the time in Orange County.

20. Comments to author by Dora Jane Tappy Cortada and Betty Tappy Barger, who grew up in the county.

21. Based on comments made in various conversations with the author by Dot and Carl Tappy, a farming family located in Uno (Madison County), Virginia, 1960s–1970s.

22. This kind of information at the county level began to become available as U.S. Census records were made public. Those for 1930 and 1940 are already avail-

able to the public; 1950's should be by the end of 2020, although the U.S. Bureau of the Census periodically releases localized data down through the most recent decennial census. Crucial to such studies of local information ecosystems are data about literacy and years of schooling, data that U.S. census records began collecting in the early nineteenth century, Margo J. Anderson, *The American Census: A Social History,* 2nd ed. (New Haven, CT: Yale University Press, 2015).

23. Their contributions have long been recognized as important, Hazel T. Craig, *The History of Home Economics* (New York: Practical Home Economics, 1946).

24. Local histories of all the counties in Central Virginia virtually ignore them or only mention them in passing, literally in one or two sentences. See, for example, Davis, *Madison County, Virginia.*

25. For example, when a furniture upholstery demonstration was held, or when a chef demonstrated new recipes and fed the attendees. Interview with Judy Ann Fray, April 7, 2016.

26. "Harry Gibb's Store Joins Madison County's History," *Madison County Eagle*, November 9, 1972, p. 1.

27. Madison County Chamber of Commerce, local telephone directories, 1980–1990.

28. Based on observations by the author in spending over a half century interacting with residents of Madison County.

29. Some of these schools had been built during the Great Depression in the 1930s with federal funding, which accounts for the large library facilities. The schools from this period were made of brick and stone and were modified periodically over the rest of the century, as occurred, for example, with Waverly Yowell Elementary School, located across Route 29 from the Town of Madison.

30. For example, one local farmwife, Dot Tappy, a respected cook in the county, handwrote three other recipes in her scrapbook, including the name to whom she attributed the instructions. Dorothy Tappy, *Kitchen Scrap Book* (Chicago, IL: The Reilly & Lee Co., 1937).

31. Interview with Judy Ann Fray, April 7, 2016.

32. Helen Zoe Veit, *Modern Food, Moral Food: Self-Control, Science, and the Rise of Modern American Eating in the Early Twentieth Century* (Chapel Hill, NC: University of North Carolina Press, 2013): 70–87.

33. U.S. Department of Agriculture, *The Home Demonstration Agent*, AIB 38 (Washington, DC: U.S. Government Printing Office, July 19151): 12.

34. Recollections by many women, some from Madison County, are documented in Karliana Brooks Sakas, *Nine Decades of Making The Best Better: A History of 4-H in Fairfax County, Virginia* (San Jose, CA: Writers Club Press, 2002).

35. Interview with Mary Linda McLearen, March 17, 2016. Her maiden name was Lamb, was raised on a farm in the county, and was active in 4-H, achieving All Star status. Her mother, Mary Lamb, was active in demonstration clubs in the 1950s and 1960s.

36. Interview with Judy Ann Fray, April 7, 2016.

37. Virginia R. Crigler graduated from Longwood College in 1929 with a B.S. in home economics, then taught in public schools until her appointment to the Extension Service in 1939.

38. After leaving the Extension Service, she continued to live in Madison, raising her children, and was active in her church, the local garden club, and promoting concerts, and volunteered in other community activities at the county, regional, and state levels. Asked if she joined a Homemakers Club after 1973, she responded, "No, had no time to do it." Madison County Extension Home Economists/FCS Agents for the period were: Virginia Rucker Crigler (1939–1968), Judy Ann Coates Fray (1968–1973), Laura S. Roach (1973–1974), Helen C. Williams (1974–1977), Jean M. Thornburn (1977–1983), Athena K. Taylor (1984–1990), Clare K. Lillard (19990–1992), and again (2014-present), Christine A. Kastan (1992–2008), and Jilian Tucker Garth (2008–2014).

39. Davis, *Madison County, Virginia*, 250.

40. The education of these home economists was relatively uniform across the nation, shaped by conventional views of women's roles, the desire to model engineering training, and the priorities of the U.S. Department of Agriculture. For a study of their training, using Iowa State College (later University), see, Amy Sue Bix, "Equipped for Life: Gendered Technical Training and Consumerism in Home Economics, 1920–1980," *Technology and Culture* 43, no. 4 (October 2002): 728–754.

41. Interview with Margaret Dawson, March 17, 2016.

42. Interview with Judy Ann Fray, April 7, 2016.

43. Brenda Estes Gore, *Facebook, copy in author's files.*

44. Sakas, *Nine Decades of Making The Best Better,* 115.

45. Mary Linda Lamb, *4-H Member's Record*, February 1971, unpaginated.

46. Considered the glue that held extension services together by both staff and residents in the county, Mrs. Sara U. Gibbs graduated from Madison County High School and from Peery Business School. She became the Extension secretary for Madison County in June 1945, and held the position for over two decades.

47. G. Allan McLearen was a textbook example of an American county agent, the most important source of new information for farmers. He graduated from the Virginia Polytechnic Institute (VPI), the state's "Ag school," in 1940 with a B.S. in dairy husbandry, served as an assistant agent in Fauquier County, then in the U.S. Army during World War II, dispatched as a captain in 1946. That year he returned to old job, this time in nearby Orange County, before beginning his decades of service as the county agent in Madison in April 1948. He died of cancer in the 1960s.

48. "Rap" Owings graduated from the University of Maryland with a degree in animal husbandry in 1953. The following year he began his career as an assistant agent for Madison and Rappahannock Counties. In 1958 he began serving full-time as the assistant agent in Madison County.

49. Citation attached to Mrs. Gene Smith Moody to James C. Bushong, May 21, 1959, copy from Virginia Cooperative Extension—Orange, Virginia, courtesy of Clare K. Lillard, Extension Agent.

50. Immediately following World War II, the Virginia State Department of Education began publishing guidelines and programs to assist teachers in educating children about nutrition, food preparation, food safety, and other related subjects, a publishing program that remained in force all through the period. One such guide was also used to train home economics teachers at Radford College, the source of many female extension agents of the period; *A Guide to Planning Homemaking Education Programs in Virginia High Schools* (Richmond, VA: State Department of Education, 1958). For a history of this initiative, *A Guide to Planning Homemaking Education Programs in Virginia High Schools*, iii, 13–14.

51. For a guide used by Radford home economics students in the 1950s into the 1970s to carry out projects that purpose see Frances M. Hettler and Isabelle R. Thomas, *Meal Management Manual* Dubuque, IA: Wm. C. Brown Company, 1951, and subsequent editions). This volume assumed students had already mastered food preparation, also a class taught at Radford College.

52. The text used at Radford College was prepared by the American Home Economics Association, *Handbook of Food Preparation* (Washington, DC: American Home Economics Association, first edition 1946, various expanded editions to the end of the century).

53. Your author counts among his life-long acquaintances nearly a half dozen home economists trained at Radford. He observed that they continued practices learned in 4-H and at Radford, including use of measuring spoons and vessels when cooking, careful attention to the setting of a dining room table, and the presentation of food at such events as Thanksgiving and Christmas, even a half-century after graduating from college. No doubt, their guests—often also products of that learning experience—put pressure on the host to perform to standards set by Crigler.

54. Extracted from annual yearbooks of the high school, *The Mahi* (Madison, VA, 1960–1967).

55. http://mchs.madisonschools.k12.va.us/teacher-websites (Accessed February 20, 2017).

56. Ibid.

57. Interview with Betty Barger, February 20, 2016. She attended Madison County High School in the early 1960s, graduated from Radford College (today Radford University) with a degree in in home economics, and spent her career as a Virginia home economist.

58. Interview with Dora T. Cortada, February 20, 2016.

59. Gabriel N. Rosenberg, *The 4-H Harvest: Sexuality and the State in Rural America* (Philadelphia: University of Pennsylvania Press, 2016): 2.

60. For an account of what girls did down to the project level, based on experiences in California that paralleled practices in Madison County during the late twentieth and early twenty-first century, see Kiera Butler, *Raise: What 4-H*

Teaches 7 Million Kids and How Its Lessons Could Change Food and Farming Forever (Berkeley: University of California Press, 2014).

61. Described by Clarion B. Trace, “Information in Everyday Life: Boys’ and Girls’ Agricultural Clubs as Sponsors of Literacy, 1900–1920,” *Information & Culture* 49, no. 3 (2014): 265–293.

62. For example, Betty and Dora Tappy, “Madison County Sisters Win Many 4-H Awards,” *Richmond Times Dispatch,* April 8, 1965. Similar news was communicated through the state’s own 4-H newsletter, *Head, Heart, Hands and Health,* published since 1917.

63. Davis, *Madison County, Virginia*, 250.

64. Dorothy Tappy to Dora T. Cortada, January 12, 1972, in possession of the author. The collection of letters consists of nearly one thousand pages, written weekly about local and family events between 1963 and 1982.

65. Some skills were never documented. For example, Dot Tappy prepared large breakfasts and lunches (known as *dinner* in the local vernacular) for workers employed on the farm that were substantial: meats, vegetables, breads, and desserts. The women who grew up in her family in the 1950s and 1960s, and relatives and friends of these children in the 1970s, were amazed at how she could in one day put together what they considered a massive Christmas meal that included a turkey, a country ham, three to four hot vegetables, a salad, hot rolls, and one to two desserts.

66. Lamb, *4-H Member’s Record*, unpaginated.

67. Ibid. When I interviewed her I asked if her mother’s role in teaching her about cooking was unusual; she said “no.” Like many mothers, Mrs. Lamb was also active as a leader and demonstrator in both the 4-H clubs and in the Demonstration Club to which she belonged.

68. Barbara Reddish Tokar to author, October 29, 2016.

69. *Cooking Favorites of Madison* (Madison, VA: Ladies Auxiliary to the Madison Volunteer Fire Department, undated, circa 1970): page C.

70. Ibid.

71. Andrew Abbott, *The System of Professions: An Essay on the Division of Expert Labor* (Chicago: University of Chicago Press, 1988).

72. In Orange County at the home of President James Madison, Montpelier, a horse race has been held the first weekend of November since before World War II. Local civic organizations used the event for fundraising, largely by selling food from local farms and homemakers from Orange, Madison, and other surrounding counties. It was not uncommon for residents to seek out foods they knew were prepared by farmwives known to them by name.

73. Barbara Reddish Tokar to author, October 29, 2016. Scientific research on how humans interact with food has validated the importance of presentation as a critical component of meals being received and consumed, Charles Spence, *Gastrophysics: The New Science of Eating* (New York: Viking,2017): 51, 61–62.

74. *Cooking favorites of Madison*, by Betty, 19, 21, 22, 25, 27, by Dora, 24.

75. Ibid., page g.

76. Ibid., page h. Regarding turkey for 250 people, it was advised to prepare seven turkeys and 75 pounds of potato and 44 pies.

77. W.S.C.S. of the Methodist Church, *Barboursville's Treasure of Personal Recipes* (Barboursville, VA: Barboursville Methodist Church, undated, circa late 1940s).

78. For examples, see Gwen McKee and Barbara Moseley, *BEST of the BEST from Virginia: Selected Recipes from Virginia's Favorite Cookbooks* (Brandon, MS: Quail Ridge Press, 1991); Junior Women's Club of Orange, Virginia, *A Taste of Virginia* (Kearney, NE: Morris Press, 1999); Etlan United Methodist Church, *Recipes and Remembrances* (Kearney, NE: Morris Press, 2003).

79. *Our Favorite Recipes* (Barboursville, VA: Pleasant Grove Baptist Church, undated, circa 1998–1999): 149.

80. Carolyn Wyman, *JELL-O: A Biography* (Orlando, FL: Mariner Books, 2001): 30–71.

81. *Favorite Recipes from Old Virginia* (Cismont, VA: St. Margaret's Chapter, Grace Church Walker's Parish, 1957): 1.

82. Sycamore Park PTO, *A Collection of Recipes* (Culpeper, VA: Sycamore Park PTO, 1978): 2.

83. Junior Women's Club of Orange, *A Taste of Tradition* (Kearney, NE: Morris Press, 1997): 9.

84. Author's wife, Dora Jane Tappy Cortada, raised in Madison County, 1940s–1960s, herself a Virginia trained home economist from Radford College.

85. Charles D. Thompson Jr., *Spirits of Just Men: Mountaineers, Liquor Bosses, and Lawmen in the Moonshine Capital of the World* (Urbana, IL: University of Illinois Press, 2011).

86. Walker Elliott Rowe, *Wandering through Virginia's Vineyards* (Baltimore, MD: Apprentice House, 2006); Richard G. Leahy, *Beyond Jefferson's Vines: The Evolution of Quality Wine in Virginia* (No city: CreateSpace Independent Publishing Platform, 2014): 112–195 for commentary on Madison County wines.

87. Virginia State Horticultural Society, *The Apple Cook Book of Virginia: 207 Distinct Recipes for Using Virginia Grown Apples* (Winchester, VA: Virginia State Horticultural Society, 1915): first page on backside of title page.

88. Virginia Federation of Home Demonstration Clubs, *Recipes from Old Virginia* (Richmond, VA: Dietz Press, 1946).

89. Mary Anne Rogers, *Favorite Recipes of the Virginians* (Montgomery, AL: Favorite Recipes Press, 1964): backside of title page. The author, a state home economist, wrote the entire text based on recipes submitted, requiring fuller instructions on preparing a dish than would normally be seen in such a publication.

90. Tappy, *Kitchen Scrap Book.*

91. Her handwriting was distinctive but had many features common to the style of the day. Some handwritten entries, however, appear just slightly different, suggesting that her mother-in-law who lived in the same house, Mary Margaret Tappy

(1862–1946), may have written those. Mary Tappy was born in Madison County and spent her entire life there, bearing and feeding 15 children and her husband.

92. If your author might add a personal comment, I was the beneficiary of over a hundred of her meals served in all four seasons of the year. I have photographs of some of these meals, which, in my humble opinion were spectacular.

93. Tappy, *Kitchen Scrap Book*, unpaginated.

94. Graves' Mountain Lodge, *Graves' Mountain Cookbook* (Syria, VA: Graves' Mountain Lodge, Inc., undated, circa late 1990s); 59. Some instructions ran to nearly a half page, see for example, p. 58.

95. Etlan United Methodist Church, *Recipes and Remembrances.*

96. Anne L. Bower, ed., *Recipes for Reading: Community Cookbooks, Stories, Histories* (Amherst, MA: University of Massachusetts Press, 1997).

97. Rather, others have focused extensively on issues related to uncertainty, ambiguity, and curiosity, although conceptions began changing in the 1960s. See, for example, A. Schultz, *The Phenomenology of the Social World* (Evanston, IL: Northwestern University Press, 1967). Most studies, although well executed, tend to be narrower than what we attempted, as in the case of studying information seeking in libraries, C. C. Kuhlthau, *Seeking Meaning: A Process Approach to Library and Information Services* (Norwood, NJ: Ablex, 1993). But see also J. D. Johnson, *Cancer-related Information Seeking* (Cresskill, NJ: Hampton Press, 1997) where he introduces the role of social norms into the discussion of information seeking.

98. Moody to Bushong, May 21, 1959.

99. Ibid.

100. Sakas, *Nine Decades of Making The Best Better,* 114–115.

101. Ann Bower, *Recipes for Reading: Community Cookbooks, Stories, Histories* (Amherst: University of Massachusetts Press, 1997).

102. W.S.C.S., *Barboursville's Treasure of Personal Recipes.*

103. VPI's library, for example, had over nine thousand publications produced by the U.S. Department of Agriculture in its collection as of August 2017. Bruce Pencek, of Virginia Tech Libraries, to author, August 2, 2017. The collection also includes publications on food, cooking, and nutrition, some published as early as 1917. Box 1 and 2, and VPI publications in Box 1 from 1932 to 1990, National Agricultural Publications, Ms2011-022, and State/Regional Home and Agricultural Publications, M2012-040, Special Collections, Virginia Tech, Blacksburg, VA.

104. Jo Anne Barton, R. F. Kelly, and P. P. Graham, *Curing Ham—Virginia Style: With Recipes for Preparing*, Bulletin 271 (Blacksburg, VA: Cooperative Extension Service, Virginia Polytechnic Institute, 1966).

105. Ladies Auxiliary, *The Madison Cookbook*, 23.

106. Jessamyn Nuehaus, *Manly Meals and Mom's Home Cooking: Cookbooks and Gender in Modern America* (Baltimore, MD: Johns Hopkins University Press, 2003): 73–99.

107. For an example of the first, see Madison County Rescue Squad Auxiliary, *Madison's Good Cookin'* (Madison, VA: North American Press, undated, circa late 1960s early 1970s) and of the second, *Favorite Recipes of the Virginians.*

108. See, for example, Walker's Parish, *Favorite Recipes from Old Virginia.*

109. Established in 1750, Ibid. Not to be confused with a Walker Methodist church located in Madison County.

110. Madison County Rescue Squad Auxiliary, *Madison's Good Cookin'*, 1.

111. Ibid.

112. *The Madison Cookbook* (Madison, VA: Ladies Auxiliary Madison Volunteer Fire Department, 1975): v.

113. Ibid.

114. *Our Favorite Recipes* (Barboursville, VA: Pleasant Grove Baptist Church, undated, circa late 1990s): ii.

115. *Walker's United Methodist Church Favorite Recipes* (Madison, VA: Walkers United Methodist Church, 1974): 1.

116. Interview with Clare K. Lillard, March 9, 2016. Lillard has worked as a home economics extension agent for Madison, Orange, and Culpeper counties on and off since the 1980s. She is currently (2016) responsible for running the regional 4-H programs.

117. Edna Lewis, *In Pursuit of Flavor* (Charlottesville: University Virginia Press, 2000, reprint of the originally edition published by Alfred A. Knopf, 1988): vii. For additional material on how African Americans worked with food in the Orange/Madison area from the 1930s to the 1970s, see Edna Lewis, *The Taste of Country Cooking* (New York: Alfred A. Knopf, 1976).

118. Lewis, *The Taste of Country Cooking,* 181–185.

119. Paragraph based on the author's personal experience in living in Orange County (1960s–1970s, visiting frequently, 1970s-present) with family connections in Madison County. I was unable to find any African American cookbooks published in Madison County. African Americans relied largely on oral transmission of information, although it was similar in content to what White women did too.

120. Interview with Judy Ann Fray, April 7, 2016.

121. Interview with Betty Barger, February 20, 2016. Barger grew up in Madison County in the 1950s and early 1960s, attended Radford College, and then served as an extension agent for several decades in other Virginia counties from the late 1960s.

122. Interview with Judy Ann Fray, April 7, 2016.

123. Cortada, "The Information Ecosystems of National Diplomacy: The Case of Spain, 1815–1936."

124. Cortada, *All the Facts.*

125. Case drew the same conclusion, when he wrote that in addition to formal sources of information people rely "on informal sources such as friends and family," Case, *Looking for Information,* 375. I draw the distinction that the ladies of Madison County used equally both formal and informal sources.

126. To use Case's phrase, "contest is central to the transfer of information," Ibid., 376.

127. Margaret A. Bogie, in Sakas, *Nine Decades of Making The Best Better,* 54.

Chapter Six

International Sales Information Ecosystems

IBM, 1920s–1980s

For there is nothing more treacherous . . . than the attempt to make precise decisions on the basis of coarse and incomplete information.

—Peter F. Drucker

Much of what constituted IBM's information ecosystem and the infrastructure to support it would look familiar to a diplomat, such as those encountered in Chapter 4. Both worked in top down run organizations, the company out of New York City (later Armonk), the foreign ministry from Madrid. Both had specific types of information they collected, moved about, and relied upon to do their daily work. Users came from similar backgrounds and shared common experiences. Each had their own institutional cultures, rituals, and ways of doing things. But differences existed, too. IBM was buffeted more by changing technologies, while diplomats more by slower unfolding political, economic, and military events. Changing technologies largely involved the arrival then transformation of computers from large expensive mainframes to inexpensive personal computers (PCs) and the connection of computers to each other by telecommunications. IBM was a much larger organization than any diplomatic corps, including Spain's. In 1925, IBM employed nearly four thousand people, in 1985, just over 405,000.[1] Like Spain in 1925, it operated in about the same number of countries, most in Europe, North and South America, and in a smattering of locations in Asia. In 1985, IBM had offices in over 125 countries, and more branch offices (sales offices) than Spain had combined in consulates and embassies. IBM was a business, the Spanish diplomatic service a government agency, spared the pressures of managing profits and losses and generation of revenues, although diplomats argued they, too, had competitors, such as rival countries during wars.

The IBM case explores how largeness in combination with a highly developed corporate culture affects information ecosystems and their infrastructures over time, and how technological innovations did the same with the flow of information, even influencing the kind collected. One quick observation: despite being a behemoth of a computer company, the dominant player in its market, technology had less of an impact on its use of information than management's actions and the influences of corporate culture. Behaviors and information used in the 1920s would have looked familiar to employees a half-century later. Unlike most of its competitors, IBM grew from a tiny company to one of the world's largest, controlling between 60 and 80 percent of the computer market.

This chapter addresses several of our framing questions. We begin with: What information was collected and used by a profession or organization? We explore that question by examining the role of information ecosystems in three parts of IBM: manufacturing, sales, and corporate headquarters. Each is sufficiently distinct from the other two to demonstrate contrasts and identify similarities and nuances. This chapter allows us to demonstrate how one can identify patterns of adoption and use, a crucial question in the study of information's history. We do that by exploring the evolution of information ecosystems and infrastructures of the sales and customer support organizations. With such a high-tech organization that operated before computers in a world of paper to an era of online digital and analog systems that eschews books, manuals, paper-based forms, and even earlier digital tools (such as terminals attached to mainframes), we can explore two other of our framing questions: What media and mediums were used to collect and store information, and how these were distributed and made available within the organization?

That this chapter explores IBM is not as important as that it probes what a large organization does with information. IBM's behavior toward information is not so different than that of other large enterprises, an observation increasingly borne out by the research of others.[2] We introduce IBM and its information ecosystem, and then explore in case study fashion the evolution of its sales and field force information system involving tens of thousands of individuals. It would be impossible to discuss IBM without explaining the role of its computing as part of our requirement to understand information infrastructures within an information ecosystem, then draw insights from the IBM case study. We conclude with a brief exploration of how to use images to understand information ecosystems and infrastructures with photographs from IBM, a medium that represents a rich source for the history of information.

INTRODUCING IBM

IBM was created in 1911 out of three smaller companies, one of which sold time recording equipment for employees checking in and out of work, another scales, and a third punch card equipment used by governments to house and analyze census data or large bodies of information, such as by insurance companies or railroads. It was named after the first letter of each component, C-T-R (Computing-Tabulating-Recording), and in 1924 changed its name to International Business Machines (IBM). It was this third leg of the company—punch cards—that shaped its business offerings in the decades to come. In 1914 C-T-R hired a new general manager, Thomas J. Watson, a sales executive who had worked at one of the iconic firms of the time, National Cash Register (NCR). NCR had developed some of the most innovative uses of information in sales and a customer service culture.[3] Watson ran IBM from 1914 until his death in 1956. He imposed on IBM practices honed at NCR, almost in wholesale fashion in his early years at IBM, including the kinds of information he believed C-T-R needed, and operational practices required to motivate his sales force, product development staffs, and manufacturing workforces. He ran the company in a near-autocratic fashion, but in the process increased revenues from $4 million in 1914 to $892 million in the year he died.[4]

Watson made several decisions that shaped the destiny of the firm and the nature of the information it would need. First, he decided that the future of IBM lay in focusing on the punch card business, that is to say, in the automation of how large organizations gathered, used, and stored information. His machines supported their move from expensive manual pen and pencil approaches to faster, less costly punch cards and keyboards, which also made tabulating numerical results and producing reports faster and easier. His second decision represented a value proposition: that for customers to use his complex, expensive equipment they needed education about its value and use, assistance—he used the word service—in determining how best to deploy his equipment to their advantage, and help in installing and maintaining the equipment. Watson's third decision, derived from his second, was to build an outstanding sales and services community and culture that would ensure implementation of his value proposition.[5] Watson remained committed to these three decisions for the rest of his life, and so too his son, Thomas J. Watson Jr., when he ran the firm until his retirement in 1971. Subsequent CEOs did as well into the 1980s. For over seven decades senior leaders believed that all parts of the enterprise had to collaborate closely together, and that this behavior required sharing information and embracing a common corporate culture.

Much has been written about IBM's corporate culture, widely admired by other business managers and the media, because of the financial results enjoyed by the firm over many decades. Every IBM memoirist and all historians of the company acknowledged that its culture was its single most important asset in addition to its motivated, well-trained, effective (many said smart) staffs across the ranks of sales, manufacturing, product development, and senior leadership.[6] IBM managers recruited the best employees they could find for all parts of the company and trained them more extensively than IBM's rivals about its products, management, sales, and uses of data processing equipment. IBM treated all employees as peers, even though there were executives, managers, and non-managers. The sales force remained the uncontested elite in the firm; yet everyone worked on straight salary, with commissions for sales, bonuses, and stock options for executives. All worked within a meritocratic culture.

In exchange for conforming and supporting the company's way of working, all were essentially assured life time employment, although it meant periodically taking on new tasks or different roles, and learning new things. Watson Sr. spoke of his company as the "IBM family" and demanded a great deal of commitment from employees, but in exchange showered them with the best collection of benefits of the time. These included medical insurance, pensions, stock purchases at discount, celebrations of work anniversaries, social events, and even partial payment of salaries to employees in military service during wars. The highly profitable company could afford these.

Everyone was taken seriously, as were expectations placed on them, the requirement for collaborative work, and obsession with customer service. Employees were expected to lead honorable private lives, to live and socialize with their customers, to dress as their customers did, and to abstain from drinking alcoholic beverages. Management was enlightened by the norms of their day. Women were more than secretaries and shop floor employees. In the 1930s they entered field services in direct support of customers, Jews were hired beginning in the 1930s, and African Americans after World War II. By the early 1960s half of IBM's business came from outside the United States, consolidated into a subsidiary called World Trade in 1949. It embraced and applied the American IBM corporate culture and operational practices and hired local nationals as employees up through the president and board of directors of each of the subsidiary country companies.

Between its founding and the early 1960s, IBM leased punch card tabulating equipment, and made a fortune selling cards used to collect and store information. Beginning in the early 1950s, the company began to develop and lease computers to these same customers as it started retiring its tabulating product line. By the early 1960s it had become a major global vendor of computers. In 1964 it introduced a line of five computers and a total of some 150 products comprising software and peripheral equipment, called the System 360, that revolutionized how corporations and governments used computers. IBM doubled its revenue in the second half of the 1960s, from $3.2 billion in 1964 to $7.2 billion in 1969, and went from 150,000 employees to over 258,000.[7] While these were challenging years, nonetheless they represented a period of growth. Key to our story is that the technology base of tabulating and even older computer systems were largely swept away by the System 360. The arrival of one hundred thousand new employees in a very short period of time, too, had to be inculcated into what was known as the "IBM Way."[8]

Across the entire period, IBM organized its work and employees in a structure that, while it changed as it grew, remained similar over time. It had factories, in the early years the largest located in Endicott then Poughkeepsie, both in New York, later smaller plants in Europe and Asia. By the late 1920s, IBM focused on manufacturing punch card equipment, including tabulators that "crunched the numbers," key punches that were like typewriters that made holes representing numbers and letters on cards, sorters that shuffled these decks of cards to produce groups of numbers for tabulators to add, subtract, and so forth, and printers to produce the "output," or results. IBM made hundreds of millions of cards, as each could only be used once. By the end of the 1930s IBM was selling a highly successful electric typewriter too, a business it remained in until the end of the 1970s, often manufactured in separate facilities in many countries. Factories had as few as several dozen employees to several thousand by the 1940s, to over eight thousand in some instances by the 1980s.

Then there was the "field force," those IBMers who worked with customers. For the entire period they consisted of two classes of employees: salesmen and field engineers. In the 1960s, a third group, known as systems engineers, who were more technical than the salesmen, but also trained in sales, came into the workforce to assist in the emerging complex world of computers. IBM established "branch offices" in country capital cities, later in other urban centers. Over time the number of branches increased worldwide from several dozen to over eight hundred by the early 1980s. In the beginning decades, branch offices might only have had a half dozen employees, but by the end of the 1970s it was not uncommon for these to have anywhere from 75 to two hundred people, with one hundred roughly the norm. If one met an IBMer (as they were known) it was probably an employee in a branch. Each office had a branch manager and as these became larger, one or two levels of management reporting to them.[9]

Because sales and services were geographically spread out, IBM established regional offices to which branches reported; "regions" reported into sales divisions, which in turn did into either "Domestic" (the U.S. side of IBM headquartered in New York) or into country IBM companies that reported into World Trade (also headquartered in the New York area). Figure 6.1 depicts the structure of the sales organization. Field engineering had a parallel structure, beginning in the 1960s. Figure 6.2 represents the entire firm in highly simplified fashion. Everyone ultimately reported into "Corporate." During Watson Sr.'s tenure scores of individuals reported directly to him. His son, Thomas Watson Jr., established the system of divisions then common in large American corporations to disperse report-

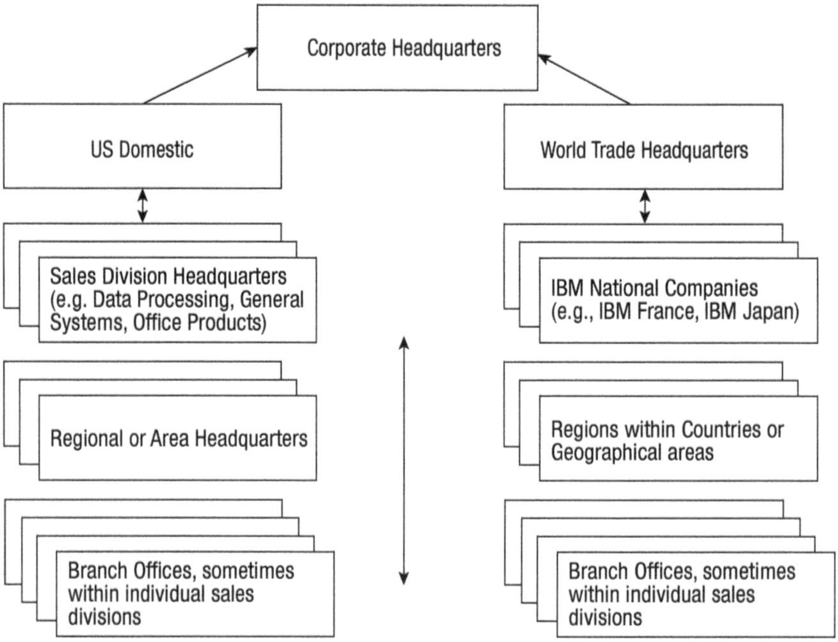

Figure 6.1. IBM Sales Organization, circa late 1940s–1980s

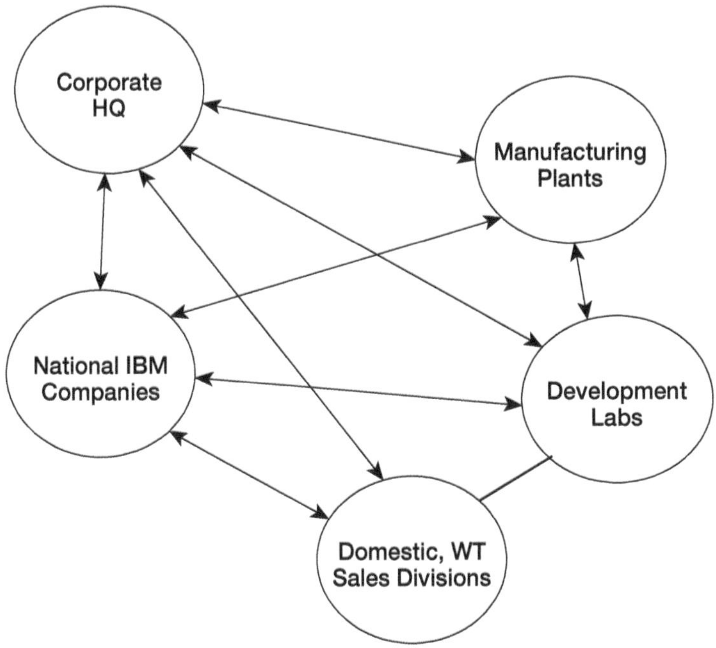

Figure 6.2. IBM's Corporate Structure, 1920s–1980s

ing and decision-making in the rapidly expanding firm. Heads of these divisions (presidents) reported into Corporate.

In the early decades, product development nestled in the factory campuses, a practice established originally in such large firms of the 1890s as Burroughs and NCR, so that engineers could collaborate, learning from each other. As the business grew more complex, IBM established laboratories that conducted scientific and engineering research, often on the same campus as manufacturing. By the 1980s IBM had about a dozen of these research and product development centers around the world. Product development often reported to a general manager responsible for the manufacture of whatever technology and products both were related to, such as software and hardware for mainframes, later separately for personal computers.

THREE INFORMATION ECOSYSTEMS: MANUFACTURING, SALES, AND CORPORATE

IBM had essentially three communities within it—manufacturing, sales and services, and corporate headquarters—each in need of its own information in order to function. Manufacturing tracked the number and types of parts it had available, on order, and in the process of being used on a manufacturing floor to build equipment. It needed information that defined schedules for producing machines—a production plan to determine what to make and when—and what parts were needed by when and where in the factory. It needed information about what machines had been built and were ready to ship, and it had to track the shipment of equipment to customers to feed data to the accounting systems of the manufacturing site and corporate. Cost accounting had become a widespread form of information gathering by the 1920s in large firms, involving collecting data on costs of parts, salaries, keeping the lights on, taxes, warehousing, and transportation expenditures, all tracked daily, weekly, monthly, quarterly, and annually. Individual factories collected their information for their site, then were combined for all of manufacturing, next presented to corporate, and ultimately reviewed with the board of directors. Down through the 1980s plant managers, then manufacturing executives by product, and ultimately the chief executive officer of the firm received this information. Corporate accountants extracted two types of data from these reports: cost of goods sold and number of units built and shipped to customers. These were then matched to the cost of sales and revenues generated by the field to calculate monthly, quarterly, and annual balance sheets of expenses versus revenues versus net income (profits) by subtracting one from the other. IBM used this information to determine taxes to pay in the United States or in a country in which manufacturing and sales occurred.

Most of the information IBMers collected was numeric, either as units of parts or machines or as costs of parts, inventory, people, and facilities. However, not all information was numeric, because IBM's factories also had to develop new machines and manufacturing processes that called for other types of information flowing into manufacturing. Between the 1910s and the 1940s, salesmen and customers discussed desired future products and episodically reported those needs to Watson Sr. If he thought an idea good he passed it on to the appropriate factory to develop. For instance, almost from the first day of his arrival at C-T-R, Watson Sr. heard about the need for a machine that could print results of tabulation of data on punch cards so that accountants could read the numbers. That led to early product innovations. In the 1940s, customers requested that IBM connect its electronic calculator (a precursor to the digital computer) to its peripheral equipment to speed information processing over earlier manual operations between machines. Most of those manual interventions were replaced by having the output of one machine transferred electronically by wires connected to other machines, until the final report (answers) were produced on cards, paper reports, or later onto magnetic tape.[10]

In addition to the highly numeric feature of business data, IBM and its customers developed a routine cadence for collecting information and its analysis. Far more than an accounting version of Tayloristic work practices, these were ways one worked. They varied, of course, by type. Daily, weekly, and monthly reviews of results achieved against targets (most of which were numeric) became a way of life for generations of employees. No job was absent such a practice of measuring actions and results, and comparing them to objectives. In time, such behavior became indistinguishable from the company's culture. One navigated through their work "by the numbers" in all countries across all levels, from the newest employee to the chairman and the board of directors. Data became the way one could determine how they were doing against qualitatively described objectives. For example, "We want to be the premier supplier of electric typewriters," (an objective of the 1930s–1960s) would be measured by what percent of all electric typewriters sold in a country came from IBM; a target might be what number had to be sold within a given year.

Beginning in the 1930s, but formalized in the 1940s within sales, manufacturing, and corporate, staffs began to mine information about customer needs to develop lists of "requirements" that management could decide to fund. This step represented a crucial evolution in the use of information at IBM, because it made possible allocation of budget and people to increasingly complex products, notably computers. "Future Products" staffs calculated costs of new offerings, estimated how many copies could be leased, then determined their expense and profits over time. That kind of information made it possible for management to arrive at decisions about what products to sell and their costs, and to determine how many people to hire with specific skills, such as computer scientists, engineers, salesmen, and so forth. In practice that process worked, although occasionally it proved bumpy because of competition within the firm for funding of alternative projects, as occurred in the 1970s when one division wanted resources to develop small computers while the mainframe manufacturing division resisted giving up people for that purpose.

Because developing a product could take years, a new concept emerged at IBM in the 1950s known as a product life cycle. Management would decide to build a new machine, for example the highly popular IBM 650. It was the first mass produced computer in the company, introduced in 1953 and sold until 1962, leasing some two thousand of these systems. During that time, it was periodically changed—improved—with new components and more software, all of which were planned. That is to say, decisions were made about what changes to make by year, with forecasts annually calculated of costs and sales, projected out one to three years in advance, all put down on paper and tracked. By the 1960s all computers, most complex industrial equipment, and even consumer electronics, built in most industries used this kind of information. Most used IBM equipment to support these kinds of data handling activities.

That was the manufacturing and product development side of IBM's information ecosystem. That information flowed to and from corporate on a weekly, monthly, and annual basis. By the end of the 1950s, overlaying this flow was a Fall Plan process whereby manufacturing, sales, and corporate put together accounting, revenue, sales, product manufacturing, and product development information into a plan that essentially said, "this is what I think we will do in the following year, following two years." Management at all levels debated and tweaked this data to arrive at a plan IBMers set out to implement in the following year, allocating budget and headcount (number of employees) in support of these plans. The cycle began in July or August and ended in November, with performance targets cascaded down through the organization, beginning in November and completed by mid-January of the next year. By the mid-1980s a Spring Plan exercise provided a mid-year assessment of progress toward achieving plans and the opportunity to adjust them as needed. By the 1990s, spring planning had become a formal company-wide practice still used today. All parts of the company participated.

Then there was the sales side of the company, which employed thousands of salesmen, systems engineers, field engineers (also called customer engineers), and administrative staffs to support them scattered across more countries than IBM had factories. To best understand their information ecosystem, we begin by looking at a branch office. Figures 6.3 and 6.4 represent the typical organization of a sales branch office, the first

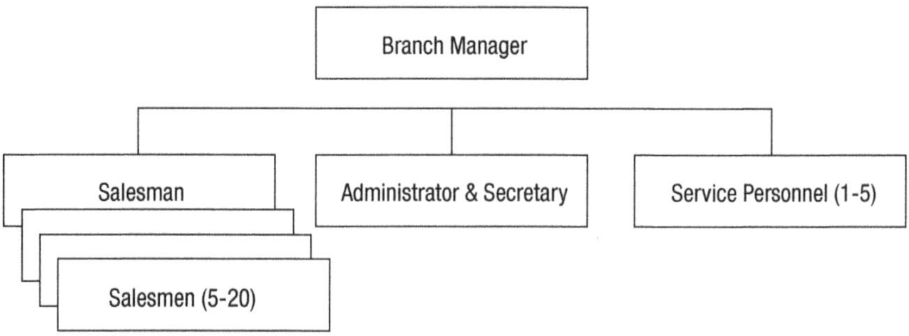

Figure 6.3. IBM Sales Branch Organization, circa 1920s

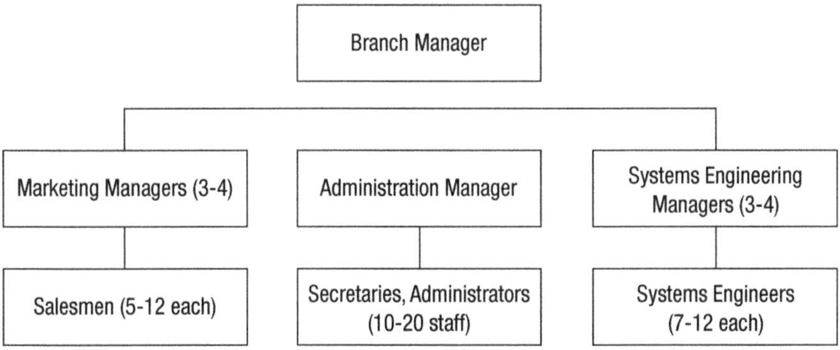

Figure 6.4. IBM Sales Branch Organization, circa 1980s

from the 1920s and the second from the 1980s. They fundamentally did not change, because their mission remained constant: to sell and support IBM's products in essentially the same way over many decades. As business grew, branch offices became bigger and more complex.[11]

In support of its branch offices, IBM created an information ecosystem that defined the activities and shaped the concerns of all participants. This ecosystem was supported by an information infrastructure. One could not work without the other. Table 6.1 lists the kinds of information a salesman needed to perform his duties by the 1930s. These remained essentially the same between the 1920s and the 1990s.

Table 6.2 lists components of the information infrastructure supporting these. The crucial change in what comprised Table 6.2 came with the shift from paper to electronic information handling beginning in the 1970s. That transformation made it possible for salesmen to perform

Table 6.1. Information Used by IBM Salesmen, circa 1920s–1980s

Cost and dimensions of punch cards
Features and lease prices of all IBM hardware
New product introductions
News about IBM corporate, divisions, and regions
Account information on organization, business results, biographies of key customers
History of IBM's relations with its individual accounts
IBM and customer telephone numbers and addresses
Customer account files, including copies of contracts
Technical "how to" information on performing studies, financial cost justification
Information on a customer's own industry
Features, prices, and advantages of competitors' products
Contacts within IBM and customer organizations to resolve issues
Computer industry news, technology trends
Branch, region, and division accounting data, personnel records

Table 6.2. Components of IBM Sales Information Infrastructures, circa 1920s–1980s

Sales manuals, telephone directories, GI manuals, product brochures
IBM corporate, division, and regional newsletters
IBM Branch Office reviews, forecasts, accounts receivable reports
Telephones, including internal Tie-line network
Internal IBM mail delivery system
Subscriptions to industry publications, including *Computerword, Datamation,* and other local and national computing publications
HONE system to support configuration of orders, training, financial analysis, proposal preparation
Administrative systems to place and track orders, issue and collect bills, monitor and spend local budget, track personnel
RETAIN system to support installation and repair of equipment by Field Engineering
IBM television network
PROFS e-mail and calendar system
Regional, divisional, and factory-located customer briefing centers
IBM and customer education centers

new functions, such as modeling financial justification of equipment for customers and "configuring" an order, that is to say, allowing software to figure out what parts and peripheral equipment were needed in order for a computer or single machine to work with others, a practice begun with brief texts in the 1930s (see Figure 6.5) The kind of information displayed in Figure 6.5 would have increased two to three fold as equipment and software became more complicated. By the end of the 1980s this infrastructure consisted of a combination of paper and electronic factors, such as a paper pamphlets and booklets describing a product and a database with the same information, a salesman's manual, which contained prices and product specifications, and contract terms often kept in the trunks of their cars, but which also existed in online systems accessible at a branch office. The types of information and their supporting infrastructure were similar, if not exactly the same, worldwide and evolved at the same pace in order to make them effective and to maintain a consistent corporate culture and way of doing business.

Beginning in 1914, all salesmen were trained in the art of selling—the persuasive conversation needed with customers—and on the features, uses, and costs of IBM's products.[12] By the end of the 1920s, IBM had codified these techniques. They continued to be taught in the late 1980s in the same way as in the 1920s. Known as the "Structured Sales Call," they focused on the acquisition of information to determine a customer's need (requirements), presenting what IBM could offer with products

PUNCHES * * * * * Page 25

ALPHABETIC DUPLICATING PUNCH

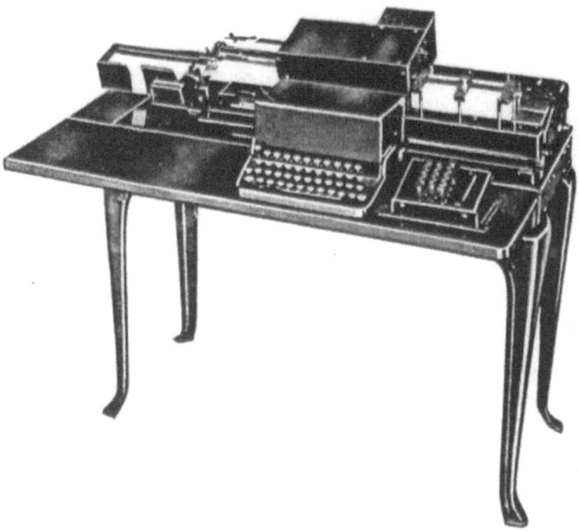

Price: 80 column $25.00 per month.

Contract: Agreement covering Alphabetic Duplicating Punches shall remain in force for one year from the date that the punches are installed ready for use and may be terminated by the customer or the company at the end of any calendar month thereafter by ninety days' previous notice in writing unless terminated by us in accordance with the stipulations of the contract.

Use: The Alphabetic Duplicating Punch is used to record both alphabetic and numerical data in tabulating cards.

Speed: The mechanical speed of operation is approximately the same as that of numerical punches. An entire card can be duplicated in approximately 7.2 seconds.

Capacity: 80 column cards only.

Standard Features: The feed and eject is the same as that of the Motor Drive Key Punch, the card reversing device being furnished as a standard feature.

The Alphabetic Duplicating Punch may be controlled by either an alphabetic or a numerical keyboard. The alphabetic keyboard is similar to that

Figure 6.5. Page from an IBM Sales Manual, circa 1930s

IBM Archives

and services to meet those, followed by discussion of ***f***eatures of IBM's "solution," ***a***dvantages to the customer of having those, then soliciting their ***r***eaction (known as the FARs). Should objections surface, and they were solicited so they could be resolved, then the salesman repeated the FAR cycle. Only once objections had been resolved could the salesman ask for the order, using any one or more of a dozen techniques to ask the question. A favorable answer led to a discussion about how to place the order and install the product. The flow of the conversation could occur in one call, as often happened when selling something relatively inexpensive such as a typewriter or later a terminal or PC, or could be a series of conversations over months or even two or three years, involving scores of meetings and conversations.[13]

Buried in that "sales cycle" at its beginning was the task of determining a customer's need for data processing. IBM employees were taught to conduct studies in a customer's organization to figure out how to "apply" (use) data processing equipment in specific operations, such as how to use punch cards to track inventory instead of a prior manual use of such tools as 3 × 5 cards and ledgers. The central task was to identify specific numbers—facts—a customer needed to gather, calculate, and report out, along with developing the data gathering and calculations required to achieve desired results. These exercises became opportunities to streamline old accounting and information handling practices, to redefine roles of employees, such as those on a factory floor who collected and disseminated information, or to implement new accounting practices, such as cost accounting that spread widely during the 1920s and 1930s, and shop floor production scheduling, made so much easier to produce in a timely fashion in the 1950s and 1960s.

These studies could take one to four months to conduct, and always involved customer personnel, periodic visits to IBM factories that hosted seminars and staffed briefing centers to share information about equipment, and conversations with legal and accounting staffs to determine terms and conditions for a sale. Many of these "T's & C's" were standard contractual offerings available by the 1910s. Customers expected their salesmen to know how one should use IBM equipment, later software too, to the advantage of their "accounts," and to keep them informed about trends in the use of IBM's latest products. That second requirement—to keep them informed about trends—led branch offices to host seminars at IBM's sales offices, briefing centers located in large cities and factories, and even in rented halls at local hotels, where they discussed technologies, features and functions, uses, and trends. That pattern of information exchange continued across the century. Hardly a month passed without one or more such briefings held for a mid- to large account. Even small customer organizations found local IBM seminars almost every month as well. Such information exchanges were frequent and well attended with active participation by both customers and IBMers exchanging information through presentations, roundtable discussions, and individualized conversations.

To facilitate ongoing dialogue, salesmen were given charge of a customer organization that no other IBMer could sell to without permission of the salesman to whom it was assigned. Any sales commission generated by any IBMer in his or her account flowed to the assigned salesman; occasionally they were duplicated to another. A "Territory Rep" had a monopoly as far as IBM was concerned. Any equipment returned to IBM cost the assigned salesman lost commissions and its value to IBM deducted from his attainment of quota, which meant he had to replace that lost value with something of equal or ideally greater value to IBM. From the 1920s through the 1970s this value was measured by using "points." One point equaled $1 dollar or 1 franc, and so forth in rental revenue per month; all quotas were stated in points. If a customer was paying IBM $1,000 per month in rental fees for all equipment, and he returned to IBM one machine no longer needed that rented for $90 per month, then the salesman had to sell something worth 90 points just to stay even, and then sell additional equipment to make his target. In our example, a salesman might receive a quota of 200 points, meaning that at the end of that year that customer had to be paying IBM $1,200 per month in leases for the salesman to make his or her target (quota). Often, as in this instance, the 90 point machine might be replaced with a bigger, more expensive one that, say for hypothetical purposes, rented for $110 per month, leaving the salesman to find an additional 180 points worth of business.

To accomplish this, salesmen needed to know their customers very well, to establish close relations with them—in the slang term used by the 1960s to "be part of the furniture," to maintain what was called "account control." Table 6.3 lists the kinds of information salesmen routinely maintained about their customers Table 6.4 information-centered activities used to maintain those close ties.

In the branch office a managerial oversight process existed that facilitated and monitored these activities. Beginning in the 1920s, on Friday afternoons salesmen and branch managers met to review their activities of the prior week, such as calls on customers, presentation of proposals, demonstrations of how equipment worked, and relations between ac-

Table 6.3. Information Branch Sales Staff Kept on Their Customers

Lists of all installed IBM products and their value in points
Lists and descriptions of how customers used IBM products
Old and current IBM proposals
Inventory of competitor's installed products
Lists of key customer contacts, including their telephone numbers, addresses, biographies, history of their relations with IBM
Documentation on prior IBM relations, contacts with customers
Account planning documentation, such as slide decks and forecasts
Customer organization charts and telephone directories
Copies of all contracts with customers
IBM field engineering contacts assigned to individual accounts
Newspaper reports on customers
Customer annual reports, internal newsletters, and publications
All IBM publications featuring one's customer
Occasional travel expense reporting (TEA—Territory Expense Accounting)

Table 6.4. Information-Centered Activities to Reinforce IBM Ties to Customers

Briefings on new products and about their implications for a customer by branch personnel
Proposal presentations by branch sales staff
Joint attendance at industry conferences with customers
Customer attendance at IBM user meetings, such as at SHARE
Customer education/briefings on products, technology and industry trends held at factories, laboratories, other branch offices, and IBM education centers
Factory visits to discuss use of potential products
Data center education for customer staffs on how to use IBM's products
Visits to other IBM customers to learn about their experiences with IBM's products and services
Calls on IBM executives or by IBM executives and experts on customers to share information and observations about their areas of expertise and interests
Joint membership in industry associations and boards
Joint collaboration in local civic organizations and charities
Distribution of IBM and commercial publications relevant to customers and IBM
Distribution of IBM press releases

counts and IBM. They discussed problems, such as how to deal with a competitor, or came up with an approach for using equipment for a customer. They planned what events—usually sales calls—would occur the following week. By the end of the 1960s, when people were organized into sales units within a branch consisting of a marketing (sales) manager and seven to 12 employees, these smaller groups held similar meetings or salesmen met one-on-one weekly with their manager. Prior to the 1960s, all salesmen were required to fill out a report on how many sales calls they made that week, documenting results of each by picking from a list of results to tick off, such as demonstration, proposal, gained or lost an order, and so forth. These data were tabulated by branch, region, and then the nation in the U.S., a practice partially implemented in other countries. This information provided a window into the ongoing activities of the sales force, allowing middle and senior management to understand what was happening in the daily activities in sales. In Watson Sr.'s day, he often came into a meeting with regional or country sales executives holding in his hand summary reports of local sales activities, sometimes to the embarrassment of the less informed audience. He was a fact-driven leader.[14]

Sales forecasts comprised a second body of information. Used since the 1910s, this class of data remained a critical component of the information world of IBM sales, as in all large companies. Every salesman, then as now, had to forecast either weekly or monthly, and annually, how much business they anticipated bringing in, measured prior to the early 1980s in points (later as revenue), and by product or service, by account, and by when. By the 1970s they also had to predict odds of a piece of business coming in, such as at 25, 50, 75, or 100 percent. For decades forecasts were divided into two categories: business committed to by a customer and forecasted equipment and software actually installed. The first information spoke to the health of the business backlog to be installed that could be used by factories to determine how many machines to build or have available by when. The second measure—installed data of when and how many points and by product—fed accounting reports of the branch, region, division, and corporation. Everyone was expected to forecast accurately, although it was more common for a community of salesmen to vary in the quality of their forecasts the most, but increasingly proved more precise as these forecasts worked their way up the organization. A forecast by a branch manager, based on aggregating all the salesmen in his or her branch and adjusted to account for varying quality of his people's forecasting skills, usually did not vary off what actually occurred, called "actuals," by more than 5 percent, often by less. Regional forecasts came in within 1 to 2 percent, division forecasts were normally 100 percent accurate. The quality of one's accuracy partially affected their annual performance appraisals that all IBMers underwent.

A third cluster of branch information concerned budgets. In all IBM organizations, these included salaries, utilities, real estate, travel and education, entertainment of customers such as for lunch, and publications and machine parts. Corporate developed and assigned budgets to divisions, divisions to regions, regions to branches, branches to individuals, all cascading down. Weekly, monthly, and quarterly tabulations of these filled IBM's information ecosystem, along with monthly and quarterly budgetary performance forecasts, paralleling the cadence of what the sales side of a branch, region, or division submitted. By the early 1930s it seemed that "everything" that could be measured, tracked, and ranked was, practices that continued until the 1990s when the idea of a branch office began evolving into new organizational constructs around product specialties, industries, and matrix structures, and less on geography.[15] These "everything" measures evolved over time, but included such items as personnel records (number of documented performance plans, performance reviews, their timings such as percent done on schedule), quantities of a particular product sold in a given year, or number of customers exposed to presentations on a subject of interest to regional or division headquarters.

Branches produced one other collection of information called the Branch Office Review. Each spring regional staff descended on their branches for a half day to two day review of operations. Branch management prepared presentations describing what their staffs were doing account-by-account, issues they were encountering, their budgets and intentions on how to spend it, employees coming and going and their issues, and training of staff and education plans for customers. Branches would plead for more resources, demonstrate they maintained "account control" to get things done, and brag, unless they were forecasting not making their targets. Regional staffs used these occasions to network and meet branch staff and to develop a deeper understanding of the rhythm of the business across the region. Regions hosted "regional reviews" attended by divisional staffs and vice presidents, even by division presidents. Reviews from branch offices on up were at the heart and soul of the sales organization, sustaining a detailed level of understanding of business to the top of the company. Accompanied by consolidated reports already described, the combined documented and oral transmission of information provided all levels of the company a rich understanding of "the business." These activities also stimulated multiple interactions with customers, adding context, because whenever reviews took place, guests at a branch or regional review also carved out time to call on customers, normally data processing managers or vice presidents of finance, sometimes customer presidents or state governors, to understand their perspective on relations with IBM and their needs and wants, further cementing ties with them.[16]

In all periods regions worked with two fundamental sets of information. The first paralleled the information collected at the branch level and consolidated to reflect a regional perspective, already discussed. A second, smaller collection allowed regions to compare and contrast performances of branch offices and to motivate improved performance by laggards. Regions published monthly rankings of branches one against the other on a series of metrics that varied over the decades, but that rated branches by sales, equipment and software installed, later revenue and all against their targets, such as percent of quota attained year-to-date. Branches were ranked from one to the lowest in a region, published and posted on bulletin boards in all offices within a region. As branch offices became larger in the 1970s, branch managers posted similar weighted rankings by sales unit. In either list, nobody wanted to be ranked in the bottom half. By the 1970s, some regions ranked individual sales managers, regardless of branch. To be number one or two in a region conferred prestige, if ever so fleeting, since the following quarter some manager could obtain a large order propelling him or her (female managers by the 1980s) to the top of the list.

One other component of information in all locations consisted of news and facts posted on bulletin boards. These included announcements of promotions, award winners, company or office events, introductions of new products, financial results reported by the national or corporate office, deaths of CEOs and other important executives, national holidays, government required postings regarding worker rights, statements such as how the office parking lot would be closed the following week due to repairs, and so forth. In the 1980s these kinds of information increasingly moved online in the form of e-mail, and in the 1990s to websites by branch, region, and so forth.

IBM's corporate information ecosystem paralleled much that existed lower in the organization that remained relatively uniform across the world, purposefully so. Corporate staff, and those at division headquarters too, used several additional types of information. By the 1930s in the United States, later in Europe, and eventually around the world, an important function of any company's headquarters staff was to understand competition, government regulations, and economic conditions. Doing so influenced the business strategy of the corporation as a whole and those of each product division (the latter which also had to understand the changing nature of technologies). "Competitive analysis," as it was known in IBM since the 1950s, involved tracking competitors' product offerings, their prices, terms and conditions, and changes in their strategy for dealing with IBM. Insights and relevant information were shared across the firm, faster by the end of the 1960s when online systems came into use in IBM worldwide.

Before 1910 and continuing to the present it was the responsibility of corporate and national headquarters to understand national government regulations affecting their business, such as taxes and safety and labor laws. They maintained a lobbying function to persuade public officials to alter regulations and laws to benefit the company.[17] By the 1970s, branch managers were expected to cultivate congressional and other legislative representatives, provincial and state governors, and other local officials for similar reasons, treating these individuals almost as if they were customers requiring "account control." As in sales, IBM employees reported up their chain of command on these issues. Every CEO, too, interacted with national leaders, including cabinet officials, prime ministers, and presidents.[18] Normally information about these activities was not shared publicly and never made it to the bulletin boards.

By the 1980s corporate officials understood that they needed the services of academically trained economists. During the 12 years of a U.S. antitrust suit against IBM dismissed in 1982, IBM's legal defense turned on the definition of what constituted the computer market, which the U.S Department of Justice accused it of dominating, constricting the ability of other firms to compete. As part of its defense team, IBM contracted with academic economists to build its case, while the U.S. Department of Justice did the same in support of its arguments.[19] With the conclusion of that case, but always concerned about potential future ones and having seen the value of economists, IBM corporate hired full time economists. By 2000, over 20 economists worked across the enterprise worldwide. At corporate, usually one or two provided senior management with economic insights on such topics as capital markets, cost of money, changing currency rates and their impact on IBM (shared also with accounting and financial staffs), global trends in national economic growth and declines and how these affected IBM's business, and economic impact of elections, wars, natural disasters, and other events. They provided such information on a monthly basis and in a standard format. Although such information was readily available from public sources, it was always marked "IBM Confidential," because it also contained assessments of what current economic indicators implied for the company's prospects. For example, if in the early 1980s interest rates for borrowing capital were rising in the United States but remaining flat in France, an IBM economist might opine that the sale of large computers in the U.S. market might slow while anticipated sales in France might continue as predicted by the field. But an executive worried about U.S. sales of mainframes might think to ask the economist how long high interest rates might last so that he (the executive) could take actions to mitigate this problem, such as lowering the price of future computer products or offering customers IBM-financed loans for their purchase.[20]

By the end of the 1940s, many of these branch, regional, division, national, and corporate information inputs had been integrated into a global infrastructure that remained intact for the next half century. This can be attributed to two circumstances. First, technological and competitive pressures did not upset how IBM was organized and managed until the second half of the 1980s, when personal computing created new rivals, customers, and economies of scale. Second, since the information ecosystem emerged and evolved out of necessity, it worked. IBM expanded through these years by revenue, profit, number of employees, increased number of countries with field offices, and prestige as an iconic enterprise. But that did not mean information needs did not change. At the specific level of facts, they did. Examining a few of these specific types of information and how they were packaged and communicated adds to our understanding of how to describe a company's information ecosystem.

EVOLUTION OF SALES AND FIELD INFORMATION SYSTEMS: CHANGES IN INFORMATION FLOWS

One example of how information flows offers a window into how facts circulated and were leveraged in a large enterprise, in this case how salesmen and field engineers (the individuals who installed and repaired equipment) used information in their work. Between the 1920s and the late 1980s, each relied on binders of information, either the "Sales Manual," used by both, or "Field Engineering Guides," for the engineers. Both were designed as small 3- to 6-ring binders that contained information needed to do their work. Pages were individually dated, such as "11-10-1955," and periodically as changes were announced new ones went to field employees, who replaced older ones with new pages, often two or three pages a month in the 1920s–early 1940s, then two or three per week during the 1950s and 1960s, as IBM retired its tabulating equipment and introduced computer products and software. Salesmen's versions included all products, components, costs, and guidance on contractual terms. Field engineering versions included the same information but also how to install and maintain these. Both included information on what machines worked with each other, that is to say, were compatible within a system of machines, an important issue especially with the arrival of computers and their larger variety of components, memories, and myriad software, even cables connecting together devices.[21] Until the 1960s, each type of publication consisted of one volume. In the 1960s they expanded into the more normal 10" by 12" three-ring format binder used by American firms, and its slightly longer version elsewhere around the world. Black binding changed to grey, and by the 1970s, a salesman's manual consisted of three volumes covering some three thousand products and issues.

An example of a salesman's manual from the 1950s is a useful one that contained information typical across the entire period. Entitled *Manual of IBM Punched Card Accounting Machines and Auxiliary Equipment*, later simply as the *IBM Sales Manual*, it was only to be used by employees, never shown to customers. Our example from the 1950s listed names of corporate officers, offered a short history of the firm, then by groups of products described each model, features, and their rental or purchase prices. As it described the information: "The data on machine features has been limited to the briefest form in order to keep the manual as compact as possible."[22] That sentence could have described all editions. These provided instructions on procedures to be used, for example, in quoting prices and terms and conditions, approvals required, and so forth. All product descriptions ran one to a half dozen pages in length and included photographs of the machines. Employees were expected to understand much of this information, which they gained through formal training and experience presenting these to customers, much the way a sales clerk in an Apple store today could explain how much memory a laptop has and features of individual software packages.

In addition to the sales and field guides that everyone seemed to carry around in the trunks of their cars, there existed another class of information first introduced in the 1930s for every product afterwards called "GI Manuals," standing for *General Information.* These thousands of GI manuals varied from several to hundreds of pages, providing blueprints of wiring and engineering drawings, instructions on how to install a device and use it, tables of codes for machines and software, and photographs and line drawings. Other GI manuals discussed uses, such as how to do accounting with specific classes of computers.[23] When IBM introduced five computers and nearly 150 peripheral machines and software that all were supposed to work with each other called the IBM System 360, the set of GI manuals accompanying these and subsequent models and editions of software occupied nearly 50 linear feet of shelving, a collection printed in tiny fonts in 8 × 10 format. Some volumes were the size of a fat New York City telephone directory. Field engineers and data center operators relied on libraries of such materials to install, run, operate, repair equipment, and use software. Large data centers employed librarians to track these along with data files generated by computers on punch cards, tape, and disk drives.

Salesmen and field engineers were sent to product schools to learn about new machines and software, where they received additional information and publications. In the case of the S/360, a typical example of this process, a field engineer about to go off to learn about the new machines in the 1960s received a pre-class briefing booklet of about 150 pages he had to master before showing up to a class that would have included a computer for hands-on learning. In the case of the *System/360 Model 20 Pre-School Student Self-Study Course,* field engineers were told it would take 14 to 18 hours to complete and that they needed to pass two examinations before being admitted to the class, a typical scenario for sales and field engineering for any education they took about any subject at IBM across the entire period. In this publication, students were exposed to the machine's data handling methods, how the hardware was organized and its "core concepts and operation," and its programming philosophy and structure (e.g., "Stored Program Concept," "Basic Flowcharting," "Instruction Formats"). It included examples and illustrations, and an index.[24]

In class they received additional materials to bring back to their home branch on how to connect and operate components, how to maintain them, and text summarizing all lectures and exercises. Both groups received technical publications they could share with customers. In the case of the System/360, when introduced on April 7, 1964, in addition to the press releases, and the typical one to four page product announcements made to IBMers in what were called "Blue Letters," for being printed on blue paper, for major new products customers received a document that looked like a press release, called "Technical Information." These provided detailed discussions of the technical make-up of the machines and software, including such facts as the electronic speed with which they operated, how much computer memory came with them, photographs, and tables of engineering data, amounting to a 24-page document.[25] Seventeen years later, when IBM introduced the Personal Computer (PC), similar publications and updates to sales manuals became available on the day of announcement (August 12, 1981).

A ubiquitous publication appeared all over IBM of enormous value that could be found in the trunks of cars, in everyone's top desk drawer in branch offices, even at home, in briefcases, and in desks assigned to IBMers in customer data centers: an IBM telephone directory. Prior to the 1990s, these publications appeared every few months around the world. Most only had telephone numbers and addresses for other IBM organizations and employees within a company or division, usually within a national company, such as IBM France or IBM Germany. These were used probably every day by a majority of field personnel throughout the period. Organized by office and division, sometimes by location, these normally included the name of the individual assigned to some responsibility. Few have survived, because like last year's telephone directory in one's home, the previous one was thrown away.[26] In addition to providing a telephone number, they reflected how the company was organized. For example, if a salesman needed to know more about a particular competitor, he could look up within his region, at corporate, or within his division the competitive intelligence group and within it have names and phone numbers. Conversations involved exchanges of information about what each knew of a particular competitor, its offerings, in which account, and for what product. The full time competitive analysis staffs, usually ex-salesmen, documented these conversations as part of tracking IBM's competitors.

Branch offices and regional headquarters always published their own directories shared with employees all over the company, but most specifically within their own organizations. Thus, a sales regional directory comprising a half dozen pages might physically be tucked into the larger IBM directory, a publication that itself could be an inch thick in any decade.

These various elements of the published physical information ecosystem—sales and GI manuals, telephone directories, training materials, bulletin board announcements, budget and sales reporting, and forecasts—made up the bulk of what field personnel worked with over many decades. Every division, country, and manufacturing site and most regions also produced weekly, monthly or quarterly newsletters across the entire period. Typical of such industrial newsletters as in other large companies, they reported milestone events, such as the manufacture of the 1000th of some product, or an extraordinary sale by an individual salesman, announced who was attending this year's sales recognition events (100 Percent Club or Golden Circle), promotions, visits by important people, and events, such as company picnics, new construction, and changes in company benefits. In addition, IBM mailed to each employee's home *THINK,* a magazine launched in the 1930s around the world in different languages to publish non-business articles by leading writers and thinkers of the day. That agenda changed in the 1970s, when it became an internal publication only, communicating the corporation's messages, featuring articles on IBM's business strategies, benefits, and highlights of success around the company to employees. *THINK* ceased publication in 1994.[27]

These various internal publications were augmented with subscriptions to industry ones, such as the weekly *Computerworld* that worked much like a city newspaper with news of events, new products, and participants in the industry. Monthly, *Datamation* provided more analysis and investigative reporting, such as surveys of how people used computers, trends in the evolution of the technology, and developments in companies in the United States. Later more specialized product trade magazines appeared, such as the widely consulted *PC Magazine.*

Before moving to a discussion of the role of computers in IBM's own information infrastructure, going back to our fundamental questions, how did all this information affect everyone's work? After the lengthy description of the various types of information available to IBMers, the first observation is that IBMers had a great deal of it available to them, certainly far more than the Spanish diplomats or the ladies of Madison County, perhaps only matched by what a high energy computer scientist might have encountered. Second, this information was highly varied and complex, not lending itself to simple generalizations. It came in multiple forms: numeric, textual, graphical, as books, manuals, several sheets of paper, broadsides, telegraph-like posting on bulletin boards, slide presentations, letters, videos, taped recordings, even through an internal television network, and e-mail to mention the most obvious. Third, IBMers lived in a push-pull world of information, one in which facts were thrust at them, such as about new products, and that required them to contribute back, such as forecasts of future sales. They pulled information into their individual work with which to perform, such as seeking instructions on how to repair a piece of equipment or accounting and tax information needed to create a compelling argument for a sale.

Information flow back-and-forth and up-and-down in the firm increased over time as its availability and need to use it, and complexity buttressed by the deployment of information handling tools did as well. These flows began early with use of typewriters, desktop calculators and tabulators in the 1910s and 1920s, deployment of computers in the 1950s, telex and online systems in the 1960s, PCs and external telecommunications networks in the 1970s, e-mail and online databases in the 1980s, and the Internet and laptops in the 1990s. The speed with which information circulated increased and intensified. For example, between the 1910s and 1950s, national postal services distributed the bulk of the company's information, except for what transpired over the telephone or in the frequent in-person meetings held all over the company. Every IBM building had a mailroom, some entire departments, as at factory sites and corporate or national headquarters. By the end of the 1960s, information moved electronically, too, speeding up the flow and volume, especially as the cost of moving data declined. Not to be overlooked was the wide use of telephones from the earliest days of the company. With the exception of shop floor staff, most employees had their own telephone numbers and seemed to use intensely every telephonic tool made available to them.

One constant transcending all decades was employee reliance on facts with which to make decisions. Branch and regional reviews more than hinted of that culture, so too the extensive training so emblematic of IBM's personnel practices. The culture of THINK by definition required all opinions, recommendations, and actions to be backed up by research and facts thoughtfully put together. To what extent was IBM unique in such behaviors? Studies of information ecosystems in other corporations are too sparse to generalize with absolute confidence. Such studies represent an important opportunity for historians to explore information ecosystems and infrastructures. However, we know that peer institutions copied practices from each other.[28] We also know that IBM promoted its own behavior as part of its branding and as a way of selling its own products.[29]

The company's tag line *Think* suggested that the business was complicated and cerebral, that much thought had to be put into how to solve problems, make sales, and support customers with complex technologies that could have significant impact on everyone's operations. Understanding what IBMers did contributes to a growing interest of historians and other scholars engaging with social theories. Usually called reflectivity, it is the study of how people did active learning as circumstances changed around them. Two historians pondering the theme of reflectivity as one insufficiently examined, Philip Scranton and Patrick Fridenson, argued that information feedback loops represented a source of insight into the behavior of an organization, a point demonstrated in this chapter.[30] Reflection enhances individual and organizational awareness of one's own views, those of rivals within the firm and competitors outside of it, various attitudes of customers, and realities imposed by regulators, economic circumstances, and ever-changing technologies.

These historians asked good questions that observing how IBM developed and ran its information ecosystems helps to answer: "How do businesses, managers, regulators, or investors change by learning? How is such learning triggered, mediated, and stored?"[31] Receiving and dealing with unwelcome news is an issue insufficiently studied, but as we saw with the weekly branch meetings, by exploring a branch's information ecosystem we gained insight into precisely that problem and how IBMers reflected on the best way to deal with these negative circumstances.

Almost as if they had embraced the central themes of information ecosystems and infrastructures, Scranton and Fridenson argued that exploring reflectivity represented an opportunity, putting "historians in a position to become increasingly aware about their conventions for gathering and assessing information, including the information that fuels research, and they may be expected to reflect on the ways in which these conventions can be altered as the character and quality of information shifts."[32]

ROLE OF INFORMATION TECHNOLOGY IN IBM'S INFORMATION INFRASTRUCTURE

The IBM case, more than the earlier studies in this book, allows us to explore how information technologies affected the flow of information within an organization and the kinds of information made available. It does not, however, allow us to document how much, as that is a function of measuring data sets and traffic currently not available to researchers and probably has not been preserved.[33] Until the late 1960s, the lion's share moved about in paper formats or through oral transmission by conversation and lectures. The speed of transmission was a function of how fast mail worked or how frequently people could gather in the same room. The two exceptions were extensive use of telephones and, earlier, the telegraph. Normally, employees rarely used the latter as it was cumbersome and expensive, and occasionally not private enough. IBMers were an impatient lot, so most did not hesitate to pick up the telephone and call someone, hence the value of the IBM telephone directory and those of one's customers.[34]

In the 1960s in a few company laboratories and spreading worldwide across the company, beginning in 1981, IBM established an internal e-mail service called PROFS (PRofessional Office System) to send messages to each other, including attached files, and to maintain online calendars. It worked, was popular, and rarely "went down." In the mid-1990s IBM replaced it with Lotus Notes, from the company of the same name that IBM had just purchased. This tool, more attractive to the eye, was about as easy to use as PROFS. It provided expanded file management capabilities, later online conferencing, and connections to the growing body of Websites and other databases used by IBMers. During the period of our case study, e-mail traveled by PROFS. E-mail in the 1980s sped up the exponential transfer of information and other communications. One could have back-and-forth dialogue about sales situations, contracting terms and conditions, and increased requests for information. Gossip, too, flowed more frequently through the system. One's personal network of connections across the firm increased dramatically, especially to include those met in IBM classes or internal meetings. E-mail became hugely popular and by the end of the decade almost all the paper mail that came in and out of IBM was customer correspondence, contracts, and proposals, and even those began electronically moving in and out of IBM in the 1990s. The old wooden mail slots that employees had used for decades remained unused by the end of the 1990s, relics of an obsoleted information infrastructure.[35]

A second effect of e-mail involved creating possible new activities. For example, in the 1980s regional and divisional staff product experts and those working in competitive analysis and sales support developed virtual networks of contacts. A mainframe expert responsible for helping salesmen fight competitors could call on branch staff to report all manner of competitive activity across a nation or continent in exchange for assistance in dealing with a competitor. That constant, daily, even hourly, feedback loop from the branches built up a large current body of information about terms and conditions, selling arguments, and features of a rival's offerings that could immediately be reported back to branch offices and be applied to defend IBM proposals and to justify changes in IBM's terms, such as prices. In pre-e-mail days all of that occurred too, just slower in a more outdated fashion, taking weeks or months to play out, often with far fewer interactions. With PROFS communications occurred more rapidly, in hours or days.

As equipment became more sophisticated in the 1960s, figuring out what machines could work with each other, what software fit on which computers, and how much computer memory everything needed, among other issues involving configuration of systems of machines and software, increasingly could no longer be done accurately enough in one's head or through some manual fashion. By the early 1970s, IBM had installed an online system that combined sales manual information with field engineering data to configure a system at a terminal online. One could order a particular computer, for instance, add such peripheral equipment as tape drives, telecommunications control units, a printer, and a raft of software, and the system would determine what one needed to add to make it all work, and to price it all out. It worked, but, because nobody fully trusted computers, even IBMers, systems and field engineers then reviewed a printout on paper of the exercise in a required review meeting—called a Systems Assurance—to make sure the system had done it properly. These printouts served as input for everyone about the activities they needed to perform to get ready for the arrival of these items at a customer's data center. These computer-generated reports became inputs into a paper-based proposal that included the configuration, its cost, and statement of benefits of IBM's recommended solution.

Online configurations were adjusted if humans found errors and then when a paper letter order came in from a customer for this equipment or software, the online version would be sent to a branch office's administrator who transmitted electronically the order to all affected factories. That data—the configuration—along with requested delivery dates instantly flowed to a factory where other employees calculated when these machines could be built and delivered, did one more check to make sure all the bits and pieces needed to work were there—another "systems assurance"—and responded back with a committed delivery date that could be communicated to a customer in writing. That order became a bill-of-materials for the factory, listing parts needed to fabricate the equipment. Since multiple factories often were involved, because each specialized in types of parts and peripheral equipment, that same data flowed immediately to other destinations in the company. Order entry had its own national network (AAS) that kept administrative staffs apprised of progress and changes in delivery dates or configurations, and delivered information that could be used by branches, regions, divisions, and corporate to forecast when revenues would start coming from the equipment based on anticipated installation dates, and tracked accounts receivables. The customer engineers (CEs) also had their own system, called RETAIN (Remote Technical Assistance Information Network), where field personnel documented problems and solutions to these that all other CEs could tap into.

Because computers were expensive capital goods running into the tens of thousands, even millions of dollars, formal financial cost justification became an approach used by IBMers to persuade customers to "invest" in this equipment. Calculations using desktop adding machines for decades and handheld H-P calculators beginning in the early 1970s depended on the personal skills and knowledge of a salesman. Then salesmen were given an online tool (*Finpac*) in which they could key in the cost and configuration of whatever they were proposing (later extracting the data directly from the configuration done on the online HONE [Hands-On Network Environment] system). HONE configurations could be sent to the AAS system directly and then off to the plants.[36] The system ran financial cost justification models that calculated tax and depreciation implications of various options for financing equipment, adding any cost justification issues a salesman wanted, such as the displaced cost of labor no longer needed because of computerized automation or lowered cost of inventory. No longer did a salesman need to rely on their varying levels of financial expertise; IBM used professional financial and accounting experts to design the system, so the quality of the analysis proved more accurate, thorough, and precise. One could now quickly do "what if" analysis, modeling alternative financial strategies, even with a customer accountant sitting by their side as they varied the data, focusing on the most appropriate financial strategy tailored to meet the needs of a customer. The system collected information by product and by how salesmen used it, which then informed programmers who maintained the system to keep it current and improve its use and relevance.

In the 1970s and continuing into the 1990s, IBM added television to its information infrastructure, much like a commercial channel, reaching into every office and other facilities in most countries. IBMers in factories, education centers, division and corporate headquarters, and in national headquarters broadcast speeches and announcements. Presentations on new products followed by education on their use and installation made up a great deal of the information content on IBM's TV. Education in such areas as IBM's rules and norms comprised another collection of programming. Salesmen could learn how to sell a particular class of products; administrators how to enter an order for equipment; yet others on how to maintain and manage their budgets; still other sessions catered to field engineers, systems engineers, and administrative staffs. These programs were convenient, saved the cost and time of traveling to classes, and were usually broadcast at times relevant to its audience, such as presentations on the day a new product was being introduced. When IBM's board of directors dismissed their chairman, John Akers, in 1993, and introduced his replacement, the announcement was broadcast live on IBM TV, perhaps the most watched internal IBM program in history. Contrast that announcement to when Thomas Watson Sr. died in 1956 after running the company for over 40 years, when it came to all IBM offices as a brief telegram, lagging behind the more rapid announcement by commercial media running the story over the radio.

The rate of appropriation of IBM's electronic infrastructure paralleled that of customers who tended to be the most aggressive users of information technology. Like them, expenditures for these had to be budgeted, typically for the following year, then installations had to be followed by training. In some instances management mandated use of a particular online application, such as product order entry or use of a master production schedule on the shop floor in a factory.[37] Both IBM and its customers used similar applications of computing, although IBMers tended to deploy these sooner and across the entire enterprise more quickly.

IBMers used their internal systems to demonstrate to customers what they, too, could do with IBM's computers. Some uses turned into products. For example, when IBM faced a 12-year long antitrust suit with the U.S. Government in the 1970s–early 1980s in which a Federal judge required IBM to make available millions of pages of documents, the company developed a database to house, manage, and retrieve these materials. In time, IBM turned this tool into a product, while lessons learned about its functionality influenced development of IBM's widely-used database management software of the 1980s, most notably IMS (IBM Information Management System), used on the majority of large mainframes around the world into the twenty-first century.[38]

WHAT VISUAL EVIDENCE CAN TEACH US ABOUT INFORMATION ECOSYSTEMS AND INFRASTRUCTURES

In many ways, this chapter relied on conventional types of materials to understand IBM's information ecosystem and infrastructure, proving that this could be done using ephemera familiar to historians. But the company also has an archive housing photographs, some well over a century old. They provide additional insight on both information ecosystems and infrastructures. A few illustrate possibilities. Using images in research across many disciplines has proven effective, particularly with respect to enhancing an understanding of context and tacit knowledge, so in practice appropriating images for the study of information fits comfortably into normal historical practice.[39]

One can argue, too, that when looked at through the lens of information ecosystems and infrastructures, they can be powerful sources of evidence and insights. Our first framing question asked what media and mediums were used to collect and store information. In IBM's case, photographs (later film and video) became important for communicating the company's messages, distributing information (e.g., what a product looked like), and preserving its history. IBM's collection of images date to the turn of the twentieth century and run into thousands of still shots and hundreds of films and videos. How can they help define IBM's information ecosystem and infrastructure over time? Examples from still shots suggest possibilities for this company and other organizations. Photographs as a form of information contribute also to a growing interest among historians to study artifacts as a way of understanding such issues as role of genders (complex equipment used by men, simpler devices by women, such as industrial machinery versus typewriters), attitudes toward work processes, and messages broadcast by organizations.[40] Their interest is closely linked to how information is exchanged in offices and factories, too, thus components of an organization's information infrastructure.[41]

Begin with Figure 6.6, an image used in advertising in 1933. It shows a wide variety of IBM products, each of which was described in one to three pages in IBM's sales manuals and that were exhibited in branch offices. The top half shows all the punch card tabulating equipment, the mid-tier smaller information devices, such as time clocks, and the lower third largely scales. By the end of the 1930s, the bottom third of the product line was gone, the mid-tier reduced in variety, and the top third the core of IBM's business for the next two decades. The image demonstrates the variety of engineering knowledge IBM had to have and the diversity of its manufacturing capabilities, largely for precision machining. It reflected the variety of information handling devices companies and government agencies used in the 1920s and 1930s. No text is really required to demonstrate those facts.

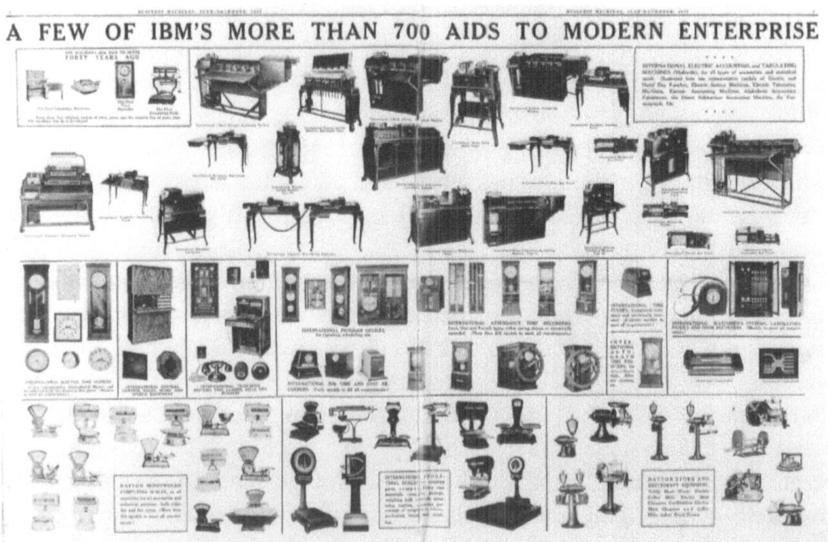

Figure 6.6. IBM Advertisement 1933
IBM Archives

Figure 6.7 tells a different story. Here we see a Field Engineer repairing a machine (IBM 402 Tabulator) in 1949. The picture hints at the complexity of the electronics by drawing our attention to that portion of the machine that shows the screwdriver and has the engineer's attention. In fact, this tabulator was a precursor to IBM's venture into computing. But notice the man. He is clean-shaven, recently had a haircut, and most important, he is wearing a suit to do maintenance work, complete with a white shirt and tie. IBM wanted its field force to look like their customers' management, to impress upon them the seriousness and high quality of its employees. This was not merely a humble machine repairman; he was an expert on data processing technology and how it could be used. He was a man to be taken seriously. By the end of the 1920s customers consulted IBM's repairmen on how best to maintain and use IBM's equipment, contributing to the ethos built over time of the company having highly skilled professionals in all manner of jobs.

Figure 6.7. IBM Field Engineer with An IBM 402 Tabulator, 1949
IBM Archives

Now compare Figure 6.8 with Figure 6.9. The first image shows IBM equipment in use in 1918. In the lower right-hand we have cabinets holding cards; they were placed there by hand. Slightly to the left is a young man feeding cards into a machine, and beyond him further up a card sorting machine. All three functions would have been required to conduct an accounting transaction involving a combination of people and machines interacting from one end of the procedure to anther. Now examine Fig-

Figure 6.8. IBM Equipment in Use, 1918
IBM Archives

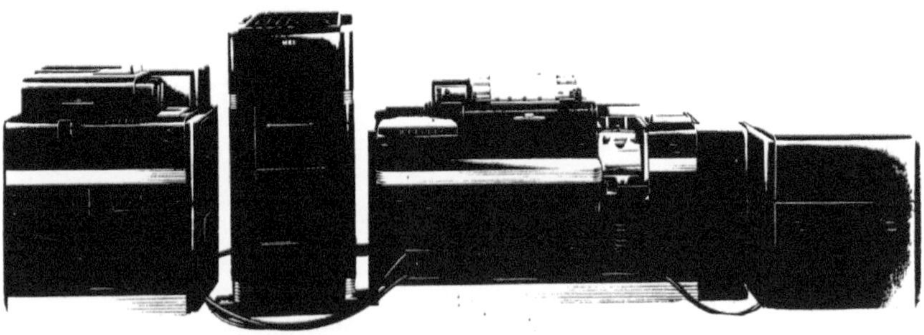

Figure 6.9. IBM Card Programmed Calculator, 1948
IBM Archives

ure 6.9, a Card Programmed Calculator (CPC) from 1948, thirty years later. The most dramatic difference communicated by this picture when compared to the earlier one is that now all the machines are connected together, not with people passing cards from one device to another, but by the machines doing that through the cables on the floor. In real life those cables would have been positioned behind the machines so as not to trip over them, but by having them in the front, the photograph emphasizes the engineering change that occurred with this generation of equipment.[42] In subsequent decades, all cables went under the floor of a data center because by then data processing equipment "talked" to each other and so involved larger numbers of them than depicted in this photograph.

Figure 6.10 shows one of IBM's earliest and most popular computers, the IBM 1401. The photograph dates from 1959 and begins to show what a computer *system* looked like in the 1960s and 1970s. Now the cables are under the floor, we no longer see the company or its customers viewing machines as individual items, rather as an integrated whole. The advanced nature of its technology is reinforced by the magnetic tapes on the desk, which were rapidly replacing punch cards as the preferred medium to store

Figure 6.10. IBM 1401, 1959
IBM Archives

information, doing so at less cost than on cards. By 1959 debates about whether to keep data on cards or tape had ended; here IBM declares victory for the more advanced medium. To the right we see tape drives that wrote to and read from tape. We still have a card processing machine in the left hand corner to indicate that this system was versatile in that it could continue to process information stored on the massive quantities of files customers still had in card form. The computer is in the middle and to its right is a printer. Everyone is looking professional and in control.

Figure 6.11 is one of the most widely seen photographs that ever came out of IBM, this one of the IBM System 360, mentioned earlier comprising 150 products introduced on April 7, 1964—the largest number ever

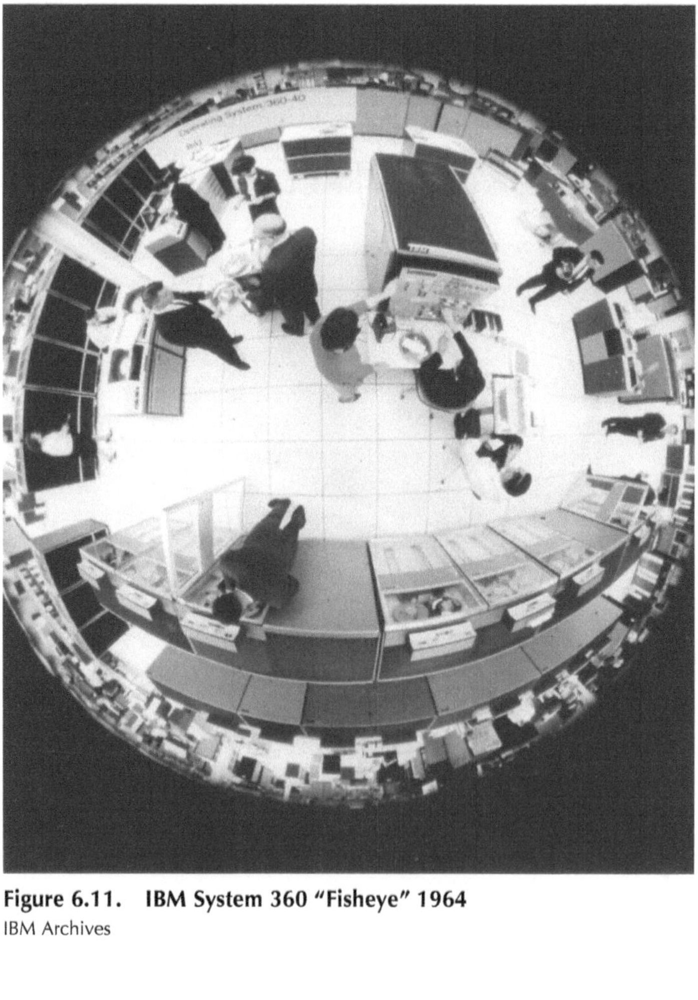

Figure 6.11. IBM System 360 "Fisheye" 1964
IBM Archives

introduced in the computer industry. Even today when Apple introduces a new hand-held device, it might bring out three to five items. This picture sends the message that this new system was comprehensive—new computers, peripheral equipment, software, procedures, and new possibilities—although most people thought the fisheye picture reflected the System 360 name when it meant 360 degrees. Look carefully and it shows an enormous variety of equipment along the periphery, speaking to the technical prowess and leadership of the company that dared to push computing technology an entire generation forward. It made all existing computers from all vendors obsolete.[43]

A challenge computer companies and computer scientists faced for over a half century was how to communicate the dramatic changes that occurred with miniaturization of computer components. One's digital watch has more power than an IBM 1401 depicted in Figure 6.10. That was only possible because of miniaturization. Hundreds of photographs were taken to try and tell that story. Figures 6.12 and 6.13 are examples from IBM. The way to read Figure 6.12 is to begin in the back, with tubes used in the 1940s to store information, glancing next to the middle with the white boards housing transistors (1950s), then down further to the two black sets of computer chips (1960s), finally to the bottom to highly integrated circuits (1970s). The message is clear: dramatic advances have been made in the miniaturization of data storage and processing components of the computer. Figure 6.13 attempts to deliver a stronger message regarding miniaturization by showing two fingers holding a computer chip. These pictures suggest what had happened to the technology in a short period of time. To customers, largely in data centers, who would have physically held these devices the picture would also have told them about specific features of the various generations of the technology, from the light bulb-like devices to the integrated circuits that looked like miniature welding projects. The text surrounding such pictures described the decline in cost for these. One Honeywell computer advertisement of the 1970s argued that if luxury automobile manufacturers had achieved the same levels of productivity as computer engineers, a Rolls Royce would only cost $5. Advertising proved highly effective in integrating images with text to communicate complex technical ideas.[44]

One final image suggests another message: simplicity for the common man. Figure 6.14 from 1981 is of IBM's first personal computer product. It is a classic example of what might immediately seem to the reader to be a sterile, lifeless image of yet another computing device. But for the historian of information, it tells much more. It announces that IBM was

Figure 6.12. Miniaturization of Computer Memories Over Time
IBM Archives

Figure 6.13. Integrated Circuit—"Computer Chip," 1970s
IBM Archives

Figure 6.14. IBM Personal Computer, 1981
IBM Archives

entering the consumer computer business—a first for the firm—and that it was doing so with a stylishly designed set of devices: keyboard, computer, monitor on top, and to the left a small printer. Miniaturization, style, and a new business venture all came together. Within two years it dominated the personal computer market. But look further. The monitor (screen) displays statistical information, suggesting that this machine could now handle "what-if" analysis of numerical data. The "killer app" in the beginning for personal computers of the late 1970s–early 1980s was its ability to work with spreadsheets. When this picture was taken the ability to use word processing was introduced by several vendors including IBM, which in time surpassed spreadsheet uses. But the nod to word processing, already evident at the time, is the text being printed on the little printer to the left. The keyboard speaks of familiarity to new users comfortable with the QWERTY keyboard of a typewriter and with the keys to the right on the keyboard in the same layout as on adding machines. The message: "You do not need to be a computer expert to use this machine," and IBM's advertising tag line, "A Tool for Modern Times."

These half dozen images are the tip of the iceberg. Corporations produced tens of thousands of movies in the twentieth century in the United States alone; amazingly, there is no history of these. But they can be even more informative, much as when watching an old Hollywood movie in which we see what rooms and street scenes looked like, how the roles of women and children were depicted, attitudes toward issues of interest to us today, and so forth. Old movies and corporate films offer contextual information about attitudes, facts, social, and business infrastructures beyond what one can learn from reading text. The argument can be made that in studying information ecosystems and infrastructures you should not overlook the power of images, that they should be viewed with the same critical eye that, say, a historian or literature professor analyzes a document or what Shakespeare meant with a turn of phrase. They should not be treated merely as superficial decorations for a text.

CONCLUSIONS

IBM's information ecosystem and infrastructure illustrate how the introduction of computing affected the kinds of information one could collect and use, the increased effects on wider use of structured information, and the nature of the digital and electronic media infrastructure underpinning IBM's evolving information world. Technology made its information ecosystem thicker and more dynamic. IBM's experience paralleled that of many other large American, Japanese, and West European corporations of the time. But this chapter told the story of a closed, highly prescribed world. What happens when that world is partially situated within a larger information ecosystem could be seen with photographs shared outside of IBM. But ask the same question with respect to a company's or university's extended information ecosystem, such as that offered by computer scientists all over the world, and we see similarities and differences. The message to take away from this chapter is the same posed by the earlier one on Spanish diplomats: that using the lens of information ecosystems and infrastructures makes it possible for historians in other fields of historiography to view their subjects in new ways, including diplomatic, political, and business historians, representatives of some of the oldest subjects of historical inquiry.

Chapter 7 illustrates possibilities to explore in larger, more diverse communities. Serving as a contrast to the closed order of the IBM case, we examine how computer scientists shared information across firms, governments, and entire nations within the context of the Cold War. We will see similarities between their behavior and those of the farm wives and children of Madison County.

NOTES

1. Emerson W. Pugh, *Building IBM: Shaping an Industry and Its Technology* (Cambridge, MA: MIT Press, 1995): 323–324.

2. A major finding about large enterprises in the second half of the twentieth century, James W. Cortada, *The Digital Hand,* 3 vols. (New York: Oxford University Press, 2004–2008); but see also, among the earliest James Beniger, *The Control Revolution: Technological and Economic Origins of the Information Society* (Cambridge, MA: Harvard University Press, 1986), and more recently, Lisa Bud-Frierman, ed., *Information Acumen: The Understanding and Use of Knowledge in Modern Business* (London: Routledge, 1994), and Margaret Levenstein, *Accounting for Growth: Information Systems and the Creation of the Large Corporation* (Stanford, CA: Stanford University Press, 1998); James W. Cortada, *All the Facts: A History of Information in the United States since 1870* (New York: Oxford University Press, 2016): 98–131, 281–325.

3. Walter A. Friedman, *Birth of a Salesman: The Transformation of Selling in America* (Cambridge, MASS: Harvard University Press, 2004); Kevin Maney, *The Maverick and His Machine: Thomas Watson, Sr. and The Making of IBM* (Hoboken, NJ: John Wiley & Sons 2003).

4. Pugh, *Building IBM,* 323–324.

5. The central focus of Maney, *The Maverick and His Machine.*

6. A key finding in James W. Cortada, "IBM," forthcoming from MIT Press.

7. Pugh, *Building IBM,* 324.

8. For the period described by an IBM sales executive, F. G. "Buck" Rogers, *The IBM Way: Insights into the World's Most Successful Marketing Organization* (New York: Harper & Row, 1986).

9. James W. Cortada, Carrying A Bag: A Memoir of an IBM Salesman, 1974–1981," *IEEE Annals of the History of Computing* 35, no. 4 (October–December 2013): 32–47.

10. Charles J. Bashe, Lyle R. Johnson, John H. Palmer, and Emerson W. Pugh, *IBM's Early Computers* (Cambridge, MA: MIT Press, 1985).

11. James W. Cortada, "IBM Branch Offices: What They Were, How They Worked, 1920s–1980s," *IEEE Annals of the History of Computing* 39, no. 3 (July–September 2017): 9–23.

12. Economists and historians are increasingly recognizing the skills and information quality of this form of conversation. The distinguished economist, Deirdre Nansen McCloskey, has termed this activity "sweet talking," the act of persuading people to make decisions and to take action, the central activity of an economy, Deirdre Nansen McCloskey, *Bourgeois Quality: How Ideas, Not Capital or Institutions, Enriched the World* (Chicago, IL: University of Chicago Press, 2016): 489–498.

13. James W. Cortada, "'There Is No Saturation Point in Education': Inside IBM's Sales School, 1970s–1980s," *IEEE Annals of the History of Computing* 37, no. 1 (January–March 2015): 56–66.

14. A few examples of these reports remain scattered about in different files at the IBM Corporate Archives, Somers, NY.

15. Jay R. Galbraith, *Designing Matrix Organizations That Actually Work: How IBM, Procter & Gamble, and Others Design for Success* (San Francisco, CA: Jossey-Bass, 2009).

16. Rogers, *The IBM Way.*

17. Alfred D. Chandler, Jr., *The Visible Hand: The Managerial Revolution in American Business* (Cambridge, MA: Harvard University Press, 1977): 494–496.

18. Discussed in considerable detail in numerous chapters by Maney, *The Maverick and His Machine* and by Thomas J. Watson Jr. and Peter Petre, *Father Son & Co.: My Life At IBM And Beyond* (New York: Bantam, 1990).

19. For IBM's defense, Franklin M. Fisher, James W. McKie, and Richard B. Mancke, *IBM and the U.S. Data Processing Industry: An Economic History* (New York: Praeger, 1983); Franklin M. Fisher and John J. McGowan, *Folded, Spindled and Mutilated: Economic Analysis and U.S. vs. IBM* (Cambridge, MA: MIT Press, 1983); for the U.S. Government's perspective, R. T. DeLamarter, *Big Blue: IBM's Use and Abuse of Power* (New York: Dodd, Mead & Co., 1986).

20. In fact, this happened. During the early 1980s, the U.S. experienced an annual inflation rate so high that loans often cost as much as 18 percent. That caused IBM to offer financing to customers since it could borrow money are lower rates than they could.

21. IBM, *Manual of IBM Punched Card Accounting Machines and Auxiliary Equipment* (New York: IBM Corporation, circa 1956) and *IBM Sales Manual* (White Plains, NY: circa 1974), both in the possession of the author. Similar items also available at IBM Corporate Archives, Somers, NY.

22. IBM, *Manual of IBM Punched Card Accounting Machines and Auxiliary Equipment,* unpaginated front matter.

23. The only known collections of these are housed at the IBM Corporate Archives, Somers, NY, and at the Charles Babbage Institute Archives in the "Cortada Papers," University of Minnesota, Minneapolis.

24. IBM, *System/360 Model 20 Pre-School Student Self-Study Course* (San Jose, CA: IBM Corporation, F. E. Education, 1966), copy in author's possession.

25. For the System 360, IBM Corporation, "IBM System/360 Combines New Microelectronic Circuits With Advanced Concepts in Computer Organization," *Technical Information*, April 7, 1964, released by the IBM Data Processing Division, White Plains, NY, copy in author's possession.

26. A handful exist at IBM Corporate Archives, Somers, NY. Author has a collection from the 1970s through the early 1990s.

27. IBM Corporate Archives, Somers, NY, keeps complete sets of all division level newsletters, company-wide newspapers and *THINK* magazine.

28. As far back as the 1880s, James Beniger, *The Control Revolution.*

29. A key finding of James W. Cortada, *IBM*, forthcoming.

30. Philip Scranton and Patrick Fridenson, *Reimagining Business History* (Baltimore, MD: Johns Hopkins University Press, 2013): 98–102.

31. Ibid., 99; also central in my larger study on IBM, Cortada, *IBM,* forthcoming.

32. Ibid., 101.

33. I have made inquiries about these issues of both the company's archivists and IT support staff several times beginning in the 1980s and mot recently in 2012. Neither kept such records.

34. Extant copies of IBM telephone directories from the 1950s through the 1990s in my collection are marked up with new numbers replacing old ones, and old names scratched out by hand replaced with new ones as well. The few preserved by the IBM Archives are in pristine condition and so do not demonstrate how they were used.

35. They remained in many mailrooms, completely ignored, not even obvious. Your author asked one mailroom employee in the early 2000s why they were still around since they took up a great deal of room. The response was "What? I donno." It obviously had not occurred to get rid of these, even though unused file cabinets and typewriters had been discarded for years.

36. Hands On Network Environment, described by W. Boos, "HONE: The IBM Marketing Support System," *IBM Systems Journal,* nos. 3/4 (1985), 189.

37. Cortada, *The Digital Hand*, a finding evident across 18 industries studied.

38. K. R. Blackman, "Technical Note: IMS Celebrates Thirty Years as an IBM Product," *IBM Systems Journal,* 37, no. 4 (1998): 596–603.

39. Douglas Harper, "Talking About Pictures: A Case for Photo Elicitation," *Visual Studies*, 17, no. 1 (2002): 13–26; John Collier and Malcom Collier, *Visual Anthropology: Photography as a Research Method* (Albuquerque, NM: University of New Mexico Press, 1986); Penny Tinkler, *Using Photographs in Social and Historical Research* (Thousand Oaks, CA: SAGE Publications, 2013).

40. Arjun Appadural, ed., *The Social Life of Things: Commodities in Cultural Perspective* (Cambridge: Cambridge University Press, 1986); Bill Brown, ed., *Things* (Chicago, IL: University of Chicago Press, 2004).

41. JoAnne Yates, *Control through Communication: The Rise of System in American Management* (Baltimore, MD: Johns Hopkins University Press, 1993); Philip Scranton and Patrick Fridenson, *Reimagining Business History* (Baltimore, MD: Johns Hopkins University Press, 2013): 57–61.

42. There are earlier photographs from the 930s that began showing cables linking tabulating equipment together. In this photograph we see that happening with what was rapidly evolving into computers.

43. Paul E. Ceruzzi, *A History of Modern Computing,* 2nd ed. (Cambridge, MA: MIT Press, 2003): 143–173.

44. William Aspray, "Marketing the Monster: Advertising Computer Technology," *Annals of the History of Computing* 8, no. 2 (1986): 127–143.

Chapter Seven

How People and Organizations Learned About Information

The Case of Computer Science and Its Users, 1945–1975

The value of any network increases in proportion to the square of the number of people using it.

—Robert Metcalfe

An information ecosystem emerged rapidly after World War II that made possible creation and sharing of information about computing and its uses around the world. Four groups of participants populated this ecosystem: engineers and scientists, vendors and suppliers of computers, customers of this technology and other users, and large organizations. While the politics of the Cold War and varying national economic conditions affected the work of all participants, a global network emerged that diffused information about computing. These agents constructed a nearly invisible information ecosystem with an underlining information infrastructure. This case study describes behavior and types of information that parallel patterns documented in Chapter 5 about the women and children of Madison County, Virginia. Both the activities of these homemakers and students and of the four classes of participants in sharing information about computing occurred at the same time, but they were physically far apart as they played out. Yet, both behaved in similar ways The approach taken in this chapter follows that used in earlier ones to define the type and role of information. First, we identify the four constituent participants. Next, and as part of doing so, we identify what information they used and activities they engaged in with this emerging body of knowledge. By this means we define the features of the ecosystem and its supporting infrastructure.

There are differences, too. The ladies of Madison County worked with an existing body of information, focusing more on its diffusion within their community and on passing it on to their children, less on creating it. When new information emerged, these new facts and practices were subsumed into a larger preexisting collection of knowledge and data. In contrast, the computing community invented its information, appropriated pre-existing methods for collecting and diffusing it, then modified these to more precisely meet their needs in the emerging field of computer science. Even its name—computer science—needed to be invented, while the residents of Madison County already had theirs—housewives and cooking—and the necessary language and way of organizing their facts to describe these, such as recipes, cookbooks, and demonstration clubs. People and institutions interested in computing had to invent new concepts, such as software, programming languages, and computer science.

In Madison County generations of participants had known each other for two centuries before the period we studied. By contrast the computer community had to form and to meet each other for the first time. They had to determine how best to interact with each other, how to depend upon, or fend off, some members of the four communities, such as vendors in competition with one another in the same ecosystem. IBM employees were significant participants in these four constituencies as engineers and scientists, salesmen, users of computers themselves, and representatives of their organizations. They joined an information ecosystem that even in the beginning outnumbered them and within two decades did so by over an order of magnitude. Even the number of countries participating in this information ecosystem exceeded those in which IBM maintained a presence. One quick example: IBM did not have a formal presence in Communist China during the period under investigation, but the Chinese had thousands of citizens familiar with computers in the 1950s–1970s. IBM did not install and maintain computers in China, but the Chinese had such machines and even used IBM's operating systems software and copies of other technologies without the firm's permission. IBM attempted to become the main focal point, the center of the emerging information ecosystem, and came close to doing so during the era of the mainframe computer (1960s–early 1980s). Technological transformations brought into the information ecosystem new participants, such as PC vendors, that kept the firm from being king of the hill. The ecosystem described in this chapter is the largest one explored in this book.

As argued throughout this book and as our framing questions suggest, after identifying the players in our case study we describe patterns of behavior. Behind the story of this chapter's information ecosystems and infrastructures is a larger one about the development of a new discipline which motivated their behavior, so that needs to be understood before proceeding much farther. We then proceed to discuss the details of how this ecosystem emerged and its form was shaped. As with the other cases, my purpose is to suggest what a study of information ecosystems and infrastructures looks like in practice. This is yet another example of demonstrating that the history of information can be studied as a specific subfield of history with one way of becoming familiar with a new topic or with a method that sheds new light on the development of a new profession and disciplines. In this case, it is about the history of computer science, just now being addressed by historians of technology and computing. There are lessons to be drawn from how the history of information is examined.

PARTICIPANTS IN THE COMPUTER SCIENCE ECOSYSTEM

Development of computers began during World War II for military purposes, largely in the United States and Great Britain. After this war computing extended to other government-sponsored experimental projects in other countries, including the Soviet Union. Government financial support, military needs of the Cold War, and rapid progress in the emergence of this technology fueled development. By the early 1950s commercial computers began appearing with American vendors early dominating this new market. By the early 1960s, many dozens of firms sold products around the world, including IBM, Burroughs, ERA, CDC, Honeywell, Remington Rand, and GE among others in the United States, still others in Western Europe. Builders of computers in the 1940s and 1950s were often electrical engineers or radio ham operators experienced with working on advanced electronics during the war.[1] On the other side of the Iron Curtain in the Soviet Union, a small cadre of engineers, too, became interested in computing, led by Segei A. Lebedev and others.[2]

Early computer developers quickly came to know each other and about their work on both sides of the Cold War. The majority of new information about computing in the 1940s centered in Great Britain and the United States, but by the mid-1950s and through the 1970s, clearly in the latter, where the largest number of experts worked. Of all the commercial firms developing and selling computers, IBM dominated both the markets in the non-communist world and the technology used behind the Iron Curtain, where Soviet computer manufacturers began standardizing on IBM's technologies in the 1960s without patent and copyright permission of the corporation. Nonetheless, eastern European engineers did developmental work too, including exploring cybernetics and use of programming languages.[3]

The most fundamental reason why computers spread around the world was not just because governments and vendors supported this work—although important—but because information about this new technology diffused among those who had to design, build, and use these early systems. They had to determine what components and know-how they needed. They put these together and explored uses of the technology. The issue of what to do with them evolved rapidly all through the period as their functions and reliability of these machines and software improved. Commercial suppliers had the added information requirement of determining how to manufacture these machines in a way that would allow them to make a profit. Until the mid-1950s, each machine was essentially built one at a time; IBM became the first vendor to develop a mass production process to make hundreds, then thousands of computers and peripheral devices, instead of dozens as had been the case before.

Because of the complexity and enormous cost of this new class of technology, diffusion of information about it, and its resultant emergence as an information ecosystem with a complementary infrastructure, the topic rapidly engaged a growing community of engineers, scientists, and business employees and others working in universities, government laboratories, and corporations in over two dozen countries by the end of the 1950s. The Cold War loomed over all of them, raising issues. For example, could an American computer engineer be candid with a Russian engineer about the practical challenges of his work, or did that violate some national security law or code of ethics? This was a new question for computer developers on both sides of the Cold War.[4] The historical record shows they shared far more information with each other than one might have thought would have occurred. Engineers related with fellow engineers, academics in one country with those in another, regardless of nationality.[5] Without sharing information, computers might not have diffused around the world, or at least not as fast they did. With hundreds doing the sharing in the mid-1940s, several thousand individuals by the early 1950s, even more thousands by the mid-1960s, and still increasing in number in subsequent years, they came from various backgrounds (engineering, science, public administration, military, and business). Membership in this particular information ecosystem kept expanding throughout the second half of the twentieth century.

In these early decades of computing, four constituencies formed this information ecosystem. The earliest members were engineers and scientists who developed computers, some peripheral equipment and software, and in the process built the first two generations of computer systems in the 1940s and 1950s. A second constituency consisted of business employees of companies in Western Europe, later Japan, who manufactured and supported computers, such as IBMers (as they were known). With the second group engaged, a third appeared: customers, often also called *users*. They quickly outnumbered the first two types of participants, creating much of the information infrastructure used by engineers and vendors, such as organizations to share information, hosting conferences that did the same, publishing on the topic, and collaborating with each other and with the first two constituencies. A fourth cohort of government and military officials funded research worldwide and included within their ranks engineers, computer scientists, managers, and users.

PATTERNS OF PRACTICES

These four groups shared several common behaviors around the world. First, their members brought into their countries information about computing technology before there were any computers in their homelands. This influx of information flowed to engineers and scientists, diffused within the organizations in which they worked, such as academic institutes, government agencies (including the military), universities, and finally flowed to potential vendors of the technology. Next, with growing awareness of emerging technologies came experiments in building such equipment, typically in universities and in some government laboratories. That experimentation stimulated internal education within these organizations about local projects and increasingly outbound to other interested engineers and potential users within a country, or even across a continent, as happened in North America and all over Western and Eastern Europe. Lastly, technical advocates and general management increasingly took notice and began stimulating demand, financial and operational commitments for acquiring the technology, and allocation of staffs to use it.[6]

Information flowed initially within the United Kingdom and United States, where the greatest amount existed and interest proved keen. The United States quickly became the largest exporter of information about computing for the rest of the century. One can trace that flow of information, much of which remained the same from one country to another, over time through events such as conferences, meetings among computer scientists, sources of publications from journals and magazines to books, and finally where companies like IBM conducted business.[7] Such an exercise allows one to generalize about activities of these four cohorts, saying, for example, that in the 1940s and 1950s they began expanding their activities and information across Western Europe, in the early 1950s–1960s in Eastern Europe, into Japan and India and Australia in the same decades, then to other parts of Asia in the 1970s and 1980s.[8]

Of that third wave, the first participants resided in South Korea, Singapore, Taiwan, Hong Kong, and finally China. Those in the 1990s and beyond included Malaysia, Thailand, the Philippines, and Vietnam. New participants among the four cohorts in other countries contributed their experiences and innovations to the global supply of information about computing, which all communities had access to, regardless of Cold War barriers or other conflicts. In South America, an area rife with economic challenges, knowledge about computing diffused too, particularly within Mexico, Brazil, and Argentina in the 1960s and 1970s, followed by a second wave of initiates to information technology that included Chile, Paraguay, Peru, Costa Rica, Trinidad, and Cuba in the 1980s–1990s.[9] Not until the late 1980s did over three-dozen African nations begin to nurture the four communities that made up the computing ecosystem.[10]

As these four communities expanded their membership, they increased their overall volume of information about computing. This could be measured by examining the number of new academic and trade journals published around the world on computing, rising rates of subscriptions for these, numbers of students in universities studying computer science, increasing volume of sales for IBM's computers, and expanding use of conferences and their growing attendance figures over time. The majority of all these activities remained open and transparent with participants engaged from all over the world, such that by the early 1960s there existed a dense global community of individuals, many of whom knew each other from other countries.[11] Each set of four cohorts had roles to play.

Engineers and scientists, always the first members of this ecosystem anywhere in the world, were the most important founding figures, because they created the largest initial body of scientific and technical information, and added to it more than any other group in the second half of the century. They were located largely in American and British academic institutions, but by the end of the 1950s in companies interested in developing computer products. Following the end of World War II, experts hosted seminars on the new technology, mostly in the United States, with attendees from Western European, British, and American government agencies and universities.[12] That practice of holding seminars became a permanent worldwide feature of their information network. This community also visited each other's sites to learn about the rapidly diversifying technologies. We now know that employees in American embassies prepared reports of these visits and projects, beginning in the 1940s.[13] Visitors included mathematicians, engineers, and scientists from the United States to Great Britain and northern Europe, even to the Soviet Union by the early 1960s, and to other government agencies, office equipment vendors, and potential users, notably insurance companies, large banks, and government agencies. Early American commercial participants included engineers from IBM, NCR, General Electric, and RCA.[14] In the late 1940s, academics and engineers began establishing journals to discuss developments in the new technology, such as the Association for Computing Machinery (ACM).[15]

Already mentioned were government engineers, scientists, and mathematicians interested in supporting Cold War objectives in the 1940s–1960s. Most academics, funded largely by government agencies, represented an extension of that community motivated as well to do the same but also by economic and scientific incentives. Engineers in corporations were keen to develop commercial computing, most aggressively in the United States and, lagging by only a few years, Western Europe. Many moved from government and academic work to establish early start-up firms, such as ERA and the Eckert-Mauchly companies in the United States. Due to the nature of the technology that we do not need to discuss here, it made sense for much of this interest to center on developing electronic components and computers, and use of computing in scientific projects in the 1940s and 1950s, later for commercial applications, such as in accounting and inventory control.[16]

This private sector cohort demonstrated a willingness to share openly what they were learning about developing such components as computer memories and how to fabricate computers together in the 1940s and early 1950s. As the Cold War intensified in the 1950s and 1960s government engineers became more circumspect about sharing "secrets" of potential military value to one side or the other. Others working in companies behaved the same way to protect the competitive advantages of their employers. These kinds of behavior slowed exchanges of information, but less than one might have thought. Meanwhile, academic computer scientists and engineers published profusely about their findings. In the 1940s and 1950s, profusely meant annually hundreds of articles, thousands in the 1960s and 1970s.[17] One estimate suggested that some 20,000 articles and other publications appeared about computers between 1945 and 1965.[18] In the next decade the volume published vastly exceeded that of the earlier period.

Their trips to see each other's projects, publication of so much material, and growing participation by thousands of individuals in the 1960s created a dense information ecosystem and supporting infrastructure of government financing and homes in universities, government research laboratories, and corporations. Trip reports made the community visible, hence, easier for new entrants to join. American delegations to Western and Eastern European sites routinely appeared in reports published by the ACM and the Computer Society.[19]

At the same time, a smaller but similar group of engineers and scientists emerged on the Communist side of the Iron Curtain, just as keen to acquire information about computing then in full bloom in the West. Most worked in engineering institutes across Eastern Europe, although many predominantly in Moscow and in East Germany. East Europeans visited American and West European colleagues, collected much information that they, too, reported on, and subscribed to all the key publications from the West. The Soviets routinely rapidly translated into Russian and some East European languages over 2,500 Western journals covering all manner of scientific and engineering subjects, including computing.[20] With Moscow becoming the center for the construction of computers, it became the information hub for the East just as in the 1940s through the 1960s U.S. coastal communities did too, notably Boston and Philadelphia in the 1940s and 1950s, then increasingly Los Angeles and Silicon Valley in the 1950s and 1960s. Soviet computing relied overwhelmingly on Western technical standards, even to the point that their mainframes in the 1960s and 1970s were essentially retro-engineered copies of IBM's popular mainframe System 360s and 370s and pirated copies of its software, and use of the popular Western European programming language, Algol.[21]

Engineers and computer scientists from around the world quickly needed to organize the rapidly expanding body of information about computers and to that end relied on specialized academic organizations, followed by commercial publishers to supply them with books and magazines, two practices that expanded throughout the period. Among the more academic engineering and user oriented providers of information, publications, and seminars were the ACM (established 1947), Data Processing Management Association (DPMA) (founded 1949), IEEE Computer Society (1951), Society for Computer Simulation (SCS) (1952), and SHARE (1955), the last of which was a user's group that published annual proceedings from conferences. SHARE became a model for user groups organized either by vendor, IBM in this case, or by type of technology, in which developers and data processing managers would meet to discuss issues and needs, to advise each other while discussing concerns with vendors in hopes of influencing development of new products and resolving existing problems. Dozens of book publishers provided user manuals and academic discourses on the technology and how best to design, build, and use them, offering these in the thousands and in all Western languages. The Soviets published many of these in translation, too.[22] What were they publishing about?

THE BIRTH OF COMPUTER SCIENCE AS A DISCIPLINE

Everything discussed in this chapter was the outward manifestation of a larger drama in play: the creation of a new academic discipline, computer science. This was a battle to gain independence from pre-existing disciplines and to shape a new one. It involved conquering old lands and finding new spaces, seizing experts in electronics and mathematics and bringing them into new academic departments, physical offices, and new roles and organizations in government, academia, and industry. This was a world war against prior thinking and the emergence of new perspectives waged in every advanced economy from the early 1950s through the end of the 1960s. By the 1970s, computer science emerged as a discipline largely independent of electrical engineering and mathematics, complete with its own curricula, academic departments now being established in many universities around the world, employees at such companies and agencies as IBM or at various European technical institutes, academic and professional associations, scholarly journals, trade magazines, and T shirts and coffee mugs. They hosted their own annual conventions, which in time became some of the largest in the world. What everyone did with information about computing and the complex infrastructures they built makes more sense when understood as an outward manifestation of the birth of computer science.

Much of the development of computer hardware—components, computers, and peripheral equipment—in the 1940s took place in academic settings by engineers and mathematicians with some involvement by electronic suppliers (such as General Electric), office equipment vendors (such as IBM), and a few startup firms. Other participants included amateur radio enthusiasts and military personnel who drifted into the subject during World War II. But in the 1950s and 1960s a concerted effort made by these individuals led to the creation of a new identity for themselves and for the work they were doing, elevating their activities into a discipline, much as one thinks of physics, engineering, or mathematics. Participants appreciated that too many government officials and scientists did not understand that computing was emerging as far more than another collection of mathematical tools. In the 1950s academic engineers and mathematicians began teaching classes on what eventually became known as software and programming, which helped to provide definition to the new topic.[23] By 1960 the software and hardware communities had been merging rapidly into what came to be called computer science. By 1963, at least 28 universities offered degrees in computer science from the bachelor to the Ph.D.[24] Their proto-computer scientists established a number of professional organizations in support of this newly emerging field. These included the Association for Computing Machinery (ACM) in 1947 that in the 1950s and 1960s did more to promote the new identity than many other organizations. The IEEE Computer Society came into being in 1970 as a consolidation of earlier groups interested in computing. In the United States the National Science Foundation (NSF) provided an enormous amount of the American government's funding for computing projects and, so, played a role in shaping the new discipline. Other organizations in the Soviet Union keen on turning cybernetics into a computing discipline at the same time played similar roles in funding and encouraging. The support the NSF gave, in particular, went far to form the field.

The proto-discipline quickly acquired identity in the 1950s and early 1960s. Briefly summarized, this happened because, to use one historian's words, they used "a variety of rhetorical and organizational strategies" to "claim scientific respectability for their field and gain control of their own funding stream within NSF," although the same comment can be made of computing's advocates in other countries, including in the USSR.[25] Americans implemented actions that included using the resources and members of the ACM to advocate establishment of a discursive boundary for the subject, defining it through papers and commentary, many published by the ACM's house organ, *Communications of the ACM.* They circulated white papers and books within the growing information ecosystem of computing comprised of academics, government officials, and private sector managers and engineers. Their activities discussed in our case study serve as witnesses to the development of a new information ecosystem and supporting infrastructure.

Central to their activities was the importance they placed on information. Historian Janet Abbate summarized how they did this:

> In addition to arguing directly for their field's scientific worthiness, ACM leaders pursued a discursive strategy of generating and disseminating information to back up their claims. Quantitative data on such topics as "scientific manpower" provided powerful ammunition for science policy struggles in 1960s America. By creating facts (statements about reality that were accepted as true and objective) on such topics, computer scientists could shape the context in which federal policy makers would consider their requests for funding.[26]

Careful, yet frequent, discussions around the world about what constituted computer science built the basis for the argument in favor of the new discipline, hence subsequently for funding to support research and staffing for it. In the process, even the definition of the notion of *science* came under debate. As one historian summed up the resulting development of computer science, "computer professionals could argue that they were scientists by virtue of having a unique subject domain within the natural world, a high level of intellectual challenge, a body of theory or technique, or even a passion for research."[27]

Much took place, which space does not permit us to discuss. However, it is important to recognize that discussions about definitions and so forth began in the 1950s. By the end of 1955, these had become an international discourse, the result of visits and conferences that created networks of personal and intellectual contacts.[28] Historians have emphasized the forms of scientific communications that gave the new subject an intellectual gravitas crucial to its acceptance, since the field was constructed at the nexus of various disciplines, such as electrical engineering, physics, chemistry, and mathematics in various universities, government agencies, countries, and corporations.[29]

Two other circumstances facilitated the successful emergence of this new discipline that can only be acknowledged here. As historians turn their attention to these, we may learn whether one was of greater importance or another; it is sufficient now, however, to acknowledge their importance. First, professors on both sides of the Atlantic and in Russia developed curricula to teach computing and it was through that process that they were able to shape the subject, such as to define courses in programming, software architectures, hardware memory systems, computer architectures (what a machine consisted of), and so forth.[30] The second was the existence of the Cold War, which motivated governments to fund development of those technologies in support of complex weapons systems, such as nuclear bombs and battlefield and air combat systems, and to facilitate mathematical/scientific data analysis and planning, called OR (Operations Research).[31] Both sides in the Cold War became by necessity and curiosity part of a global information ecosystem, whose activities are described below.

Cold War considerations may have been more important than creating classes, because the former involved large numbers of individuals and massive quantities of funding for both the definition phase of identifying computer science as a discipline and then in turning it from an intellectual exercise into the development and use of computers worldwide.[32] The West tended to think of computing as about software and hardware, while the Soviets favored cybernetics, a more intellectual discourse in the 1950s–1960s. For them, cybernetics was less about a body of scientific information and more a dialectic in support of communism, compromising its scientific value in the eyes of many computing experts in the West.[33] At the same time, the Soviets built an information infrastructure to acquire Western scientific and engineering knowledge. It included the capability of translating into Eastern European languages articles from some 2,500 Western journals on all manner of science (not just computing), a mechanism for distributing these quickly to appropriate institutes, universities, factories, and other government agencies, and the exchange of information with the West discussed below. The discussion of alternative views of computing—computer science versus cybernetics—ended by the start of the 1980s. Historian Ksenia Tatarchenko brought down the curtain on the drama played out among the protagonists of the Cold War with the simple conclusion that "cybernetics' loss was a gain for the up-and-coming discipline of computer science," because it "drew on the universality, international authority, and administrative power of an already established discipline, that of mathematics." This same historian added, computer science "was predicated on the international flow of knowledge."[34] Put less elegantly, computer science led to development of machines and software useful to governments, their military, and everyone's businesses. The world eventually concluded that computer science translated into functioning machines and improved operations.[35]

With the essential story of the emergence of computing as a body of information in mind, we can now turn to a more focused identification of the participants, to the information ecosystems they populated, and to the infrastructures they created to facilitate development, dissemination, and appropriation of this new class of scientific and engineering facts. Who now did most of the work of nurturing information ecosystems and infrastructures?

SUPPLIERS OF COMPUTERS: VENDORS AND PUBLIC ORGANIZATIONS

By 1960 some six thousand large computers existed around the world, with the vast majority installed in North America and Western Europe. Electronics and office supply firms used prior knowledge of electronics augmented with additional skills in what eventually became known as programming by the mid-1950s to build an industry that installed thousands of machines each year in the 1960s and 1970s. First generation of products went to existing customers of earlier data processing machines as they, too, built on prior experience to understand how best to use the new technology, relying on such older technologies as punch card tabulators, electronic calculators, and adding machines.[36] Multinational vendors were able to leverage economies of scale and larger communities of technically knowledgeable staffs to build and maintain these systems, and to maintain access to customers who were logical candidates to acquire computers. Of these, IBM was the biggest. Their information ecosystem was embedded in the densest community of computer experts, the northeastern United States and in Western Europe, where employees, customers, government officials, and experts in universities and other vendors interacted the most. They taught each other about the technology, following practices dating to the 1890s when their predecessors and their institutions first learned about typewriters, adding machines, punch card equipment, and other business equipment.[37] Recall from Chapter 6 about IBM that its employees were often part of a larger ecosystem.

Figure 7.1 graphically situates IBM—one of the largest organizations in the world of computing—inside the broader information ecosystem, illustrating the key connectors between IBM and everyone else in the computer community. Various types of people plugged into the larger ecosystem, which, because of its size, accurately conveys that it enveloped IBM, subsuming even this big company into a larger world. Customers and other interested participants always outnumbered IBM whether measured by number of people involved, competitors of the firm, or other organizations that used or developed the technology. Computers, and their continued development and use, forced expansion of the ecosystem. The overlap of bubbles suggests particularly intense connections and their size the relative number one to another. Table 7.1 lists the kinds of information they exchanged around the world, while Table 7.2 the types of organizations that participated in the Atlantic community.

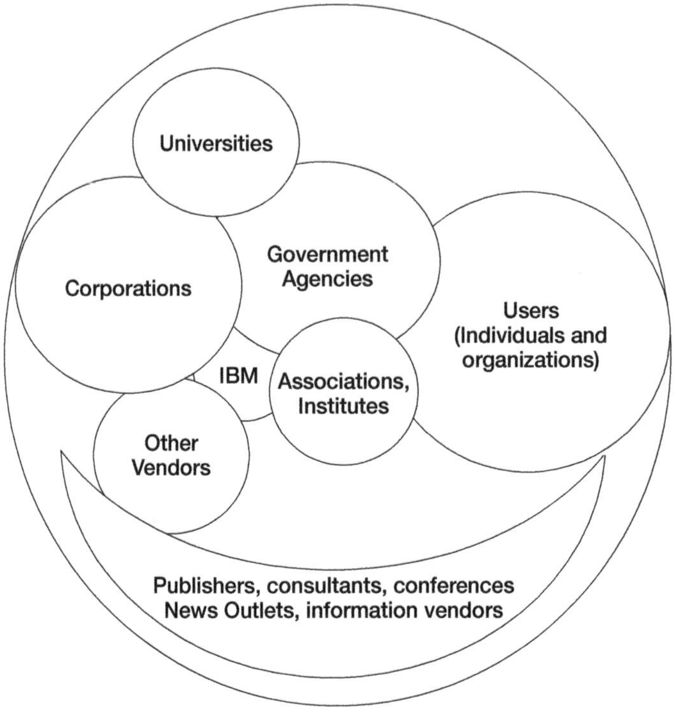

Figure 7.1. IBM in the Greater Computer Information Ecosystem, 1950s–1980s

Table 7.1. Sample Types of Information Shared, 1945–1975

Hardware	*Software*
Architectures/designs	Operating systems
Features	Utility tools
Prices	File management and databases
Maintenance	Maintenance
Programming	*Operations*
How-to	Running equipment
Pros and cons of languages	Change management
Experiences with each	Personnel needs and training
Applications	*Managerial*
Business uses	Project management
Cost justification	Personnel practices
Selection processes	Vendor relations
Training	Legal, privacy, data security

Table 7.2. Sample Types of Participating Organizations in Atlantic Community, 1945–1975

Academic	*Public Sector*
Engineering schools	Military branches
Electrical engineering departments	Census bureaus
Mathematics departments	Weather agencies
Physics departments	Economic development
Technical universities	Atomic energy agencies
Discipline associations	Intelligence agencies
	Law enforcement
Computing Industry	*User Organizations*
Association for Computing Machinery	GUIDE, Share for IBM
Data Processing Management Association	DECUS for Digital Computing
Computer Society	Joint Users Group (JUG) for Univac
American Federation of Information Processing Societies	National Computer Conference
Consultants	*Laboratories*
Hardware manufacturers	Bell Laboratories
Service Bureaus	Bletchley Park
Software firms	U.S. National Bureau of Standards

What did all the participants do to share information? Hundreds of vendors "pitched" the features and uses of their products to technical staffs in all Fortune 1000 companies and large government agencies in customer conference rooms, at their own branch offices and education centers, in university classrooms, and at conferences. Other participants did the same, taking advantage of pre-existing bricks-and-mortar infrastructures to provide venues for such discourses. In the years between the 1940s and the beginning of the 1980s their ecosystem probably involved, worldwide, several million people. Professors discussed how to develop new technologies, software, computer architectures, programming languages, and designs of information databases. Engineers at IBM participated in these dialogues too, such as with academics at Princeton University, MIT, Harvard University, and California Institute of Technology in the United States, and in Great Britain with scientists and engineers at Oxford and Cambridge Universities, and at the University of Warwick. IBM's product developers worked closely with American military and large information handling agencies to fund and develop equipment, especially in the early years of the 1950s. Participants included the U.S. Bureau of the Census and the U.S. Department of the Navy, but there were over a dozen others involved too, in addition to British and French agencies. IBMers participated in similar conversations behind the Iron Curtain on rare occasions in Poland and East Germany.

Members of this ecosystem routinely showed up at each other's conferences. One meeting, say, with one hundred participants might include a handful of IBM employees. As the company began staffing specialized research labs (ultimately a dozen around the world) with engineers and computer scientists strongly connected to academic and other engineering associations and universities, they shared information.[38] Many participants seemed to have been trained at the same universities and it was not uncommon for people to move around the ecosystem to various employers. For example, MIT employed over one thousand people working on the world's largest computer system in the early 1950s (Whirlwind), the majority of who migrated to other universities and computer companies over the next decade, but continued to participate in the exchange of information and jobs. The same occurred in other early American computer start-ups, such as at ERA and Eckert-Mauchly Computer Corporation.

All vendors supported this information ecosystem with massive quantities of gray publications, a collection of materials barely studied by historians.[39] Every commercial computer and peripheral device was accompanied by several types of publications: technical descriptions of what comprised the equipment and its software, user manuals instructing operators and programmers on how to operate equipment and use software, additional information for field engineers on how to install and repair products, still other publications for salesmen about uses of computing (called *applications*), thousands of short case studies of successful installations and benefits to customers, and sales materials. IBM's publications alone totaled over 20,000 titles, most of which circulated without charge from the company in large quantities through the computer ecosystem via the pre-existing infrastructure of its network of branch offices and salesmen, conferences, and briefing centers located in cities and company factories. The number of events and copies of publications far exceeded what academics and many government officials were accustomed to in their work.[40] Industry associations distributed similar materials that they produced, such as those published by the Computer Society and ACM. It was not uncommon for thousands of organizations to use such materials to inform their own understanding and use of computers.[41]

In sum, institutional members of the computer information ecosystem included a rich variety of participants: employees of government agencies, IT industry associations, royal and other national academies and institutes, and lobbyist organizations. They provided early leadership in promoting and disseminating information about the new technology. By the 1960s, however, their role diminished as user groups increased in size along with the frequency of their exchanges. IBM thought of them as customers, academics as part of their routine discipline-specific associations, and customers as their own professional and industry groups. However way they viewed themselves, as a group they became the largest contingent of the information ecosystem and so must be discussed. They constituted a community of several million people by the 1980s.

USERS OF COMPUTERS

Users (i.e., customers, technical staff) of computers always played a proactive role in the dissemination and use of information about computing. Because it seemed their experience with computers normally involved newly developed technologies, they quickly settled into the habit of assisting each other, just as users of smart phones today teach each other how to download apps or adjust settings. Customers explained to vendors what they needed; engineers communicated back and forth to figure out what to invent next, or about how to fix problems; consumers did the same with suppliers of PCs, laptops, and smart phones.[42]

From the beginning permanent crucial members of the information ecosystem were user groups. Like auto clubs dedicated to specific automobiles forming clubs to share information about Ford cars or European sports cars, users of IBM or Univac equipment, for example, formed their own organizations to help each other and to share information.[43] They used the tried and tested mechanism of annual and regional conventions that mimicked the format of scholarly association annual meetings, replete with book displays, others by vendors, private meetings between suppliers and customers in hotel rooms, convention-wide general meetings and smaller presentations devoted to specific topics, and publication of thousands of fat volumes of proceedings. In the United States some of the largest of these gatherings were the regional and national meetings of the Data Processing Management Association (DPMA) and the National Computer Conference (NCC). The NCC sometimes had as many as 20,000 annual participants between 1973 and 1985, building on smaller regional conferences held by other groups as early as the 1950s.[44]

The more vendor-specific ones included those focused on IBM, such as SHARE (not an acronym, rather meaning to *share* information) and GUIDE (Guidance of Users of Integrated Data-Processing Equipment) with thousands of attendees that met for decades. These events became major focal points for the exchange of information and conversations about all manner of computer science, hardware and software, and for resolving technical and operational and managerial problems. Users of Burroughs equipment worked through CUBA, while Univac customers joined USE, and for smaller systems DECUS (Digital Equipment Computer Users). Users managed these organizations and their events, and vendors participated in the conventions and provided financial support. Many associations had regional chapters, which held more frequent local meetings. The same occurred in Europe, later in Asia. They published their presentations or, like SHARE, published white papers. Many were kept in three-ring binders, filling up more than a bookshelf per decade per organization.[45]

GUIDE was the largest of these, with membership by companies or agencies, not individuals. Forty-four companies banded together to establish GUIDE in 1956. By 1980 it had a membership of 2,400 companies and government agencies; each used IBM equipment.[46] Members encouraged each other how best to use IBM's products and representatives of these members formed thick personal networks of thousands of people all over the world. Task forces defined their needs, communicated with various parts of IBM (largely laboratories, product developers, and sales), ran training programs, and documented best practices. GUIDE met twice a year and by the mid-1980s it was common to see four thousand people attend such gatherings.[47] SHARE did the same. Formed in 1954 in Los Angeles, by 1980 it had 1,500 member organizations and operated the same way.[48] Both focused on technical and operational matters concerning IBM, while DPMA worried more about operational and managerial issues.

All proved successful because often the most relevant sources of information about computing were users—customers—for others and vendors, the latter uncovering what customers wanted next, what issues they faced, and so forth. These organizations solved the problem of communications having become too slow in one-on-one personal meetings so typical of the 1940s and early 1950s that no longer satisfied the needs of, now, thousands, later tens of thousands then millions, of people populating the information ecosystem. In time, all these various organizations, vendors, and universities invigorated the information ecosystem with additional features to their infrastructure, notably stocking university and corporate libraries with thousands of journals, proceedings, trade magazines, and books about all manner of computing.[49] Institutions and vendors began forming similar libraries in Western and Eastern Europe in the 1960s and 1970s and in Asia in the 1970s–1980s, evidence of their relevance to their local computing information ecosystems.

BROAD TRENDS IN THE DEVELOPMENT OF COMPUTING'S INFORMATION WORLD

In the period 1 from 945–1975 two information ecosystems and their supportive infrastructures emerged focused on computing. Each functioned similarly to the other. Both borrowed so many practices and often information from each other that it almost seemed as if instead of two there might have only been one global information ecosystem. The first rested on both sides of the Atlantic, in North America and in Western Europe. One could argue that Japan participated in this ecosystem after 1950, since it relied almost entirely on participants of the Atlantic ecosystem. The Atlantic ecosystem consisted of thousands of organizations in over two dozen countries, including all the advanced industrialized economies of that time, all the democracies too. Americans dominated this ecosystem with their vendors, notably IBM, and the United States, which had more computers per capita than any other country and the largest economy too. The Atlantic ecosystem and its infrastructure were massively larger than the second one.

The second clustered behind the Iron Curtain with Russia serving the same role as the United States within the Soviet Bloc, the U.S.S.R. Western Russia, East Germany, Poland, and to a lesser extent Hungary were active participants, with China joining during the 1970s. In contrast centers of activities included on the Atlantic side both coasts of the United States, Toronto in Canada, central and southern England, Nordic countries, Germany, Netherlands, and pockets in France. But dozens of countries combined participated in one way or another in these two ecosystems. Historians now know that over half the nations of the world participated since the late 1950s, even though that often meant less than several hundred people in a country in the beginning, for example in India.[50] The Atlantic ecosystem exported far more information to the Soviet ecosystem than it received back. The infrastructures used by both proved extensive, but the Soviet one was more finely tuned to harvest emerging new information from the West in a timely, routine manner. Both adopted similar mechanisms for doing that, but the Soviets more frequently better funded translation services. They used embassy personnel to acquire publications, assigned spies to gather information, and recruited surrogates to arrange for illegal transfers of hardware and software to the U.S.S.R.

A surprising feature of the ecosystem was how quickly it emerged and expanded. One can understand, say, a hundred electrical engineers and physicists gathering in Boston or Philadelphia in the 1940s to share what they knew, even to host conferences in 1946–1949 attended by a score of individuals who knew each other. But it was another matter when, by the early 1950s, that population was expanding into thousands, then by the early 1960s to tens of thousands, and in the 1970s into several million. Growth and density of the ecosystem paralleled that massive increase in the installation of computers that occurred simultaneously. Encouraging expansion of the ecosystem, of course, was the rapid transformation of all information technologies and their uses. While that confluence of circumstances involved changing knowledge about technologies and opportunities to apply them, the need to know more about how to do so did too. Understanding developed along with innovations in electronics, components, emergence of computer science, programming, and software. One circumstance fed another in a tightly wrapped feedback loop that picked up momentum and spread out like rings from a stone thrown in a pond.

Over time individual participants played on an ever-larger stage while appearing diminutive on it. Using IBM as an example, this was a company with just over 30,000 employees in 1950 as it began entering the commercial computer business and with nearly 289,000 in the mid-1970s when in the thick of it all it remained only one of thousands of institutional members. IBM's staff was an order of magnitude smaller population than the total ecosystem, although its employees were profoundly influential within it. Generations of IBM engineers benefited from their personal participation in this ecosystem; indeed, it would have been impossible for the company to succeed in the computer business without their participation.[51] Individual IBMers also took up leadership positions in many of these organizations, populating committees, chairing others, and serving on boards of directors, even as their presidents. IBM consistently encouraged this kind of extra-curricular activity to remain in the center of the activity and influential.

IMPLICATIONS

There are several implications to consider for the study of the history of information ecosystems and infrastructures and about the history of technology and science. These networks of influence could be small, as in the case of historians of computing discussed in Chapter 3, the women in Chapter 5, or earlier in Chapter 4 with Spain's diplomats. But like IBM's sales force, the diplomats were also part of a larger ecosystem with its widely accepted norms and infrastructures. We did not explore the wider world of the Spanish diplomats, but it paralleled many of the patterns described in this chapter. The size of an ecosystem apparently does not constrain its successful operation, rather normalizing patterns of behavior across a larger community. Here, Indians, Chinese, Russians, Americans, British, and French participated in and benefited from the experience, as measured by the extent of their appropriation of computing. The computing community described here and in earlier chapters was part of a much larger information ecosystem of a nation or continent, as I discovered when writing a history of how Americans used information.[52]

However, as an information ecosystem expands in size, historians have to pay more attention to what the ecosystem's members already knew: what organizations, their formal and information mechanisms for communicating amongst each other, events, and even data transmission technologies needed for the ecosystem to function. The ladies of Madison County did not need some overarching organization, although one could argue they had one with extension agents, but the computer people did. The Spaniards largely needed their foreign office ministry, IBMers their company, the latter even if in the period from 1945 through the 1950s it was still a mid-sized global manufacturing firm. The point is, the bigger the community, the more it needed to work within the structure of social professional norms and to enhance their infrastructure with magazines, journals, books, and, in the post 1975 period, with telecommunications.[53]

This chapter illustrated how an information ecosystem, and its supporting infrastructure, could be tied to a much larger story, in this case to the Cold War. As in every case study, information is the life blood of human activity, and so tracking what specifically moved from one person to another, how that was done, its speed of transmission and timing, and effects is the crucial next step in enhancing our understanding of many historical episodes. This chapter has demonstrated how to connect small and large organizations to an information ecosystem. They often were the creators and sustainers of information infrastructures, because these were tied closely to the reason for the existence of such organizations. It did not matter if they were government agencies, companies, or industry and academic societies. The behavior was the same and so we have examples of how to gain access to the specific information they used and, just as important, how they added to or altered the nature of that data. In short, they provided the context of how much information was created and applied.

In the next chapter we explore the exact opposite, what happens in a small information ecosystem, in this instance that of the family historian. Even in this instance, we see a bigger than obvious ecosystem and the role of an outsized information infrastructure. This case study offers up yet another, but different, type of information ecosystem. It offers another lesson, too: an individual can create an information ecosystem and construct a supportive infrastructure without consciously knowing what they are doing. We can define specifically the information that drives creation of both and document how information and its use evolve over time by using the research approaches proposed in this book.

NOTES

1. James W. Cortada, *The Digital Flood: The Diffusion of Information Technology Across the U.S., Europe, and Asia* (New York: Oxford University Press, 2012), and its extensive bibliographic discussion, 733–768.
2. Boris N. Malinovsky, *Pioneers of Soviet Computing* (published electronically, 2010), available at http://www.sigcis.org/files/malinovsky/2010.pdf (Accessed 12/24/2019).
3. John Impagliazzo and Eduard Proydakov, eds., *Perspectives on Soviet and Russian Computing: First IFIP WG 9.7 Conference, SoRuCom 2006, Petrozavodsk, Russia July 3–7, 2006* (Berlin: Springer-Verlag, 2011).
4. I explore such issues in more detail in James W. Cortada, "When Knowledge Transfer Goes Global: How People and Organizations Learned About Information Technology, 1945–1970," *Enterprise and Society* 14, no. 1 (2014): 68–102 and in, "How New Technologies Spread: Lessons from Computing Technologies," *Technology and Culture* 54, no. 2 (April 2013): 229–261.
5. A key finding of Cortada, *The Digital Flood.*
6. For 16 country case studies, Ibid.
7. Archivists at the Charles Babbage Institute at the University of Minnesota have assembled a collection of over 10,000 books and a large collection of proceedings and journals that make such statements possible to make. An easy technique is to trace the translations of key works in the field, the vast majority of which originated in the United States and then were translated into other languages.
8. Cortada, *The Digital Flood,* 195–237, 546–570.
9. Jorge Aguirre and Raúl Carnota, *Historia de la Informática en Latinoamérica y el Caribe: Investigaciones y testimonies* (Rio de Cuarto: Universidad de Rio Cuarto, 2009).
10. Wout Ottevanger, Jan van den Akker, and Leo de Feiter, *Developing Science, Mathematics, and ICT Education in Sub-Saharan Africa: Patterns and Promising Practices* (Washington, DC: World Bank, 2007).
11. Cortada, "When Knowledge Transfer Goes Global," 68–102.
12. Described in more detail in Cortada, *The Digital Flood,* 45–50.

13. Prepared by American intelligence agents, commercial attaches, and academic experts invited to visit and report on local conditions. In addition to such reports located in embassy country files (U.S. Department of State records, U.S. National Archives). Two other conveniently available collections of such reports are the Blackman Papers, National American History Museum, Smithsonian Institution, and the Goodman Papers at the Charles Babbage Institute, University of Minnesota.

14. Various country reports in Blackman Papers, Boxes 216 and 217, National American History Museum, Mathematics Branch, Smithsonian Institution.

15. On its own information ecosystem and infrastructure, see Thomas J. Misa, ed., *Communities of Computing: Computer Science and Society in the ACM* (No City: Association for Computing Machinery, 2017).

16. On business motives, for example, see John Aris, "Inventing Systems Engineering," *IEEE Annals of the History of Computing* 22 no. 3 (2000): 4–15.

17. H. J. van der Aa, ed., *International Computer Bibliography: A Guide to Books on the Use, Application and Effect of Computers in Scientific, Commercial, Industrial and Social Environments,* 2 vols (Amsterdam: Studiecentrum voor Informatica, 1968–1971); FUNDP NAMUR. *Belgian Computing Literature*. Brussels: FUNDP NAMUR, circa 2008.

18. Various titles as these were published in 73 reports, supported by Deutsche Forschungegemeinschaft—DFG (1954–1966). A complete set available at the IBM Laboratory Library, Zurich, Switzerland.

19. Often reported on by industry watchers, such as AUERBACH, *European Information Technology*, and by academic and government experts, Seymour E. Goodman, "Computing and the Development of the Soviet Economy," in U.S. Congress, Joint Economic Committee, *A Compendium of Papers Submitted to the Joint Economic Committee Congress of the United States* (Washington, DC: U.S. Government Printing Office, 1979), vol. 1 and his "Soviet Computing and Technology Transfer: An Overview," *World Politics* 31, no. 4 (July 1979): 539–570; also academics and engineers publishing trip reports, such as John W. Car III, Alan J. Perlis, James E. Robertson, and Norman R. Scott, "A Visit to Computation Centers in the Soviet Union," *Communications of the ACM* 2, no. 3 (1959): 8–20.

20. Segei P. Prokhorov, "Computers in Russia: Science, Education, and Industry," *IEEE Annals of the History of Computing* 21, no. 3 (1999): 4–15; Eugene Gros, *Russian Books on Automation and Computers* (London: Scientific Information Consultants, 1967).

21. N. C. Davis and Seymour E. Goodman, "The Soviet Bloc's Unified System of Computers," *Computing Surveys* 10, no 2 (June 1978): 93–122. See also, Richard W. Judy, *The Riad Computers of the Soviet Union and Eastern Europe, 1970–1985: A Survey and Comprehensive Analysis* (Indianapolis, IN: Hudson Institute, March 1986).

22. Examples of journals include, with their launch date, *Mathematical Tables an Other Aids to Computation* (1943–1960), *Computers and Automation* (1951), *Association for Computing Machinery Journal* (1954), *Datamation* (1957), *IBM*

Journal of Research and Development (1957), *Computer Journal* (1958), and *Computerworld* (1967). For further details on this aspect of the information ecosystem, James W. Cortada, *The Computer in the United States: From Laboratory to Market, 1930 to 1960* (Armonk, NY: M. E. Sharpe, 1993), 102–112.

23. Janet Abbate, "From Handmaiden to 'Proper Intellectual Discipline': Creating a Scientific Identity for Computer Science in 1960s America," in Thomas J. Misa, ed. *Communities of Computing: Computer Science and Society in the ACM* (San Rafael, CA: ACM Books, 2017): 25–46 and for a discussion of the origins of the phrase, Ibid., 14.

24. W. F. Atchison and J. W. Hamblen, "Status of Computer Sciences Curricula in Colleges and Universities," *Communications of the* ACM 7, no. 4 (1964): 226–227. For a thorough account of the emergence of computer science, Paul Ceruzzi, *A History of Modern Computing,* 2nd ed. (Cambridge, MA: MIT Press, 2003): 13–46.

25. Abbate, "From Handmaiden to 'Proper Intellectual Discipline,'" 45.

26. Ibid., 39.

27. Ibid., 45.

28. William Aspray, "International Diffusion of Computer Technology, 1945–1955," *IEEE Annals of the History of Computing* 8, no. 4 (1986): 351–360.

29. The most vocal historian of this thesis is A. Akera, *Calculating a Natural World: Scientists, Engineer, and Computers during the Rise of US Cold War Research* (Cambridge, MA: MIT Press, 2008).

30. Sebastian Dziallas and Sally Fincher, "The History and Purpose of Computing Curricula (1960s–2000s)," in Misa, *Communities of Computing*, 91–109.

31. Ksenia Tatarchenko, "The Anatomy of an Encounter: Transnational Mediation and Discipline Building in Cold War Computer Science," in Ibid., 199–227. Russia, within the USSR, led the charge for all of Communist Europe and provided the most extensive training and financial support for computing from the late 1940s to 1989.

32. James W. Cortada, *The Digital Flood: The Diffusion of Information Technology Across the U.S., Europe, and Asia* (New York: Oxford University Press, 2012): 251–276.

33. Geoffrey C. Bowker, "How to be Universal: Some Cybernetic Strategies, 1943–1970," *Social Studies of Science* 23, no. 1 (1993): 107–127. Ronald R. Kline has studied the history of cybernetics both from the perspective of its intellectual contents and its failure to achieve the same disciplinary recognition as computer science, *The Cybernetic Moment: Or Why We Call Our Age the Information Age* (Baltimore, MD: Johns Hopkins University Press, 2015). For a history of Soviet cybernetics that pays more attention on what information was collected, organized, and acted upon, and thus feels more like the story I tell in this chapter, see Slave Gerovitch, *From Newspeak to Cyberspeak: A History of Soviet Cybernetics* (Cambridge, MA: MIT Press, 2002).

34. Tatarchenko, "The Anatomy of an Encounter,"211.

35. A key conclusion I argued more thoroughly in James W, Cortada, *The Digital Hand: How Computers Changed the Work of American Manufacturing, Transportation, and Retail Industries* (New York: Oxford University Press, 2004): 3–65.

36. In the pre-computer era, large organizations and academics used data processing equipment, such as tabulators, calculators, and adding machines, building in the process information ecosystems similar to what existed after arrival of the computer. I have described this world more thoroughly in Cortada, *Before the Computer: IBM, NCR, Burroughs, and Remington Rand and the Industry They Created, 1865–1956* (Princeton, NJ: Princeton University Press, 1993).

37. Thomas J. Watson, Jr. and Peter Petre, *Father Son & Co.: My Life at IBM and Beyond* (New York: Bantam, 1990), 241–242, 246, 346–352; James W. Cortada, *Before the Computer*, 89–186.

38. IBM World Trade Corporation, *Annual Report 1969*, 24–25.

39. "Gray publications" refers to those that are not normally publically available, or conventionally accessible through libraries, for example. These can range from casual reports to massively detailed monographic publications rigorously adhering to academic standards. Examples include preprints and white papers. I was able to prepare a three-volume history of how nearly 20 American industries used computers based considerably on such materials, James W. Cortada, *The Digital Hand,* 3 vols. (New York: Oxford University Press, 2004–2008).

40. Many documents, and even book-length publications, were published in editions of tens of thousands of copies. Publications your author was responsible for producing in the 1990s always appeared in the tens of thousands of copies, both paper and digital, diffused around the world. Articles in trade publications normally were distributed to two hundred to four hundred thousand subscribers by trade magazines by the 1970s.

41. Large collections of such materials exist at IBM's Corporate Archives and the Charles Babbage Institute at the University of Minnesota, and there is a growing collection of some 10,000 items at the Computer History Museum at Mountain View, California. Sarah Wilson, "Guide to the Computer Collections of Computing Manuals and Marketing Materials," describes over 440 linear feet of materials, available at http://www.computerhistory.org/collections/accession/102634420 (Accessed December 28, 2019).

42. Cortada, *The Computer in the United States*, 102–124.

43. Thomas Haigh in a series of studies explored their issues, "Sources for ACM History: What, When, Why," *Communications of the ACM* 50, no. 5 (May 2007): 36–41; "Inventing Information Systems: The Systems Men and the Computer," *Business History Review* 75, no. 1 (Spring 2001): 15–61; but see also, Nathan Ensmenger, "Power to the People: Toward a Social History of Computing," *IEEE Annals of the History of Computing* 23, no. 1 (January–March 2001): 94–96; "Letting the 'Computer Boys' Take Over: Technology and the Politics of Organizational Transformations," *International Review of Social History* 48 (2003):

153–180; A. Akera, "Voluntarism and the Fruits of Collaboration: The IBM User Group, Share," *Technology and Culture* 42 (2001): 710–736.

44. Paul Korzenoiwoski, "NCC Past to Present: A Barometer of Industry Progress," 8.

45. Examples of such collections are preserved at the Charles Babbage Institute, University of Minnesota, including one of the few preserved sets of SHARE and GUIDE publications.

46. Akera, "Voluntarism and the Fruits of Collaboration: The IBM User Group, Share," 710–736.

47. T. F. O'Leary, Jr., "GUIDE," in Anthony Ralston and Edwin D. Reilly, Jr., eds., *Encyclopedia of Computer Science and Engineering* (New York: Van Nostrand Reinhold, 1983), 670–671.

48. Paul Armer, "SHARE—A Eulogy to Cooperative Effort," *Annals of the History of Computing* 2, no. 2 (April 1980): 122–129.

49. The largest collection of these can be found at the Charles Babbage Institute at the University of Minnesota. For a series of bibliographies of such materials, see James W. Cortada, *A Bibliographic Guide to the History of Computing, Computers, and the Information Processing Industry* (Westport, CT: Greenwood Press, 1990), *Second Bibliographic Guide to the History of Computing, Computers and the Information Processing Industry* (Westport, CT: Greenwood Press, 1996), and *A Bibliographic Guide to the History of Computer Applications, 1950–1990* (Westport, CT: Greenwood Press, 1996).

50. The extent of the diffusion of computing was a central finding of Cortada, *The Digital Flood.*

51. An observation made evident when reading histories of IBM's technology histories, Charles J. Bashe, Lyle R. Johnson, John H. Palmer, and Emerson W. Pugh, *IBM's Early Computers* (Cambridge, MA: MIT Press, 1985); Emerson W. Pugh, Lyle R. Johnson, and John Palmer, *IBM's 360 and Early 370 Systems* (Cambridge, MA: MIT Press, 1991).

52. James W. Cortada, *All the Facts: A History of Information in the United States since 1870* (New York: Oxford University Press, 2016).

53. This is not a new idea. As early as 1988 sociologist Andrew Abbott began pointing this out in his seminal study, *The System of Professions: An Essay on the Division of Expert Labor* (Chicago, IL: University of Chicago Press, 1988) and further in his *Chaos of Discipline* (Chicago, IL: University of Chicago Press, 2001), 121–156.

Chapter Eight

Tiny Information Ecosystems and Infrastructures

Genealogists and Family Historians

> *In all of us there is a hunger, marrow deep, to know our heritage—to know who we are and where we came from. Without this enriching knowledge, there is a hollow yearning. No matter what our attainments in life, there is still a vacuum, an emptiness, and the most disquieting loneliness.*
>
> —Alex Haley, author of *Roots*

Millions of families worldwide have a family historian. The work before us is how best to study family history and its memory.[1] In China and Japan documented genealogies have preserved accounts of some families for over a thousand years; the same is true for noble families in Europe. In the United States, wealthy families became interested in the subject in Victorian times and after World War II millions of additional people in the middle class.[2] Academics generally dismiss this sub-field of history as hobby, but it is serious business. Ancestry.com, the largest Internet-based genealogical company, operates in over 30 countries, has over 3 million paid subscribers for its services (largely online databases), maintains one hundred million family trees, provides access to over 19 billion documents, and has scanned over two hundred million photographs, documents, and family histories. It generates over $1 billion in revenue, making it a large corporation by any measure.[3] Surveys suggest that in the United States, 75 percent of all families have dabbled in genealogy.[4]

Because most people are only interested in their own family's history, a family historian has both a small audience and equally a tiny team to assist in their research. Wealthy families hire professional genealogists and, sometimes, family historians to dig for details. Everyone else is on their own to figure out how best to conduct the research, although aided by a large body of "how-to" information, at least since World War II in the United States, Great Britain, and Western Europe.[5] In this chapter we explore the work and information family historians engage with, focusing on the American experience because, as with adoption of computing, residents in the United States proved early aggressive adders of information technologies to their information infrastructures. We see what appears to be a smaller information ecosystem than those discussed in earlier chapters, but a large infrastructure. Fewer individuals serve at the center of these ecosystems, but they cannot operate without bodies of information that are large, diverse, and disparate to a far greater extent than those of the hundreds of ladies of Madison County, or the several thousand Spanish diplomats and tens of thousands of IBM employees. How do family historians operate? What do they do with information, two hundred indeed what information do they need? Why do they rely on so much data when they are scaling research to meet needs of only their family? Keeping in mind, too, the guiding questions posed in Chapter 1, we discuss their mediums and identify patterns of adoption and use, effects on their work, and describe features of their information.

To cover this sweep of issues and questions, we begin by defining what genealogists and family historians do, followed by a short discussion of the important impact of the Internet on their work. Then we describe their information infrastructure, as it is more than just the Internet, and conclude with a discussion of the challenges faced by genealogists and family historians. Examples illustrate their activities. By inference, this chapter demonstrates that when viewing the work of family historians through the lens of information ecosystems and infrastructures, an approach works that should be useful to professional historians in appreciating the strengths and weaknesses of the methods applied by genealogists. It turns out, family historians are more rigorous in their research than historians willingly acknowledge.[6] In this observation, I am not alone. Others have reached similar conclusions, arguing as I do that genealogical methods are not so radically different than what scholars use in their disciplines.[7]

But first, clarification of a couple of definitions helps in understanding this world of information seekers. A *genealogist* is an individual who describes "a line of descent traced continuously from an ancestor."[8] They define generations of ancestors, documenting names of parents and children within a family, generation after generation.[9] They focus largely on birth and death dates of individuals and how they related to other members of a family, such as to grandfathers and grandmothers, parents, children, aunts and uncles, cousins, and so forth. A second term—*family historians*—refers to people who do the same research but take an extra step to study what these individuals did, where they lived, their life experiences, and collective history of the clan. The term *family history* encompasses the work of both and is often used interchangeably with genealogy. Their efforts come close to some of the interests, focus, and methods of historians and anthropologists that date to the dawn of the twentieth century.[10] People studying their family's past normally begin by following the biblical practice of documenting who "begat" whom before filling in stories about the experiences of their ancestors. As they flush out details about members of their family, it becomes possible to explore a family's history. Very quickly, both roles—genealogist and family historian—merge, explaining why the terms are used interchangeably, including here.

WHAT GENEALOGISTS AND FAMILY HISTORIANS DO

Their primary objective is to collect information about the genealogy and history of their family and to communicate their findings to other members of the family, less so to outsiders.[11] The life cycle of their work is fairly uniform. Someone begins by collecting genealogical information. In the United States that normally starts by looking at a handed-down family Bible whose center pages contain names of ancestors, birth and death dates, and marriages. Next, conversations with the elders of the family reveal names of other members, usually back about 120 years, although fuzzier as the data goes further back in time. Such conversations frequently introduce misinformation unintentionally, largely the result of bad memories. Sometimes the process starts with these conversations, followed by examining the "family Bible." Next, family documents are normally collected and studied. Then the researcher begins a long process of examining census records, those of churches, published histories, and so forth, discussed further below. This step can take the rest of the lifetime of the family genealogist, although a half dozen years is not unreasonable to get its basic outlines worked out back two or three hundred years. Gaps in the data stall the reconstruction of family trees—the primary deliverable of the genealogist—while normally remaining incomplete.[12]

Preparing iterations of family trees consumes a genealogist's time as they revise these with their incorporation of new information. They begin with today's generation and work backwards in time to parents, grandparents, and across an entire generation to include brothers and sisters of one's grandparents and the children issuing from that generation. They roll back in time as far as they can go. If from a Catholic family, since the Church required its priests to keep baptismal, death, and marriage records beginning in the 1500s, one can get back to the mid-1500s before encountering significant gaps in extant data, assuming that their family's parishes in Europe did not burn down. A similar process applies to socially elite Asian families. The process is iterative as researchers validate the accuracy of such data as names, birth and death dates, and where people lived, correcting errors and adding details. This phase requires extensive communications with different sources of information, such as parish priests and archivists. It can necessitate travel to government agencies around the world, such as to county courthouses in the United States and to provincial archives and parishes in Europe or Latin America. The arrival of the Internet with its massive quantities of information did not eliminate the need for these kinds of activity; it just facilitated it.

Glenn Rouse, an Australian of British descent exemplifies this iterative pattern of collecting names, data, of going back and forth to validate birthdates and relations to one-another individuals. In his own words: "I am very much a proud genealogist and have built a huge tree of over 20 years of dedication, devotion, endless days and nights of coffee-fuelled research, now over 13,000 people. My research has taken me to many countries of the world, never dreamt I would meet ancestral cousins, walked the paths my ancestors walked."[13] What was he hunting for? "I have over 13,000 people on my page, mostly related; but also gathering information not just on the direct person, but their family history. They are spread from both my father's and mother's ancestries, as their ancestors came to Australia between 1842 and 1862; I am still researching my maternal grandmother's family tree and have gone back to the sixteenth century Lancashire." He was enthusiastic about finding out, "that some of my earlier (*sic*) were originally Quaker farmers . . . my 10th great-grandfather Robert Lucas, his wife Elizabeth Cowgill left Lancashire and emigrated to Pennsylvania where he died in 1688."[14] For a close circle of friends and family he posted information about his ancestors on Facebook. Many family historians collect photographs of their ancestors and this genealogist is no exception. In July 2017, he came across the photograph of a young member of his family killed in Flanders, Belgium, in the same month that one hundred thousand other young men died. The picture of his ancestor is stunning in his British uniform: clean-cut, young, looking quite normal, as so many other people readers know. But read how he described him: "Just found this photo of my maternal grandfather's 5th cousin, 2nd Lt Philip Henry Habershon 9th battalion, King's Royal Rifle Corps (great-grandson of Sarah Gillbee), killed in action 25 Sep 1915 in Flanders, Belgium aged 22."[15] Note the facts he valued: full name, exact relationship to other members of the family in detail, and age. It was not an isolated case of precision on his part. He earlier posted a photograph of his grandmother: "Today, 15 July, 111 years ago today, my grandmother Elizabeth Glenburn Knoll Rouse was born in Ballarat East, Victoria."[16] Rouse behaved like a family historian.[17]

A second phase involves augmenting genealogical details with information about one's employment history, where they were raised, their personalities, and events in their lives. This is when they collect and identify photographs of people, places, and events, gather and study letters written by family members, and sweep up surviving ephemera that can range from school report cards to old contracts and business records, military and work files, old newspaper clippings, publications by ancestors, and so forth. That job is never completed. By this phase the family genealogist is organizing paper and digital files by generation or individual and begins to share their findings with the family.[18]

A genealogist of a British family (Barlow) that emigrated to the United States in the early 1800s and in the early 1900s moved to Havana, Cuba, has for decades accumulated bits-and-pieces, typical of what family historians do: "Joe Barlow's Cadiz manganese mine in Cuba," citing from Google books a reference of a mine he owned, its size, and its description: "The deposits are situated at an altitude of about 1250 ft. (381 m.) on a high ridge about 100 yd. (91 m.) from a precipice overlooking Rio Giesa," and so forth.[19] This finding was not trivial, as she was trying to reconstruct his various entrepreneurial activities in Cuba, which included mines and successfully developing Havana suburbs, which made it possible to send his son to a private military academy in the United States. This family historian disseminated this seemingly obscure piece of information throughout her family on the same day that she uncovered it.[20] The point is that each morsel of detail was relevant and celebrated. Communications normally begin by telling stories, a favorite way of doing this for hundreds of years, but over the past century, too, through the mail, written histories, and in recent decades using e-mail, social media, and self-published accounts. All became components of their diverse information infrastructure.[21] Use of oral traditions, of story-telling, employed by families is similarly applied by corporations for the same purposes.[22]

Organizational skills prove crucial to their success. Cardboard boxes full of unstructured files that only made sense to them, but not to anyone else, are common problem for the rest of the family. With the availability of software tools and the Internet, increased order came, since software provided pre-defined formats for information (such as where to type a birth date) and standardized databases. On rare occasions, these historians write up what they have learned as narrative family histories, as family albums of illustrations with detailed descriptions of the protagonists, or as transcriptions of handwritten diaries and letters in typed format that could be replicated and shared within the family and with copies donated to local and state/provincial historical societies. Some of these three types of compilations are published as books by the individual for private consumption or by commercial, historical society, or university presses. Just for the United States, there are tens of thousands of such compilations; increasingly the same can be said about the work of European family historians working after World War II than before when only the rich and a few upper-middle classes habitually engaged in such activities.

For an example of today's engagement, there is the case of the Etten family of the Rhineland, a branch of which settled in Racine, Wisconsin (USA). A report on the evolution of this family written by a member, Pat Savage Etten, describes the birth and death dates of individuals, when they emigrated to the United States, and to whom they married. For one example of many she noted, "Michael, born 1837 in Germany came to U.S. 1873, residing in Kankakee Township, Kankakee County, Illinois," with data drawn from U.S. Census Records. Her report was well annotated, as one would expect in a scholarly study. She listed the various descendants with similar information. She included in her report facsimiles of German emigrant passenger lists of people arriving at American ports, photographs of members of the family in Germany and in the United States, and a detailed family tree. A typical entry to that tree is for Johann "Jean" Etten: "66 (b. 22 Jun 1773—Walsdorf, Daun, Rheinland-Pfalz, Germany d.Aft 1834—Walsdorf, Daun, R. Germany." She was interested in this man as part of a larger tree devoted to one Peter Etten (born about 1700). She included copies of marriage licenses and photographs of Roman Catholic First Communion events of the children.[23]

The extent to which such researchers worked alone remains unclear. Extant evidence suggests they did, that they rarely collaborated with others in their families, although most occasionally engaged members to share information and to contribute ephemera to the family information ecosystem. However, they talked extensively to librarians and archivists, but rarely shared their findings with other amateur genealogists the way, say, academic historians normally do by making presentations at conferences and within their own departments. But they helped each other. A common practice was to share specific data about ancestors, also about how to go about the work. For example, here is the advice given by an American relative to another:

> I put in my own minimalist trees on Ancestry.com and I think also on the LDS Family History site, just to create some visibility so other researchers could find me. I've emailed you tons of items from those sources over the years so you probably have the printouts in your files. Hunting down new tidbits is a lot of fun and I still turn to that as new databases come on line.[24]

Her insight on the work effort, too, is common and worth noting:

> I find the process of data entry very tedious and lonely work, and hard to continue because of the big mess of papers that need to be accessible as you go. It seems like every time I got into it, something would come up and I'd have to put everything away. I'd suggest you assemble what you have and then hire someone to do the data input. Quality control and editing is something I wouldn't mind working on as enough of the info is in my head that I can spot a lot of errors easily.[25]

When they shared practices, these were occasional events, more frequently the result of reading "how-to" manuals or submitting to the online processes called for by genealogical services, such as by Ancestry.com. These two quotes beg for more detail. What did their world—ecosystem—look like?

THEIR INFORMATION ECOSYSTEMS

The information ecosystem of a genealogist or family historian consists of five types of records, a collection that hardly varied over the past two centuries in the Western world. They come in different formats, normally on paper, increasingly as digitized files. Family trees are the most obvious, because they document the relationship of individuals to each other by generation over time. Almost every genealogist begins by collecting this kind of information and normally presents that data either in the form of a tree-like image with branches or as a hierarchical chart, much like one sees representing various departments and divisions of a corporation or government agency. At a minimum for each member of a family tree, one typically annotates a person's full name (first, middle, last) and birth and death dates, lines to indicate connections to the names of their parents, and other lines to point out the names of each of their children and siblings.

A second body of information comprises photographs and other images of members of the family trees. For members of the twentieth century, those are relatively easy to accumulate, far more difficult back in time when fewer photographs and sketches were made. Images are data, because they humanize the names and communicate much about the social standing and life style of people. They can provide insights of a more tacit nature, too, such as character, attitudes, and intelligence. Collecting images of their homes, workplaces, and communities in which they lived adds to that tacit knowledge, especially about their sense of self identity, just as do photographs of one's current family. Methods for using such evidence are widespread and accepted.[26]

A sample illustrates their value. James Gillbee (1794–1878) was born into a financially comfortable family in Kent, England. While traveling to Puerto Rico from Saint Kitts, the ship he sailed on sank during a violent storm. He floated at sea for three days before being picked up. He lived in Ponce, Puerto Rico, for the rest of his life and prospered with a sugar plantation. The family story was that he was badly sunburned on the voyage and temporarily blinded by the sun.[27] He was tough and in good health, considered smart, and became wealthy. There are no medical records but a few financial ones about him. However, there is a photograph of him, taken in the 1860s (Figure 8.1) while on a business trip. It was customary for upper class Puerto Rican and Spanish families to document their images with both oil portraits and the new technology of the day—photography. Look at it. Explore his demeanor and face, clearly not that of a weak person, rather of a vigorous individual. Observe his clothes and fob; symbols of a prosperous individual. We might go further, as encouraged by cultural anthropologists, to even discern in his facial features the look of a man familiar with the rigors of the world. Family documents reinforced his reputation as practical and successful.

A third type of information, often massive in quantity in comparison to the first two, consists of facts about business transactions, performance as students, milestone events (such as baptisms, graduations, marriages, funerals), and military service. These are captured in such documents as wills, military and employment records, school report cards, diaries, family letters, obituaries, and other correspondence. Many stories told about family members often enter a genealogist's information ecosystem by way of letters, e-mail, and social media answering specific questions about the family.[28]

Work records constitute an important, fourth, often detailed collection of information. The most obvious are military service records, which nations

Figure 8.1. James Gillbee

preserve in considerable detail for hundreds of years. In the case of Spanish and British veterans, for example, one can find some records of officers dating back a thousand years, for U.S. military to the Revolutionary War of the 1770s. These kinds of facts document appointments, promotions, recognition of meritorious service, what units they served in, battles and campaigns results of court martials, and the amount of their pensions. Similar records are frequently preserved for public servants. It is not uncommon for personnel records of government employees since the 1700s to include appraisals too, and other data comprising hundreds of pages.

It was important for genealogists to understand the context of their documentation. One example suffices to illustrate the point. Spanish military officers were required for centuries to demonstrate that they had no Jewish or African ancestors, by law their "purity of blood" (*limpieza de sangre*). To do so required they accumulate notarized testimonial letters from officials and priests to that effect and the same for their proposed wives, to marry whom they had to obtain permission from the military. Generations of officers accumulated such files they submitted to the Spanish government. These records were also necessary in order to receive honors and privileges. One observer of this practice explained that by the 1700s, families were "concerned with maintaining its (*sic*) status and obtaining more honors, marrying a stranger was riskier than marrying a close relative."[29] The needed documentation to prove purity now serve as detailed sources of genealogical information.[30]

Typical was Colonel Francisco Xavier Colas y de Aguilar. His military records covered the period from December 6, 1731 to the end of 1763. They are incomplete, because the army transferred him to Santiago de Cuba as commander of the local artillery in 1766 or 1767 and that transfer did not appear in his personnel file.[31] His career proved fruitful and on July 12, 1765, after a series of routine promotions, he became a lieutenant colonel of artillery. During his career he served as an officer in the conquest of the kingdoms of Naples and Sicily; operated in the campaigns in Savoy and Lombardy and transferred to Catalonia, then subsequently to Mallorca, Navarra, and the coasts of Santander and Galicia. Each of the Italian assignments involved extensive combat and various sieges requiring his skills in artillery. He married a native of Sicily, Leonor Catani Croca (Croché),[32] who also came from a military family. We know these details because of the purity requirements, the records kept of his promotions, and the background of his intended wife. Their combined records amounted to over one hundred pages of genealogical and personnel files, testimonials, and routine administrative documentation, such as his orders to transfer to Cuba. The archives of the various Spanish kingdoms are full of such materials.[33] By understanding their context, one would know to search them for family history.

A fifth category of information dating from the 1930s is sound and movie images, showing individuals at various stages of their lives, documenting events, what their homes looked like, and projecting tacit insights about their personalities and life styles. Because the ephemera used to preserve these kinds of information are fragile, specifically film, tape recordings, CDs, and DVDs, families demonstrated they were willing to spend considerable time and money to reformat this information on ever-newer media, such as moving recordings from reel-to-reel tapes and cassettes to CDs, and not just by the family historian. This desire to preserve such records spawned companies to convert analog files to digital formats, such as home movies to digital DVDs or to the "cloud," slides and prints to digital files.[34]

Genealogists and family historians try to obtain copies of all five of these kinds of information, whether in the original (most prized) or as copies. Table 8.1 lists typical types of information a family historian collects, Table 8.2 the kinds of physical records that contain such data. Genealogical guides focus more on the content of Table 8.2 for obvious tactical reasons, but both are always on the mind of an historian. They go back and

Table 8.1. Types of Information Gathered by Genealogists and Family Historians

Names	Images of people, property
Birth and death dates	Records of major family events
Parent's names	Data and history of residences, communities
Grandparents' names	News accounts of individuals
Birth locations	Family values and beliefs
Academic records	Religious affiliations
Military activities	Political and social attitudes
Business profiles	Migrations to other countries
Conversations	Dates and details of migratory experiences
Communications	Business records of employers, owners
Financial worth	Attitudes towards contemporary events
Inventories of possessions	Hobbies, interests, sports

Table 8.2. Types of Physical Records Collected by Genealogists and Family Historians

Birth and death certificates	Biographies
Adoption papers	Obituaries
Marriage certificates	Census
Divorce records	Military personnel files
Death certificates	Drivers licenses
Report cards, diplomas	Criminal records
Property deeds	Wills
Family letters	Diaries and scrap books
Photographs	Paintings and prints
Emigration and travel records	Books, newspapers, magazines
Tax filings	Medical records
Oral histories	Movies and other recordings
Tombstone data	Ship passenger lists
Probate records	Family trees
Possessions of identified owners	E-mail correspondence

forth between one and the other as they iteratively collect information, revisiting familiar sources when enlightened by new nuggets of data, say, about an individual, on where they may have lived, who they married, and so forth. As with the Barlow mine in Cuba, data collected can be obscure, but hardly trivial.

Lesser known bodies of information can prove useful but detailed, such as that collected about a clan. Often paralleling information about individuals and their relations to each other is a large correspondence conducted by family historians with relatives, librarians, archivists, alumni offices of schools and universities, book dealers, and other individuals who touched the lives of the family. These are inquiries about extant records, such as the availability of baptismal certificates from a church. These include inquiries to relatives about the existence of photographs, other documents, or concerning individuals.[35] Their correspondence mirrors project files in a business archive. Experienced family historians keep these organized by individuals discussed, generation, or location.[36] Besides informing the research, these serve to enlighten the next historian within their family about sources already explored, so as not to repeat research, such as writing to the same church for baptismal records already determined by the previous family historian as having been destroyed in some long-ago fire.

How family historians interact with all manner of information illustrates the value to them of such data, demonstrating why information infrastruc-

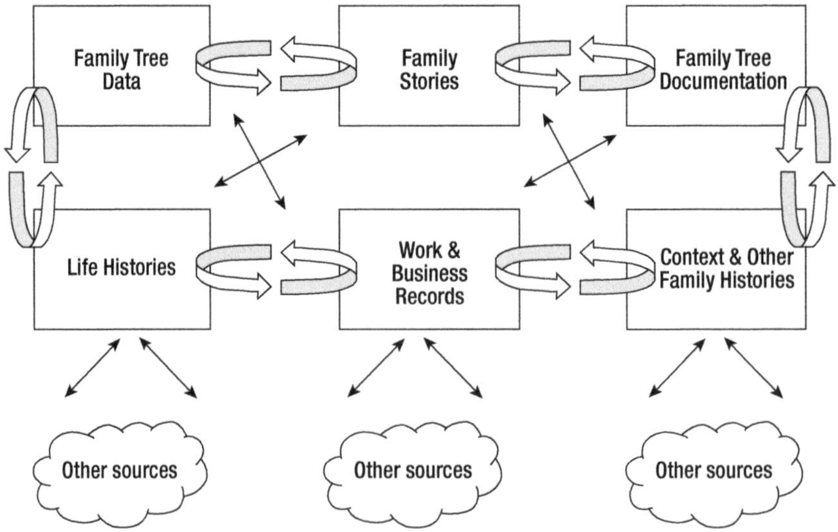

Figure 8.2. Iterative Research Cycle of a Family Historian

tures are so important and so large. Figure 8.2 illustrates at a high level the flow among a family historian and a subject's information. It is also a representation of their genealogical information ecosystem. Research on a family is like completing a puzzle, because there exist pieces of incomplete information, such as the year of birth for someone. Another common gap to fill is the identities of someone's parents or siblings. Just as frustrating is that many members of a family may have the same name, because the variety of first names did not increase dramatically until the twentieth century. Frequent changes in last names usually involved irritating misspellings, such as Tappe for Tappy, which raises the question if they are of the same family, the first a potentially French rendition, the second British or Irish. In most societies, parents named their children after themselves, grandparents, aunts, or uncles. Last names changed to conform to another nation's norms, such as when a Spaniard named Francisco now went by Frank in the United States, or a long Central European last name was reduced in length. But many other reasons occur, such as a woman keeping or changing her name when she married, others to avoid racial profiling, or to enhance their economic competitiveness.[37] Whatever the reason, name changes are problematic, yet another research topic for family historians who need to find out why the change occurred. Was it an error of transcription (quite common in all periods of written history) or purposeful?

Before family historians began relying on PCs and later the Internet, they lived in a world of vast paper records scattered all over the world. A reminder of a point made earlier, the research cycle for the entire project or for a piece of it usually begins with storytelling, when one member verbally communicates what they know about an individual or a branch of a family, beginning with the most current information, backfilling content about earlier times, such as about ones' parents, then about their parents, and so forth. Such storytelling often is the spark inspiring someone to start documenting his or her family's history and that leads to the reality that crucial records are scattered all over a country or continent. Before the Internet, that individual would gather extant documentation, such as family bibles and letters, then follow up by trips to libraries that have genealogical finding aids and histories. But that was barely a start.

Next come trips to regional archives, churches, and local government records offices, such as to county clerks in the United States, or municipal and church offices in Europe. Newspapers quickly become a major source at this stage of the research and on both sides of the Atlantic at large national libraries and universities, and in the United States, the U.S. Library of Congress, which began microfilming these and distributing copies to regional libraries. By the early 1980s, there were 42 state genealogical societies as well in the United States that became useful sources of information and advise on research matters.

Throughout the twentieth century many thousands of "how to" guidebooks and articles helped family researchers. They shared common information gathering techniques. These included instructions on what kinds of information should be gathered (as in Table 8.1), lists of types and by name libraries and archives that contained such facts, discussions about how to determine the accuracy of data from various sources, on creating research agendas and strategies, how best to organize information and ephemera, how to write family history, and bibliographies of other finding aids and guides. In the second half of the century, specialized book-length guides appeared, too, on how to conduct genealogical research on African American families, or on those of Hispanic or Catholic descent.[38]

This iterative research process proved slow and normally took years, even decades, and never ended, because members of the family were born while others died. Basic problems involved two features of the information: it was always fragmentary and physically scattered about the world. One might learn that an ancestor was baptized in a village in northeastern Spain in 1789, then in the provincial archives 60 miles away that this individual obtained a passport to travel to Puerto Rico in 1816, then that he landed in Ponce, Puerto Rico six months later, then from a tombstone on a nearby plantation that he died in 1868. First there was a baptismal certificate from a small church, then a register of passports at a provincial archive, then a ship record for Ponce probably located in the archives in Seville, Spain (just south of Madrid), a tombstone outside Ponce, learned about from local land records that indicated this individual had a plantation, and from another book on the social history of the area that people pointed out that families usually buried their dead on their property or in a Catholic sanctified graveyard, and so on. This situation is normal with almost every individual, particularly in societies that experienced enormous turbulence, such as wars or even the more mundane mobility of North America communities since the seventeenth century. The fragmentation that so characterized the nature of the information also accounts for the large amount of communications that genealogists engage in over many years. Concentrated collections of archival materials devoted to one family are the exceptions.

The objective is to recreate a factual record of individuals, then groups of people—often referred to as nuclear families (father, mother, children)—then by period or generations. The paper trail by category of data collection (person, family) involves acquiring photographs, ephemera of their lives (such as school transcripts, military records, photographs), and writing down or recording stories, all organized the way the various "how-to" manuals almost universally suggest.

A precious, often factually inaccurate source of information family historians included in their collection of data, is whatever elderly relatives recall.[39] There is a race to get to them while their minds are still reasonably clear to find out about their own lives and those of their parents and aunts and uncles, followed by their accounts of earlier generations. These family members are asked about the life stories of as many of these individuals as they can recall, their names, birth and death dates, and very importantly, who they were related to and the names of their children, and who they married. Determining where all these hundreds of people lived that the elderly could remember becomes an important effort too. Often the family historian will regret not getting to someone before they died, or before they could identify old photographs (subject, place, circumstance, and date). It is such a widespread problem that we do not need examples to make the point; most families face this issue.[40]

Memories are never precise so whatever is learned is often written down, but then needs to be verified through extant documents, such as baptismal or court records. Verification often results in the extended research conducted that take years. Gaps in knowledge of an elderly person can be frustrating, too, such as their inability to recall the name of a sibling of their grandparents or the children's names of an aunt. The challenge for family historians is their own limits of competency. Some, indeed many, have the reputation of accepting at face value what they are told, without verifying, while at the other extreme some adhere to legal standards of evidence verification. Discrepancies in facts and interpretations of even minor facts consume hours, days, and years to resolve, leading academic historians to discount the quality of much of this research as unreliable. Retracing facts back-and-forth becomes the stuff of family lore served up by the clan's historian as they try to determine the missing pieces of a story and where to hunt for the answer, hence the notion many articulated that "doing" family history was about solving a never-ending puzzle. Figure 8.2 is a simple summary of the bulk of what these historians do.

THE IMPACT OF THE INTERNET ON FAMILY HISTORY INFORMATION ECOSYSTEMS

In the 1980s personal computers became available and the Internet in the 1990s to genealogists and family historians. No set of technologies so profoundly or quickly changed the work of family historians, particularly genealogists, as these two technologies. It would be difficult to overstate their importance for the process or to any group described in this book. While the technology preceded their use by family historians, it was when they became available to individuals at affordable prices in forms that one could use without being a computer specialist that we could see these people using them. A key development involved the connection of computers to telecommunications, which made it possible to transfer information from one place to another. By the late 1980s, a genealogist could acquire a PC and communicate over a telephone line with another computer that had a great deal of useful information.

While technology was necessary, it was insufficient, because family historians needed content, not just connections. With the Internet, massive files useful to family historians could be created by libraries and archives of their own holdings, while smaller data sets relevant to one family could be too by individuals, augmented by a family historian and other members of the clan. That data could be shared with other relatives in the same way. By the early 2000s, sharing involved all manner of traditional information: facts, family trees, photographs, and other images of documents, such as letters and other ephemera.

As early as the 1980s PC software became available that allowed family historians to collect and organize quickly information, using spreadsheets, datasets, database tools, and word processors. The nearly simultaneous availability of word processors brought with it not only the benefits already enjoyed through use of a typewriter but increased speed and ease of typing, storing, editing, and transmission of text. By the early 2000s, one could merge texts with images, scan manuscripts, extract tables from spreadsheets and database packages, and embed them in text. Database software made it possible for non-technically oriented family historians to collect, sort, display, and share thousands of pieces of information, such as needed for a family tree, as in the case of Glenn Rouse in Australia.[41]

When specialized software packages designed for genealogists began to appear in the 1990s, genealogists quickly appropriated these to create what had before been a time consuming exercise. Updates, a constant activity, could now be done quickly and new family trees printed. Those old messy hand scribbled family trees on big white cardboard charts or pieces of paper taped together rapidly became a thing of the past with software producing legible, neatly typed displays of family trees. In the new century, such software made it possible to populate files behind names in a family tree that one could go to in order to store everything that it had about an individual and conversely, access—"click on"—that name to read what was known about that person. People were now able to organize and access better organized information more conveniently. Handbooks about how to use the Internet often included diskettes with specialized software tools.[42]

Libraries and archives moved vast quantities of genealogical information online: baptismal and death records from around the world, military records, municipal files, permits, telephone directories, newspapers, magazines, business registers, travel records, and immigration files, to mention a few. Elsewhere I described this development as a "data tsunami."[43] That was in 2011; a decade later the amount of material available online more than doubled. Much of it was accessible for free, conveniently from the comfort of one's home office through their PC, laptop, or tablet without requiring a computing background. Commercial websites became available, accessible for a subscription fee, such as Ancestry.com. Family historians swarmed over these kinds of material, often reducing the amount of time to accumulate information by years. Instead of having to go from one country to another to visit parish archives, increasingly they did so from home. One could look up the address of a parish priest, e-mail him with inquiries, and have a response back in a few days with the requested facts having been looked up and scanned by a hopefully cooperative priest. Family trees that took a decade or two to put together could now be assembled in weeks and months.

The tool is becoming effective for other forms of research. For example, if one were to acquire an old property in, say, Wisconsin, such as a small farm with a 150 year old stone house, the temptation to understand its history might be irresistible. After going through normal land title and deed records, one would only know who owned the farm house before them, little about who lived on the property, or about their lives. Take the home located at 632 Center Road, Rutland, Wisconsin, built in 1855 by one Samuel Hunt. In 1868 he sold the property to another family that lived on it until the early 1890s, and so it went until the present owners, Elizabeth and Eric Bachhuber, who acquired it in 2011 with the intention of restoring it to its past prime. Local press celebrated its sale as one of the oldest properties sold that year.[44] Deed records took about a half-day to examine on microfilm. But then there was the question of who the residents were over the years. That is where genealogical research methods turned up information that gave the property life. From U.S. Census records the new owners learned that the various previous farmer had married and had various aged children. They learned what other professions and jobs were held by the farmers, everyone's ages, where they came from before moving onto the property, how big their farm was (it changed in size over the past 170 years), and where their children went to school.[45] All those various data were located in digital databases and were collected with less than 40 hours of work. Local tax records were both on microfilm and in the original bound volumes, which added information about property values.[46] A four-hour oral history interview conducted with Charles Burch, a child who lived on the farm in the 1950s, filled in details about what the family did, who lived on the property as early as the 1930s and as late as the 1970s, about their personalities and behaviors, and what they raised on the land.[47]

The center of the research was the farm, the families simply secondary players in its story, but family history filled many details. That kind of history made it possible to document various additions and changes to the original farm house, a century-old tobacco shed and a dairy barn, while dismissing local stories that could not be documented, such as an addition supposedly built out of the wood from a dismantled one-room school house that could never be identified.[48] The bulk of the non-online research occurred at the nearby Oregon Area Historical Society, a typical American local historical society largely focused on supporting the needs of local genealogists. Volunteers there reported that their most widely used collections included property tax records, others on school attendance, local newspapers, obituary files, still others documenting early settlers in southern Wisconsin, and its growing collection of photographs of people, buildings, streets, and events.

Across the United States also in a small town, Orange, Virginia, a similar historical society existed. Established in 1965 as the Orange County Historical Society, it too experienced similar demands for family records, often used, too, to document the history of properties, some of which dated to the 1710s.[49] This is also the same county from which James Madison (1751–1836), fourth president of the United States (1809–1817), came from and where his home, Montpelier, is now a major historic site. Both this historical society and the one in Oregon, Wisconsin, collected the same kinds of information visitors consulted.[50]

As the number of organizations posting information on the Internet increased, family historians tapped into these new sources to enhance their work. Geographic information systems (GIS) contained databases of maps of underground sewer and water pipes, street maps accessible online, and other data describing buildings designed for use by engineers in towns and cities, but now consulted by family historians too. Ship passenger lists became especially useful for tracking migrations of individuals from one country to another, establishing the date when someone came, say, to the United States and who else traveled on their ship (e.g., their children, spouses).[51] Transcribing cemetery and tombstone texts became a popular local historical society project, so too posting on the Web. Data on tombstones are highly prized by genealogists, because they tend to have fewer factual errors than paper documents. Posting wills and property deeds, long highly regarded sources of information by genealogists, became a convenient source to tap online in the early years of the twenty-first century on both sides of the Atlantic from Canada to the bottom of South America, from Spain to the Nordic countries. Finally, a variety of other records made it online: business directories published by cities, genealogical histories and their journals, and websites of discussion groups.

In the early 2000s, dozens of startup companies catered to the needs of family historians, most notably Ancestry.com.[52] They became platforms, websites, to which subscribers could go where either online files existed, or information that would direct them to other online sites, such as those operated by government agencies. Family historians so enthusiastically embraced the use of these websites that these became large businesses that could afford to take on projects to digitize paper files, such as church records. That is how Ancestry.com became a source of information for tens of millions of subscribers.

With such Internet sites family historians could search indexes, vital records, statistics and census and immigration records; tap into massive online genealogical databases rapidly becoming available, such as those of the Latter Day Saints; create personal family history pages; explore a growing number of searchable databases, which were especially useful for exploring large government data sets, high school yearbooks, and local newspapers; participate in genealogical discussion groups to discuss research challenges with other family historians; explore library catalogs online that used to be on cards accessible only by visiting the physical library; and download and print information and images of original records.[53]

Family historians became some of the most intensive users of historical records of all kinds, exploring a large variety of disparate sources of information. Family history is often comprised of thousands of bits of information from a vast array sources that when combined provide an understanding about a family or individual. That fragmented, even trivial feature of much genealogical information made the ability to search numerous databases one of the most important reasons for appropriating the Internet. Family historians would have been reluctant to fly to a distant city to examine immigration records to determine when one ancestor arrived in the United States, but proved eager to access an online source for that one single date—when someone came to the United States. That same day they could then access another searchable database to see if that person was drafted into the U.S. Army during World War I, which would otherwise have required another trip to Washington DC, only to learn that some of those records were housed in St. Louis, Missouri, but possibly burned in a massive fire. Such expenditures of time and money shrank dramatically with the availability of searchable databases.[54]

How extensively did they use the Internet? Ancestry.com reported that between 2006 and 2008—the period of initial massive adoption of the Internet by genealogists—family historians created more than 7.5 million family trees and more than 725 million profiles linked to those trees. It reported over 6.5 million visitors and an excess of 10 million photographs uploaded to its site, while over 150 million hints and comments were added.[55] Those numbers continued to increase over the next decade. Today, it is routine for family historians to work with such databases along with more traditional paper ephemera.

Parallel to these digital developments, an entirely new class of information became available: DNA. The ability for commercial enterprises to sample a person's DNA, when coupled to ethnic and demographic collections of DNA that originated in the 1990s, meant that if one compared their DNA to those of others in large digital databases, an analyst could determine where their ancestors came from. The National Geographic Society launched one of the first such initiatives and as its database of samples from around the world increased, it became easier to explain to someone that, say, their ancestors came out of Africa 60,000 years ago, migrated up the right hand side of the Mediterranean through what today is Syria, then moved westward into Europe, then down into the Iberian peninsula 30,000 years ago.[56] In time other organizations, too, offered such services, including Ancestry.com.

By 2016, African Americans, whose nearly 390,000 ancestors arrived in the New World as slaves and whose subsequent genealogy was not documented by slave owners, could at least learn from what parts of Africa they originated, adding to their understanding about their family history.[57] One lesson already learned is that most African Americans have white ancestry, indicating that far more white slave owners engaged sexually with their "property" than otherwise thought.[58] That realization offered the prospect of finding some records drawn from the white side of their families. The emblematic case of U.S. President Thomas Jefferson having children with one of his slaves is now seen as more typical than exceptional.[59]

In summary, just since the late 1990s, the types and volume of information available to family historians expanded exponentially, thanks to the availability of the Internet, software tailored to their needs, and inexpensive PCs, tablets, smart phones, and communications. The amount of time needed to conduct research dropped dramatically, along with its cost in money, time, and effort. Those circumstances stimulated interest and consequently increased consumption of relevant and obscure bodies of information by family historians. Underpinning their work was their reliance on a massive complex information infrastructure.[60]

THEIR INFORMATION INFRASTRUCTURES

Recall Figure 2.2 (p. 42) depicting the two components of an information infrastructure. One part is physical, ranging from books and bookshelves and libraries to the postal service, bookstores and office supply stores, PCs, and so forth. The second part consists of information. Both components can exist in part within the walls of an organization, such as the Spanish foreign ministry, or almost all within one large ecosystem, as in IBM's world. In the example of the family historian, it mirrors more what the women and children of Madison County encountered, a combination of formal structures (schools and agricultural extension services) and looser networks (friends and neighbors). With the family historian, we have the loosest infrastructure of all, held together, as suggested by Figures 8.3 and 8.4, in the mind of the researcher. Presenting graphic

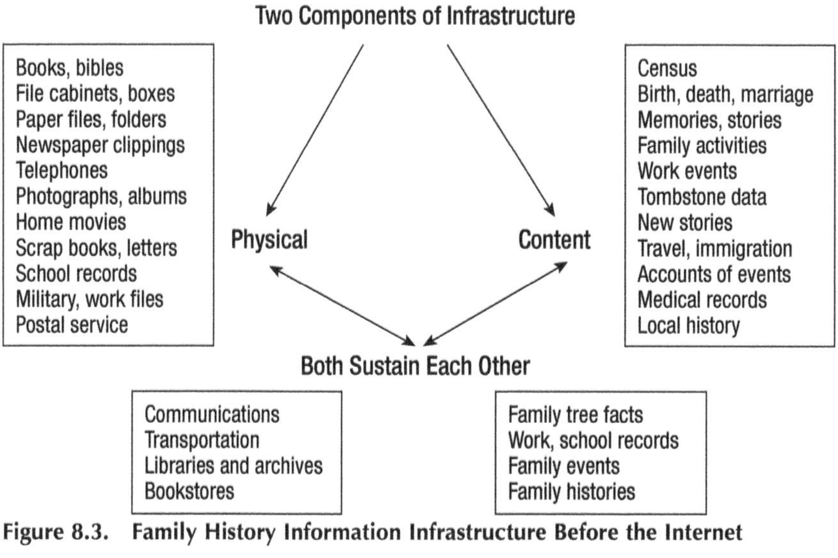

Figure 8.3. Family History Information Infrastructure Before the Internet

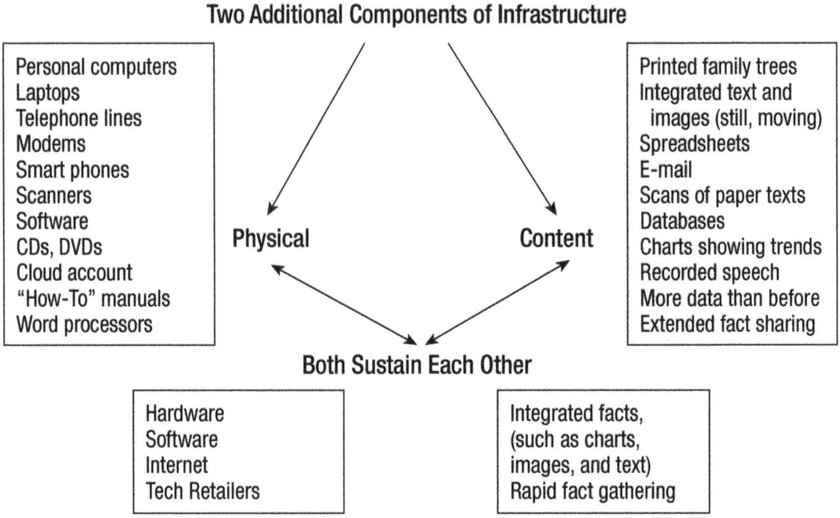

Figure 8.4. Family History Information Infrastructure After the Arrival of the Internet

representations implies his or her information was a far more formal structured infrastructure, but nothing could be farther from the truth. For every family historian it was unique, tailored to meet his or her needs, a reflection of what they had used so far. The construct was probably intuitive, not as obvious as we describe over the next pages.

These changed over time, too. For example, including in the infrastructure, say, a church or two might have made sense for a half dozen years in pre-Internet times, as a researcher worked with those organizations to mine files for baptismal, marriage, death, and cemetery records, but once gathered, they were never called upon again for help. These churches would drop out of the researcher's infrastructure, replaced with new ones, such as a business or military archive, or local historical society. The infrastructure always remained dynamic, requiring a historian of information examining any community and its records to understand how these evolved over time. That is why the case of the pre- and post-Internet period in the work of a family historian was useful to study. The change was dramatic, explicit, and currently evident. But the same happened in earlier times. Remember what happened when Spanish diplomats began using the telegraph, later the telephone in Chapter 4? Researchers latched onto new communications tools almost as fast as they appeared and became affordable.[61]

Information infrastructures are cobbled together by their users, tailored to meet their needs, and used to the best of their abilities. Family historians are not employees of large corporations that can provide these. All infrastructures have two facets, regardless of their size or purpose. One is physical, the other is content (information). For the family historian the physical has always consisted mainly of paper ephemera, such as those listed to the left of Figure 8.3.

But there are other components. A second is physical, including file cabinets, boxes, albums of photographs, and newspaper articles. Since information moves about, reliable postal delivery and access to transportation to libraries and archives are also important elements of the infrastructures, represented here as a third component. To the degree these work and their speed of operation is taken into account, the work of the family historian is affected just as in the case of the Spanish diplomats. Access to telephones at affordable prices remains important, playing the same role as for the Spaniards and IBM employees. Recall early in this chapter I pointed out that correspondence related to research can be almost as voluminous as the actual documentation about the family, hence the importance of reliable postal service and e-mail. Fourth are the institutions historians rely on: public and government libraries, local and national archives, church offices, university libraries, specialized bookstores, chambers of commerce, and record keeping services of an ancestor's employer, among others.

Each of these four elements of the physical side of the infrastructure affect the degree to which each other can be used. Government regulations regarding access to military or personnel records is an obvious example, but so too, availability of church records, or the hours in which an archive is open, even whether or not it had a photocopier onsite, or allowed one to use their smartphone to take photographs.[62] Cost of transportation to a place in the infrastructure remains a mitigating factor affecting the degree to which a family historian improves the quality and quantity of information he or she can collect.

The right hand side of Figure 8.3 speaks to the content itself, a subject that can be seen as the facts themselves, although realistically more as the physical formats in which information is stored, such as on a piece of paper or in a book. Each format has its own structure by which information is presented, such as how a recipe is described on a 3 × 5 card or in a notebook, birth and death dates in a Bible, or on a family tree. Each collection of norms, which, as we saw with recipes, means certain pieces of information are excluded by custom, such as how to bake rolls or cure a ham since all women in Madison County were assumed to know how to perform those tasks. The historian routinely works with these various formats, often collecting originals or copies of all manner of ephemera. A family historian with original contracts or wills from the fifteenth century finds that even the shape of the document varies considerably from those prepared in the twentieth century, and that is before one even discusses what kind of information each contained. The ability to work with these various components of an infrastructure suggests two others for historians to account for insufficiently touched upon in this chapter: knowledge about the times and history in which a particular ancestor lived, and, more urgently, a researcher's ability to read information in multiple languages.[63] In addition, handwriting changed over time, including the shapes of letters.

This linguistic challenge can be overcome by leveraging one's information ecosystem, something the historian of information should look for. As a family historian identifies that a family came from another country, the absolutely guaranteed circumstance with anyone's clan located in North and South America, in ex-European colonies, and even in parts of southeastern Europe and along contested geographies, such as China's borders, is that one will encounter records in another language that must be understood within the context of another culture. As an example, turn to the German-American experience. German emigrants to the United States constituted the largest European group to come to North America. Over five million came to the United States between 1820 and 1914, accounting for roughly a third of all emigrants.[64] That meant many American family historians would run into the linguistic barrier of having to work not only in the German language, but also with handwriting styles sharply different than those practiced today by English and German–speaking record keepers. Using our example of the Barlow-Etten family as an example, we see how one's information ecosystem expanded. Barlow was of British descent, Etten German. As the Barlow family's historian, Nina Winkler was busy at work in the United States in the 1990s–2000s, and expanded her research to that of her husband's family, Winkler, who was also of German descent. In Germany another family historian was doing the same for the Ettens, Nelly Gerhards. In 1995 she had put together a short account of the Etten family. Her history included family trees, birth and death notices, and a substantial collection of images of official documents and photographs. Everything was in German. The two family historians discovered each other and began to communicate, largely in English.[65] They shared files. Many were virtually illegible to Winkler, less so to Gerhards. Then in 1997 Nina Winkler and her husband, Edward, traveled to Germany to meet their German counterparts to trade information, understand texts, and gather copies of documents and photographs (see Figure 8.5). This included accumulating information about the Winkler clan.

Figure 8.5. German-American Family Reunion

The German side of the family had members who spoke English and a correspondence ensued for over a decade. For example, in 1998 Gerhards reported findings of a visit to a local archives related to Ed Winkler's family: "A chronicle of 1896 says Leonhard Winkler was a school teacher in Gutenstetten from 1813 to 1825. Besides teaching, he listed the debt/costs that were caused by 6000 Russians who marched through Gutenstetten on their way to the battle of Waterloo against Napoleon." "Helmut Reib would be willing to follow up. . . . What do you think? Shall we go ahead?"[66] In short, the Barlow-Etten-Winkler information ecosystem had expanded from the United States to Germany; earlier links to British records offices existed. The Americans easily overcame the language barrier, while initiating a continuous flow of information that by 2015 had resulted in the accumulation of over two hundred pages of data and documents, and several dozen photographs of nineteenth and twentieth century relatives. With the exception of the exchange of e-mails, the bulk of this family research was done without benefit of the Internet's wide availability.

Everything about the pre-Internet infrastructures displayed in Figure 8.3 exists in the world presented in Figure 8.4. The pieces of the information ecosystem that make up components in Figure 8.4 are parts of the larger ecosystem reflected in Figure 8.3 that are added, because they never fully replaced the older network. The post office still delivers books, while the researcher is checking on Google Books (a major source) over the Internet. A Civil War soldier's original letters to his wife may eventually be scanned into a digital file, but probably has not been, as millions were written, but only tens of thousands digitized. In our current century many local historical societies busily scan these now that digital scanning is easy, fast, and inexpensive. Not all photographs can be downloaded from a smartphone or Facebook. Too many remain in paper format as originally printed and even worse, unidentified, leaving millions of people anonymous to history and to their families. So today's family historian works with a paper-based infrastructure in which information remains on paper that is physically moved about, transported, and touched in a world in which digital files are also part of the mix of their activities. Rarely can one find a family historian who operates fully in a digital world without recourse to paper. Yet, the volume of information provided by the digital component of the information infrastructure is growing rapidly.

Recipes were still formatted the same way on the Internet as in earlier paper versions; one still needed to read in the languages of their ancestors; and the same kinds of information were collected and organized in similar ways, such as inquiries of traditional sources and updates to family trees. There were new activities, too, that made retrofitting the digital infrastructure into the pre-existing one important, some already listed: quickly searching massive databases for little bits of information buried in thousands of pages of material; probing databases from all over the world from the convenience of one's kitchen table; being able to revisit archival and published sources repeatedly to verify information previously gathered, or that now becomes relevant thanks to the unearthing of some other fact. It is that ability to move increasingly back and forth through sources quickly and easily that so distinguished the digital style of work, along with its speed and lowered cost of research. So, along with the file cabinets, cardboard boxes, and bookshelves, the infrastructure now includes scanners, PCs, Internet connections, smartphones with cameras, and a couple of fat paper and digital manuals on how to conduct Internet-based genealogical research.[67]

CHALLENGES FACING GENEALOGISTS AND FAMILY HISTORIANS

The long shadow of inaccurate information hovers over the work of the genealogist and family historian. It comes in all forms: misinformation, inaccurate or alternative facts, purposeful obfuscation, or suppression of the truth. For generations there existed enough evidence of this problem to make family history suspicious, labeled as "myths," "folklore," and "legends." Today, when credentialing is so highly prized, people conducting research about their families are often branded as "amateurs," lacking "critical thinking," or not practicing the discriminatory skills so prized by "trained" researchers adorned with advanced academic degrees and whose publications are not self produced but published by established academic and trade publishers. A reading of genealogical and family "how-to" guides offer evidence to the contrary. So too would a check on the backgrounds of some of these researchers. Lawyers and doctors, even academic historians, do this kind of research, applying their ethical standards and professional methodologies, resulting in high levels of accuracy and intellectual rigor. One's relative promulgating myths or lies about the family increasingly seems anachronistic as the number of valuable databases becomes what even the greater "amateur" relies upon as they migrate to online tools that fill in data drawn from searches of reliable databases.[68]

But bad data survives, infecting information ecosystems, regardless that more people today have a college degree in the Western World than a generation ago, and that so many subscribers to Internet tools are knowledge workers themselves. A mistaken entry into a family bible made in the nineteenth century survives to the present, so too misspelling of a name or statement of age scribbled by a harried census taker. Transcription and spelling errors are camouflaged by time and changing handwriting styles, uncovered through painstaking cross checking of numbers and names. Even university students are admonished not to believe everything they see on the Internet. So too the genealogist to remain wary of printed and handwritten data.[69] The critical judgment required in one era is still needed in ours. A highly regarded professionally trained genealogist, Elizabeth Powell Crowe, warned those using the Internet for research to be wary: "A source isn't a primary source unless you've held the original document in your hand."[70] While her admonition may seem a bit extreme to those not family historians, the fear of the fake that resonated so strongly with her does too with serious family historians. Her original document could have inaccurate information, too. She reminded that cross checking facts remains the only way to ensure accuracy: "In my opinion, you must evaluate what you find on the Internet, just as you evaluate what you find in a library, courthouse, or archive."[71]

When examining the information ecosystem and supporting infrastructure of the family historian, we see that today's researcher straddles two worlds, that of paper and digital files. In practice the latter is an extension of the former, often overlapping with the same information existing in both. One can argue this is not about straddling information, but about ecosystems and their infrastructures becoming dramatically larger or integrated. But to state the obvious: not everything is yet on the Internet. Most Catholic Church records are not, nor most European newspapers, pre-1980 local municipal and county records in any country, or the majority of state, provincial, and national government records. The U.S. Congress essentially dismissed the librarian of the Library of Congress in 2016 for not placing enough materials on the Web, appointing instead a professional librarian, Carla Hayden, with at least some experience making materials available over the Internet. Colonial records from European archives are just now making it onto the Internet. One faces the situation in which the majority of Latin American colonial records from when Christopher Columbus came in 1492, through the 1820s, when these colonies gained independence, remain bundled with red ribbons on miles of shelves in Seville, Spain.

Other sources of information, both accurate and misleading, essential to the family historian are often difficult to obtain. The ones I am thinking of are histories of towns and counties, often written by priests, ministers, county clerks, lawyers, and occasionally a teacher or self-trained local historian. Often printed locally, rarely peer-reviewed, not always available in public or state libraries, and published in very limited quantities, they are often detailed and useful. But they are difficult to find. Often one still needs to travel to a location and hope there is a local historical society, which then will have copies to consult. More than just useful to find a relative's name listed, and possibly containing information about their activities, is the contextual information they provide about the times in which an ancestor lived. Increasingly, these can be compared to histories of an entire region or state prepared by local academic historians, thereby increasing one's confidence regarding the accuracy of local information. So, librarians, archivists, and genealogists continue to be members of a family historian's information ecosystem and infrastructure.[72]

This case study of the genealogist/family historian is less about a pre- and post-Internet information ecosystem, which is often a paradigm favored by historians, sociologists, and media experts to describe changing information landscapes, and more about the old and the new co-existing side-by-side. It is not a new idea—it was recently demonstrated by David Edgerton in his study of pre-digital technologies in use with newer ones, in his book *The Shock of the Old.*[73] Yet, one information landscape affects the other. The Canadian seer of modern uses of the media, Marshall McLuhan, observed in 1964, "A new medium is never an addition to an old one, nor does it leave the old one in peace. It never ceases to oppress the older media until it finds new shapes and positions for them."[74] McLuhan was reacting to the emerging role of television, which we now know did not displace radio or printed matter, as so many thought would happen in the early 1960s. This case study suggests co-existence, yet also convergence and blending, as the information infrastructure for family historians continues to expand with the complexity and diversity of the components of its supporting information infrastructure. This occurs regardless of how many people are at the center of it all. In answer to the question that launched this chapter, information ecosystems and infrastructures may start small then expand in pursuit of a larger narrative, regardless of the size of the community that use them. One individual needs as many as dozens or thousands of people in the same information ecosystem. In this case there are no obvious boundaries to their information ecosystems or infrastructures.

The experience of the genealogists/family historians demonstrates three additional observations. First, they work within a complex, often large information ecosystem without the benefit or burden of being part of some overarching organization, such as an employer. They can work with highly diverse information with only incremental sporadic help from relatives, librarians, and archivists. Second, their patterns of behavior are remarkably similar across time and space. The Germans, our Australian Glenn Rouse, the American Nina Winkler, and so many others could connect, trade information, and focus on similar data collecting priorities. Third, because of that similarity of purpose and work, we could apply the concept of studying information ecosystems and infrastructures to come to those first two conclusions. The approach facilitated understanding what they did and the information they gathered and used. As in our other case studies, information and its underlying information ecosystems offered participants information, context, and identity. Family ties and identities were reinforced as a direct result of participation within the familial information ecosystem.

With this chapter we end our case studies and turn our attention to a summary of the case for exploring information ecosystems and their infrastructures, and muse about the future prospects of this approach.

NOTES

1. Alon Confino, "Collective Memory and Cultural History: Problems of Method," *American Historical Review* 102, no. 5 (December 1997): 1386–1403.

2. U.S. Library of Congress has over 40,000 genealogies and over the local histories, most of which have some family history, http://www.loc.gov/rr/genealogy/lhgcoll.html (Accessed 3/18/2019).

3. Thomas MacEntee, "The Truth Behind Ancestry.com's Recent Subscriber Losses," July 24, 2014, https://www.linkedin.com/pulse/20140724231020-31267915-the-truth-behind-ancestry-com-s-recent-subscriber-losses; "Ancestry.com Facts," https://www.ancestry.com/corporate/about-ancestry/company-facts (both accessed 2/8/2019); for statistics also see https://www.ancestry.com/corpo rate/about-ancestry/company-facts (Accessed April 5, 2020).

4. Described in more detail in James W. Cortada, "Genealogy as a Hobby," in William Aspray and Barbara M. Hayes, eds., *Everyday Information: The Evolution of Information Seeking in America* (Cambridge, MA: MIT Press, 2011), 157–184.

5. Jules Hudson and Nick Barratt, "The Rise of Family History," *History Today* 57, no. 4 (2008), 20–21; David G. Null, "Genealogy and Family History in the Academic Library." *Journal of Academic Librarianship* 11, no. 1 (1985): 29–33. For evidence that such publications have been around for a long time with a detailed bibliography published long before the arrival of the Internet and today's "how-to" literature, see Russell E. Bidlack, "Genealogy Today," *Library Trends* 32, no. 1 (1983): 7–23. Amazon.com lists nearly 250,000 publications related to the topic.

6. An observation long understood by archivists and librarians, Gail R. Redmann, "Archivists and Genealogists: The Trend Toward Peaceful Coexistence," *Archival Issues* 18, no. 2 (1993): 121–132.

7. See for example, Srdjan Vucetic, "Genealogy as a Research Tool in International Relations," *Review of International Studies* 37 (2011): 1295–1312; its use in the study of politics, Larry Shiner, "Reading Foucault: Anti-Method and the Genealogy of Power-Knowledge," *History and Theory* 21, no. 3 (October 1982): 382–398.

8. *Oxford English Dictionary,* https://en.oxforddictionaries.com/definition/genealogy.

9. The work is driven by their motives and interests, Ronald Bishop, "In the Grand Scheme of Things: An Exploration of the Meaning of Genealogical Research," *Popular Culture* 41, no. 3 (June 2008): 393–412.

10. See for example, the classic study by W. H. R. Rivers, "The Genealogical Method of Anthropological Inquiry," *Sociological Review* 3 (1910): 1–12.

11. Mandy P. Hendry and Andrew M. Ledbetter, "Narrating the Past, Enhancing the Present: The Associations Among Genealogical Communication, Family Communication Patters, and Family Satisfaction," *Journal of Family Communication* 17, no. 2 (2017): 117–136.

12. P. Darby and P. Clough, "Investigating the Information-Seeking Behavior of Genealogists and Family Historians," *Journal of Information Science* 39 (2013): 73–84.

13. Glenn Ross to author in a series of Facebook messages, 2015–2017.

14. Both quotes from Glenn Rouse posted to his Facebook account, July 20, 2017.

15. Ibid.

16. Ibid.

17. Shared behavior that has been documented as far back as the Middle Ages, Daniel Woolf, *The Social Circulation of the Past: English Historical Culture, 1500–1730* (Oxford: Oxford University Press, 2003): 73–98; Mary Madden, *America's Online Pursuits: The Changing Picture of Who Is Online and What They Do* (Pew Internet and American Life Project, December 21, 2003), http://www.pewinternet.org/2003/12/22/americas-online-pursuits/ (Accessed 3/18/2019); Wendy M. Duff and Catherine A. Johnson, Where Is the List with All the Names? Information-Seeking Behavior of Genealogists," *The American Archivist* 66 (Spring/Summer 2003): 79–95.

18. Elizabeth Yakel and Deborah A. Torres, "Genealogists as a 'Community of Records,'" *The American Archivist* 70 (Spring/Summer 2007): 93–113.

19. Ernest F. Burchard, "Manganese-Ore Deposits in Cuba," *Transactions of the American Institute of Mining, Metallurgical and Petroleum Engineers,* 63 (1920): 85.

20. Nina Winkler to James W. Cortada, June 7, 2016.

21. See the entire issue of *Journal of Family Communications* devoted to this topic, 10, no. 1 (2010).

22. May E. Boyce, "Organizational Story and Storytelling: A Critical Review," *Journal of Organizational Change Management* 9, no. 5 (1996): 5–26.

23. "Research Report #227054—Savage, 5 May 1997," copy in author's possession.

24. Nina Winkler to Monica Ballard, April 11, 2015, in author's possession.

25. Ibid.

26. Joanna Cohen Scherer, "Historical Photographs as Anthropological Documents: A Retrospective," *Visual Anthropology* 3, nos. 2–3 (1990): 131–155; Melissa Banta and Curtis Hinsley, *From Site to Sight: Anthropology, Photography and Imagery* (Cambridge, MA: Peabody Museum Press, 1986); Richard Chalfen, *Snapshot: Versions of Life* (Bowling Green, OH: Bowling Green State University Popular Press, 1987); James Borchert, "Analysis of Historical Photographs: A Method and a Case Study," *Studies in Visual Communication* 7, no. 4 (Fall 1981): Article 3, available at https://repository.upenn.edu/cgi/viewcontent.cgi?article=1142&context=svc (Accessed 3/18/2019).

27. James N. Cortada to Francisco A. Scarano, November 5, 1984, Cortada Family Archives.

28. For how this is done, Ann P. Turnbull, Barbara J. Friesen, and Carmen Ramirez, "Participatory Action Research as a Model for Conducting Family Research," *Research and Practice for Persons with Severe Disabilities* 23, no. 3 (1998): 178–188; Drew Smith, *Social Networking for Genealogists* (Baltimore, MD: Genealogical Publishing Company, 2009); George G. Morgan, *How to*

Do Everything Genealogy, 3rd ed. (San Francisco, CA: McGraw-Hill Osborne Media, 2012): 417–430.

29. Alina García-Lapuerta, *La Belle Créole: The Cuban Countess Who Captivated Havana, Madrid, and Paris* (Chicago, IL: Chicago Review Press, 2014), 19.

30. One finding of the research done on Cortada and other related families regarding this class of documentation across the centuries (1500s–1800s) for all branches of the families studied in Spain and in the Caribbean was the high degree of accuracy of information, particularly in the naming and identification of relatives and dates of their baptismals and deaths.

31. Military record in Colas Papers, Cortada Family Archives.

32. There are multiple spellings of this name. *Croche* is the Catalan phonetic writing of the Italian surname *Croce*. The Croce family of Milan were prominent in Spain's service during the sixteenth century. It is quite possible that the lady in question was born in Italy but that he met her while serving in Aragon.

33. In the case of the Spanish military, there are guides to such records useful to genealogists, as exist in other countries as well. See, for example, Enrique de Ocerin, *Indice de los Expedientes matrimoniales de militares y marinos que se conservan en el Archivo General Military (1761–1865),* 2 vols (Madrid: C.S.I.C., 1959–1967).

34. For examples, DigMyPics, FotoBridge, iMemories, ScanCafe, QA Video Services, and Digital Transfer Services. For a larger list, see http://www.dmoz.org/search?q=home+movies+preservation&all=no&t=reference&cat=all (Accessed 2/20/2019).

35. For an account of a nearly 70-year case, see James W. Cortada, *History Hunting: A Guide for Fellow Adventurers* (Armonk, NY: M. E. Sharpe, 2012):85–112.

36. Curiously, this parallel file of correspondence that accompanies actual family documents has not been discussed by students of the genealogical process, let alone by those exploring the research methods used by historians. The instances I have seen of detailed family genealogical projects over the past forty years in the United States and in Western Europe always included such voluminous correspondence files.

37. See, for example, Stanley J. Zagraniczny, "Some Reasons for Polish Surname Changes," *Polish American Studies* 20, no. 1 (January–June 1963): 12–14; Moa Bursell, "Name Change and Destigmatization among Middle Eastern Immigrants in Sweden," *Ethnic and Racial Studies* 35, no. 3 (2012): 471–487; Claudia Goldin, "Making a Name: Women's Surnames at Marriage and Beyond," *Journal of Economic Perspectives* 18, no. 2 (Spring 2004): 143–160.

38. For example, see Jessie Carney Smith, *Ethnic Genealogy: A Research Guide* (Westport, CT: Greenwood Press, 1983); Gale Group, *Hispanic American Genealogical Sourcebook* (Farmington Hills, MI: Thomson Gale, 1994); James M. Beidler, *Trace Your German Roots Online* (Georgetown, ON: Family Tree Books, 2016); Franklin Carter Smith and Emily Anne Croom, *A Genealogist's Guide to Discovering Your African-American Ancestors. How to Find and Record Your Unique Heritage* (Baltimore MD: Genealogical Publishing Company, 2009).

39. Faulty memory is a serious problem in all walks of life and has been studied sufficiently by academic researchers to present any historian with an understanding of the issue. For that insight see Daniel L. Schacter, *The Seven Sins of Memory: How the Mind Forgets and Remembers* (Boston, MA: Houghton Mifflin, 2001).

40. Considerable research has been done on this issue, but one of the most useful studies that has a direct bearing on genealogical research is the minor classic by Daniel L. Schacter, *The Seven Sins of Memory: How the Mind Forgets and Remembers* (New York: Mariner Books, 2002).

41. On July 17 he posted to his Facebook account, "My research has taken me to many countries of the world, never dreamt I would meet ancestral cousins, walked the paths my ancestors walked."

42. Scores appeared. Some of the most widely circulated included Ralph Roberts, *Genealogy via the Internet: Tracing Your Family Roots Quickly and Easily. Computerized Genealogy in Plain English (*Alexander, NC: Alexander Books, 1998); Richard S. Wilson, *Publishing Your Family History on the Internet* (La Habra, CA: Compuology, 1999); Matthew L. Helm and April Leigh Helm, *Your Official America Online Guide to Genealogy Online* (Dulles, VA: AOL Press, 2000); Matthew L. Helm and April Leigh Helm, *Genealogy Online for Dummies* (Foster City, CA: IDG Books, 1999); Terri Stephens Lamb, *SAMS Teach Yourself Today e-Genealogy: Finding Your Family Roots Online* (Indianapolis, IN: SAMS/Macmillan, 2000); Thomas Jay Kemp, *Virtual Roots 2.0: A Guide to Genealogy and Local History on the World Wide Web* (Wilmington, DE: Scholarly Resources, 2003); Elizabeth Powell Crowe, *Genealogy Online* (New York: Osborne/McGraw-Hill, 2002); Myra Vanderpool Gormley and Tana Pedersen Lord, *The Official Guide to Rootsweb.com* (Provo, UT: Generations Network, 2007). Many of these publications went through multiple editions to keep up with the rapidly evolving capabilities and content of the Internet.

43. Cortada, "Genealogy as a Hobby," 172.

44. Karen Rivedal, "Some Highlights from 2011," *Wisconsin State Journal*, January 28, 2012, p. D1, D3.

45. See, for example, U.S. Federal Census Records for each decade from 1840 to 1940; *Dane County Deed Books of Records*, U.S. Department of the Interior, "National Register of Historic Places Inventory—Nomination Form," August 11, 1982, Prepared by Diane H. Filipowicz, May, 1982, Wisconsin Historical Society; Florice Paulson, *Oregon School District: Rural and Village Schools, 1846–1998* (Oregon, WI: Oregon Area Historical Society, 1998).

46. "Tax Roles Dane County," Series 90, reel # 1, but others down to the mid-twentieth century, Wisconsin Historical Society.

47. Interview with Charles Burch by James W. Cortada, July 1, 2017.

48. Paulson, *Oregon School District.*

49. About this society see, https://www.orangecovahist.org/about-us.html (Accessed 2/23/2019).

50. For similar information about the Oregon, Wisconsin organization, see http://oregonareahistoricalsociety.org/about-us/ (Accessed 2/23/2019).

51. See, for example, the large collection of these now available online from Ancetry.com at http://www.ancestry.com/cs/us/Immigration-Records (Accessed 2/23/2018).

52. George G. Morgan, *The Official Guide to Ancestry.com* (Provo UT: Ancestry Publishing, 2008).

53. Diane K. Kovacs, *Genealogical Research on the Web* (New York: Neal-Schuman, 2002) captures the wonder of the "new" way of doing research on the Internet as compared to the "old" way of pre-Internet days.

54. The Ellis Island immigration and travel files in New York house as estimated 51 million records. When the database became available for the first time, millions of people attempted to access it that week, crashing the database. On weekends access still (2018) can be slow as it has become one of the most widely accessed genealogical websites in the United States.

55. E-mail from Sussane M. Bonnor (Senior Public Relations Manager, Ancestry.com) to author, October 21, 2008.

56. "National Geographic Geno 2.0," *PC,* October 20, 2015, http://www.pcmag.com/article2/0,2817,2490077,00.asp (Accessed February 20, 2019); Blaine T. Bettinger, *The Family Tree Guide to DNA Testing and Genetic Genealogy* (Georgetown, ON: Family Tree Books, 2016).

57. There even existed a specialized service, African Ancestry, http://www.africanancestry.com/home/ (Accessed February 20, 2019). One normally hears that 10.7 million slaves arrived, but that larger number is for all of the New World; most went to the Caribbean and to South America.

58. Katarzna Bryc, Eric Y. Durand, J. Michael Macpherson, David Reich, and Joanna L. Mountain, "The Genetic Ancestry of African Americans, Latinos and European Americans across the United States," *American Journal of Human Genetics* 96, no. 1 (8 January 2015): 37–53; Deborah A. Bolnick et al., "The Science and Business of Genetic Ancestry Testing," *Science* 318 (19 October 2007): 399.

59. Annette, Gordon-Reed, *Thomas Jefferson and Sally Hemings: An American Controversy* (Charlottesville, VA: University of Virginia Press, 1999).

60. We may be observing Internet-savvy family historians entering a new phase in their use of Internet sources to collect information, including use of visualization tools and Big Data analytics, George G. Morgan and Drew Smith, *Advanced Genealogy Research Techniques* (New York: McGraw-Hill, 2013); James W. Cortada, "New Approaches to the History of Information: Ecosystems, Infrastructures, and Graphical Representations of Information," *Library and Information History* 32, no. 3 (August 2016), 179–202.

61. Two early studies documented this pattern of behavior, Kristin E Martin, "Analysis of Remote Reference Correspondence at a Large Academic Manuscripts Collection," *American Archivist*, 64, (2001), 17–42; Wendy M. Duff and

Catherine A. Johnson, "A Virtual Expression of Need: An Analysis of E-mail Reference Questions," Ibid., 64 (2001), 43–60.

62. While visiting a church in Vic, Spain, I found documents that I wanted to copy, but the church not having a photocopier. The priest walked me down the street to the police station which did and which was gracious enough to allow me to use.

63. For your author to study his family's history required a working knowledge of Latin, Old Catalan and contemporary Catalan, Medieval and modern Spanish, and English. A little Danish and some Russian would not have hurt to have, and so remain limitations (boundaries) of another type characterizing the information infrastructure.

64. Richard J. Evans, *The Pursuit of Power: Europe 1815–1914* (New York: Viking, 2016): 348.

65. The major correspondence occurred as preparation for a meeting between Winkler and the German family, Nelly Gerhards to Nina Winkler, August 27, 1997, copy in author's possession.

66. Nelly Gerhards to Ed Winkler, December 2, 1998, copy in author's possession.

67. Wendy Duff and Catherine Johnson, "Where is the list with all the names? Information-seeking Behavior of Genealogists," *American Archivist*, 66 (2003), 78–95.

68. Christine Garrett, "Genealogical Research, Ancestry.com, and Archives" (Unpublished M.A. thesis, Auburn University, 2010); Dick Eastman, "What's in the Future for Genealogy?" Ancestry Magazine (2002), www.ancestry.com/learn/library/article.aspx?article=6826 (Accessed 3/18/2019).

69. As one student of the problem warned, "One issue which should concern genealogists who find records on the Internet is the authenticity of the documents. It is often difficult to ascertain whether or not primary records have been altered (either inadvertently or intentionally) in the digitization process. Additionally, genealogists must be as leery of secondary and tertiary sources published on the Web as they are of their paper counterparts, using them as guides to locate primary documents and the facts they contain," Eastman, "What's in the Future for Genealogy?"

70. Crowe, *Genealogy Online,* 12–13.

71. Ibid., 14.

72. Elizabeth Shown Mills, "Genealogy in the 'Information Age': History's New Frontier?" National Genealogical Society Quarterly Centennial Issue 91 (2003), 261 and 267.

73. David Edgerton, *The Shock of the Old: Old Technology and Global History Since 1900* (London: Profile Books, 2006).

74. Quoted in David Sax, *The Revenge of the Analog: Real Things, and Why They Matter* (New York: Public Affairs, 2016), vii.

Part Three

WAY FORWARD

Chapter Nine

The Case for Information Ecosystems and Infrastructures and Lessons Learned

Historical research to this day remains unorganized, and the historian is expected to make his own instruments or do without them; and so with wooden ploughs we continue to draw lonely furrows, most successfully when we strike sand.

—Sir Lewis Bernstein Namier

The purpose of this book is to illustrate how the study of information's history can proceed by reconstructing and examining information ecosystems and their supporting infrastructures. While it is not the only path to move forward with in this newly emerging aspect of history, it points to a way to address a central problem historians face, and for that matter, scholars in other disciplines, by improving specificity for what otherwise is a broad, sprawling, ill-defined subject called information. When specific in approaching the subject with a sharper definition, we can better identify tactical steps to describe its forms, magnitude, and influence on individuals and groups of people. This book's objective is advanced by illustrating how one could apply the proposed strategy for research through the mechanism of exploring a range of case studies.

The framing questions introduced in Chapter 1 are tools to stimulate development of relevant research agendas. They are not canons to be observed, although they are useful to historians studying information's history. Clio's followers can add others to the collection as experience warrants. However, the idea of thinking of information as forming ecosystems and supporting networks is quite specific. I have demonstrated that these exist, regardless of framing questions or methodological and historiographical approaches to the study of information. They are real and they need to be identified and described. Once such basic work is done, it becomes more sensible to parse and analyze different types of information with the understanding of what such exercises mean within the context of human use. In short, much of what is proposed follows the classic steps of scientific research: observe and describe existing conditions.

We have three remaining tasks to accomplish in this chapter. First, I summarize the case for studying the history of information's ecosystems and infrastructure, resting on the examples of how that can be done presented in earlier chapters. Next, these case studies spun off lessons about information and its history worth gathering into one integrated discussion. Third, we need to acknowledge that this approach has its limits, so we define some of the most obvious, and in the process, suggest opportunities for other forms of historical research about the history of information.

THE CASE FOR STUDYING INFORMATION THROUGH ECOSYSTEMS AND INFRASTRUCTURES

There are at least six reasons for approaching the study of information through the lens of ecosystems and infrastructures. We are aware of these because as historians turn increasingly to the history of information, they are learning that the subject has its own characteristics. These features are shaped by the questions they ask, drawn from other aspects of history and disciplines. It is normal, for example, when presenting a point of view that readers will ask for more, but not until they read the text to which they are reacting, such as happens with a book reviewer. For example, in an earlier book I wrote about the history of information in the United States in which I applied the ecosystem/infrastructure model. In an otherwise favorable review, one historian of cultural and social history, Steven Lubar, wrote that, "He's convinced me, in a general way; but he hasn't spelled out the ways" and that after I wrote a 656 page book! He behaved quite normally, too, when asking for more discussion, such about race and gender.[1] So, why is our approach useful?

First, it is simple. While it may seem almost heuristic, it is, nonetheless, easy to grasp. Our introduction of the approach in Chapter 1 was short. The framing questions are obvious, serving as a checklist of what to explore. The objective was to be as intuitive and obvious as possible, because scholars can be an impatient lot and want to dive into a topic quickly with confidence. The experience of putting together the case studies, and the earlier one Lubar reviewed, demonstrated this approach is simple. Many of the information ecosystems and infrastructures already exist. Overlaying on them information they use leads to a description of an ecosystem. It turns out, all existing, visible, known ecosystems have an information component. It is just that these information components are often subsumed in the ecosystem as other aspects are highlighted by historians, such as the role of individuals or organizations. Here I am suggesting that attention in existing ecosystems turn to the role of information, rather than, say, that of people, describing features of the information, how they are used, and so forth, all within an ecosystem. The supporting infrastructure becomes more evident, as well as the relationship of one piece to another, such as the role of a physical postal system to e-mail, in which both are used simultaneously.

Second, it is applicable to many times, places, and circumstances. Our case studies illustrate how the approach works with post-Napoleonic Era diplomats, computer scientists, children, farm wives, IBM salesmen, and historians. If you read the cases, you would find a similar of structure in all. Paul Miranti, a business historian, described this approach better than I could: "the tractability of Cortada's notions about information makes possible their general applicability in evaluating other eras and milieus."[2] Combined between the book he reviewed and this current one, the approach worked in describing over three dozen cases since the eighteenth century. It meets the test of a transferable method applicable in multiple circumstances. There is value in having a technique that works—what a doctor calls a protocol, what a business manager "best practices" for a process, an engineer a proven method.

Third, it works to set information within its socio-cultural context. One of the challenges historians face in exploring information is how best to imbed facts (data, knowledge, wisdom, lessons learned) into the lives and activities of individuals. That is the ecosystem part of the model, because it does not work unless the researcher pays attention to its socio-cultural context. For example, with the farm wives and children of Madison County, information made no sense unless we understood what these people did—farming and preparing for careers and lives in agriculture through schooling and 4-H—so as to uncover the relevance of specific types of information, such as recipes. The Cold War influenced what kinds of information about computing, science, and engineering moved back and forth across the Iron Curtain, and even the speed and volume of its flow. Knowing what a salesperson does and how they are rewarded for their work is crucial in understanding, say, sales forecasting or arguments put to a customer for why they should acquire a computer. Miranti added that while attractive to business managers, the approach might make historians uncomfortable, because armed with the socio-cultural context of information, it ties "the past to the present," and thus "adumbrates the probable direction of future change."[3] In short, the ecosystem/infrastructure approach might give non-historians so much confidence that they would want to use findings from such an exercise to predict future events. That is a step too far for historians, but not for economists, business school professors, business consultants, and industry pundits.

Fourth, it is flexible. One can add or subtract issues to explore. In the case of the Spanish diplomats we paid great attention to the publications they relied on (Chapter 4), farmwives their social events (Chapter 5), added in a discussion of photographs and what they have to teach us in the case of IBM (Chapter 6), explored how information could be co-located in an industry (Chapter 2), and how vastly scattered bits and pieces of information were pulled together with an infrastructure by family historians (Chapter 8). One can be as detailed as they want. For example, in one earlier study, it was possible to set the context and describe what information various professionals needed over the course of a century in less than one thousand words each, while in the case of the Madison housewives we could dig so deeply that it required twenty times the amount of text to cover the same topic.[4]

Fifth, it makes information specific and relevant. In every case study, we explored collections of information normally not discussed by historians to any significant degree. For example, try and find in any diplomatic history much, if any, discussion about consular laws and administrative rules, or even how one should go about writing a treaty. You will be hard pressed to do so, yet to write about a diplomat's information ecosystem and its supporting infrastructure, it was crucial that we were able to integrate what otherwise was ignored information into the history of Spanish diplomacy. Where would one find a discussion of why certain recipes were simply ignored in Virginia cookbooks? Here we learned that everyone knew how to bake rolls or cook a ham, but not necessarily how to bone it. That widespread shared knowledge, for example, carried with it insights about eating habits and the cultural interplay of food and social behavior. Again, we face the same task: linking specific information into daily work practices. Seen in the abstract, a VPI publication on cooking pork would seem obscure, indeed arcane, but within the context of what farm wives and their husbands did it is important, indeed a magnificent example of over two hundred such publications produced by VPI and the U.S. Department of Agriculture distributed in Madison County between the early

1930s and 1990. It is the forced specificity imposed on the historian that both populates the ecosystem and its supporting infrastructure, but also brings into the general history of human participants new evidence about their daily lives.

Sixth, experience with the Internet suggests that information is not just situated in ephemera or in one's head, but also in an information network. David Weinberger, an expert on the features of the Internet at Harvard University, became one of the first observers to point out that information resides in a network too, not just in one's head or on paper. In his words, "the Internet enables groups to develop ideas further than any individual could. This moves knowledge from individual heads to the networking of the group."[5] That reality stimulated much research about the role of the Internet, surfacing observations that connect more people together than earlier social, professional, or technology-based networks, that include much more diverse participants that are both professional and amateur, that accumulate vast quantities of information more available via links than earlier networks, and that scale more dramatically.[6] Other observers reinforced these observations, recently for example, Eric T. Meyer and Ralph Schroeder: "science and scholarship advancing as part of a network of partially overlapping instruments and the data sources that they manipulate and that, even if they do not form part of a single unit, are nevertheless accessible via a single network."[7] They predicted networks would continue to expand and become more fluid in form and content, yet remaining, too, "polymorphous." Information technology makes it possible to gather and use larger datasets of greater complexity.[8] Awareness of such possibilities has encouraged organizations to purposefully expand their use of such networks.[9]

Such insights can inform research on pre-Internet uses of this latest technology. Recall from Chapter 4 about the Spanish diplomats where we discussed how documents moved between the New World and Madrid, often taking a three-year round trip from when an official in Central America asked for a decision and the time when he received it from Spain. Students of that earlier network studied the role of ships, overland horseback delivery services, procedures for dealing with delays, and creation of filing systems. They dealt with the same issues as students of the Internet. One could almost see hyper-linked behavior attached to documents as they moved through the slow infrastructure as readers added comments on the margins or attached other documents (information) to these. Given that the studies of earlier networks were conducted at the same time as those about the Internet, when these researchers were familiar with online tools and datasets, it is difficult to imagine that information networking was not influential in shaping their research agendas.[10] The combination of all these scholars' work reinforces the importance of both studying networks as specific topics but also, as demonstrated in our book, in combination with information ecosystems to describe more fully interactions between people and facts.

THE ARC OF THE BOOK AND A FEW LESSONS LEARNED

If you read this book cover-to-cover, you were exposed to the basic elements of information history pertinent to the proposed exploration of ecosystems and infrastructures. That was the role of the first two chapters. Chapter 3 explored how historians sensitive to information ecosystems and infrastructures dealt with the issue of managing information they needed and studied. The diplomats in Chapter 4 present a case study to begin putting together the pieces of the proposed way of studying information history. The chapter does this by showing what it looks like when we explore the combined history of ecosystems and infrastructures.

With Chapter 5—the homemakers of Madison County—it should be obvious that participants are more varied, nuanced, brought together differently than before, hence fresh and innovative, yet, like a fine meal, well executed and integrated. Everything in this case is there on purpose, and the reader is able to handle the extra level of detail required to understand the broader topic of ecosystems and infrastructures that justified the topic in the first place.

Chapter 6, much shorter than 5, should now seem almost familiar, because it parallels the story told about the Spanish diplomats. This chapter reinforces two messages. First, that it is possible for people working within any large organization to respond to use of information in similar ways. That finding is crucial for accepting the proposed approach to the study of information's history. Without that acceptance, we do not have a strategy that can be broadly applied to the whole of human history, let alone smaller groups, such as people in one nation, time, and in one or more organizations. Second, that the experience of the Spanish diplomats provides essential context with which to know what to look for when studying a new group, such as IBM's employees, whose activities are poorly understood by historians, and even then only by a tiny group. That context makes it possible to judge the quality of the presentation of the IBM experience, hence that of any other historian writing about information ecosystems of a community. Just as experienced cooks did not have to write out every little step in their scrapbooks on how to make rolls, so too in this chapter we did not have to go through the same level of detail as presented about the Spaniards. The role of the seventh chapter is to explore less defined other communities besides IBM engaged in creating and using information about computers. An important introduction here is the discussion in parallel with ecosystems and networks in the development of a new field of knowledge—computer science—which is difficult to understand without thinking in terms of ecosystems and infrastructures.

How might we study the experience of the opposite—a small cohort of individuals, such as a family, or even just one person, such as a family historian? Does our approach apply effectively enough here? Answering such questions with one final case study is the role of Chapter 8. Most genealogists are amateurs, wives and uncles that most families have who are keepers of the clan's history. Professional historians snub them, thinking of them as "amateurs" just as a chef at a five star restaurant might discount the cooking skills of most people, or a medical doctor the work of a shaman. *Une violation du notre culture!* Yet as the chapter demonstrates, and as we know from personal experience, there are many fine amateur historians. Family historians develop their own information ecosystems and infrastructures. They use the latest techniques to do data mining and analysis, relying on information technology made available by the occupants in chapters 6 and 7, perhaps even the kinds of people populating Chapter 5, many of whom were both interested in genealogy and understood that the combined two constituted important aspects of their larger social structure. Many family historians and their broader ecosystem are advancing methods of historical research, perhaps in some ways faster than the professionals.

OPPORTUNITIES AND LIMITS

As historians focus increasingly on the history of information *per se*, and not just on its ephemera and other physical forms, they will probably do two things: co-opt methods to do so from prior practice and shift their emphasis. Often when historians discuss knowledge, information, and data they talk about objects, such as what kinds of books were published and how many were distributed and read, and study the emergence of public libraries, the layout of book pages, invention of paragraphs and chapters, and the topics published. Thousands of such studies crowd our bookshelves and bibliographies. There is nothing wrong with this activity, but it represents only a piece of information's history, what I have argued was more the physical part of information infrastructures. What now has to happen is that we extract from those physical objects what was contained in them—information—to examine its features, forms, movement, and transformation, much the way scholars did when studying, for example, the history of the book.

That is how we get to our other notion: co-opting pre-existing historiographical techniques. We can treat information (facts, data) as protagonists with their own behaviors and characteristics, just as we have books and computers. In a recent study of American history, in one chapter I treated information as a human being, providing a biography of it from childhood through its teenage years to adulthood. Referees for the publisher considering publishing this book thought that technique creative and effective.[11] What had long been a supporting actor in the drama of the human existence was now promoted to lead actor. This shift in thinking requires that we deemphasize discussing the physical object itself. This is difficult to do since we were trained to talk about those items, for example, "In 1925 Adolph Hitler published his manifesto, *Mein Kampf* in which he outlined his ideas for a new order." Historians in our approach to information would spend more time discussing Hitler's ideas and information, where these came from, and how they shaped his behavior and that of his circle of cohorts, relegating the fact that these appeared in a book to a footnote. Diffusion and application of his thinking would play center stage.[12]

But information, like everything else, needs context, a footing, hence the convenience of the right hand side of the infrastructure (content) graphic (Figure 2.2 p. 42) then situated within an information ecosystem. If the truth be known, ecosystems and infrastructures are, as the slightly facetious epigraph to this chapter suggests, tools, an information scaffolding of convenience. In future years, we will need something different analogous to a bucket truck used by tree cutters and electrical utility companies, rather than a building's scaffolding. That new requirement is probably pointing us to what family historians have begun to experiment with: visualization, data mining, and data analytics. As researchers co-opt tools routinely used in their work lives, these will be appropriated for their own family projects. Professional historians, archivists, librarians, and scholars in the humanities and social sciences will do that too; they always have.[13] Such techniques have long helped business and government managers to make decisions about otherwise complex or fuzzy issues.[14]

Styles for presenting information should change as well, as historians continue to strive for specificity and clarity when explaining that which we cannot touch. Information is invisible, a conjure of our minds, and not physical, like a rock or piece of wood. But even like rocks and wood, they eventually evaporate after dramatic transformation. To accomplish giving information a near-tangible clarity, they turn increasingly to graphical representations of their ideas, a practice long in evidence in business, economic, and scientific literature, less so in the humanities and history. This book you are reading is filled with simple figures, few by the standards of, say, business books, even "how-to" volumes on genealogy, but more than a serious history book might contain. Can you argue that the ideas explored here would have been easier to understand without them? For those fortunate enough to have a family historian, armed with a family tree scribbled on paper, they understand the near impossibility of knowing who was related to whom of several hundred ancestors without such a graphical representation. That notion applies to so many subjects.

The most obvious broad example in wide use of the idea of presenting information in visual formats is, of course, how numbers are graphically spread before us like a feast. The leading expert on the use of graphical representations of numbers, Edward R. Tufte, should have a wider audience among students and historians of information. His numerous books on the subject were published by a small press, often difficult to acquire, expensive, yet gorgeous, so worth the effort to study. As he correctly notes, use of pictures to represent information is a relatively new development, especially for numbers. He argues that, "modern data graphics can do much more than simply substitute for small statistical tables. At their best, graphics are instruments for reasoning about quantitative information. Often the most effective way to describe, explore, and summarize a set of numbers—even a very great set—is to look at pictures of those numbers."[15] The same logic applies to non-numerical information, as humbly demonstrated in our book about communities of information users applied in many disciplines and professions.[16]

Software tools are essential to the conceptualization and presentation of such images. Finding ways to digitize increasing amounts of facts, such as numbers and names, and defining their relationship to each other (classic spreadsheet functions), is clearly on the immediate horizon for students of information. This is not a celebratory cheer for the Internet so much as it is an acknowledgement of what software can do to collect and manipulate, then present, ever-larger collections of information. On the other hand, the Internet is now the repository of orders of magnitude more facts than were available even at the dawn of the new century. Historians will find it increasingly compulsory to consult ever-larger collections of archival and other information sources.[17] That is where software tools that search large files can help. But, this is more than about additional homework; it is about different possibilities. Will the hunt for a broader history of information be possible, such as writing a history of how all of Europe used information for over five hundred years, rather than a group or eighteenth century Scottish intellectuals over the course of a thirty-year period? Since information permeates all manner of human activity, the question has to be asked in the context of envisioning the future use of new methodologies for the study of information's history.

There are limits, of course, to viewing the history of information through the lens of an ecosystem and its underlying infrastructure, even though the approach can embrace a great deal, as we saw with the brief analysis of photographs and the more detailed reconstruction of social networks of farm wives. One limitation is the sublimation of information's complexity. Two examples from the farm wives make the point. In Chapter 5 I mentioned that one of the topics discussed at Demonstration Club events was canning of fruits, vegetables, and meats as an instance almost pulled casually from a possible list of over two hundred discussed at such events. It was presented, however, because all farm wives engaged in the practice. In that chapter the topic of canning was tangential to the main subject: ecosystems and networks. But look at the subject by itself and a far different picture emerges. In the 1930s considerable progress was made in understanding the chemical transformation that occurs in the cooking and preservation of food, building on a century of scientific/chemical analysis. In that decade home economists received two revised editions of booklets describing safe and effective methods of canning they were urged to communicate rapidly to homemakers. They did this through a combination of lectures, demonstrations, and distribution of these pamphlets. Let us examine one of those publications, this one originally published in 1936 then revised in 1938.

Home Canning of Fruits Vegetables and Meats is a 38-page densely packed pamphlet.[18] It puts on one page as much text as would a densely-published academic monograph. It includes eight tables of facts, lists, and numeric information. Examples include "Approximate capacity of steam pressure canners of various sizes" (p. 7), "Pounds of steam pressure in canner and approximate corresponding degree of temperature, under standard conditions at sea level" (p. 7), "Proportions of sugar and water for light, medium, and heavy syrups" (p. 19), and "Timetable for processing fruits, tomatoes, and other acid foods" (pp. 24–25). These are not light-hearted data sets. The topics discussed are predictable, such as "processing to destroy enzymes and micro-organisms," "equipment and methods," "steps in canning," and canning for specific types of fruits, vegetables, and meats. This booklet ends with a list of nine other similar publications in a series entitled "Farmers Bulletin No. . . . ," with such titles as *Home Storage of Vegetables* (No. 879), *Homemade Fruit Butters* (No. 900), and *Making Fermented Pickles* (No. 1438).[19]

By any reasonable definition this is a technical manual. Consider the text on destroying enzymes and micro-organisms that, just as with a college textbook, first educates about the nature of the problem being addressed in this "how-to" manual:

> All fresh fruits, vegetables, and meats contain substances called enzymes. Up to a certain point these enzymes bring about desirable changes in foods. They cause fruits and vegetables to ripen normally and the tissues of meats to become more tender as they are held in storage; but if allowed to go on unchecked enzymes hasten the decay of foods. The low temperature of cold storage retard[s] the action of enzymes, and the heat of cooking or canning destroys them entirely.[20]

The rest of the pamphlet reads in a similar way: issues at hand are explained, along with effects and actions one can or should take, and results to look for. Most readers of this pamphlet in the 1930s and 1940s were women without a high school degree. Yet they treated this level of detail as normal. A generation later, the same kind of scientific "how-to" publications kept appearing in Madison County homes. For example, *Family Fare: A Guide to Good Nutrition* (1971) provided 91 pages of densely-packed information and a list of yet other publications of similar length and content, ranging from *Calories and Weight* to *Fruits in Family Meals* to *Conserving the Nutritive Values in Foods.*[21] Most women had a small collection of such publications in a kitchen drawer.[22]

There is one other related potential limitation to the approach that should be acknowledged, and that weighed on my mind when writing the case studies for this book. It is an issue that plagues all historical research, but appeared more obvious here, since the focus on describing ecosystems and infrastructures feels as if constraining the sprawling subject of information. Put as a question, do we run the risk of being too broad, too shallow, or not deep enough in our analysis of information? When proposing a methodological approach with which to study any topic, the temptation to adhere to that convention in order to demonstrate it, to convince others to apply it, to illustrate its advantages, can lead one to other issues essential to the topic at hand, but limit alternative possibilities of technique or issues to explore. To counter those potential problems, developing richly turned case studies remains critical. It is why spending so much time understanding context is crucial. In each case study the reader had to wade through background context to an extent some might have found unnecessary, such as descriptions of farming life in Madison County, the high-tech world of computer historians, IBM sales and research, the struggles of computer scientists to create a new discipline, the family historian fighting off unintended falsehoods promulgated by relatives ignorant of the facts perpetuating a mythology of the family or who had already become feeble-minded. Context is a useful antidote to all these issues.

So too credentialing, which has a vast literature that need not detain us here, because when it was relevant to a case study, we discussed it. We do not yet, however, have a good understanding of the effects credentialing has on the shape of an information infrastructure. We may learn more soon, however, because observers of the Internet's use are paying attention to the interactions of experts and amateurs, or to use their words, "crowdsourcing" or "networking knowledge," normally within the context of "scaling knowledge and networking."[23] César Hidalgo, of MIT's Media Lab, in exploring the relationship among atoms, energy, and information—the three things that make up the universe—argued that "our need to form networks, however, emerges from one important consideration: the limited ability of humans to embody knowledge and knowhow," which requires, therefore, that to overcome our limitations, "we need to collaborate." That means whoever provides information and is willing to share it is prized, and participates in *de facto* or *de jure* networks.[24] It is not clear if our focus on ecosystems and infrastructures lends itself to causing researchers to describe the comings and goings of participants in these. To a large extent in this book, participants and their activities were described almost as set pieces, as static activities, much like a photograph captures a moment in time we know would be more realistically presented as a motion picture. It is an old problem for historians and social scientists, since they must describe unfolding events as activities in motion. This is something they know how to do and so our approach can be tied to their normal work habits. Do other disciplines know how to do the same? We do not know for sure.

SOME FINAL THOUGHTS

Much that is suggested here will sound comfortably familiar, even not new and that is a good thing, because studying the role of information should not be all that mysterious. Librarians, archivists, historians, sociologists, economists, media experts, computer scientists, information specialists, business professors, managers, and lawyers have been working on this topic for a long time. The difference today is that it now has a name (*nome*), an emerging identity with caché: Information History. That awareness is quite helpful, because once recognized as something it can attract methods, best practices, and value more easily than before, because names are information magnets.

We have the example of the effects in the case of global trade. Prior to the 1980s, for several thousand years almost all societies and regions engaged in global trade. Some of that commerce involved the manufacture of parts then transferred elsewhere to be made into new products. Examples include cotton from Egypt shipped to England in the nineteenth century, where it was made into cloth. That cloth went to the United States for the manufacture of clothing. But that activity of moving subassemblies about did not have a name and until it did how it was done remained relatively unchanged. But global trade became the focus of intense improvement to optimize costs and speed. In the 1980s it acquired a name, *supply chains*. Almost instantly, manufacturing firms began to think of these activities in more structured ways and learned more precisely what to outsource to other countries to make, where to assemble pieces most cost effectively, and how best to transport final products to customers. Manufacturing changed radically, then how entire companies organized other aspects of their work in the 1990s. The latter new twist of events resulted in the adoption of yet a new name for the wider effort, *reengineering the corporation*.[25]

Today Apple iPhones are based on U.S.-developed technology (much of it funded by the U.S. Department of Defense), designed in Silicon Valley, manufactured in Asia, then delivered to Apple stores worldwide. Another example: no automobile driven in the West is made in one country, not since the early 1980s. Scholars and managers could now look at the totality of the activities involved in what constituted supply chains and, when they did, see differences in how they functioned rather than global trade in general. Their analysis became specific, their issues more pinpointed, and in the process a new subfield of manufacturing and distribution came into being. The cost of goods declined worldwide, contributing to global inflation remaining essentially benign for over a quarter century. We face a similar circumstance with the study of information.

I brought the historian's lens to the discussion of information ecosystems and infrastructures with this book. Others will do so with their own disciplinary perspectives. In the process we will learn much about the role of information in ways not appreciated before, just as supply chains went through their own period of discovery after being recognized, opening a new and important field of management. These are the building blocks of modern society to be studied. Now it is your turn to do the same.

NOTES

1. Steven Lubar, "Review: *All the Facts*," *IEEE Annals of the History of Computing* 39, no. 1 (January–March 2017): 8.
2. Paul Mirani, "*All the Facts: A History of Information in the United States since 1870* (Review)," *Business History Review* 91, no. 1 (April 2017): 186.
3. Ibid.
4. For the short cases, "What a Construction Worker Knew in the Late 1800s," (page 62), "What Farmers Had to Know by 1870," (pages 68–69), "What Electricians Needed to Know, 1920s–1940s," (page 128), "Growth in Medical Information in America: Evolution in a Doctor's Training, 1870–1940," (pages 181–182, "What It Took to Advance in Police Work, 1959," (page 255), "What It Took to Be a Kindergarten and Elementary School Teacher in 1949," (page 275), James W. Cortada, *All the Facts: A History of Information in the United States Since 1870* (New York: Oxford University Press, 2017).
5. David Weinberger, *Too Big to Know: Rethinking Knowledge Now That Facts Aren't the Facts, Experts Are Everywhere, and the Smartest Person in the Room Is the Room* (New York: Basic, 2011): 45–46.
6. Features nicely summarized in Ibid., 47–68.
7. Eric T. Meyer and Ralph Schroeder, *Knowledge Machines: Digital Transformations of the Sciences and Humanities* (Cambridge, MA: MIT Press, 2015): 215–216.
8. Ibid., 216.
9. Shane Greenstein, *How the Internet Became Commercial: Innovation, Privatization, and the Birth of a New Network* (Princeton, NJ: Princeton University Press, 2015); Lee Rainie and Barry Wellman, *Networked: The New Social Operating System* (Cambridge, MA: MIT Press, 2012).
10. Arndt Brendecke, *Imperio de información: Funciones del saber en el dominio colonial español* (Madrid: Iberoamericana, 2012); Sylvia Sellers-García, *Distance and Documents at the Spanish Empire's Periphery* (Stanford, CA: Stanford University Press, 2014).
11. James W. Cortada, *All the Facts: A History of Information in the United States Since 1870* (New York: Oxford University Press, 2016), 28–47.
12. For a facsimile of the process applied, see Ian Kershaw, *Hitler: 1889–1936 Hubris* (New York: W. W. Norton, 1999).

13. A key finding in Cortada, *All the Facts*.

14. For two case studies, one dealing with a cholera epidemic and the other the decision to launch the space shuttle, *Challenger*, see Edward R. Tufte, *Visual and Statistical Thinking: Displays of Evidence for Making Decisions* (Cheshire, CT: Graphics Press, 1997).

15. Edward R. Tufte, *The Visual Display of Quantitative Information,* 2nd ed. (Cheshire, CT: Graphics Press, 2001), unpaginated in "Introduction," first page.

16. For hundreds of examples of an enormous variety of representations of information in visual formats, see Ibid., also Edward R. Tufte, *Envisioning Information* (Cheshire, CT: Graphics Press, 1990) and *Visual Explanations: Images and Quantities, Evidence and Narrative* (Cheshire, CT: Graphics Press, 1997). For a practical "how-to" book relevant to scholars interested in the history of information, see Cole Nussbaumer Knaflic, *Storytelling with Data: A Data Visualization Guide for Business Professionals* (Hoboken, NJ: John Wiley & Sons, 2015).

17. Christine L. Borgman, *Scholarship in the Digital Age: Information, Infrastructure, and the Internet* (Cambridge, MA: MIT Press, 2007).

18. Louise Stanley and Mabel C. Steinbarger, *Home Canning of Fruits, Vegetables, and Meats,* Farmers' Bulletin No. 1762 (Washington, DC: U.S. Department of Agriculture, 1938).

19. Ibid., 37.

20. Ibid., 2.

21. The list of other sources is posted on the back of the cover of, Consumer and Food Economics Research Division, Agricultural Research Service, *Family Fare: A Guide to Good Nutrition* (Washington, DC: U.S. Department of Agriculture, 1971).

22. For example, in the case of Dot Tappy of Uno, Virginia, on the occasion of her death in 1980, she had in one drawer her kitchen scrapbook and a handful of U.S. Department of Agriculture pamphlets, all showing signs of wear, some undated mimeographed collections of recipes, another on how to wash walls, and a pamphlet written by Mary L. Thompson, a VPI Food Specialist, *Homemade Desserts,* Bulletin 197 (Blacksburg, VA: VPI and U.S. Department of Agriculture, January 1952). That publication had her name on it written in her own hand, in possession of her daughter Dora.

23. See, for example, Weinberger, *Too Big to Know,* 14–16, 52–54, 61–62.

24. César Hidalgo, *Why Information Grows: The Evolution of Order, from Atoms to Economies* (New York: Basic Books, 2015): 180–181.

25. The best selling business book of the decade introduced the new name, Michael Hammer and James Champy, *Reengineering the Corporation: A Manifesto for Business Revolution* (New York: HarperBusiness, 1993).

Index

www.ingramcontent.com/pod-product-compliance
Ingram Content Group UK Ltd.
Pitfield, Milton Keynes, MK11 3LW, UK
UKHW012035150926
475560UK00001B/25

9 781538 148549